S O C I A L I S T
R E G I S T E R
2 0 0 4

THE SOCIALIST REGISTER
Founded in 1964

EDITORS:
LEO PANITCH
COLIN LEYS

Visit our website at:
http://www.yorku.ca/org/socreg/
for a detailed list of all our issues, order forms and an online selection of
past prefaces and essays,

...and join our listserv by contacting
socreg@yorku.ca
for a discussion of the essays from this volume and issues relevant to socialists.

SOCIALIST REGISTER 2004

THE NEW IMPERIAL CHALLENGE

Edited by LEO PANITCH and COLIN LEYS

MERLIN PRESS
FERNWOOD PUBLISHING
MONTHLY REVIEW PRESS

First published in 2003
by The Merlin Press Ltd.
PO Box 30705
London
WC2E 8QD

© The Merlin Press, 2003

British Library Cataloguing in Publication Data is available from the British Library

ISSN: 0081–0606

Published in Europe by The Merlin Press
0850365 35 X Paperback
0850365 34 1 Hardback

Published in the USA by Monthly Review Press
1 58367 099 8 Paperback

Published in Canada by Fernwood Publishing
1 55266 118 0 Paperback

Typeset by Jon Carpenter
Printed in the UK by Antony Rowe, Chippenham

CONTENTS

PREFACE

This, the 40th volume of the *Socialist Register*, was originally planned in the spring of 2001, well before September 11, 2001, let alone the 2003 invasion of Iraq. It seemed to us that an increasingly serious limitation of contemporary socialist thought was its lack of conceptual tools capable of analyzing the nature of imperialism today, rather than recycling theories developed in a much earlier era. Our aim was to produce a volume that would help make socialist theory and analysis realistic, and socialist activism focused and coherent, in the opening years of a new century marked by US-led globalization and a new and more overt form of US imperialism.

The need for theory to inform practice is particularly acute at times of rapid and comprehensive change such as we are now experiencing. Perhaps the arbitrary division of time into centuries makes any 'turn of the century' seem a moment of exceptional change, yet it is striking that so many socialist thinkers had precisely the same feeling a hundred years ago, when imperialism was also a chief focus of their concern. Many non-Marxists as well as Marxists at that time saw global capitalism as in flux, or in crisis, and imperialism as its newly-defining moment. The range of thinkers involved then, and the scope of the work they undertook, should have warned us not to embark lightly on the similar task we were proposing to undertake a hundred years later, but it was only when we started commissioning contributions that we realized fully how much it was a task for many volumes, by many authors. Our response was to decide that we could at least devote two successive volumes to the theme.

The title of the *Socialist Register 2004*, 'The New Imperial Challenge', refers not only to the new challenges to human well-being and self-determination presented by American imperialism today, but also the challenge to the left to develop a better theory of imperialism and its relation to globalized capitalism. The 2005 *Socialist Register*, tentatively entitled 'The New Imperial Order', will explore the cartography of contemporary imperialism – its nature and its impact in various regions of the world – with a particular focus on finance and culture.

Our decision to take up the issue of imperialism was made only too timely by subsequent events. Bush's declaration of a 'war on terror' after the destruction of the World Trade Centre, followed by the United States' assumption of a right to wage 'pre-emptive wars', reflect the unrivalled military power of the USA, deployed by a rightwing administration with unprecedented global ambitions and willing to use that power with remarkably little thought for the consequences. This indeed calls for urgent and realistic assessment – especially since the US is also rapidly developing ever more devastating armaments, including space-based weapons which, as Noam Chomsky chillingly puts in his essay in this volume, 'may well bring biology's experiment with human intelligence to an inglorious end.' Indeed war-making – whether by the US itself, or by the states to which US weaponry is exported – seems almost to have become a 'natural' manifestation of American capitalism.

The logic of this is not new. In his study of the allies' mass bombing of Germany in World War II, *On the Natural History of Destruction*, W.G. Sebald describes how the bombing campaign was the product of a vast technical and organizational mobilization which took on its own implacable momentum, brushing aside the mounting evidence that in spite of its unspeakable cost in civilian lives and the total destruction of German cities it was militarily ineffective. The personnel involved, from arms factory workers to the bomber crews themselves, could be involved only on the basis of accepting, in one way or another, that the entire process was somehow natural. Sebald cites the reaction of a US Air Force officer, Brigadier Frederick L. Anderson, who was interviewed by a German journalist in Halberstadt in 1952. When asked if it would have made any difference if the town had flown a huge white flag of surrender from the top of its tallest church spire, Anderson replied that the bombs were 'expensive items'; 'in practice', he said, 'they couldn't have been dropped over mountains or open country after so much labor had gone into making them at home.' No one contemplating the assembly of overwhelming US military power in the Persian Gulf, in 1991 and again in 2003, could doubt that a similar logic is again at play today. It is not easy to dismiss Sebald's concluding question: whether the human catastrophes produced so regularly and predictably by this industrially-driven logic should not be thought of as 'anticipations' of 'the point at which we shall drop out of what we have thought for so long to be our autonomous history and back into the history of nature.'

We do not believe such a cataclysmic outcome is inevitable. We take heart from Eric Hobsbawm's much-cited overview of the new American empire, in the June 2003 issue of *Le Monde Diplomatique*, which concludes with the thought that 'the only thing of which we are absolutely certain is that historically it will be a temporary phenomenon, as all … other empires have been.' Clearly, however, its defeat in good time depends on the left's ability to identify the contradictions – economic, political and ecological – of twenty-first century imperialism, and to develop effective counter-strategies in light of them. Unless the left can do this, the main response may increasingly – and ever more tragically – come from reactionary and atavistic elements. For despite its seemingly overwhelming oppressive power, American imperialism is beset by serious problems. One is the sheer cost, even for the US, of maintaining the military strength required for its new imperial ambitions. Another is the improbability of the total world order – pro-American, consumerist, resting stably on a veneer of electoral democracy – which the Bush administration appears to envisage, and the counter-productive nature of the use of brute force to achieve this unlikely political end. Even more important, perhaps, is the delegitimation that is increasingly likely to befall all the governments which the US must rely upon to govern its global empire. To find ways to intervene effectively in light of these contradictions, and to develop the capacities to do so, is the true imperial challenge to humanity.

Among our contributors, Sam Gindin holds the Packer Visiting Chair in Social Justice at York University, Toronto; Aijaz Ahmad teaches in the School of Political Studies at Jawaharlal Nehru University, New Delhi. David Harvey is with the Centre for Place, Culture, and Politics and teaches in the Anthropology Programme at the Graduate Center of the City University of New York. Greg Albo teaches Political Science at York University; and Noam Chomsky is Emeritus Professor of Linguistics at the Massachusetts Institute of Technology. Amy Bartholomew teaches in the Department of Law, and Jennifer Breakspear is a graduate student in its Legal Studies programme, at Carleton University in Ottawa. Paul Rogers teaches Peace Studies at Bradford University; and Michael Klare teaches Peace & World Security Studies at Hampshire College in Amherst, MA. Tina Wallace is a research associate in International Gender Studies, Queen Elizabeth House, Oxford University; and John Bellamy Foster teaches in the Department of Sociology at the University of Oregon, where Brett Clark is a graduate student. John Saul is Professor Emeritus of Political Science at York University. Emad El-Din Aysha writes for *The Egyptian Gazette* and until recently taught at the American University in Cairo. Bob Sutcliffe is an independent economic researcher who until recently taught at the University of the Basque Country in Bilbao.

Every preface to the *Register* over the past forty years has included the caveat that neither the editors nor the contributors necessarily agree with everything that appears in the volume. In introducing this caveat in their preface to the 1964 volume, Ralph Miliband and John Saville explained that they thought it was necessary to make clear that the editors' own 'definite and committed point of view', which obviously coloured their choice of contributors as well as what they themselves wrote, would in no way 'imprison discussion with a narrow framework.' We are pleased that the 'wide range of ideas and arguments' this policy was intended to promote continues to characterize the *Register*, and not least its 40th volume, and we thank all our contributors for making this possible.

We also want to thank Tony Zurbrugg and Adrian Howe at Merlin Press, not only for their hard work and skill in editing this volume, but for continuing, and indeed enhancing, the intimate relationship between Merlin Press and the

Socialist Register established by Merlin's founder, Martin Eve. Among the numerous improvements they have introduced have been imaginative new cover designs, and we are especially grateful to Louis Mackay for designing one for this volume that brilliantly captures what is perhaps the new American empire's most distinctive yet also most problematic characteristic, of seeking to rule through other states. A note he sent to us, in relation to the question of which countries' flags ought to be featured on the cover, expressed this rather aptly: 'It seems to me that the imperial order that is aspired to is one in which American power is unchallenged, and unchallengeable ... That would require North Korea and its fellow traveller on the axis of evil, France, to fall into line. I think the image works better if it includes countries that are not already allies, but are destined to become allies, in a world in which the US has *only* allies at the level of nation states. Then enemies can only be within.'

That the *Register* has flourished for four decades has been due to regular infusions of new blood – not least through the innovation in 1996 of contributing editors. We want particularly to thank both our contributing and our corresponding editors – including Bill Fletcher, Jr, currently Executive Director of the Trans-Africa Forum in Washington, D.C., who joined us as a new contributing editor last year – for their advice on this volume. We are also especially grateful to Alan Zuege, one of our contributing editors at York University, for once again deploying his exceptional skills as editorial assistant for this volume. Finally, we want to thank our contributing editor George Comninel for monitoring the list-serv *socialist-register@yorku.ca* (where items of interest on current affairs are posted daily and where discussions of *Register* essays are encouraged), and Marsha Niemeijer for maintaining the *Socialist Register* website *http://www.yorku.ca/socreg/*.

The *Socialist Register*'s 40th anniversary comes immediately after the *Economist*'s 160th. Long before the *Register* reaches that venerable age we trust that it will have become a journal of mainstream popular opinion. As it enters its fifth decade, this is what keeps all of us going.

July 2003
L.P.
C.L.

GLOBAL CAPITALISM AND AMERICAN EMPIRE

LEO PANITCH AND SAM GINDIN

'American imperialism… has been made plausible and attractive in part by the insistence that it is not imperialistic.'

Harold Innis, 1948[1]

The American empire is no longer concealed. In March 1999, the cover of the *New York Times Magazine* displayed a giant clenched fist painted in the stars and stripes of the US flag above the words: 'What The World Needs Now: For globalization to work, America can't be afraid to act like the almighty super-power that it is'. Thus was featured Thomas Friedman's 'Manifesto for a Fast World', which urged the United States to embrace its role as enforcer of the capitalist global order: '…the hidden hand of the market will never work without a hidden fist…. The hidden fist that keeps the world safe for Silicon Valley's tech-nologies is called the United States Army, Air Force, Navy and Marine Corps.' Four years later, in January 2003, when there was no longer any point in pretending the fist was hidden, the *Magazine* featured an essay by Michael Ignatieff entitled 'The Burden': '…[W]hat word but "empire" describes the awesome thing that America is becoming? …Being an imperial power… means enforcing such order as there is in the world and doing so in the American interest.'[2] The words, 'The American Empire (Get Used To It)', took up the whole cover of the *Magazine*.

Of course, the American state's geopolitical strategists had already taken this tack. Among those closest to the Democratic Party wing of the state, Zbigniew

Brzezinski did not mince words in his 1997 book, *The Grand Chessboard: American Primacy and Its Geostrategic Imperatives*, asserting that 'the three great imperatives of geo-political strategy are to prevent collusion and maintain security dependence amongst the vassals, to keep tributaries pliant, and to keep the barbarians from coming together.'[3] In the same year the Republican intellectuals who eventually would write the Bush White House's National Security Strategy founded the Project for a New American Century, with the goal of making imperial statecraft the explicit guiding principle of American policy.[4]

Most of what passes more generally for serious analysis in justifying the use of the term 'empire' in relation to the US today is really just an analogy, implicit or explicit, with imperial Rome. On the face of it, this is by no means absurd since, as an excellent recent book on the Roman Empire says, 'Romanization' could indeed be

> understood as the assimilation of the conquered nations to Roman culture and political worldview. The conquered became partners in running the empire. It was a selective process that applied directly only to the upper level of subject societies but it trickled down to all classes with benefits for some, negative consequences for others…. Roman supremacy was based on a masterful combination of violence and psychological persuasion – the harshest punishment for those who challenged it, the perception that their power knew no limits and that rewards were given to those who conformed.[5]

But an analogy is not a theory. The neglect of any serious political economy or pattern of historical determination that would explain the emergence and reproduction of today's American empire, and the dimensions of structural oppression and exploitation pertaining to it, is striking. It serves as a poignant reminder of why it was Marxism that made the running in theorizing imperialism for most of the twentieth century. But as a leading Indian Marxist, Prabhat Patnaik, noted in his essay 'Whatever Happened to Imperialism?', by 1990 the topic had also 'virtually disappeared from the pages of Marxist journals' and even Marxists looked 'bemused' when the term was mentioned. The costs of this for the left were severe. The concept of imperialism has always been especially important as much for its emotive and mobilizing qualities as for its analytic ones. Indeed, in Patnaik's view, rather than 'a theoretically self-conscious silence', the 'very fact that imperialism has become so adept at "managing" potential challenges to its hegemony made us indifferent to its ubiquitous presence.'[6] Yet the left's silence on imperialism also reflected severe analytic problems in the Marxist theory of imperialism. Indeed, this was obvious by the beginning of the 1970s – the last time the concept of imperialism had much currency – amidst complaints that the Marxist treatment of imperialism 'as an undifferentiated global product of a certain stage of capitalism' reflected its lack of 'any serious historical or sociological dimensions'.[7] As Giovanni Arrighi noted in 1978, 'by the end of the 60s, what had once been the *pride* of Marxism – the theory of imperialism – had become a tower of Babel, in which not even Marxists knew any longer how to find their way.'[8]

The confusion was apparent in debates in the early 1970s over the location of contemporary capitalism's contradictions. There were those who focused almost exclusively on the 'third world', and saw its resistance to imperialism as the sole source of transformation.[9] Others emphasized increasing contradictions within the developed capitalist world, fostering the impression that American 'hegemony' was in decline. This became the prevalent view, and by the mid-1980s the notion that 'the erosion of American economic, political, and military power is unmistakable' grew into a commonplace.[10] Although very few went back to that aspect of the Marxist theory of inter-imperial rivalry that suggested a military trial of strength, an era of intense regional economic rivalry was expected. As Glyn and Sutcliffe put it, all it was safe to predict was that without a hegemonic power 'the world economy will continue without a clear leader...'[11]

There was indeed no little irony in the fact that so many continued to turn away from what they thought was the old-fashioned notion of imperialism, just when the ground was being laid for its renewed fashionability in the *New York Times*. Even after the 1990-91 Gulf War which, as Bruce Cumings pointed out, 'had the important goal of assuring American control of... Middle Eastern oil', you still needed 'an electron microscope to find "imperialism" used to describe the U.S. role in the world.' The Gulf War, he noted, 'went forward under a virtual obliteration of critical discourse egged on by a complacent media in what can only be called an atmosphere of liberal totalism.'[12] This continued through the 1990s, even while, as the recent book by the conservative Andrew Bacevich has amply documented, the Clinton Administration often outdid its Republican predecessors in unleashing military power to quell resistance to the continuing aggressive American pursuit of 'an open and integrated international order based on the principles of democratic capitalism.' Quoting Madeleine Albright, Clinton's Secretary of State, in 1998: 'If we have to use force, it is because we are America. We are the indispensable nation,' and, in 2000, Richard Haas, the State Department's Director of Policy Planning in the incoming Bush Administration, calling on Americans finally to reconceive their state's 'global role from one of a traditional nation state to an imperial power', Bacevich argues that the continuing avoidance of the term imperialism could not last. It was at best an 'astigmatism', and at worst 'an abiding preference for averting our eyes from the unflagging self-interest and large ambitions underlying all U.S. policy'.[13]

By the turn of the century, and most obviously once the authors of the Project for a New American Century were invested with power in Washington D.C., the term imperialism was finally back on even a good many liberals' lips. The popularity of Hardt and Negri's tome, *Empire*, had caught the new conjuncture even before the second war on Iraq. But their insistence (reflecting the widespread notion that the power of all nation states had withered in the era of globalization) that *'the United States does not, and indeed no nation state can today, form the center of an imperialist project'* was itself bizarrely out of sync with the times.[14]

The left needs a new theorization of imperialism, one that will transcend the limitations of the old Marxist 'stagist' theory of inter-imperial rivalry, and allow for a full appreciation of the historical factors that have led to the formation of a unique American informal empire. This will involve understanding how the American state developed the capacity to eventually incorporate its capitalist rivals, and oversee and police 'globalization' – i.e. the spread of capitalist social relations to every corner of the world. The theory must be able to answer the question of what made plausible the American state's insistence that it was not imperialistic, and how this was put into practice and institutionalized; and, conversely, what today makes implausible the American state's insistence that it is not imperialistic, and what effects its lack of concealment might have in terms of its attractiveness and its capacity to manage global capitalism and sustain its global empire.

RETHINKING IMPERIALISM

There is a structural logic to capitalism that tends to its expansion and inter-nationalization. This was famously captured in Marx's description in the *Communist Manifesto* of a future that stunningly matches our present: 'The need of a constantly expanding market for its products chases the bourgeoisie over the whole surface of the globe. It must nestle everywhere, settle everywhere, establish connections everywhere... it creates a world after its own image.' But affirming Marx's prescience in this respect runs the risk of treating what is now called globalization as inevitable and irreversible. It must be remembered that Marx's words also seemed to apply at the end of the nineteenth century, when, as Karl Polanyi noted, '[o]nly a madman would have doubted that the international economic system was the axis of the material existence of the human race'.[15] Yet, as Polanyi was concerned to explain, far from continuing uninterrupted, there were already indications that the international economic system of the time was in the early stages of dissolution, and would soon collapse via two horrific world wars and the implosion of the Great Depression.

The postwar reconstruction of the capitalist world order was a direct response on the part of the leading capitalist states to that earlier failure of globalization. Through the Bretton Woods infrastructure for a new liberal trading order the dynamic logic of capitalist globalization was once again unleashed. During the brief post-war 'golden age' – through the acceleration of trade, the new degree of direct foreign investment, and the growing internationalization of finance – capitalist globalization was revived, and was further invigorated through the neoliberal response to the economic crisis of the 1970s. The outcome of this crisis showed that the international effects of structural crises in accumulation are not predictable *a priori*. Of the three great structural crises of capitalism, the first (post-1870s) accelerated inter-imperialist rivalry and led to World War One and Communist revolution, while the second crisis (the Great Depression) actually reversed capitalism's internationalizing trajectory. Yet the crisis of the early 1970s was followed by a deepening, acceleration and extension of capitalist globalization. And while this promoted inter-regional economic competition, it did not produce anything like the old inter-imperial rivalry.

What this erratic trajectory from the nineteenth to the twenty-first century suggests is that the process of globalization is neither inevitable (as was conventionally assumed in the latter part of the nineteenth century and as is generally assumed again today), nor impossible to sustain (as Lenin and Polanyi, in their different ways, both contended). The point is that we need to distinguish between the expansive tendency of capitalism and its actual history. A global capitalist order is always a contingent social construct: the actual development and continuity of such an order must be problematized. There is a tendency within certain strains of Marxism, as in much bourgeois analysis, to write theory in the present tense. We must not theorize history in such a way that the trajectory of capitalism is seen as a simple derivative of abstract economic laws. Rather, it is crucial to adhere to the Marxist methodological insight that insists, as Philip McMichael has argued, that it is necessary to '*historicize theory*, that is to problematize globalization as a relation immanent in capitalism, but with quite distinct material (social, political and environmental) relations across time and time-space... Globalization is not simply the unfolding of capitalist tendencies but a historically distinct project shaped, or complicated, by the contradictory relations of previous episodes of globalization.'[16]

Above all, the realization – or frustration – of capitalism's globalizing tendencies cannot be understood apart from the role played by the states that have historically constituted the capitalist world. The rise of capitalism is inconceivable without the role that European states played in establishing the legal and infrastructural frameworks for property, contract, currency, competition and wage-labour within their own borders, while also generating a process of uneven development (and the attendant construction of race) in the modern world. This had gone so far by the mid-to late nineteenth century that when capital expanded beyond the borders of a given European nation-state, it could do so within new capitalist social orders that had been – or were just being – established by other states, or it expanded within a framework of formal or informal empire. Yet this was not enough to sustain capital's tendency to global expansion. No adequate means of overall global capitalist regulation existed, leaving the international economy and its patterns of accumulation fragmented, and thus fuelling the inter-imperial rivalry that led to World War I.

The classical theories of imperialism developed at the time, from Hobson's to Lenin's, were founded on a theorization of capitalist economic stages and crises. This was a fundamental mistake that has, ever since, continued to plague proper understanding.[17] The classical theories were defective in their historical reading of imperialism, in their treatment of the dynamics of capital accumulation, and in their elevation of a conjunctural moment of inter-imperial rivalry to an immutable law of capitalist globalization. A distinctive capitalist version of imperialism did not suddenly arrive with the so-called monopoly or finance-capital stage of capitalism in the late nineteenth century, as we argue below. Moreover, the theory of crisis derived from the classical understanding of this period was mistakenly used to explain capitalism's expansionist tendencies. If capitalists looked to the export of capital as well as trade in foreign markets, it was not so much because centralization and concentration of capital had ushered in a new stage marked by the falling rate of profit, overaccumulation and/or undercon-sumption. Rather, akin to the process that had earlier led individual units of capital to move out of their original location in a given village or town, it was the accelerated competitive pressures and opportunities, and the attendant strate-gies and emerging capacities of a developing capitalism, that pushed and facilitated the international expansionism of the late nineteenth and early twen-tieth centuries.

The classical theorists of imperialism also failed to apprehend adequately the spatial dimensions of this internationalization. They made too much of the export of goods and capital to what we now call the 'third world', because the latter's very underdevelopment limited its capacity to absorb such flows. And they failed to discern two key developments in the leading capitalist countries themselves. Rather than an exhaustion of consumption possibilities within the leading capi-talist countries – a premise based on what Lenin's pamphlet *Imperialism* called 'the semi-starvation level of existence of the masses' – more and more Western working classes were then achieving increasing levels of private and public consumption.[18] And rather than the concentration of capital in these countries limiting the introduction of new products so that 'capital cannot find a field for profitable investment',[19] the very unevenness of on-going competition and tech-nological development was introducing new prospects for internal accumulation. There was a deepening of capital at home, not just a spreading of capital abroad.

Far from being the highest stage of capitalism, what these theorists were observing was (as is now obvious) a relatively *early* phase of capitalism. This was so not just in terms of consumption patterns, financial flows and competition, but also in terms of the limited degree of foreign direct investment at the time, and the very rudimentary means that had then been developed for managing the contradictions associated with capitalism's internationalization.

It was, however, in their reductionist and instrumental treatment of the state that these theorists were especially defective.[20] Imperialism is not reducible to an economic explanation, even if economic forces are always a large part of it. We need, in this respect, to keep imperialism and capitalism as two distinct concepts. Competition amongst capitalists in the international arena, unequal exchange and uneven development are all aspects of capitalism itself, and their relationship to imperialism can only be understood through a theorization of the state. When states pave the way for their national capitals' expansion abroad, or even when they follow and manage that expansion, this can only be understood in terms of these states' relatively autonomous role in maintaining social order and securing the conditions of capital accumulation; and we must therefore factor state administrative capacities as well as class, cultural and military determinations into the explanation of the imperial aspect of this role.

Capitalist imperialism, then, needs to be understood through an extension of the theory of the capitalist state, rather than derived directly from the theory of economic stages or crises. And such a theory needs to comprise not only inter-imperial rivalry, and the conjunctural predominance of one imperial state, but also the structural pene-tration of former rivals by one imperial state. This means we need to historicize the theory, beginning by breaking with the conventional notion that the nature of modern imperialism was once and for all determined by the kinds of economic rivalries attending the stage of industrial concentration and financialization asso-ciated with turn-of-the-century 'monopoly capital'.

In fact, the transition to the modern form of imperialism may be located in the British state's articulation of its old mercantile formal empire with the informal empire it spawned in the mid-nineteenth century during the era of 'free trade'. Schumpeter's theory of imperialism as reflecting the atavistic role within capitalism of pre-capitalist exploiting and warrior classes, and both Kautsky's and Lenin's conception that mid-nineteenth century British industrial capital and its policy of free trade reflected a 'pure' capitalism antithetical or at least 'indifferent' to imperial expansion,[21] all derived from too crude an understanding of the sepa-ration of the economic from the political under capitalism. This lay at the root of the notion that the replacement of the era of free competition by the era of finance capital had ended that separation, leading to imperialist expansion, rivalry and war among the leading capitalist states.

Like contemporary discussions of globalization in the context of neoliberal 'free market' policies, the classical Marxist accounts of the nineteenth century era of free trade and its supersession by the era of inter-imperial rivalry also confus-ingly counterposed 'states' and 'markets'. In both cases there is a failure to appreciate the crucial role of the state in making 'free markets' possible and then to make them work. Just as the emergence of so-called 'laissez faire' under mid-nineteenth century industrial capitalism entailed a highly active state to effect the formal separation of the polity and economy, and to define and police the domestic social relations of a fully capitalist order, so did the external policy of free trade entail an extension of the imperial role along all of these dimensions on the part of the first state that 'created a form of imperialism driven by the logic of capitalism'.[22]

As Gallagher and Robinson showed 50 years ago, in a seminal essay entitled 'The Imperialism of Free Trade', the conventional notion (shared by Kautsky, Lenin and Schumpeter) that British free trade and imperialism did not mix was belied by innumerable occupations and annexations, the addition of new colonies, and especially by the importance of India to the Empire, between the 1840s and the 1870s. It was belied even more by the immense extension, for both economic and strategic reasons, of Britain's 'informal empire' via foreign investment, bilateral trade, 'friendship' treaties and gunboat diplomacy, so that 'mercantilist techniques of formal empire were being employed in the mid-

Victorian age at the same time as informal techniques of free trade were being used in Latin America. It is for this reason that attempts to make phases of imperialism correspond directly to phases in the economic growth of the metropolitan economy are likely to prove in vain...'[23] Gallagher and Robinson defined imperialism in terms of a *variable political function* 'of integrating new regions into the expanding economy; its character is largely decided by the various and changing relationships between the political and economic elements of expansion in any particular region and time.'

> ...In other words, it is the politics as well as the economics of the informal empire which we have to include in the account... The type of political lien between the expanding economy and its formal and informal dependencies... has tended to vary with the economic value of the territory, the strength of its political structure, the readiness of its rulers to collaborate with British commercial and strategic purposes, the ability of the native society to undergo economic change without external control, the extent to which domestic and foreign political situations permitted British intervention, and, finally, how far European rivals allowed British policy a free hand.[24]

This is not to say there are not important differences between informal and formal empire. Informal empire requires the economic and cultural penetration of other states to be sustained by political and military coordination with other independent governments. The main factor that determined the shift to the extension of formal empires after the 1880s was not the inadequacy of Britain's relationship with its own informal empire, nor the emergence of the stage of monopoly or 'finance capital', but rather *Britain's inability to incorporate the newly emerging capitalist powers of Germany, the US and Japan into 'free trade imperialism'*. Various factors determined this, including pre-capitalist social forces that did indeed remain important in some of these countries, nationalist sentiments that accompanied the development of capitalist nation-states, strategic responses to domestic class struggles as well as geo-political and military rivalries, and especially the limited ability of the British state – reflecting also the growing separation between British financial and industrial capital – to prevent these other states trying to overturn the consequences of uneven development. What ensued was the rush for colonies and the increasing organization of trade competition via protectionism (tariffs served as the main tax base of these states as well as protective devices for nascent industrial bourgeoisies and working classes). In this context, the international institutional apparatuses of diplomacy and alliances, British naval supremacy and the Gold Standard were too fragile even to guarantee equal treatment of foreign capital with national capital within each state (the key prerequisite of capitalist globalization), let alone to mediate the conflicts and manage the contradictions associated with the development of global capitalism by the late nineteenth century.

No less than Lenin, by 1914 Kautsky had accepted, following Hilferding's

Finance Capital, that 'a brutal and violent' form of imperialist competition was 'a product of highly developed industrial capitalism.'[25] Kautsky was right to perceive, however, that even if inter-imperial rivalry had led to war between the major capitalist powers, this was not an inevitable characteristic of capitalist globalization. What so incensed Lenin, with his proclivity for over-politicizing theory, was that Kautsky thought that all the major capitalist ruling classes, after 'having learned the lesson of the world war', might eventually come to revive capitalist globalization through a collaborative 'ultra-imperialism' in face of the increasing strength of an industrial proletariat that nevertheless still fell short of the capacity to effect a socialist transformation. But Kautsky himself made his case reductively, that is, by conceiving his notion of ultra-imperialism from, as he repeatedly put it, 'a purely economic standpoint', rather than in terms of any serious theory of the state. Moreover, had Kautsky put greater stress on his earlier perception (in 1911) that 'the United States is the country that shows us our social future in capitalism', and discerned the capacity of the newly emerging informal American empire for eventually penetrating and coordinating the other leading capitalist states, rather than anticipating an equal alliance amongst them, he might have been closer to the mark in terms of what finally actually happened after 1945. But what could hardly yet be clearly foreseen were the developments, both inside the American social formation and state as well as internationally, that allowed American policy makers to think that 'only the US had the power to grab hold of history and make it conform.'[26]

THE AMERICAN REPUBLIC:
'EXTENSIVE EMPIRE AND SELF-GOVERNMENT'

The central place the United States now occupies within global capitalism rests on a particular convergence of structure and history. In the abstract, we can identify specific institutions as reflecting the structural power of capitalism. But what blocks such institutions from emerging and what, if anything, opens the door to their development, is a matter of historical conjunctures. The crucial phase in the reconstruction of global capitalism – after the earlier breakdowns and before the reconstitution of the last quarter of the twentieth century – occurred during and after World War II. It was only after (and as a state-learned response to) the disasters of Depression and the Second World War that capitalist globalization obtained a new life. This depended, however, on the emergence and uneven historical evolution of a set of structures developed under the leadership of a unique *agent*: the American imperial state.

The role the United States came to play in world capitalism was not inevitable but nor was it merely accidental: it was not a matter of teleology but of capitalist history. The capacity it developed to 'conjugate' its *particular* power with the *general* task of coordination' in a manner that reflected 'the particular matrix of its own social history', as Perry Anderson has recently put it, was founded on 'the attractive power of US models of production and culture... increasingly unified in the sphere of consumption.' Coming together here were, on the one hand, the invention in the US of the modern corporate form, 'scientific management' of the labour process, and assembly-line mass production; and, on the other, Hollywood-style 'narrative and visual schemas stripped to their most abstract', appealing to and aggregating waves of immigrants through the 'dramatic simplification and repetition'.[27] The dynamism of American capitalism and its worldwide appeal combined with the universalistic language of American liberal democratic ideology to underpin a capacity for informal empire far beyond that of nineteenth century Britain's. Moreover, by spawning the modern multinational corporation, with foreign direct investment in production and services, the American informal empire was to prove much more penetrative of other social formations.

Yet it was not only the economic and cultural formation of American capitalism, but also the formation of the American state that facilitated a new informal empire. Against Anderson's impression that the American state's constitutional structures lack the 'carrying power' of its economic and cultural ones (by virtue of being 'moored to eighteenth century arrangements')[28] stands Thomas Jefferson's observation in 1809 that 'no constitution was ever before as well-calculated for extensive empire and self-government.'[29] Hardt and Negri were right to trace the pre-figuration of what they call 'Empire' today back to the American constitution's incorporation of Madisonian 'network power'.[30] This entailed not only checks and balances within the state apparatus, but the notion that the greater plurality of interests incorporated within an extensive and expansive state would guarantee that the masses would have no common motive or capacity to come together to check the ruling class.[31] Yet far from anticipating the sort of decentred and amorphous power that Hardt and Negri imagine characterized the US historically (and characterizes 'Empire' today), the constitutional framework of the new American state gave great powers to the central government to expand trade and make war. As early as 1783, what George Washington already spoke of ambitiously as 'a rising empire'[32] was captured in the Federalist Paper XI image of 'one great American system superior to the control of all transatlantic force or influence and able to dictate the terms of connection between the old and the new world!'[33]

The notion of empire employed here was conceived, of course, in relation to the other mercantile empires of the eighteenth century. But the state which emerged out of the ambitions of the 'expansionist colonial elite',[34] with Northern merchants (supported by artisans and commercial farmers) and the Southern plantation-owners allying against Britain's formal mercantile empire, evinced from its beginnings a trajectory leading to capitalist development and informal empire. The initial form this took was through territorial expansion westward, largely through the extermination of the native population, and blatant exploitation not only of the black slave population but also debt-ridden subsistence farmers and, from at least the 1820s on, an emerging industrial working class. Yet the new American state could still conceive of itself as embodying republican liberty, and be widely admired for it, largely due to the link between 'extensive empire and self-government' embedded in the federal constitution. In Bernard DeVoto's words, 'The American empire would not be mercantilist but in still another respect something new under the sun: the West was not to be colonies but states.'[35]

And the 'state rights' of these states were no mirage: they reflected the two different types of social relations – slave and free – that composed each successive wave of new states and by 1830 limited the activist economic role of the federal state. After the domestic inter-state struggles that eventually led to civil war, the defeat of the plantocracy and the dissolution of slavery, the federal constitution provided a framework for the unfettered domination of an industrial capitalism with the largest domestic market in the world, obviating any temptation towards formal imperialism via territorial conquest abroad.[36] The outcome of the Civil War allowed for a reconstruction of the relationship between financial and industrial capital and the federal state, inclining state administrative capacities and policies away from mercantilism and towards extended capitalist reproduction.[37] Herein lies the significance that Anderson himself attaches to the evolving juridical form of the American state, whereby 'unencumbered property rights, untrammeled litigation, the invention of the corporation' led to

> what Polanyi most feared, a juridical system disembedding the market as far as possible from ties of custom, tradition or solidarity, whose very abstraction from them later proved – American firms like American films – exportable and reproducible across the world, in a way that no other competitor could quite match. The steady transformation of international merchant law and arbitration in conformity with US standards is witness to the process.[38]

The expansionist tendencies of American capitalism in the latter half of the nineteenth century (reflecting pressures from domestic commercial farmers as much as from the industrialists and financiers of the post-civil war era) were even more apt to take informal forms than had those of British capitalism, even though they were not based on a policy of free trade. The modalities were initially similar, and they began long before the Spanish-American War of 1898, which is usually seen as the start of US imperial expansion. This was amply documented in a paper boldly called 'An Indicator of Informal Empire' prepared for the US Center for Naval Analysis: between 1869 and 1897 the US Navy made no less than 5,980 ports of call to protect American commercial shipping in Argentina, Brazil Chile, Nicaragua, Panama, Columbia and elsewhere in Latin America.[39] Yet the establishment of colonies in Puerto Rico and the Philippines and the annexation of Hawaii 'was a deviation … from the typical economic, political and ideological forms of domination already characteristic of American imperialism.'[40] Rather, it was through American foreign direct investment and the modern corporate form – epitomized by the Singer Company establishing itself as the first multinational corporation when it jumped the Canadian tariff barrier to establish a subsidiary to produce sewing machines for prosperous Ontario wheat farmers – that the American informal empire soon took shape in a manner quite distinct from the British one.[41]

The articulation of the new informal American empire with military intervention was expressed by Theodore Roosevelt in 1904 in terms of the exercise of 'international police power', in the absence of other means of international control, to the end of establishing regimes that know 'how to act with reasonable efficiency and decency in social and political matters' and to ensure that each such regime 'keeps order and pays its obligations': '[A] nation desirous both of securing respect for itself and of doing good to others [Teddy Roosevelt declared, in language that has now been made very familiar again] must have a force adequate for the work which it feels is allotted to it as its part of the general world duty... A great free people owes to itself and to all mankind not to sink into helplessness before the powers of evil.'[42]

The American genius for presenting its informal empire in terms of the framework of universal rights reached its apogee under Woodrow Wilson. It also reached the apogee of hypocrisy, especially at the Paris Peace Conference, where Keynes concluded Wilson was 'the greatest fraud on earth'.[43] Indeed, it was not only the US Congress's isolationist tendencies, but the incapacity of the American presidential, treasury and military apparatuses, that explained the failure of the United States to take responsibility for leading European reconstruction after World War One. The administrative and regulatory expansion of the American state under the impact of corporate liberalism in the Progressive era,[44] and the spread of American direct investment through the 1920s (highlighted by General Motor's purchase of Opel immediately before the Great Depression, completing the 'virtual division' of the German auto industry between GM and Ford)[45] were significant developments. Yet it was only during the New Deal that the US state really began to develop the modern planning capacities that would, once they were redeployed in World War II, transform and vastly extend America's informal imperialism.[46]

Amidst the remarkable depression-era class struggles these capacities were limited by 'political fragmentation, expressed especially in executive-congressional conflict, combined with deepening tensions between business and government...'[47] America's entry into World War II, however, not only resolved 'the statebuilding impasse of the late 1930s' but also provided 'the essential underpinnings for postwar U.S. governance.' As Brian Waddell notes in his outstanding study of the transition from the state-building of the Depression to that of World War II:

> The requirements of total war... revived corporate political leverage, allowing corporate executives inside and outside the state extensive influence over wartime mobilization policies... Assertive corporate executives and military officials formed a very effective wartime alliance that not only blocked any augmentation of the New Dealer authority but also organized a powerful alternative to the New Deal. International activism displaced and supplanted New Deal domestic activism.

Thus was the stage finally set for a vastly extended and much more powerful informal US empire outside its own hemisphere.

THE AMERICAN RECONSTRUCTION OF A CAPITALIST WORLD ORDER

The shift of 'U.S. state capacities towards realizing internationally-interventionist goals versus domestically-interventionist ones'[48] was crucial to the revival of capitalism's globalizing tendencies after World War II. This not only took place through the wartime reconstruction of the American state, but also through the more radical postwar reconstruction of all the states at the core of the old inter-imperial rivalry. And it also took place alongside – indeed it led to – the multiplication of new states out of the old colonial empires. Among the various dimensions of this new relationship between capitalism and imperialism, the most important was that *the densest imperial networks and institutional linkages, which had earlier run north-south between imperial states and their formal or informal colonies, now came to run between the US and the other major capitalist states.*

What Britain's informal empire had been unable to manage (indeed hardly to even contemplate) in the nineteenth century was now accomplished by the American informal empire, which succeeded in integrating all the other capitalist powers into an effective system of coordination under its aegis. Even apart from the U.S. military occupations, the devastation of the European and Japanese economies and the weak political legitimacy of their ruling classes at the war's end created an unprecedented opportunity which the American state was now ready and willing to exploit. In these conditions, moreover, the expansion of the informal American empire after World War II was hardly a one-way (let alone solely coercive) imposition – it was often 'imperialism by invitation'.[49]

However important was the development of the national security state apparatus and the geostrategic planning that framed the division of the world with the USSR at Yalta,[50] no less important was the close attention the Treasury and State Department paid during the war to plans for relaunching a coordinated liberal trading regime and a rule-based financial order. This was accomplished by manipulating the debtor status of the US's main allies, assisted by the complete domination of the dollar as a world currency and the fact that 50% of world production was now accounted for by the U.S. economy. The American state had learned well the lesson of its post-World War I incapacity to combine liberal internationalist rhetoric with an institutional commitment to manage an international capitalist order. Through the very intricate joint planning of the British and American Treasuries during the war[51] – i.e. through the process that led to Bretton Woods – the Americans not only ensured that the British were 'accepting some obligation to modify their domestic policy in light of its international effects on stability', but also ensured the liquidation of the British Empire by 'throwing Britain into the arms of America as a supplicant, and therefore subordinate; a subordination masked by the illusion of a "special relationship" which continues to this day'.[52]

But it was by no means only the US dollars that were decisive here, nor was Britain the only object of America's new informal empire. A pamphlet inserted in *Fortune* magazine in May 1942 on 'The U.S. in a New World: Relations with Britain' set out a program for the 'integration of the American and British economic systems as the foundation for a wider postwar integration':

> ... if a world order is to arise out of this war, it is realistic to believe that it will not spring full-blown from a conference of fifty states held at given date to draw up a World Constitution. It is more likely to be the gradual outgrowth of the wartime procedures now being developed... If the U.S. rejects a lone-wolf imperialism and faces the fact that a League of Nations or some other universal parliament cannot be set up in the near future...[this] does not prevent America from approaching Britain with a proposal for economic integration as a first step towards a general reconstruction procedure. Unless we can reach a meeting of minds with Britain and the Dominions on these questions it is utopian to expect wider agreement among all the United Nations.[53]

This pamphlet was accompanied by a lengthy collective statement[54] by the editors of *Fortune* and *Time* and *Life* magazines which began with the premise that 'America will emerge as the strongest single power in the postwar world, and...it is therefore up to it to decide what kind of postwar world it wants.' They called, in this context, for 'mutual trust between the businessman and his government' after the tensions of the New Deal, so that government could exercise its responsibilities both 'to use its fiscal policy as a balance wheel, and to use its legislative and administrative power to promote and foster private enterprise, by removing barriers to its natural expansion...' This would produce 'an expansionist context in which tariffs, subsidies, monopolies, restrictive labor rules, plantation feudalism, poll taxes, technological backwardness, obsolete tax laws, and all other barriers to further expansion can be removed.' While recognizing that 'the uprising of [the] international proletariat... the most significant fact of the last twenty years... means that complete international free trade, as Cobden used to preach it and Britain used to practice it, is no longer an immediate political possibility', nevertheless free trade between the US and the Britain would be 'a jolt both economies need' and on this basis 'the area of freedom would spread – gradually through the British Dominions, through Latin America, perhaps someday through the world. For universal free trade, not bristling nationalism, is the *ultimate* goal of a rational world.' And in terms that were uncharacteristically direct, the editors called this a new imperialism:

> Thus, a new American 'imperialism', if it is to be called that, will – or rather can – be quite different from the British type. It can also be different from the premature American type that followed our expansion in the Spanish war. American imperialism can afford to complete the work the British started; instead of salesmen and planters, its representatives can be brains and bulldozers, technicians and machine tools. American imperi-

alism does not need extra-territoriality; it can get along better in Asia if the tuans and sahibs stay home… Nor is the U.S. afraid to help build up industrial rivals to its own power… because we know industrialization stimulates rather than limits international trade… This American imperialism sounds very abstemious and high-minded. It is nevertheless a feasible policy for America, because friendship, not food, is what we need most from the rest of the world.

The immense managerial capacity the American state had developed to make this perspective a reality was nowhere more clearly confirmed than at the Bretton Woods conference in 1944. The Commission responsible for establishing the IMF was chaired and tightly controlled by the 'New Dealer' Harry Dexter White for the American Treasury, and even though Keynes chaired the Commission responsible for planning what eventually became the World Bank, and though the various committees under him were also chaired by non-Americans, 'they had American rapporteurs and secretaries, appointed and briefed by White', who also arranged for 'a conference journal to be produced every day to keep everyone informed of the main decisions. At his disposal were 'the mass of stenographers working day and night [and] the boy scouts acting as pages and distributors of papers' – all written in a 'legal language which made everything difficult to understand [amidst] the great variety of unintelligible tongues'. This was the 'controlled Bedlam' the American Treasury wanted in order to 'make easier the imposition of a *fait accompli*.' It was in this context that every delegation finally decided 'it was better to run with the US Treasury than its disgruntled critics, "who [Keynes put it] do not know their own mind and have no power whatever to implement their promises."' The conference ended with Keynes's tribute to a process in which 44 countries 'had been learning to work together so that "the brotherhood of man will become more than a phrase." The delegates applauded wildly. "The Star Spangled Banner" was played'.[55]

With the IMF and World Bank headquarters established at American insistence in Washington, D.C., a pattern was set for international economic management among all the leading capitalist countries that continues to this day, one in which even when European or Japanese finance ministries and central banks propose, the US Treasury and Federal Reserve dispose.[56] The dense institutional linkages binding these states to the American empire were also institutionalized, of course, through the institutions of NATO, not to mention the hub-and-spokes networks binding each of the other leading capitalist states to the intelligence and security apparatuses of the US as part of the strategy of containment of Communism during the Cold War. These interacted with economic networks, as well as with new propaganda, intellectual and media networks, to explain, justify and promote the new imperial reality.

Most of those who stress the American state's military and intelligence links with the coercive apparatuses of Europe and Japan tend to see the roots of this in the dynamics of the Cold War.[57] Yet as Bacevich, looking at American policy from the perspective of the collapse of the USSR, has recently said:

To conceive of US grand strategy from the late 1940's through the 1980's as 'containment' – with no purpose apart from resisting the spread of Soviet power – is not wrong, but it is incomplete...[S]uch a cramped conception of Cold War strategy actively impedes our understanding of current US policy...No strategy worthy of the name is exclusively passive or defensive in orientation...US grand strategy during the Cold War required not only containing communism but also taking active measures to open up the world politically, culturally, and, above all, economically – which is precisely what policymakers said they intended to do.[58]

What an exclusive concentration on the foreign policy, intelligence and coercive apparatuses also obscures is how far the American 'Protectorate System' (as Peter Gowan calls it), was part of actually 'alter[ing] the character of the capitalist core.' For it entailed the 'internal transformation of social relations within the protectorates in the direction of the American "Fordist" system of accumulation [that] opened up the possibility of a vast extension of their *internal markets*, with the working class not only as source of expanded surplus value but also an increasingly important consumption centre for *realizing* surplus value.'[59] While the new informal empire still provided room for the other core states to act as 'autonomous organizing centres of capital accumulation', the emulation of US technological and managerial 'Fordist' forms (initially organized and channelled through the post-war joint 'productivity councils') was massively reinforced by American foreign direct investment. Here too, the core of the American imperial network shifted towards to the advanced capitalist countries, so that between 1950 and 1970 Latin America's share of total American FDI fell from 40 to under 20 percent, while Western Europe's more than doubled to match the Canadian share of over 30 percent.[60] It was hardly surprising that acute outside observers such as Raymond Aron and Nicos Poulantzas saw in Europe a tendential 'Canadianization' as the model form of integration into the American empire.[61]

None of this meant, of course, that the north–south dimension of imperialism became unimportant. But it did mean that the other core capitalist countries' relationships with the third world, including their ex-colonies, were imbricated with American informal imperial rule. The core capitalist countries might continue to benefit from the north–south divide, but any interventions had to be either American-initiated or at least have American approval (as Suez proved). Only the American state could arrogate to itself the right to intervene against the sovereignty of other states (which it repeatedly did around the world) and only the American state reserved for itself the 'sovereign' right to reject international rules and norms when necessary. It is in this sense that only the American state was actively 'imperialist'.

Though informal imperial rule seemed to place the 'third world' and the core capitalist countries on the same political and economic footing, both the legacy of the old imperialism and the vast imbalance in resources between the Marshall Plan and third world development aid reproduced global inequalities. The space was afforded the European states to develop internal economic coherence and growing domestic markets in the post-war era, and European economic integration was also explicitly encouraged by the US precisely as a mechanism for the 'European rescue of the nation-state', in Alan Milward's apt formulation.[62] But this contrasted with American dislike of import-substitution industrialization strategies adopted by states in the south, not to mention US hostility to planned approaches to developing the kind of auto-centric economic base that the advanced capitalist states had created for themselves before they embraced a liberal international economic order. (Unlike the kind of geostrategic concerns that predominated in the American wars in Korea and Vietnam, it was opposition to economic nationalism that determined the US state's involvement in the overthrow of numerous governments from Iran to Chile.). The predictable result – given limits on most of the third world's internal markets, and the implications of all the third world states competing to break into international markets – was that global inequalities increased, even though a few third world states, such as South Korea, were able to use the geostrategic space that the new empire afforded them to develop rapidly and narrow the gap.

Still, in general terms, the new informal form of imperial rule, not only in the advanced capitalist world but also in those regions of the third world where it held sway, was characterized by the penetration of borders, not their dissolution. It was not through formal empire, but rather through the reconstitution of states as integral elements of an informal American empire, that the international capitalist order was now organized and regulated. Nation states remained the primary vehicles through which (a) the social relations and institutions of class, property, currency, contract and markets were established and reproduced; and (b) the international accumulation of capital was carried out. The vast expansion of direct foreign investment worldwide, whatever the shifting regional shares of the total, meant that far from capital escaping the state, it expanded its dependence on *many* states. At the same time, capital as an effective social force within any given state now tended to include both foreign capital and domestic capital with international linkages and ambitions. Their interpenetration made the notion of distinct national bourgeoisies – let alone rivalries between them in any sense analogous to those that led to World War I – increasingly anachronistic.

A further dimension of the new relationship between capitalism and empire was thus the *internationalization of the state*, understood as a state's acceptance of responsibility for managing its domestic capitalist order in way that contributes to managing the international capitalist order.[63] For the American imperial state, however, the internationalization of the state had a special quality. It entailed defining the American national interest in terms of acting not only on behalf of its own capitalist class but also on behalf of the extension and reproduction of global capitalism. The determination of what this required continued to reflect the particularity of the American state and social formation, but it was increasingly inflected towards a conception of the American state's role as that of ensuring the survival of 'free enterprise' in the US itself through its promotion of free enterprise and free trade internationally. This was classically articulated in President Truman's famous speech against isolationism at Baylor University in March 1947:

> Now, as in the year 1920, we have reached a turning point in history. National economies have been disrupted by the war. The future is uncertain everywhere. Economic policies are in a state of flux. In this atmosphere of doubt and hesitation, the decisive factor will be the type of leadership that the United States gives the world. We are the giant of the economic world. Whether we like it or not, the future pattern of economic relations depends upon us... Our foreign relations, political and economic, are indivisible.[64]

The internationalization of the Americans state was fully encapsulated in National Security Council document NSC-68 of 1950, which (although it remained 'Top Secret' until 1975) Kolko calls 'the most important of all postwar policy documents'. It articulated most clearly the goal of constructing a 'world environment in which the American system can survive and flourish... Even if there were no Soviet Union we would face the great problem... [that] the absence of order among nations is becoming less and less tolerable.'[65]

THE RECONSTITUTION OF AMERICAN EMPIRE IN THE NEOLIBERAL ERA

This pattern of imperial rule was established in the post-war period of reconstruction, a period that, for all of the economic dynamism of 'the golden age', was inherently transitional. The very notion of 'reconstruction' posed the question of what might follow once the European and Japanese economies were rebuilt and became competitive with the American, and once the benign circumstances of the post-war years were exhausted.[66] Moreover, peasants' and workers' struggles and rising economic nationalism in the third world, and growing working class militancy in the core capitalist countries, were bound to have an impact both on capital's profits and on the institutions of the post-war institutional order.

In less than a generation, the contradictions inherent in the Bretton Woods agreement were exposed. By the time European currencies became fully convertible in 1958, almost all the premises of the 1944 agreement were already in question. The fixed exchange rates established by that agreement depended on the capital controls that most countries other than the US maintained after the war.[67] Yet the very internationalization of trade and direct foreign investment that Bretton Woods promoted (along with domestic innovations and competition in mortgages, credit, investment banking and brokerage that strengthened the capacity of the financial sector within the United States) contributed to the restoration of a global financial market, the corresponding erosion of capital controls, and the vulnerability of fixed exchange rates.[68]

Serious concerns over a return to the international economic fragmentation and collapse of the interwar period were voiced by the early sixties as the American economy went from creditor to debtor status, the dollar moved from a currency in desperately short supply to one in surplus, and the dollar-gold standard, which had been embedded in Bretton Woods, began to crumble.[69] But in spite of new tensions between the US and Europe and Japan, the past was not replayed. American dominance, never fundamentally challenged, would come to be reorganized on a new basis, and international integration was not rolled back but intensified. This reconstitution of the global order, like earlier developments within global capitalism, was not inevitable. What made it possible – what provided the American state the time and political space to renew its global ambitions – was that by the time of the crisis of the early seventies American ideological and material penetration of, and integration with, Europe and Japan was sufficiently strong to rule out any retreat from the international economy or any fundamental challenge to the leadership of the American state.

The United States had, of course, established itself as the military protectorate of Europe and Japan, and this was maintained while both were increasingly making their way into American markets. But the crucial factor in cementing the new imperial bond was foreign direct investment as the main form now taken by capital export and international integration in the post-war period. American corporations, in particular, were evolving into the hubs of increasingly dense host-country and cross-border networks amongst suppliers, financiers, and final markets (thereby further enhancing the liberalized trading order as a means of securing even tighter international networks of production). Even where the initial response to the growth of such American investment was hostile, this generally gave way to competition to attract that investment, and then emulation to meet 'the American challenge' through counter-investments in the United States.

Unlike trade, American FDI directly affected the class structures and state formations of the other core countries.[70] Tensions and alliances that emerged within domestic capitalist classes could no longer be understood in purely 'national' terms. German auto companies, for example, followed American auto companies in wanting European-wide markets; and they shared mutual concerns with the American companies inside Germany, such as over the cost of European steel. They had reason to be wary of policies that discriminated in favour of European companies but might, as a consequence, compromise the treatment of their own growing interest in markets and investments in the United States. And if instability in Latin America or other 'trouble spots' threatened their own international investments, they looked primarily to the US rather than their own states to defend them.

With American capital a social force within each European country, domestic capital tended to be 'dis-articulated' and no longer represented by a coherent and independent national bourgeoisie.[71] The likelihood that domestic capital might challenge American dominance – as opposed to merely seeking to renegotiate the terms of American leadership – was considerably diminished. Although the West

European and Japanese economies had been rebuilt in the post-war period, the nature of their integration into the global economy tended to tie the successful reproduction of their own social formations to the rules and structures of the American-led global order. However much the European and Japanese states may have wanted to renegotiate the arrangements struck in 1945, now that only 25% of world production was located in the U.S. proper, neither they nor their bourgeoisies were remotely interested in challenging the hegemony that the American informal empire had established over them. 'The question for them', as Poulantzas put it in the early seventies, 'is rather to reorganize a hegemony that they still accept...; what the battle is actually over is the share of the cake.'[72]

It was in this context that the internationalization of the state became particularly important. In the course of the protracted and often confused renegotiations in the 1970s of the terms that had, since the end of World War II, bound Europe and Japan to the American empire, all the nation states involved came to accept a responsibility for creating the necessary *internal* conditions for sustained *international* accumulation, such as stable prices, constraints on labour militancy, national treatment of foreign investment and no restrictions on capital outflows. The real tendencies that emerged out of the crisis of the 1970s were (to quote Poulantzas again) 'the internalized transformations of the national state itself, aimed at taking charge of the internationalization of public functions on capital's behalf.'[73] Nation states were thus not fading away, but adding to their responsibilities.

Not that they saw clearly what exactly needed to be done. The established structures of the post-1945 order did not, in themselves, provide a resolution to the generalized pressures on profit rates in the United States and Europe. They did not suggest how the U.S. might revive its economic base so as to consolidate its rule. Nor did they provide an answer to how tensions and instabilities would be managed in a world in which the American state was not omnipotent but rather depended, for its rule, on working through other states. The contingent nature of the new order was evidenced by the fact that a 'solution' only emerged at the end of the seventies, two full decades after the first signs of trouble, almost a decade after the dollar crisis of the early seventies, and after a sustained period of false starts, confusions, and uncertain experimentation.[74]

The first and most crucial response of the Nixon administration, the dramatic end to the convertibility of the American dollar in 1971, restored the American state's economic autonomy in the face of a threatened rush to gold; and the subsequent devaluation of the American dollar did, at least temporarily, correct the American balance of trade deficit. Yet that response hardly qualified as a solution to the larger issues involved. The American state took advantage of its still dominant position to defend its own economic base, but this defensive posture could not provide a general solution to the problems facing all the developed capitalist economies, nor even create the basis for renewed US economic dynamism.[75] By the end of the seventies, with the American economy facing a flight of capital (both domestic and foreign), a Presidential report to Congress (describing itself as 'the most comprehensive and detailed analysis of the competitive position of the United States') confirmed a steep decline in competitiveness – one that it advised *could* be corrected, but not without a radical reorientation in economic policy to address the persistence of domestic inflation and the need for greater access to savings so as to accelerate investment.[76]

The concern with retaining capital and attracting new capital was especially crucial to what followed. The opening up of domestic and global capital markets was both an opportunity and a constraint for the American state. Liberalized finance held out the option of shifting an important aspect of competition to the very terrain on which the American economy potentially had its greatest advantages, yet those advantages could not become an effective instrument of American power until other economic and political changes had occurred. The American state's ambivalence about how to deal with the growing strength of financial capital was reflected in its policies: capital controls were introduced in 1963, but were made open to significant 'exceptions'; the Euro-dollar market was a source of concern, but also recognized as making dollar holdings more attractive and subsequently encouraging the important recycling of petro-dollars to the third world. The liberalization of finance enormously strengthened Wall Street through the 1970s and, as Duménil and Lévy have persuasively shown, proved crucial to the broader changes that followed.[77] But this should not be seen as being at the expense of industrial capital. What was involved was not a 'financial coup', but rather a (somewhat belated) recognition on the part of American capital generally that the strengthening of finance was an essential, if sometimes painful, price to be paid for reconstituting American economic power.[78]

The critical 'turning point' in policy orientation came in 1979 with the 'Volcker shock' – the American state's self-imposed structural adjustment program. The Federal Reserve's determination to establish internal economic discipline by allowing interest rates to rise to historically unprecedented levels led to the vital restructuring of labour and industry and brought the confidence that the money markets and central bankers were looking for. Along with the more general neoliberal policies that evolved into a relatively coherent capitalist policy paradigm through the eighties, the new state-reinforced strength of finance set the stage for what came to be popularly known as 'globalization' – the accelerated drive to a seamless world of capital accumulation.

The mechanisms of neoliberalism (the expansion and deepening of markets and competitive pressures) may be economic, but neoliberalism was essentially a *political* response to the democratic gains that had been previously achieved by subordinate classes and which had become, in a new context and from capital's perspective, barriers to accumulation. Neoliberalism involved not just reversing those gains, but weakening their institutional foundations – including a shift in the hierarchy of state apparatuses in the US towards the Treasury and Federal Reserve at the expense of the old New Deal agencies. The US was of course not the only country to introduce neoliberal policies, but once the American state itself moved in this direction, it had a new status: capitalism now operated under 'a new form of social rule'[79] that promised, and largely delivered, (a) the revival of the productive base for American dominance; (b) a universal model for restoring the conditions for profits in other developed countries; and (c) the economic conditions for integrating global capitalism.

In the course of the economic restructuring that followed, American labour was further weakened, providing American capital with an even greater competitive flexibility vis-à-vis Europe. Inefficient firms were purged – a process that had been limited in the seventies. Existing firms restructured internally, outsourced processes to cheaper and more specialized suppliers, relocated to the increasingly urban southern states, and merged with other firms – all part of an accelerated reallocation of capital within the American economy. The new confidence of global investors (including Wall Street itself) in the American economy and state provided the US with relatively cheap access to global savings and eventually made capital cheaper in the US. The available pools of venture capital enhanced investment in the development of new technologies (which also benefited from public subsidies via military procurement programs), and the new technologies were in turn integrated into management restructuring strategies and disseminated into sectors far beyond 'high tech'. The US proportion of world production did not further decline: it continued to account for around one-fourth of the total right into the twenty-first century.

The American economy not only reversed its slide in the 1980s, but also set the standards for European and Japanese capital to do the same.[80] The renewed confidence on the part of American capital consolidated capitalism as a global project through the development of new formal and informal mechanisms of international coordination. Neoliberalism reinforced the material and ideological conditions for guaranteeing 'national' treatment for foreign capital in each social formation, and for 'constitutionalizing' – by way of NAFTA, European Economic and Monetary Union and the WTO – the free flow of goods and capital (the WTO was a broader version of GATT, but with more teeth).[81] The American economy's unique access to global savings through the central place of Wall Street within global money markets allowed it to import freely without compromising other objectives. This eventually brought to the American state the role, not necessarily intended, of 'importer of last resort' that limited the impact of slow-downs elsewhere, while also reinforcing foreign investors' and foreign exporters' dependence on American markets and state policies. The Federal Reserve, though allegedly concerned only with domestic policies, kept a steady eye on the inter-national context. And the Treasury, whose relative standing within the state had varied throughout the post-war era, increasingly took on the role of global macro-economic manager through the 1980s and 1990s, thereby enhancing its status at the top of the hierarchy of US state apparatuses.[82]

The G-7 emerged as a forum for Ministers of Finance and Treasury officials to discuss global developments, forge consensus on issues and direction, and address in a concrete and controlled way any necessary exchange rate adjustments. The US allowed the Bank for International Settlements to re-emerge as major international coordinating agency, in the context of the greater role being played by increasingly 'independent' central bankers, to improve capital adequacy standards within banking systems. The IMF and the World Bank were also restructured. The IMF shifted from the 'adjustment' of balance of payments problems to addressing structural economic crises in third world countries (along the lines first imposed on Britain in 1976), and increasingly became the vehicle for imposing a type of conditionality, in exchange for loans, that incorporated global capital's concerns. The World Bank supported this, although by the 1990's, it also focused its attention on capitalist state-building – what it called 'effective states'.[83]

The reconstitution of the American empire in this remarkably successful fashion through the last decades of the twentieth century did not mean that global capitalism had reached a new plateau of stability. Indeed it may be said that dynamic instability and contingency are systematically incorporated into the reconstituted form of empire, in good part because the intensified competition characteristic of neoliberalism and the hyper-mobility of financial liberalization aggravate the uneven development and extreme volatility inherent in the global order. Moreover, this instability is dramatically amplified by the fact that the American state can only rule this order through other states, and turning them all into 'effective' states for global capitalism is no easy matter. It is the attempt by the American state to address these problems, especially vis-à-vis what it calls 'rogue states' in the third world, that leads American imperialism today to present itself in an increasingly unconcealed manner.

BEYOND INTER-IMPERIAL RIVALRY

We cannot understand imperialism today in terms of the unresolved crisis of the 1970s, with overaccumulation and excess competition giving rise again to inter-imperial rivalry. The differences begin with the fact that while the earlier period was characterized by the relative economic strength of Europe and Japan, the current moment underlines their relative *weakness*. Concern with the American trade deficit seems to overlap both periods, but the context and content of that concern has radically changed. Earlier, the American deficit was just emerging, was generally seen as unsustainable even in the short run, and was characterized by foreign central bankers as exporting American inflation abroad. Today, the global economy has not only come to live with American trade deficits for a period approaching a quarter of a century, but global stability has come to depend on these deficits and it is the passage to their 'correction' that is the threat – this time a deflationary threat. In the earlier period, global financial markets were just emerging; the issue this raised at the time was their impact in undermining existing forms of national and international macro-management, including the international role of the American dollar. The consequent explosive development of financial markets has resulted in financial structures and flows that have now, however, made 'finance' itself a focal point of global macro-management – whether it be enforcing the discipline of accumulation, reallocating capital across sectors and regions, providing the investor/consumer credit to sustain even the modest levels of growth that have occurred, or supporting the capacity of the US economy to attract the global savings essential to reproducing the American empire.

In this context, the extent of the theoretically unselfconscious use of the term 'rivalry' to label the economic competition between the EU, Japan (or East Asia more broadly) and the United States is remarkable. The distinctive meaning the concept had in the pre-World War I context, when economic competition among European states was indeed imbricated with comparable military capacities and Lenin could assert that 'imperialist wars are absolutely inevitable',[84] is clearly lacking in the contemporary context of overwhelming American military dominance. But beyond this, the meaning it had in the past is contradicted by the distinctive economic as well as military integration that exists between the leading capitalist powers today.

The term 'rivalry' inflates economic competition between states far beyond what it signifies in the real world. While the conception of a transnational capitalist class, loosened from any state moorings or about to spawn a supranational global state, is clearly exceedingly extravagant,[85] so too is any conception of a return to rival national bourgeoisies. The asymmetric power relationships that emerged out of the penetration and integration among the leading capitalist countries under the aegis of informal American empire were not dissolved in the wake of the crisis of the Golden Age and the greater trade competitiveness and capital mobility that accompanied it; rather they were refashioned and reconstituted through the era of neo-liberal globalization. None of this means, of course, that state and economic structures have become homogeneous or that there is no divergence in many policy areas, or that contradiction and conflict are absent from the imperial order. But these contradictions and conflicts are located not so much in the relationships between the advanced capitalist states as *within* these states, as they try to manage their internal processes of accumulation, legitimation and class struggle. This is no less true of the American state as it tries to manage and cope with the complexities of neo-imperial globalization.

Nor does the evolution of the European Union make the theory of inter-imperial rivalry relevant for our time.[86] Encouraged at its origins by the American state, its recent development through economic and monetary union – up to and including the launching of the Euro and the European Central Bank – has never been opposed by American capital within Europe, or by the American state. What it has accomplished in terms of free trade and capital mobility within its own region has fitted, rather than challenged, the American-led 'new form of social rule' that neoliberalism represents. And what it has accomplished in terms of the integration of European capital markets has not only involved the greater penetration of American investment banking and its principle of 'shareholder value' inside Europe, but has, as John Grahl has shown, been 'based on the deregulation and internationalization of the US financial system.'[87]

The halting steps towards an independent European military posture, entirely apart from the staggering economic cost this would involve (all the more so in the context of relatively slow growth), were quickly put in perspective by the war on the former Yugoslavia over Kosovo – supported by every European government – through which the US made it very clear that NATO would remain the ultimate policeman of Europe.[88] But this only drove home a point over which pragmatic European politicians had never entertained any illusions. Dependence on American military technology and intelligence would still be such that the US itself sees '[a]n EU force that serves as an effective, if unofficial, extension of NATO rather than a substitute [as] well worth the trouble.'[89] And on the European side, Joschka Fischer, Germany's Foreign Minister, has similarly acknowledged that '[t]he transatlantic relationship is indispensable. The power of the United States is a decisive factor for peace and stability in the world. I don't believe Europe will ever be strong enough to look after its security alone.'[90] Indeed, it is likely the very appreciation of this reality within European elite circles that lies at the heart of their oft-expressed frustrations with the current American leadership's tendency to treat them explicitly as merely 'junior' partners. Though it has been argued that the end of the Cold War left Europe less dependent on the American military umbrella and therefore freer to pursue its own interests, this same development also left the US freer to ignore European sensitivities.

As for East Asia, where Japan's highly centralized state might be thought to give it the imperial potential that the relatively loosely-knit EU lacks, it has shown even less capacity for regional let alone global leadership independent of the US. Its ability to penetrate East Asia economically, moreover, has been and remains mediated by the American imperial relationship.[91] This was particularly rudely underlined by the actions of the American Treasury (especially through the direct intervention of Rubin and Summers) in the East Asian crisis of 1997-98, when it dictated a harsh conditionality right in Japan's back yard.[92] Those who interpreted Japan's trade penetration of American markets and its massive direct foreign investments in the US through the 1980s in terms of inter-imperial rivalry betrayed a misleadingly economistic perspective. Japan remains dependent on American markets and on the security of its investments within the US, and its central bank is anxious to buy dollars so as limit the fall of the dollar and its impact on the Yen. And while China may perhaps emerge eventually as a pole of inter-imperial power, it will obviously remain very far from reaching such a status for a good many decades. The fact that certain elements in the American state are concerned to ensure that its 'unipolar' power today is used to prevent the possible emergence of imperial rivals tomorrow can hardly be used as evidence that such rivals already exist.

During the 1990s, not only the literal deflation of the Japanese economy, but also the slow growth and high unemployment in Europe stood in stark contrast with the American boom. So much was this the case that if Donald Sassoon was right to say that 'how to achieve the European version of the American society was the real political issue of the 1950s',[93] so it once again seemed to be the case in the 1990s, at least in terms of emulation of US economic policies and shareholder values. Now, with end of that boom, and the growing US trade and fiscal deficit, new predictions of American decline and inter-imperial rivalry have become commonplace. But the question of the sustainability of the American empire cannot be answered with such short-term and economistic measures, any more than they could in the 1970s, when Poulantzas properly disdained

> the various futurological analyses of the relative 'strength' or 'weakness' of the American and European economies, analyses which pose the question of inter-imperialist contradictions in terms of the 'competitiveness' and actual 'competition' between 'national economies'. In general, these arguments are restricted to 'economic criteria' which, considered in themselves, do not mean very much, ...and [yet such analyses] extrapolate from these in quite an arbitrary manner.[94]

This is not to say that the current economic conjuncture does not reveal genuine economic problems for every state in global capitalism, including the American. These problems reflect not the continuation of the crisis of the 1970s, but rather new contradictions that the dynamic global capitalism ushered in by neoliberalism has itself generated, including the synchronization of recessions, the threat of deflation, the dependence of the world on American markets and the dependence of the United States on capital inflows to cover its trade deficit. There is indeed a systemic complexity in today's global capitalism that includes, even at its core, instabilities and even crises. Yet this needs to be seen not so much in terms of the old structural crisis tendencies and their outcomes, but as quotidian dimensions of contemporary capitalism's functioning and, indeed, as we argued above, even of its successes.

The issue for capitalist states is not preventing episodic crises – they will inevitably occur – but containing them. The American imperial state has, to date, demonstrated a remarkable ability to limit the duration, depth, and contagion of crises. And there is as yet little reason to expect that even the pressure on the value of the dollar today has become unmanageable. This is what lies behind the confidence of Andrew Crockett, general manager of the Bank for International Settlements and chairman of the Financial Stability Forum (comprising central bankers, finance ministry officials and market regulators from the G7 states) that 'they have the network of contacts, [and] the contingency plans, to deal with shocks to the markets.'[95] Of course such confidence does not itself guarantee that the US Treasury and Federal Reserve, which worked closely with their counterparts in the other core capitalist states during the war on Iraq (whatever their governments' disagreements over that war) just as they did immediately after the disruption of Wall Street caused by the terrorist attacks of September 11,[96] will always have the capacity to cope with all contingencies. We would, however, argue that the future development of such capacities is not ruled out by any inherent *economic* contradictions alone.

The crisis that has produced an unconcealed American empire today lies, then, not in overaccumulation leading back to anything like inter-imperial rivalry, but in the limits that an informal empire based on ruling through other states sets for a strategy of coordinated economic growth, even among the advanced capitalist countries. In these liberal democratic states, the strength of domestic social forces – in spite of, and sometimes because of, the internationalization of domestic capital and the national state – has limited the adoption of neoliberalism (as seen, for example, in the difficulties experienced by the German state in introducing flexible labour markets, or the inertia of the Japanese state in restructuring its banking system). This has frustrated the 'reforms' that capital sees as necessary, along the lines of the American state's own earlier restructuring, to revive economic growth in these countries so as to allow them to share the burden of absorbing global imports and relieving pressure on the American trade deficit. It is also by no means obvious, despite the energy that capitalists in each country have invested in securing these 'reforms', that they would, by themselves, prove to be the magic bullets that would produce renewed growth. And their full intro-duction could in any case generate far more intense class struggles from below – though it must be said that these would need to generate something approaching a fundamental transformation in class and state structures to generate a new alter-native to neoliberalism and break the links with the American empire.

UNCONCEALED EMPIRE: 'THE AWESOME THING AMERICA IS BECOMING'

To the extent that there is a crisis of in imperialism today, it is best conceived as Poulantzas conceived the earlier crisis of the 1970s:

> What is currently in crisis is not directly American hegemony, under the impact of the 'economic power' of the other metropolises, whose rise would, according to some people have erected then automatically into equivalent 'counter-imperialisms', but rather imperialism as a whole, as a result of the world class struggles that have already reached the metropol-itan zone itself. ... In other words it is not the hegemony of American imperialism that is in crisis, but the whole of imperialism under this hege-mony.[97]

The notion of 'world class struggles' is no doubt too loose, and in another sense too restrictive in light of the diverse social forces now at play, to capture how the contradictions between the third world and the American empire are currently manifesting themselves. It is nevertheless the case that the most serious problems for 'imperialism as a whole' arise in relation to the states outside the capitalist core. Where these states are – as in much of the third world and the former Soviet bloc – relatively undeveloped capitalist states yet increasingly located within the orbit of global capital, the international financial institutions, as well as the core capitalist states acting either in concert or on their own, have intervened to impose 'economically correct' neoliberal structural 'reforms'. In the context of financial liberalization, this has meant a steady stream of economic crises. Some of these could be seen as a functionally necessary part of neoliberalism's success (as may perhaps be said of South Korea after the Asian crisis of 1997-8), but all too often these interventions have aggravated rather than solved the problem because of the abstract universalism of the remedy. Whatever neoliberalism's successes in relation to strengthening an already developed capitalist economy, it increasingly appears as a misguided strategy for capitalist development itself. As for so-called 'rogue states' – those which are not within the orbit of global capitalism so that neither penetrating external economic forces nor international institutions can effectively restructure them – direct unilateral intervention on the part of the American state has become increasingly tempting. It is this that has brought the term 'empire' back into mainstream currency, and it is fraught with all kinds of unpredictable ramifications.

In this context, the collapse of the Communist world that stood outside the sphere of American empire and global capitalism for so much of the post-war era has become particularly important. On the one hand, the rapid penetration and integration by global capital and the institutions of informal American empire (such a NATO) of so much of what had been the Soviet bloc, and the opening of China, Vietnam, and even Cuba to foreign capital and their integration in world markets (even if under the aegis of Communist elites), has been remarkable. It has also removed the danger that direct US intervention in states outside the American hemisphere would lead to World War III and nuclear Armageddon. The fact that even liberal human rights advocates and institutions through the 1990s have repeatedly called for the US to act as an international police power reflected the new conjuncture. But, on the other hand, both the hubris and sense of burden that came with the now evident unique power of the American state led it to question whether even the limited compromises it had to make in operating through multilateral institutions were unnecessarily constraining its strategic options, especially in relation to 'rogue states' outside the orbit of the informal empire.

The 'loneliness of power' was increasingly involved here. The felt burden of ultimate responsibility (and since 9/11 the much greater sensitivity to US vulnerability as a target of terrorism at home as well as abroad), promotes the desire to retain full 'sovereignty' to act as needed. This is what underlies the increasingly unconcealed nature of American imperialism. The problem it now faces in terms of 'conjugating its particular power with the general task of coordination' (to recall Anderson's incisive phrase), can clearly be seen not only in relation to the economic contradictions of neoliberalism discussed above, but also in the growing contradictions between nature and capitalism (as revealed, for example, not only in the severe problems of carbon emissions that the Kyoto Accord is supposed to address, but also in the problem of oil reserves addressed by the Cheney Report, discussed by Michael Klare in another essay in this volume).

These issues are multiplied all the more by the role the American imperial state now has come to play (and often to be expected to play) in maintaining social order around the whole globe. From the perspective of creating a 'world environment in which the American system can survive and flourish', the under-standing of the 1950 National Security Council document NSC-68 that '[e]ven if there were no Soviet Union we would face the great problem... [that] the absence of order among nations is becoming less and less tolerable' anticipated what has finally become fully clear to those who run the American empire. George W. Bush's own National Security Strategy document of September 2002 (intimations of which were surfacing inside the American state as soon as the Soviet bloc collapsed)[98] had a long pedigree.

Just as neoliberalism at home did not mean a smaller or weaker state, but rather one in which coercive apparatuses flourished (as welfare offices emptied out, the prisons filled up), so has neoliberalism led to the enhancement of the coercive apparatus the imperial state needs to police social order around the world. The transformation of the American military and security apparatus through the 1990s in such a way as to facilitate this (analyzed by Paul Rogers elsewhere in this volume) can only be understood in this light. (US unilateralism in the use of this apparatus internationally is hardly surprising if we consider how the activities of the coercive apparatuses of states at a domestic level are protected from exten-sive scrutiny from legislatures, and from having to negotiate what they do with non-coercive state apparatuses.)

All this was already apparent in the responses to 'rogue states' under the Bush I and Clinton administrations. The US did work hard to win the UN's support for the 1990-91 Gulf War and oversaw the long regime of sanctions against Iraq that the American state insisted on through the 1990s. But other governments sensed a growing unilateralism on the part of the U.S. that made them increas-ingly nervous, if only in terms of maintaining their own states' legitimacy. The Gulf War had shown that the United Nations could be made to serve 'as an imprimatur for a policy that the United States wanted to follow and either persuaded or coerced everybody else to support,' as the Canadian ambassador to the UN put it at the time. This playing 'fast and loose with the provisions of the UN Charter' unnerved 'a lot of developing countries, which were privately outraged by what was going on but felt utterly impotent to do anything – a demonstration of the enormous US power and influence when it is unleashed.'[99]

Yet at the very same time, it also made American strategists aware just how little they could rely on the UN if they had to go to such trouble to get their way. The United Nations, by its very nature as a quasi-parliamentary and diplo-matic body made up of all the world's states, could not be as easily restructured as were the Bretton Woods institutions after the crisis of the 1970s. This, as evidenced in the repeated use of the American veto in the Security Council since that time, was a constant irritant. And while NATO could be relied on as a far more reliable vehicle for the American war on the former Yugoslavia over Kosovo (with the added benefit of making clear to the Europeans exactly who would continue to wield the international police power in their own backyard), even here the effort entailed in having to keep each and every NATO member onside was visibly resented within the American state itself.

Bush's isolationist rhetoric in the 2000 election campaign, questioning the need for American troops to get involved in remote corners of the globe, was bound to be reformulated once Bush was actually burdened with (and appropriately socialized in) the office of a Presidency that is now as inevitably imperial as is it domestic in nature. For this, the explicitly imperial statecraft that the geopolitical strategists close to the Republican Party had already fashioned was ready and waiting. September 11 alone did not determine their ascendancy in the state, but it certainly enhanced their status. Their response has revealed all the tensions in the American state's combination of its imperial function of general coordination with the use of its power to protect and advance its national interests. Defining the security interests of global capitalism in a way that also serves the needs of the American social formation and state becomes especially tricky once the security interests involved are so manifestly revealed as primarily American. This means that while threats to the US are still seen by it as an attack on global capitalism in general, the American state is increasingly impatient with making any compromises that get in the way of its acting on its own specific definition of the global capitalist interest and the untrammelled use of its particular state power to cope with such threats.

Perhaps the most important change in the administrative structure of the American empire in the transition from the Clinton administration to the Bush II administration has been the displacement of the Treasury from its pinnacle at the top of the state apparatus. The branches of the American state that control and dispense the means of violence are now in the driver's seat; in an Administration representing a Republican Party that has always been made up of a coalition of free marketeers, social conservatives and military hawks, the balance has been tilted decisively by September 11th towards the latter.[100] But the unconcealed imperial face that the American state is now prepared to show to the world above all pertains to the increasing difficulties of managing a truly global informal empire – a problem that goes well beyond any change from administration to administration.

This could turn out to be a challenge as great as that earlier faced by formal empires with their colonial state apparatuses. The need to try to refashion all the states of the world so that they become at least minimally adequate for the administration of global order – and this is now also seen as a general condition of the reproduction and extension of global capitalism – is now the central problem for the American state. But the immense difficulty of constructing outside the core anything like the dense networks that the new American imperialism succeeded in forging with the other leading capitalist states is clear from the only halting progress that has been made in extending the G7 even to the G8, let alone the G20. For the geopolitical stratum of the American state, this shows the limits of any 'effective states' approach outside the core based on economic linkages alone.

This explains not only the extension of US bases and the closer integration of intelligence and police apparatuses of all the states in the empire in the wake of September 11, but the harkening back to the founding moment of the post-1945

American empire in the military occupations of Japan and Germany as providing the model for restructuring Iraq within the framework of American empire. The logic of this posture points well beyond Iraq to all states 'disconnected from globalization', as a U.S. Naval War College professor advising the Secretary of Defense so chillingly put it:

> Show me where globalization is thick with network connectivity, financial transactions, liberal media flows, and collective security, and I will show you regions featuring stable governments, rising standards of living, and more deaths by suicide than murder. These parts of the world I call the Functioning Core… But show me where globalization is thinning or just plain absent, and I will show you regions plagued by politically repressive regimes, widespread poverty and disease, routine mass murder, and – most important – the chronic conflicts that incubate the next generation of global terrorists. These parts of the world I call the non-integrating Gap… The real reason I support a war like this is that the resulting long-term military commitment will finally force America to deal with the entire Gap as a strategic threat environment.[101]

In this 'Gap' are listed Haiti, Colombia, Brazil and Argentina, Former Yugoslavia, Congo and Rwanda/Burundi, Angola, South Africa, Israel–Palestine, Saudi Arabia, Iraq, Somalia, Iran, Afghanistan, Pakistan, North Korea and Indonesia – to which China, Russia and India are added, for good measure, 'as new/integrating members of the core [that] may be lost in coming years.' The trouble for the American empire as it inclines in this strategic direction is that very few of the world's 'non-core' states today, given their economic and political structures and the social forces, are going to be able to be reconstructed along the lines of post-war Japan and Germany, even if (indeed especially if) they are occupied by the US military, and even if they are penetrated rather than marginalized by globalization. What is more, an American imperialism that is so blatantly imperialistic risks losing the very appearance of not being imperialist – that appearance which historically made it plausible and attractive.

The open disagreements over the war on Iraq between the governments of France, Germany and even Canada, on the one hand, and the Bush administration, on the other, need to be seen in this light. These tensions pertain very little to economic 'rivalries'. The tensions pertain rather more to a preference on the part of these states themselves (in good part reflective of their relative lack of autonomous military capacity) for the use of international financial institutions, the WTO and the UN to try to fashion the 'effective states' around the world that global capitalism needs. But the bourgeoisies of the other capitalist states are even less inclined to challenge American hegemony than they were in the 1970s. Indeed many capitalists in the other states inside the empire were visibly troubled by – and increasingly complained about – their states not singing from the same page as the Americans. In any case, the capitalist classes of each country, including the US (where many of the leading lights of financial capital, such as

Rubin and Volcker, were openly disturbed by the posture of the Bush administration on the war as well as economic policy), were incapable of expressing a
unified position either for or against the war. Once again we can see that what
is at play in the current conjuncture is not contradictions between national bourgeoisies, but the contradictions of 'the whole of imperialism', implicating all the
bourgeoisies that function under the American imperial umbrella.

These contradictions pertain most of all to the danger posed to the broader
legitimacy of the other capitalist states now that they are located in a framework
of American imperialism that is so unconcealed. The American empire has
certainly been hegemonic vis-à-vis these states, their capitalist classes and their
various elite establishments, but it has never entailed, for all of the American
economic and cultural penetration of their societies, a transfer of direct popular
loyalty to the American state itself. Indeed, the American form of rule – founded
on the constitutional principle of 'extensive empire and self-government' – has
never demanded this. The economic and cultural emulation of the American
way of life by so many ordinary people abroad may perhaps properly be spoken
of as hegemony in Gramsci's terms. But however close the relationship between
the American state and capitalist classes and their counterparts in the informal
empire, this did not extend to anything like a sense of patriotic attachment to the
American state among the citizenry of the other states. Nor did the American
state ever take responsibility for the incorporation, in the Gramscian sense of
hegemony, of the needs of the subordinate classes of other states within its own
construction of informal imperial rule. Their active consent to its informal imperial rule was always mediated by the legitimacy that each state could retain for
itself and muster on behalf of any particular American state project – and this has
often been difficult to achieve in the case of American coercive interventions
around the globe over the past fifty years. A good many of these states thus
distanced themselves from the repeated US interventions in Latin America and
the Caribbean since 1945, and indeed since 1975, not to mention the American
subversion of governments elsewhere, or the Vietnam War.

In this sense the unpopularity of American military intervention – and even
its lack of endorsement by other advanced capitalist states – is not new. But this
dimension of the imperial order is proving to have particularly important consequences in the current conjuncture. The American state's war of aggression in
Iraq – so flagrantly imperial and so openly connected to a doctrine that expresses
the broader aim of securing a neoliberal capitalist order on a global scale – has
evoked an unprecedented opposition, including within the capitalist core states.
Yet even in France and Germany where the opposition is highest, many more
people today attribute 'the problem with the US' as due to 'mostly Bush' rather
than to the 'US in general'. This suggests that the possibility of a 'benign
imperium' still exists even in the other advanced capitalist countries.[102] But
insofar as the conditions making for American military intervention clearly transcend a given administration, and insofar as a benign imperium can hardly prove
to be more than an illusion in today's world, this is a currency that could be less

stable than the American dollar. This is especially significant: since the American empire can only rule through other states, the greatest danger to it is that the states within its orbit will be rendered illegitimate by virtue of their articulation to the imperium. To be sure, only a fundamental change in the domestic balance of social forces and the transformation of the nature and role of those states can bring about their disarticulation from the empire, but the ideological space may now be opening up for the kind of mobilization from below, combining the domestic concerns of subordinate classes and other oppressed social forces with the anti-globalization and anti-war movements, that can eventually lead to this.

It is the fear of this that fuels, on the one hand, the pleas of those who entreat the imperium to be more benign and to present itself in a more multilateralist fashion, at least symbolically; and, on the other hand, the actions of those who are using the fear of terrorism to close the space for public dissent within each state. This is especially so within the United States itself. The old question posed by those who, at the founding of the American state, questioned whether an extended empire could be consistent with republican liberty – posed again and again over the subsequent two centuries by those at home who stood up against American imperialism – is back on the agenda. The need to sustain intervention abroad by mobilizing support and limiting opposition through instilling fear and repression at home raises the prospect that the American state may become more authoritarian internally as part of it becoming more blatantly aggressive exter-nally. But the unattractiveness of an empire that is no longer concealed in its coercive nature at home as well as abroad suggests that anti-imperialist struggles – even in the rich capitalist states at the heart of the empire as well as in the poor ones at its extremities – will have growing mass appeal and force.

NOTES

We wish to thank Greg Albo, Cenk Aygul, Patrick Bond, Dan Crow, Robert Cox, Bill Fletcher, Stephen Gill, Gerard Greenfield, Khashayar Khooshiyar, Martijn Konings, Colin Leys, Eric Newstadt, Chris Roberts, Donald Swartz and Alan Zuege for their comments on a draft of this essay. A good many of their comments have been incorporated here; others we will only be able to address as part of our book project on this topic.

1   'Great Britain, The United States and Canada', Twenty-First Cust Foundation Lecture, University of Nottingham, May 21, 1948, in H. Innis, *Essays in Canadian Economic History*, Toronto: University of Toronto Press, 1956, p. 407.
2   The Friedman manifesto appeared in the *New York Times Magazine* on March 28, 1999, and the Ignatieff essay on January 5, 2003. Ignatieff adds: 'It means laying down the rules America wants (on everything from markets to weapons of mass destruction) while exempting itself from other rules (the

Kyoto protocol on climate change and the International Criminal Court) that go against its interests.'

3   *The Grand Chessboard*, New York: Basic Books, 1997, p. 40.

4   See 'Rebuilding America's Defenses: Strategy, Forces and Resources For a New Century', A Report of the Project for the New American Century. http://www.newamericancentury.org/publicationsreports.htm; and *The National Security Strategy of the United States of America*, Falls Village, Connecticut: Winterhouse, 2002.

5   Antonio Santosuosso, *Storming the Heavens: Soldiers, Emperor, and Civilians in the Roman Empire*, Westview: Boulder, 2001, pp. 151-2.

6   *Monthly Review* 42(6), 1990, pp. 1-6. For two of those who insisted, from different perspectives, on the need to retain the concept of imperialism, see Susan Strange, 'Towards a Theory of Transnational Empire', in E-O. Czempiel and J. Rosenau, eds., *Global Changes and Theoretical Challenges*, Lexington: Lexington Books, 1989, and Peter Gowan, 'Neo-Liberal Theory and Practice for Eastern Europe', *New Left Review*, 213, 1995.

7   Gareth Stedman Jones, 'The Specificity of US Imperialism' *New Left Review*, 60 (first series), 1970, p. 60, n. 1.

8   Giovanni Arrighi, *The Geometry of Imperialism*, London: NLB, 1978, p. 17. What in good part lay behind the left's disenchantment with the concept of imperialism was the extent to which the words that opened Kautsky's infamous essay in 1914 – the one that so attracted Lenin's ire – increasingly rang true: 'First of all, we need to be clear what we understand from the term imperialism. This word is used in every which way, but the more we discuss and speak about it the more communication and understanding becomes weakened.' 'Der Imperialismus', *Die Neue Ziet*, Year 32, XXXII/2, Sept 11th, 1914, p. 908. Only the last part of this famous essay was translated and published in *New Left Review* in 1970. Thanks are due to Sabine Neidhardt for providing us with a full translation. Note Arrighi's use of almost identical words in 1990: 'What happened to the term imperialism is by the time it flourished in the early 1970s, it had come to mean everything and therefore nothing.' See 'Hegemony and Social Change', *Mersham International Studies Review*, 38, 1994, p. 365.

9   Bob Rowthorn, 'Imperialism in the Seventies: Unity or Rivalry', *New Left Review*, 69, 1971.

10   'In recent years no topic has occupied the attention of scholars of international relations more than that of American hegemonic decline. The erosion of American economic political and military power is unmistakable. The historically unprecedented resources and capabilities that stood behind United States early postwar diplomacy, and that led Henry Luce in the 1940s to herald an "American century," have given way to an equally remarkable and rapid redistribution of international power and wealth. In the guise of theories of "hegemonic stability," scholars have been debating the extent of hegemonic decline and its consequences.' G. John Ikenberry, 'Rethinking

the Origins of American Hegemony', *Political Science Quarterly*, 104(3), 1989, p. 375. Among the few critics of this view, see Bruce Russett, 'The Mysterious Case of Vanishing Hegemony. Or is Mark Twain Really Dead?', *International Organization*, 39(2), 1985; Stephen Gill, 'American Hegemony: Its Limits and Prospects in the Reagan Era', *Millenium*, 15(3), 1986; and Susan Strange, 'The Persistent Myth of Lost Hegemony', *International Organization*, 41(4), 1987.

11 Andrew Glyn and Bob Sutcliffe, 'Global But Leaderless', *Socialist Register 1992*, London: Merlin, 1992, p. 93.

12 Bruce Cumings. 'Global Realm with no Limit, Global Realm with no Name', *Radical History Review*, 57, 1993, pp. 47-8. This issue of the journal was devoted to a debate on 'Imperialism: A Useful Category of Analysis?'.

13 Andrew L. Bacevich, *American Empire: The Realities and Consequences of U.S. Diplomacy,* Cambridge, MA: Harvard University Press, 2002, pp. x, 3, 219.

14 Michael Hardt and Antonio Negri, *Empire*, Cambridge, MA: Harvard University Press, 2000, p. xiv, emphasis in text. See our review essay, 'Gems and Baubles in Empire', *Historical Materialism*, 10, 2002, pp. 17-43.

15 *The Great Transformation*, Beacon, Boston: 1957, p. 18.

16 Philip McMichael, 'Revisiting the Question of the Transnational State: A Comment on William Robinson's "Social theory and Globalization"', *Theory and Society*, 30, 2001, p. 202.

17 Just how far this fundamental mistake continues to plague the Left can be discerned from the fact that even those who insist today that the old theory of imperialism no longer can be made to fit contemporary global capitalism, nevertheless accept it as explaining the pre-World War One imperialism. This has been most recently seen in the way Hardt and Negri completely follow Lenin and Luxemburg in this respect, arguing that capitalism by its very nature confronts a contradiction in trying to realize surplus value: workers get less than what they produce (underconsume), so capital must look outside its own borders for markets. Since this is a problem in each capitalist country, the 'solution' requires constant access to markets in *non-capitalist* social formations. The focus on non-capitalist markets is reinforced by the need for the raw materials to feed workers and supply production at home. But the successful realization of the surplus and the expansion of production simply recreate the contradiction or crisis of underconsumption as a crisis of overproduction. This forces capital 'abroad' to find outlets for its surplus capital. That overall search for foreign markets, materials and investment opportunities involves the extension of national sovereignty beyond its borders – imperialism – and at the same time tends to bring the outside world 'in' (i.e. into capitalism). And so the crisis of underconsumption/overproduction is simply regenerated on a larger scale.

18 '[I]f capitalism could raise the living standards of the masses, who in spite of the amazing technical progress are everywhere still half-starved and poverty stricken, there could be no question of a surplus of capital.... But if capi-

talism did these things it would not be capitalism; for both the uneven development and a semi-starvation level of existence of the masses are fundamental and inevitable conditions and constitute premises of this mode of production.' V.I. Lenin, *Imperialism: The Highest Stage of Capitalism*, in *Selected Works*, Volume I, Moscow: Progress Publishers, 1970, p. 716.

19   *Ibid.*

20   See John Willoughby, *Capitalist Imperialism: Crisis and the State*, New York: Harwood Academic Publishers, 1986, esp. pp. 7-8; and earlier, put more circumspectly, Harry Magdoff, *The Age of Imperialism*, New York: Monthly Review Press, 1969, esp. p. 13.

21   See John Kautsky, 'J.A. Schumpeter and Karl Kautsky: Parallel Theories of Imperialism', *Midwest Journal of Political Science*, V(2), 1961, pp. 101-128; and Lenin, *Imperialism*, p. 715.

22   Ellen Meiksins Wood, *Empire of Capital*, London: Verso, 2003, p. 72.

23   John Gallagher and Ronald Robinson, 'The Imperialism of Free Trade', *The Economic History Review*, VI(1), 1953, p. 6. They explicitly challenged Lenin's view that the move towards responsible government in the colonies that coincided with the era of free trade did not mean that the policy of 'free competition' entailed 'that the liberation of the colonies and their complete separation from Great Britain was inevitable and desirable' in the opinion of leading bourgeois politicians. This reflected, they argued, a conventional misconception that free trade rendered empire 'superfluous', which severely misconstrued the significance of changes in constitutional forms. As Gallagher and Robinson put it: '[R]esponsible government far from being a separatist device, was simply a change from direct to indirect methods of maintaining British interests. By slackening the formal political bond at the appropriate time, it was possible to rely on economic dependence and mutual good-feeling to keep the colonies bound to Britain while still using them as agents for further British expansion.' *Ibid.*, p. 2.

24   *Ibid.*, pp. 6-7.

25   All the quotations of Karl Kautsky here are from John Kautsky, 'J.A. Schumpeter and Karl Kautsky', pp. 114-116, except for the one on his economic reductionism, where we have used the wording of *New Left Review*'s 1970 partial translation of 'Der Imperialismus', p. 46. For the best exposition of Kautsky's conception of 'ultra-imperialism', see Massimo Salvadori, *Karl Kautsky and the Socialist Revolution, 1880-1933*, London: NLB, 1979, pp. 169-203.

26   These are the words of a biographer of Dean Acheson, as quoted by William Appleman Williams, *Empire as a Way of Life*, New York: Oxford University Press, 1980, p. 185.

27   Perry Anderson, 'Force and Consent', *New Left Review*, 17, 2002, p. 24.

28   *Ibid.*, p. 25. See also Daniel Lazare's *The Frozen Republic*, New York: Harcourt Brace, 1996 which fails to distinguish between the democratic constraints and domestic policy gridlocks that the old elitist system of checks

and balances produces and the remarkable informal imperial 'carrying power' of the American constitution in the sense argued here.

29 Quoted in Williams, *Empire as a Way of Life*, p. 61. Jefferson had already come to accept Madison's 'expansionist' perspective that republican liberty was not incompatible with an extended state, nor with a strong federal government. As DeVoto sums up Jefferson's trajectory: '...after 1803, the phrase "the United States" in Jefferson's writings, usually plural up to now, begins increasingly to take a singular verb.' Bernard DeVoto, *The Course of Empire*, Lincoln: University of Nebraska Press, 1983 (1952), p. 403.

30 See Hardt and Negri, *Empire*, chapter 2.5.

31 See John F. Manley, 'The Significance of Class in American History and Politics', in L.C. Didd and C. Jilson, eds., *New Perspectives on American Politics*, Washington, D.C.: Congressional Quarterly Press, 1994, esp. pp. 16-19.

32 Quoted in Williams, *Empire as a Way of Life,* p. 43.

33 *The Federalist Papers*, No. 11 (Hamilton), Clinton Rossiter, ed., New York: Mentor, 1999, p. 59.

34 See Marc Engel, *A Mighty Empire: The Origins of the American Revolution*, Ithaca: Cornell University Press, 1988.

35 DeVoto, *The Course of Empire*, p. 275.

36 See Charles C. Bright, 'The State in the United States During the Nineteenth Century', in C. Bright and S. Harding, eds., *Statemaking and Social Movements*, Ann Arbor: University of Michigan Press, 1984.

37 See the first two chapters of Gabriel Kolko's *Main Currents in Modern American History*, New York: Harper & Row, 1976; and Bright, 'The State', esp. pp. 145-153.

38 Anderson, 'Force and Consent', p. 25.

39 S.S. Roberts, 'An Indicator of Informal Empire: Patterns of U.S. Navy Cruising on Overseas Stations, 1869-97', Center for Naval Analysis, Alexandria, Virginia, n.d., cited in Williams, p. 122.

40 Stedman Jones, 'The Specificity', p. 63.

41 See L. Panitch, 'Class and Dependency in Canadian Political Economy', *Studies in Political Economy*, 6, 1980, pp. 7-34; W. Clement, *Continental Corporate Power*, Toronto: McLelland & Stewart, 1977; and M. Wilkins, *The Emergence of Multinational Enterprise*, Cambridge, Mass: 1970. Jefferson had justified the war of 1812 (sparked by American concerns that the British were encouraging Indian resistance to western expansion) in these terms: 'If the British don't give us the satisfaction we demand, we will take Canada, which wants to enter the union; and when, together with Canada, we shall have the Floridas, we shall no longer have any difficulties with our neighbors; and it is the only way of preventing them.' The passage from the urge to continental expansion though internal empire to expansion through informal external empire, with Canada representing the model of successful American imperialism in the twentieth century, was marked, almost exactly

100 years later, when President Taft spoke in terms of 'greater economic ties' being the way to make Canada 'only an adjunct of the USA.' See Williams, pp. 63-4, 132.

42   Quoted in G. Achcar, *The Clash of Barbarisms*, New York: Monthly Review Press, 2002, p. 96.

43   Letter to Duncan Grant, quoted in Nicholas Fraser, 'More Than Economist', *Harper's Magazine*, November, 2001, p. 80. The issue here, of course, was the American state's refusal to forgive Allied war debts, with all the consequences this entailed for the imposition of heavy German reparations payments. See Michael Hudson's *Super Imperialism: The Economic Strategy of American Empire*, New York: Holt, Rinehart and Winston, 1971.

44   See R. Jeffery Lustig, *Corporate Liberalism: The Origins of American Political Theory 1890-1920*, Berkeley: University of California Press, 1982; and Stephen Skowronek, *Building a New American State: The Expansion of National Administrative Capacities 1877-1920*, New York: Cambridge University Press, 1982.

45   See Kees van der Pijl, *The Making of an Atlantic Ruling Class*, London: Verso, 1984, p. 93.

46   This was glimpsed by Charles and Mary Beard even before the war in their analysis of the passage from the old 'Imperial Isolationism' to the newer 'Collective Internationalism' in their *America in Midpassage*, New York: Macmillan, 1939, Volume I, Ch. X, and Vol, II, Ch. XVII.

47   This and the subsequent quotations in this section are all from Brian Waddell, *The War against the New Deal: World War II and American Democracy*, De Kalb: Northern Illinois University Press: 2001, pp. 4-5. See also, Rhonda Levine, *Class Struggles and the New Deal*, Lawrence: University Press of Kansas, 1988.

48   Brian Waddell, 'Corporate Influence and World War II: Resolving the New Deal Political Stalemate', *Journal of Political History*, 11(3), 1999, p. 2.

49   Geir Lundestad, 'Empire by Invitation? The United States and Western Europe, 1945-52', *Journal of Peace Research*, 23(3), September, 1986; and see van der Pijl, *The Making*, chapter 6.

50   See Gabriel Kolko, *The Politics of War: The World and United States Foreign Policy 1943-1945*, New York: Random House, 1968.

51   See Eric Helleiner, *States and the Reemergence of Global Finance*, Ithaca: Cornell, 1994.

52   Robert Skidelsky, *John Maynard Keynes: Fighting for Freedom, 1937-1946*, New York: Viking, 2001, pp. xxiii.

53   *The United States in a New World: I. Relations with Britain. A series of reports on potential courses for democratic action. Prepared under the auspices of the Editors of Fortune*, May, 1942, pp. 9-10.

54   'An American Proposal', *Fortune*, May 1942, pp. 59-63.

55   All the quotations in this paragraph are derived from Skidelsky's account, pp. 334, 348, 350-1, 355.

56 The very words which senior officials at the German Bundesbank used in an interview we conducted in October, 2002.

57 Martin Shaw, *Theory of the Global State*, Cambridge, U.K.: Cambridge University Press, 2000.

58 Bacevich, *American Empire*, p. 4.

59 Peter Gowan, 'The American Campaign for Global Sovereignty', *Socialist Register 2003*, London: Merlin, 2003, p. 5.

60 Michael Barratt Brown, *The Economics of Imperialism*, Middlesex, UK: Penguin, 1974, pp. 208-9.

61 See Raymond Aron, *The Imperial Republic: The United States and the World 1945-1973*, Cambridge, MA: Winthrop, 1974, esp. pp. 168 and 217; and N. Poulantzas, *Classes in Contemporary Capitalism*, London: NLB, 1974, esp. pp. 39 and 57.

62 Alan S. Milward, *The European Rescue of the Nation-State*, London: Routledge, 2000.

63 See Robert Cox, *Production, Power and World Order*, New York: Columbia University Press, 1987, esp. p. 254. Cf. N. Poulantzas, *Classes,* p. 73.

64 Address on Foreign Economic Policy, Delivered at Baylor University, March 6, 1947, Public Papers of the Presidents, http://www.trumanli-brary.org/trumanpapers/pppus/1947/52.htm. On the preparations for this crucial speech, see Gregory A. Fossendal, *Our Finest Hour: Will Clayton, the Marshall Plan, and the Triumph of Democracy*, Stanford: Hoover Press, 1993, pp. 213-5.

65 Quoted in Williams, p. 189; and see Gabriel Kolko, *Century of War*, New York: The New Press, 1994, p. 397.

66 The special post-war conditions included the application of technologies developed during the war; catch up to American technology and methods (the gap had already been rising during the thirties and obviously accelerated during the war); pent-up demand; subsidized investments for rebuilding and the productivity effect of new facilities – all providing enormous scope for accumulation after the destruction of so much value during the Depression and the War. See Moses Abramowitz, 'Catching Up, Forging Ahead, and Falling Behind', *Journal of Economic History*, 46(2), June, 1986, and also 'Rapid Growth Potential and Realization: The Experience of the Capitalist Economies in the Postwar Period' in Edmund Malinvaud, ed., *Economic Growth and Resources,* London: Macmillan, 1979. Also crucial was the unique role of the American state in opening up its market, providing critical financial assistance, and contributing to international economic and political stability internationally.

67 The interwar collapse of the gold standard had demonstrated that capital mobility and democratic pressures from below, which limited any 'automatic' adjustment process, were incompatible with stable exchange rates.

68 On the relationship between the collapse of the gold standard, capital mobility, and the development of democratic pressures, see Barry

Eichengreen, *Globalizing Capital: A History of the International Monetary System*, Princeton: Princeton University Press, 1996, Chapters 2-3. On the developments within US finance itself in the 1970s, and their impact abroad, see Michael Moran, *The Politics of the Financial Services Revolution*, London: Macmillan, 1991.

69   Looking back to that period, two Vice-Presidents of Citibank, observed 'it is not surprising that economists were so sure in the late 60's and early 70's that the breakdown of fixed exchange rates would further weaken economic links between countries.' See H. Cleveland and R. Bhagavatula, 'The Continuing World Economic Crisis', *Foreign Affairs,* 59(3), 1981, p. 600. See also Louis Pauly's observation that, at the time, '[i]nternational monetary disarray appeared quite capable of restoring the world of the 1930s'. Louis B. Pauly, *Who Elected the Bankers?*, Ithaca: Cornell University Press, 1997, p. 100.

70   The 'induced reproduction of American monopoly capitalism within the other metropolises…implies the extended reproduction within them of the political and ideological conditions for [the] development of American imperialism.' N. Poulantzas, 1974, p. 47.

71   'It is this dis-articulation and heterogeneity of the domestic bourgeoisie that explains the weak resistance, limited to fit and starts, that European states have put up to American capital'. *Ibid.*, p. 75.

72   *Ibid.*, p. 87.

73   *Ibid.*, p. 81. On the internationalization of the state, see also Cox, *Production, Power, And World Order*, pp. 253-267.

74   At one time or another, policy during the seventies included import surcharges, attempts at international co-operation on exchange rates, wage and price controls, monetarism, and fiscal stimulus.

75   A *New York Times* reporter captured the unilateralist aggressiveness driving the American response: 'What is entirely clear is that the United States in a single dramatic stroke has shown the world how powerful it still is… in breaking the link between the dollar and gold and imposing a 10% import tax, the United States has shown who is Gulliver and who the Lilliputians… by "Lilliputians" are meant not the Nicaraguans or Gabons but West Germany, Japan, Britain, and the other leading industrial nations', cited by H.L. Robinson, 'The Downfall of the Dollar' in *Socialist Register 1973*, London: Merlin Press, 1973, p. 417.

76   *Report of the President on U.S. Competitiveness*, Washington: Office of Foreign Economic Research, U.S. Department of Labour, September, 1980.

77   G. Duménil and D. Lévy, 'The Contradictions of Neoliberalism' in *Socialist Register 2002*, London: Merlin, 2002.

78   Our interviews with key industrial and financial figures, including, in September 2001, Richard Wagoner, CEO of General Motors and, in March 2003, Paul Volcker, the former Chairman of the Federal Reserve who also

led the negotiations with Chrysler have confirmed us in this view. In spite of the fact that the auto industry was hit especially hard by the high interest rates, high dollar, and reduction in consumer demand that came with the shift to financial liberalization, industry executives considered this direction as being the only alternative through the eighties and nineties.

79 The term is from G. Albo and T. Fast's 'Varieties of Neoliberalism' paper presented to the Conference on the Convergence of Capitalist Economies, Wake Forest, North Carolina September 27-29, 2002.

80 See S. Gindin and L. Panitch, 'Rethinking Crisis', *Monthly Review*, November, 2002.

81 See Stephen Gill, *Power and Resistance in the New World Order*, London: Palgrave-Macmillan, 2003, pp. 131ff. and pp. 174ff.

82 See Leo Panitch, 'The New Imperial State', *New Left Review*, 2, 2000.

83 See Leo Panitch, '"The State in a Changing World": Social-Democratizing Global Capitalism?', *Monthly Review,* October, 1998.

84 Lenin, preface to the French and German editions of *Imperialism,* p. 674.

85 Compare W. Ruigrok and R. van Tulder, *The Logic of International Restructuring*, London: Routledge, 1995 (esp. chs. 6 & 7) against W.I. Robinson, 'Beyond Nation-State Paradigms', *Sociological Forum*, 13(4), 1998; and see the debate on Robinson's 'Towards a Global Ruling Class?', *Science and Society*, 64(1), 2000 in the 'Symposium' in 65(4) of that journal, 2001-2.

86 The argument here is much further elaborated in L. Panitch and S. Gindin, 'Euro-capitalism and American Empire', *Studies in Political Economy*, Fall 2003.

87 John Grahl, 'Globalized Finance: The Challenge to the Euro', *New Left Review*, 8, 2001, p. 44. See also his outstanding paper, 'Notes on Financial Integration and European Society', presented to conference on The Emergence of a New Euro-Capitalism, Marburg, October 2002. On the increasing adoption of American management practices in Europe, see M. Carpenter and S. Jefferys, *Management, Work and Welfare in Western Europe*, London: Edward Elgar, 2000.

88 See Peter Gowan, 'Making Sense of NATO's War on Yugoslavia', *Socialist Register 2000*, London: Merlin, 2000.

89 W.A. Hay and H. Sicherman, 'Europe's Rapid Reaction Force: What, Why, And How?', *Foreign Policy Research Institute*, February, 2001.

90 *Economist,* May 27, 2003.

91 See Dan Bousfield, 'Export-Led Development and Imperialism: A Response to Burkett and Hart-Landsberg', *Historical Materialism*, 11(1), 2003, pp. 147-160. The counter argument, in terms of Japan's 'leadership from behind' was best set out in G. Arrighi and B. Silver, ed., *Chaos and Governance in the World System*, Minneapolis: University of Minnesota Press, 1999.

92 See Panitch, 'The New Imperial State'.

93 Donald Sassoon, *One Hundred Years of Socialism*, London: I.B. Taurus, 1996, p. 207.

94 Poulantzas, *Classes*, pp. 86-7.
95 *Financial Times*, March 26, 2003.
96 Our interviews at the Bundesbank and the UK Treasury in October 2002 confirm this. Indeed, there often appears to be more contact across the Atlantic between these bureaucrats and their counterparts in the US than there is among the various departments within these institutions.
97 *Classes in Contemporary Capitalism*, p. 87.
98 See Peter Gowan, 'The American Campaign', pp. 8-10.
99 'The United Nations after the Gulf War: A Promise Betrayed', Stephen Lewis interviewed by Jim Wurst, *World Policy Journal*, Summer 1991, pp. 539-49.
100 The increased influence gained by the military, coercive and security apparatuses in the wake of September 11 could be seen in that the first victory of the new war was scored at home, against the US Treasury. It involved breaking the latter's long-standing resistance (lest it would demonstrate the continuing viability of capital controls) to freezing bank accounts allegedly connected to terrorist organizations (which mechanisms the US state has always known about since it was involved in establishing these to facilitate money transfers to many of its favoured terrorists in the past).
101 Thomas P.M. Barnett, 'The Pentagon's New Map: It Explains Why We're Going to War and Why We'll Keep Going to War', *Esquire*, March, 2003 (available at the U.S. Naval War College website at http://www.nwc.navy.mil/newrules/ThePentagonsNewMap.htm).
102 See the report on the Pew Global Attitudes Survey in the *Financial Times*, June 4, 2003, which shows that in France and Germany, where only 43% and 45% respectively have 'a favourable image of the US' today, 74% of respondents in each country attribute the problem with the US to 'mostly Bush' as opposed to only 25% to the 'US in general' or to 'both'. Interestingly, in those advanced capitalist countries where the US image is more positive (Canada 63%, the UK 70%) there is nevertheless a higher percentage than in France or Germany who see 'the problem with the US' as due to the 'US in general' or 'both' (32%) rather than 'mostly Bush' (60%). As for countries like Indonesia and Turkey, where 'a favourable image of the US' has fallen from 75% and 53% respectively to only 15% today in both countries, it may be worth noting that whereas 45% of Turks attribute the problem to the 'US in general' or 'both', only 27% of Indonesians do so, in contrast with the 69% who see the problem as 'mostly Bush'.

IMPERIALISM OF OUR TIME

Aijaz Ahmad

I begin with the phrase 'imperialism of our time' as homage to Michal Kalecki who wrote his seminal essay 'Fascism of Our Time' at the juncture when the American far right had made a serious bid for the Presidency with the emergence of Barry Goldwater as the Republican candidate in the 1964 US election. Kalecki did not refer to Mussolini directly, although he might have, since it was after all Mussolini who first said that fascism is simply that form of rule in which government unites with 'corporations' – a term which for Mussolini meant something not unlike what President Eisenhower meant when warning of the US government's convergence with the 'military-industrial complex'. Kalecki's analysis did suggest, however, that in its extreme form industrial capitalism does have an inherent fascist tendency, and he wondered what fascism would look like if it ever came to the United States in conditions of prosperity and stable electoral democracy. Kalecki's intent was not to suggest that the US was becoming fascist, nor do I mean to imply that we are living in fascist times. Nonetheless, one of the salient features of the present conjuncture is that the United States, the leading imperialist country with historically unprecedented global power, is today governed by perhaps the most rightwing government in a century. The chickens of the most hysterical forms of authoritarianism that the US has been routinely exporting to large parts of the globe seem to be coming home to roost, with national as well as global consequences, including military consequences.

I also use the simple phrase 'imperialism of our time' with the more modest aim of avoiding terms like 'New Imperialism' which have been in vogue at various times, with varying meanings. Imperialism has been with us for a very long time, in great many forms, and constantly re-invents itself, so to speak, as the structure of global capitalism itself changes. What is offered here is a set of provisional notes toward the understanding of a conjuncture, 'our time', which is itself a complex of continuities and discontinuities – and, as is usual with conjunctures, rather novel. I shall first offer a series of proposition and then, in the remaining space for this article, some further elaboration of these points.

I

The fundamental novelty of the imperialism of our time is that it comes after the dissolution of the two great rivalries that had punctuated the global politics of the twentieth century, namely what Lenin called 'inter-imperialist rivalry' of the first half of the century as well as what we might, for lack of a better word, call the inter-systemic rivalry between the US and the USSR that lasted for some seventy years. The end of those rivalries concludes the era of politics inaugurated by the First World War and it is only logical that the sole victor, the United States, would set out most aggressively to grab all possible spoils of victory and to undo the gains that the working classes and oppressed nations of the world had been able to achieve during that period.

This new face of imperialism arises not only after the dissolution of the great colonial empires (British and French, principally) and colonial ambitions of the other, competing capitalist countries (Germany and Japan, mainly) but also the definitive demise of the nationalism of the national bourgeoisie in much of the so-called Third World (anti-colonialism, wars of national liberation, the Bandung project, non-alignment, the protectionist industrialising state) which had itself been sustained considerably by the existence of an alternative pole in the shape of the communist countries. The three objectives for which the US fought a war of position throughout the twentieth century – the containment/disappearance of communist states, its own primacy over the other leading countries, the defeat of Third World nationalism – have been achieved.

Far from being an imperialism caught in the coil of inter-imperialist rivalries, it is the imperialism of the era in which (a) national capitals have interpenetrated in such a manner that the capital active in any given territorial state is comprised, in varying proportions, of national and transnational capital; (b) finance capital is dominant over productive capital to an extent never visualized even in Lenin's 'export of capital' thesis or in Keynes' warnings about the rapaciousness of the rentiers; and (c) everything from commodity markets to movements of finance has been so thoroughly globalized that the rise of a global state, with demonstrably globalized military capability, is an objective requirement of the system itself, quite aside from the national ambitions of the US rulers, so as to impose structures and disciplines over this whole complex with its tremendous potential for fissures and breakdowns.

Empires without colonies have been with us, in one corner of the globe or another, throughout the history of capital, sometimes preceding military conquest (commercial empires), at other times coming after decolonization (South America after the dissolution of Spanish and Portuguese rule), and sometimes taking the form for which Lenin invented the term 'semi-colonial' (Egypt, Persia etc). However, this is the first fully post-colonial imperialism, not only free of colonial rule but antithetical to it; it is unlikely that the current occupation of Iraq will translate itself into long-term colonial rule, however long the quagmire may last and even if the superhawks of the Pentagon take US armies into Syria, Iran or wherever. It is not a matter of an ideological preference for 'informal' empire over 'formal' empire, so-called. It is a structural imperative of the current composition of global capital itself, as Panitch and Gindin argue in this volume. The movement of capital and commodities must be as unimpeded as possible but the nation-state form must be maintained throughout the peripheries, not only for historical reasons but also to supplement internationalization of capitalist law with locally erected labour regimes so as to enforce what Stephen Gill calls 'disciplinary neoliberalism' in conditions specific to each territorial unit.

The singular merit of Luxemburg's theory of imperialism was that, unlike Hilferding or Lenin or Bukharin, she sought to ground her theory in the larger theory of the capitalist mode of production itself and therefore focused on the question of the relationship between industrial and agricultural production which had been a notable feature of the Marxist theory of capitalism as such. One of her key propositions was that colonialism was not a conjunctural but a necessary aspect of the globalization of the law of value because capitalist zones require non-capitalist zones for full realization of surplus value; but she also went on to say that once capitalism has reached the outer reaches of the globe a crisis would necessarily ensue thanks to the increasing disappearance of non-capitalist zones. This latter inference would appear to be unwarranted, historically and even logically. Combined and uneven development does not strictly require that the peripheries remain 'non-capitalist', i.e., outside the global operation of the law of value. In actual history, the era of classical colonialism divided the world between an industrial core and a vast agricultural hinterland. Then, however, the dissolution of the great colonial empires and the postwar restructuring of global capital opened a new era in which the world was increasingly divided between advanced and backward industrial zones, while particular countries and continents were themselves divided between islands of the most advanced forms of finance and industrial production, on the one hand, and the most backward forms of agricultural production, on the other. At the extreme poles within the so-called 'Third World', one witnessed not only the stunning capitalist breakthrough in countries like Taiwan and South Korea but also, in contrast, the regression of parts of sub-Saharan Africa to levels below those obtaining at the time of decolonization. This transcontinental production of extreme inequalities is rife with potential for perennial violence, hence the need for state systems that guarantee extreme forms of extra-economic coercion. Meanwhile, one can witness across large parts of Asia and Africa all the processes of primitive accumulation and forced proletarianization that Marx specified in his famous chapter on the question, with reference mainly to England, and one remembers the central role he assigns to the state in the process, which, in his words, 'begat' the conditions for capitalist production 'hothouse-fashion'. To the extent that relatively similar processes are duplicated in a number of countries under regimes of both nation-state and globalized management (the World Bank, the WTO, etc.), in a system that is itself trans-national, a supervening authority above national and local authorities is again an objective requirement of the system as a whole; hence the tight fit among the multi-lateral institutions, the US state and the local managers of other states.

At the broadest level of generalization, one could say that it took two world wars to decide whether the US or Germany would inherit the British and French empires and thus transform itself into the leader of the bloc of advanced capitalist countries, and hence the centre of a global empire. It is significant that while the German vision was mired in the primitive notions of a worldwide colonial empire, the US, already under Woodrow Wilson, was championing the dissolution of colonialism and the 'right of nationalities', an ideological precursor for today's imperialism of 'democracy' and 'human rights'. And, it was after World War I, as the centre of global finance shifted decisively from London to New York and the Bolshevik Revolution arose to challenge global capitalism as a whole, that the US positioned itself as the leader of the 'Free World', as was symbolized by Wilson's dominating presence at Versailles as well as the leading role the US always played in the containment-of-communism crusades, especially after the Second World War.

Precisely at the time when the US has achieved all its long-standing objectives, including the objective of full dominance over its partners in the advanced capitalist world, there has arisen in some circles the expectation of an 'inter-imperialist rivalry' between the US and EU as competing centres of global capitalist production, with reference mainly to the size of the European economy as well as a futuristic projection of an East Asian power, be it Japan or China or a bloc of East Asian states. This seems fanciful. The most the Europeans do in the Third World is look for markets and investment opportunities. There is no power projection, for the simple reason that there is no power. Not only is the US military power far greater than that of all of Europe combined, it also has a military presence in over a hundred countries of the world, in sharp contrast to Germany or even France, and NATO goes only where the US tells it to go. This military supremacy over its would-be rivals is supplemented then by the overwhelming power of its currency and finance, and its dominance over the global production of techno-scientific as well as social-scientific intelligentsias, and its global cultural and ideological reach through its dominance over mass entertainment and (dis)information.

The US fought as hard against radical Third World nationalism, as it did against communism during the second half of the century. Having championed decolonization as a precondition for the emergence of a globally integrated empire under its own dominion, it set its face against national liberation movements, whether led by communists (as in Indochina) or by radical nationalists (as in Algeria); against non-alignment (the rhetoric of 'for us or against us' of Bush Jr. today comes straight out of John Foster Dulles' speeches during the 1950s); as well as against particular nationalist regimes, be it Nasser's or Nkrumah's or Sukarno's or even Prince Sihanouk's in Cambodia. Instead, it kept monarchies in power where it could and imposed dictators wherever it needed to. The failure of the national-bourgeois project in the Third World has all kinds of domestic roots but the implacable undercutting of it by the US was a very large part of it. One now tends to forget that in his postwar vision, Keynes himself had recommended not only state restrictions on rentiers in the advanced capitalist countries, but also regular long-term transfers of capital to the underdeveloped countries to guarantee real growth, and hence domestic peace, and hence stability of the global capitalist system as a whole, not to speak of more prosperous markets for the advanced capitalist countries' own commodities. This latter recommendation was rejected out of hand by the US which kept a tight control over the making of the Bretton Woods architecture. This undercutting of the national-bourgeois project – precisely because the project required high levels of protectionism, tariffs, domestic savings and state-led industrialization, with little role for imperialist penetration – certainly made all those states much weaker in relation to foreign domination but also made those societies much more angry and volatile, eventually even susceptible to all kinds of irrationalism, with little popular legitimacy for the indigenous nation-state. This phenomenon itself has required not only globalized supervision but also an increasingly *interventionist* global state. Little fires have – more and more – to be put out everywhere and now the whole system has to be 're-ordered', as Bush and Blair keep saying. The Cold War was never cold for many outside the NATO and Warsaw Pact zones, and US military interventions in the Third World, direct and indirect, was a routine affair throughout that period. Now, winning the Cold War has opened the way not to world peace but for an ideology of permanent interventionism on part of the United States: 'a task that never ends', as Bush put it some ten days after the 11 September catastrophe.

Defeat of all the forces which Hobsbawm cumulatively and felicitously calls 'the Enlightenment left' – communism, socialism, national liberation movements, the radical wings of social democracy – has led to a full-blown ideological crisis across the globe. Race, religion and ethnicity – re-packaged as just so many 'identities'– are now where class struggles and inter-religious, inter-racial, trans-ethnic solidarities once used to be, and a politics of infinite Difference has arisen on the ruins of the politics of Equality. Postmodernism is rife with thematics taken over from European irrationalism and with nostalgia for the pre-modern. Indeed, this idea of the pre-modern as the postmodern solution for problems of modernity is even more widespread, with far more murderous consequences, in the peripheries of the capitalist system, be it the ideologies of the Hindu far right in India, the sundry fundamentalisms of Islamic mullahs, or the millenarian ideologies of those who brought us September 11th. Terrorism is now where national liberation used to be, and the US today chases these handful of terrorists as assiduously and globally as it used to chase phalanxes of revolutionaries until not long ago. Nor is it a matter any longer of the peripheries. The United States itself is gripped today by a peculiar, cabal-like combination of Christian fundamentalists, zionists, far right neo-conservatives and militarists.

It is here that the specificity of the current Bush regime in the United States lies. We shall return to the fact that the US has fought a war of position not just against communism throughout much of the twentieth century, not only against radical nationalisms in the second half of that century but also, crucially, for its own dominance over its capitalist rivals and in pursuit of a role for itself as the sole architect of the global capitalist system. In that sense, of course, the current Administration continues a much older project, and some of the most aggressive of its policies can be traced back to not only Bush Sr. or Ronald Reagan but to Clinton and Carter as well. The first specificity of this regime lies in the fact that, thanks to the dissolution of the Soviet bloc, this is the first time in human history that a single imperial power is so dominant over all its rivals that it really has no rival, near or far, precisely at the time when it has the greatest capacity to dominate the globe; Clinton in this calculus appears as a transitional figure and Bush Jr's Presidency, the first US Presidency of the twenty-first century, seems to coincide fully with this moment when history's greatest concentration of force can be exercised without any restraint. That is the objective moment of this Presidency. The second specificity is that never in the post-1914 epoch has so concentrated a force of the far right taken hold of the governing institutions of the US state, a force so overdetermined in their ideology and projects that they recognize no limits to their own venality or criminality or global ambition. They are in their own way quite as millenarian as the most irrational member of Al Qaida but, unlike Al Qaida, they have power – more power than anyone else on earth. Thus it is that their actions by and large conform to the logic of capital but also may well exceed that logic.

II

To properly understand where imperialism stands today its necessary to begin by reconsidering Lenin's conception – hardly a theory, one might add – of 'inter-imperialist rivalry'. His thinking on this subject arose in the course of a conjunctural analysis required by an intense debate over whether a world war was imminent or not, the line that European social democracy was to adopt in case war did break out, the question of voting over war credits in the various countries (notably Germany), the question of what revolutionary possibilities might or might not open up in the event of a war and what kind of a power bloc (class alliances) the revolutionary parties were to try to constitute in that event, and where – if anywhere – the likelihood of a revolution would be the greatest. The notable feature of this conception was that it was not rooted in the dynamics of the capitalist mode of production nor a historical analysis of the competition that gave rise to recurring conflicts among colonial powers from the beginning. As a conjunctural analysis, however, Lenin's position proved to be unassailable. The First World War, contrary to what Kautsky, the master theoretician of German social democracy, believed, soon led to the Second, meanwhile creating a situation where the Bolshevik Revolution could be successful. At the end of the war, countries like Germany and Italy did witness a level of revolutionary militancy that was not to be matched again during the inter-war period. And it was in consequence of that war and the Bolshevik Revolution that anti-colonial mass movements arose in a number of Asian and African countries, with the alliance of proletariat, peasantry and left-wing intelligentsia – which Lenin had recommended at the time – becoming a common feature of those movements, whether led by communists or not. Nor is there much doubt that as a latecomer to advanced capitalism without being a 'colony-holding state' (Luxemburg's phrase), Germany was keen on a re-division of the colonial world.

The acuity of Lenin's *conjunctural* analysis, and the recommendations on matters of strategy he drew from it, has nothing to do with whether or not he was right on other things, like export of capital, etc. The idea of 'inter-imperialist rivalry' was in fact much more closely integrated with the idea of 'the weakest link' (more revolutionary possibility in Russia than in Germany, for example), the political strategy of multi-class alliances based on the strategic alliance of the proletariat and the peasantry (a great innovation in Marxist revolutionary theory for backward countries: Stalin's fatal crime that he broke that alliance), and the national-colonial question (the possibility of anti-colonial revolutions thanks to the weakening of the colonizing bourgeoisies, the rise of mass anti-colonial movements after the First World War, general decolonization after the second). One can appreciate the merits of the conjunctural analysis and the accompanying political theory without having to subscribe to the letter of the whole of the economic theory with which he sought to buttress it.

The conception of 'inter-imperialist rivalry', however, presupposed a stage in the global evolution of the capitalist mode of production in which national capitals are essentially discrete in nature and with little inter-penetration. And, it therefore presupposed a kind of state that represents the national bourgeoisie as such, in competition with other national bourgeoisies and their states. Rooted as the conception was in a debate over the inevitability and imminence of war among these competing and discretely organized states, 'rivalry' itself had a meaning far exceeding mere competition because it excluded the possibility of even any lasting collaborative competition *in those circumstances*. The idea that war was imminent similarly presupposed some equivalence, or at least illusion of equivalence, in levels of military capability, i.e. the rivals had to be seen to be erecting military structures that were capable of fighting each other.

This brief excursus on Lenin serves to make a point: one cannot lift the conception of 'inter-imperialist rivalry' out of a conjunctural analysis of almost a century ago. As one now re-visits those texts, one is struck by their belonging to a different epoch, entirely. The specificity of the conjuncture in the imperialism of our time, as different from Lenin's, is that its core – consisting of advanced capitalist countries – is comprised of neither rivals nor equals. The total population and the collective GNP of the EU is certainly equal to that of the United States, marginally greater in fact. That's where the matter ends, however. It has no centralized state structure even remotely comparable to that of the US, no singular language, no standing army or security structure of its own, no foreign policy that is binding on member states, and its laws supersedes national laws only certain circumscribed fields. Its proposed constitution in 2003 was so bound by conditionalities and ifs and buts that it looked more like a statement of principle and vision than a proper constitution. The Brussels bureaucracy, the new Euro, and a whole host of good intentions seem to be the unifying factors.

All this became transparent during the decision-making process over the invasion of Iraq. Britain threw in its lot with the US, with complete disregard of even procedural consideration for the EU but in keeping with the role of loyal subordinate that the US imposed upon it soon after the second World War, and from which neither Wilson nor Thatcher nor Blair have ever deviated. Then, as France and Germany sought to distinguish themselves from that position and the US Defence Secretary Rumsfeld dismissed them contemptuously as 'old Europe', everyone from Derrida to Habermas marched to television studios to express dismay on Europe's behalf. Eventually, Rumsfeld did line up Britain, Italy, Spain, Portugal and a host of little/new countries of 'Europe' on his side, and it was in the Azores that Bush made the final decision to ignore the Security Council and proceed with the invasion. Equally significant is the fact that in the last round of negotiations at the Security Council before the invasion began, the Franco-/German alliance proposed a thirty-day warning to Saddam (and the inspectors) after which they too were willing to condone the invasion. Bush pointedly snubbed them by keeping to the schedule set by the Pentagon and ignoring the Security Council from that point on. The US instructed the UN to withdraw its inspectors forthwith and Kofi Annan, the Secretary-General of the United Nations, did not even bother to call the Security Council in session, even though the inspectors had been sent there not by the US but by a Security Council Resolution; Annan simply instructed the inspectors to comply with US orders. Hans Blix, the chief inspector, was to say later that he had long believed that Iraq had no weapons of mass destruction and the whole thing was a charade anyway. Once the invasion got into full swing, even the Franco-German alliance began to pray publicly for a quick US victory and, only slightly less publicly, began begging for contracts for European firms in the 'reconstruction' of Iraq. When the US decided to establish itself as the occupying force and grant the UN no appreciable role in it, the Franco-German alliance complied.

Meanwhile, on the completely different issue of a Belgian law which grants Belgian courts the jurisdiction to try foreign nationals for war crimes, a stern warning from Rumsfeld that he might move the NATO headquarters from Brussels if the laws were not changed brought a swift promise of compliance from the Belgian government. So much for the claim by high-minded European intellectuals that respect for universal human rights is an integral aspect of the emerging European identity. Belgium apparently has no right to have laws of its own even on issues such as war crimes, even though these laws have no relevance to global trade, finance or commercial contracts. The doctrine of limited sovereignty that is emerging as a major component in US policy, with its vast implications for the new imperial constitutionalism, is to be applied, apparently, not only to the Third World countries but even, selectively, to Europe's own ability to promulgate laws for itself.

In the theoretical field, developments of this kind concretely bring into question the Negri/Hardt conception of a supra-national 'sovereignty', which, according to them, has been so thoroughly globalized that it is hard to locate it anywhere in particular, just as this 'sovereignty' is to be opposed by a 'multitude' which too is beyond class or any other determinate identity or boundary. In actual reality, it is of course the United States that claims a sovereign right to act in its own interests (which it calls 'defence') while flouting the sovereignty of others, so that the sovereignty of the imperial state seems boundless. Indeed, it was Ms. Albright, a former professor at Georgetown University, who became the first high official of US administration, as Clinton's Secretary of State, to expound the notion that 'nationality' as well as 'sovereignty' belong to an outdated repertoire of political theory and need to be abandoned in view of new structures of globalization and imperatives of 'humanitarian intervention'.

The declaration of the Bush administration that it has the sovereign right to make war – what it calls 'pre-emptive war' – against any or all states that it perceives as a threat, while reserving the right to judge what constitutes a threat, is in fact an extension of a doctrine already in place since earlier Administrations. What we are witnessing is the making of an imperial sovereignty claimed for itself by a state which is at once the state of a nation as well as a globalized state of contemporary capitalism. The US arrogates to itself a limitless sovereignty which is arbitrary by nature, and can only exist in so far as its might is so superior to that of all others that its action would necessarily go unchallenged by other components of the global state system however resentful they might be otherwise.

While we are still on the question of inter-imperialist rivalry, as contrasted to the global sovereignty of the US imperium, it is worth recalling that there is yet another, even less plausible and more or less futuristic idea which locates this rivalry not in the Atlantic zone but the Pacific zone, so that the rival arises not from Europe but from East Asia. In an earlier version, the rivalry was to come from Japan but the deeply crisis-ridden nature of its current economy, contrasted with the remarkable growth rates sustained by the Chinese economy over the past more than a decade, seems to have shifted the attention to China. This too is implausible, however. Whatever its recent rates of growth, the scale of the Chinese economy is nothing compared with that of the EU, and whatever the immense size of its land army, the high-tech component of its military capability is still far behind even that of Russia. The preponderant role of its military establishment is internal, with respect to management of civil society and dominance over other institutions of state; for the rest, its war-making capabilities are largely defensive in character. Its economic growth itself has aggravated internal social contradictions, along fault-lines of class and region, and China will be lucky if it can survive, through this extremely difficult and lop-sided growth period, in its present territorial shape, and may face increasing mass unrest along class lines as well. One can be fairly certain that the US will exploit that internal unrest to foster separatist movements, especially in the outlying regions such as Xinjiang, just as it closely watches Tibet as a possible staging area. Meanwhile the remorseless export orientation of the Chinese economy has served to integrate it deeply into the US consumer market, so that China today is beset by the nightmare that if there is a full-scale American recession Chinese exports will decline dramatically and its economy will consequently grind to a halt. Integration of China into the US-dominated global system as a way of increasing its dependency is an imperative that Bush Sr. and Clinton well understood. The current Administration may pursue a policy (in which India is likely to play an important role) of forcing upon China stupendous expenditures on building its military defences, taking those resources away from economic growth and thus exacerbating internal conflicts. In any case, China is extremely vulnerable to the United States, militarily and economically, and any idea of it as competitor is fanciful at best.

III

Unlike inter-imperial rivalry, the question of colonialism is – or should be – central to our thinking today. In the history of imperialism, the role of colonialism – generally conceptualized these days in terms of a contrast between 'formal' and 'informal' empires – remains a contentious issue. Four initial observations can be offered without fear of much contradiction, except from devoutly Westocentric circles. First, colonialism was not an incidental, epiphenomenal or episodic feature of the development of capitalism, and the neglect of this fact has marred much Marxist theory of capitalism; colonialism was from the beginning an intrinsic part of the primitive accumulation of capital and former colonies continue to play this role in the primitive accumulation of capital on the global scale in postcolonial imperialism of even today (primitive accumulation, as David Harvey argues elsewhere in this volume, being a constant feature of capitalism throughout its history, right up to the present conjuncture). Second, there is a sharp contrast between different kinds of colonialism, as for example between settler colonialism (which succeeded in the Americas and Australia but failed in Africa) and the so-called colonies which were occupied, administered and exploited by bourgeoisies so external to them that they never put their roots down in the conquered lands (the experience of most colonies in Asia and Africa). Some of the white settlements in the temperate zones made a transition to advanced capitalism (notably North America and to an extent Australia-New Zealand) while others did not (South America). None of the occupied-but-unsettled colonies did, not even India which arguably had some potential at the moment of colonization. Much capital and technology was transferred to the settler colonies, very little to the unsettled ones. All this had rather consequential effects on the class structure of the respective sub-systems. The settler-colonies which made the capitalist transition are marked by the dominance of industry over agriculture, and they have a demographic balance in which the employed greatly outnumber the army of the unemployed; in those which did not make that transition, the army of the unemployed and the indifferently employed tend to exceed the employed sections of the working class.

Third, the so-called 'informal' empire (imperialism without colonies) has been a recurring feature from the beginning, and full-scale colonialist conquest often came as an aftermath of other forms of imperialist exploitation. Coastal outposts in western Africa, combined with raids and incursions into the interior, were enough to empty it of much of its population via the slave trade and to disrupt its economic networks; conquest of the interior came much later. Even the beginnings of territorial conquest of India came very much later than the establishment of coastal outposts for purposes of commercial imperialism, and the full territorial conquest – not to speak of the transition from a possession of the East India Company to a crown colony – took a hundred years; by contrast, ninety years were to elapse between full conquest and decolonization.

Fourth, the global history of 'formal' and 'informal' empires – not to speak of colonial conquest and decolonization – is parallel but non-synchronic. Latin America was fully decolonized well before the interiors of Africa and Asia were fully colonized; the history of Anglo-American rivalry over the 'informal' empire in Latin America after decolonization predates the rise of mass anti-colonial movements in Asia and Africa by roughly a century. The fact that Latin American states originated in settler-colonial formations while most states in Asia and Africa did not experience even the attempt to impose that form has had enormously differentiated consequences for the development of languages, cultures, religions, demographic compositions, etc. in the respective continents. And some of the consequences of imperialism were rather similar in 'formal' and 'informal' empires so far as the colonized territories and the 'semi-colonies' (Lenin's term) are concerned. India shifts to the status of a crown colony in the 1830s; Turkey, never colonized, undertakes modern bourgeois reforms under the Tanzimat at roughly the same time; by the 1920s both had developed remarkably similar property relations, legal structures, reform movements etc, not to speak of the modes of dependence on Europe (e.g., debt servitude) with the difference that India had been colonized and Turkey not.

The United States occupies a unique place in this whole history of colonialism. It was the only former colony that turned itself into an empire, but even during the nineteenth century when colonizing was quite the fashion in Europe, the US sought not to colonize Latin America but to dominate it. Born in genocidal annexation of vast territories, its initial Thirteen Colonies made a revolution, turned themselves into a nation, wrote for themselves a constitution which combined stirring rhetoric of what we today call 'human rights' with defence of slavery, so that the settlers could now go on doing what they were doing anyway – race-based slavery for the plantations, profits from the triangular trade, commerce and industry concentrated mostly on the eastern seaboard, petty commodity production in New England – without having to share profits with the 'mother country'. The expansionist ideology that arose out of it was annexationist rather than colonial in the European sense; what lay beyond the frontier was there to take, and frontiers could be extended through much of the nineteenth century. To the west, only the Pacific proved to be the limit; to the south and north, borders with Mexico and Canada were determined in warfare and annexation of territory, not conquering these neighbours as colonies. Unlike the 'colony-holding' states of Europe it never had the problem of surplus labour; it constantly accumulated for itself a massive surplus of resources. European colony-holders exported their populations to achieve a favourable demographic balance; the US thrived on importing slaves, skilled labourers and vast intellectual resources from other countries. Its first 'informal' empire was in the Americas itself, while the heart of the empire lay in the annexed territories that were constantly converted into more and more national territory; empire and nation were, in that originating moment, one.

IV

The US entered World War I not for re-division of the colonial world but as arbiter of European disputes, and emerged out of it as the first among equals. The Nazis initiated the Second World War with the ambition of turning the whole world into a vast and permanent German colony. Once the US entered the Second World War, it explicitly adopted the goal of persuading – or forcing – all the 'colony-holding' states to unburden themselves of the colonies and get on with the business of joining a unified capitalist empire on the global scale. Later, the US was to fight and fund many wars, the most lethal and protracted ones in Indochina of course, but never to colonize, only to obtain client regimes and make the world safe for capitalism.

The post-Second World War settlement was based on a combination of a clear-cut US leadership and a complex network of multilateral institutions. The most useful were the institutions – such as the IFIs and NATO – which the US could control more firmly. The UN was always treated as a necessary and useful nuisance because the USSR had veto power in the Security Council and because membership in the General Assembly was so numerous that, in the heyday of communism and Third World nationalism, majorities were not always easy to obtain; there even came a fleeting moment, in the 1970s, when UN itself became a forum for the pursuit of Third World nationalist projects through such subsidiary organizations as the UNCTAD. Now that those adversaries have been vanquished, a paradoxical situation has arisen in which the UN itself has become much more pliant but the US is now so determined to take the management of the capitalist world into its own hands that it is undermining not only the UN, but even, on occasion, the IMF and the World Bank which had been until recently among its chief instrumentalities for governance of, especially, the Third World. With hindsight, one can now see that the great emphasis on multilaterism in the past was itself perhaps a function of the fact that the US faced challenges from communism and Third World nationalism and needed at least an institutional framework in which to buttress the unity and consent of its chief allies behind its own leadership. Now, with those challenges gone, the leadership firmly secured, and a much more belligerent US Administration in office, many aspects of this multilateralism are being allowed to lapse. Bush Jr's hysterical assertions of US imperial sovereignty stand in sharp contrast to the trilateralism of his father.

A very underrated aspect of the global hegemony the US established after the Second World War was the role its knowledge industry came to play in training and nurturing large elements of the ruling strata in the Third World, directly in its own institutions on US soil and indirectly through 'national' institutions located in the Third World itself, through supply of teachers, syllabi, grants, research equipment, libraries and so forth. Marx once remarked that a ruling class is stable only to the extent that it presses the best minds of the subordinate classes into its service. As it emerged as clear leader of the capitalist countries after the Second World War, at a moment when European empires were being dissolved in Asia and Africa, the US developed the largest, best funded, richest academic establishment ever known to humankind, and systematically set out to bring key intellectual strata from the newly decolonized countries into its own academic institutions, across the diverse fields of physical and technical sciences, social sciences and the humanities, arts, diplomacy, jurisprudence and so on. Many stayed on and became part of the intellectual powerhouse of the United States itself; from the 1960s onwards, certainly, the stupendous 'brain drain' from the Third World (principally Asia) gained momentum (as, by contrast, fewer European intellectuals were now inclined to migrate out of their increasingly prosperous and politically stable continent).

Those who returned became the home country's economists, scientists, diplomats, bureaucrats, professors, politicians, businessmen. By comparison, the role of the European countries in the intellectual formation of the postcolonial Third World intelligentsia declined sharply, and domestic institutions were re-fashioned to correspond as closely as possible to their American counterparts. The American imperial project was of course greatly aided by the fact that English became during this period something of a world language, thanks to the fact that it was the language of the two predominant imperial powers of the nineteenth and twentieth centuries. The net result was that large parts of the state institutions in Third World dependencies were taken over simply through the intellectual takeover of many of their key personnel. The American worldview became the practical common sense for those personnel. Nor was this a matter of practical affairs alone. There was an attendant training of sense and sensibility, of literary and artistic taste, of patterns of consumption, the telecasting and absorption of news, the duplication of forms in the entertainment industry. Most European intellectuals are known in much of Africa and Asia today through their American re-packaging. The only Latin American literature that arrives in the bookshops of Delhi is that which has been translated, annotated, commented upon and published in the United States. The only 'universal' musical forms today are the ones that either come from the US or are local duplicates and variants of the American form. Postmodernization of the world is actually Americanization of the world, with considerable degree of local colour and imitative originality no doubt. A good degree of this imitative originality can be seen in Europe too.

V

That, however, is not the only impact modern imperialism has had on the cultural and ideological spheres in the Third World. A general outbreak of irrationalism across large areas of the former colonies and semi-colonies is the other consequence of the defeat of the original anti-colonial project.

National liberation movements against colonialism and imperialism had risen within a determinate field of force, which was constituted on the one hand by anachronistic hierarchies of their own societies and foreign rule which was itself much too complicit with those hierarchies – and on the other hand, inspiration from the radical side of Modernity: the Enlightenment ideas of secular reason and the right of every social entity to emancipate itself through the exercise of that reason; the practical example of the relatively emancipated social life in industrialized societies; the ideas of the Bolshevik Revolution which had exploded upon the world just as these mass movements were coming into being and which itself inspired new mass movements. As such, they were, generally speaking, secular reform movements – secularization of religion itself was often an objective – as well as anti-colonial movements. As mass movements, their notable achievement was that they brought into the political field collective social actors which had never acted politically in the past. And as national movements for independence and social change, they sought to bring together diverse elements of society which otherwise belonged to different ethnic, religious and linguistic groups.

This was obviously not the only kind of opposition that grew against colonialism. A traditionalizing backlash in defence of the older social hierarchies was common enough, as hostile to secularizing reform movements as to colonialism. However, as one looks at a broad landscape – from North Africa, through West and South Asia up to Indochina – one is struck by how dominant the secularizing and reforming, even revolutionary, tendencies were. This would include Arab nationalism as much as the Indian anti-colonial movement, and the same was of course true of such reformist regimes as that of Ataturk which founded the modern Turkish state. Mass communist parties were a phenomenon not at all restricted to countries such as Vietnam where the communist-led national liberation triumphed, but also in a whole range of countries, from Iraq and Sudan to India, Malaya and Indonesia. Muslim societies seem to have been rather hospitable to communist ideas, while entities like the Egyptian Muslim Brotherhood and the Indian RSS remained marginalized until the last quarter of the twentieth century. One might add that political Islam was nurtured in all those societies by the US from the 1950s onward as a bulwark against communism, with eventually disastrous effects in Afghanistan and beyond. In class terms, meanwhile, such movements usually represented an alliance of the urban middle classes and the peasantry, and were led by the intelligentsia arising out of the former who were themselves aligned with the national-bourgeois project.

What, then, happened to this project after independence? That is a complex story, but as a broad generalization, one could say that every national bourgeois regime that arose after decolonization in the larger agrarian societies had a stark choice of alignment between imperialism and the peasantry, and in every instance it betrayed the peasantry. This is a theme of great significance. Gramsci argued that the European bourgeoisie that went through the experience of the French Revolution became so thoroughly frightened by the prospect of the peasantry carrying its own revolution to its logical end that no bourgeoisie was ever again to play a revolutionary role against the landholding classes. In the agrarian economies of the larger former colonies certainly, agrarian revolution was the only way out of imperialist dependence and lack of that revolution lies at the heart of the defeat of the national bourgeois project and the eventual acceptance of imperialist dictation and the formation of neoliberal regimes by the local bourgeoisies. This internal factor was certainly decisive in India, where the post-colonial state 'begat' quite a powerful industrial/financial bourgeoisie 'hothouse-fashion' and created a widespread class of rich farmers in the countryside – but never emancipated the vast bulk of the poor and landless peasantry. That type of state itself began to decay by the mid-70s, and when the appropriate moment arrived the bourgeoisie cut loose from the project of state-led growth strategies and reconciled itself to a greatly subordinated status in the structure of global capitalism. A major external factor contributing to the fate of the national-bourgeois project was the existence of the Soviet bloc which provided key supports for it in terms of technological inputs, finance and markets; the demise of the Soviet bloc also ended what little had remained of that project. Imperialist pressure was in any case the largest element in the demise of that project.

The defeat and/or decline of the democratic, secular, anti-colonial nationalism has given rise, in a host of countries, from India to Egypt to Algeria, to hysterical, irrationalist forms of cultural nationalism and atavistic hysteria. I have been arguing elsewhere in my writings that in the whole history of modern nationalism, from the early years of the nineteenth century onward, there has been a ferocious struggle between the Enlightenment project of equal citizenship and rational self-emancipation on the one hand, and the romanticist, identitarian, racialistic, religiously bigoted nationalisms. What we are seeing today is that the defeat of the Enlightenment project has necessarily led to the rise of savage identities based on race or religion. As Clara Zetkin once put it, fascism is a just reward for the failure to make the revolution.

This brings us to Al Qaida. In the Arab world, where the zionist state was a chief instrumentality of US imperialism, it was in the crucible of the Six Day

War of 1967 – Israel's professedly 'pre-emptive' invasion of Egypt, instant destruction of its Air Force, occupation of the Sinai – that the radical-nationalist project of Nasserism collapsed; the re-stabilization of the monarchies and resurgence of political Islam in the Arab world can be dated back to that catastrophe. Defeat of the left and of the secular-democratic forces of national liberation in Palestine accounts for the latter-day rise of Hamas and the suicide bombers. In Iran, the destruction of the communist movement and forces of secular nationalism by the joint efforts of the CIA and Shah's secret police paved the way for the Islamic regime to fill the vacuum and hijack the anti-monarchical, reformist sentiments of the Irani people. In Afghanistan, the US sponsored an elaborate, ferocious war against the reformist regime brought about by the communist forces, assembled a huge international force of Islamicist extremists to fight against communism and brought to the world stage the so-called 'mujahideen', the Taliban, Osama bin Laden and the rest; that is the monster of its own making that came to haunt the United States on 11th September 2001.

VI

We may now, finally, return to the question with which we began, namely wherein lies the specificity of Bush Jr's regime. It does not lie, in the first instance, in the invasion of either Afghanistan or Iraq. In the case of Afghanistan, the US has only come back to profit from the war it initiated in 1978, under Carter, against the then new and deeply secular regime of the People's Democratic Party of Afghanistan (PDPA), through their Islamicist proxies who called themselves 'mujahideen' ('fighters of the faith'); Brzezinski, Carter's National Security Advisor, has written that he sponsored that war with the explicit objective of drawing in the Soviets – and the Soviets obliged by walking into the trap. Taliban (literally, 'students') arose from among the youngsters and children who grew up in the refugee camps that the war itself had produced; they were trained in seminaries established with the express purpose of producing more 'fighters of the faith' in American service; and the regime of their Islamicist faction was foisted upon that wretched and bleeding country by the Pakistani intelligence agencies upon US advice. The so-called 'Arab Afghanis', among whom Osama was a leader, were CIA agents recruited to fight the Soviets. When the Taliban refused to cooperate fully with the US in its designs on Central Asian oil, the US decided to invade. Niaz Naik, the dean of Pakistan's diplomatic corps, said on the BBC that he had been told by the Americans during the summer of 2001 that invasion would begin in October. The events of 11th September came between the making of the design and its execution.

War against Iraq began not in 2003 but in the course of the so-called 'Gulf War', in 1991, which continued through sanctions and no-fly zones, for over a decade – longer than the combined duration of the First and Second World Wars – under three consecutive US Presidents, two Republicans (father and son) and one Democrat (Clinton, the 'New Democrat' who inspired 'New Labour' across the Atlantic). It was during the Clinton Presidency that the US Congress passed the Iraq Liberation Act, in 1998. When the sanctions regime was estimated by some UN agencies to have killed half a million Iraqi children, and journalists asked Clinton's Secretary of State Madeleine Albright whether their death was worth the price of upholding the sanctions, she said 'the price was worth it'. The so-called no-fly zones in northern and eastern Iraq were declared by Boutros Boutros-Ghali, the UN Secretary-General, to be illegal, and yet under that scheme the Anglo-American bombardment of Iraq became the longest aerial campaign since the Second World War; in 1999 alone 1800 bombs were dropped and 450 targets hit. Cumulatively, over some twelve years, the tonnage dropped on Iraq came to equal seven Hiroshimas.

'Regime change' is a catchy phrase, and the Bush Administration has undoubtedly raised it to the status of a legitimate right of imperial sovereignty. However, the US has been doing it for decades. It did so in Iraq itself when the CIA helped overthrow the progressive regime of Abd al-Karim Kassem in 1964 and brought in the Ba'ath party regime ('We came to power on a CIA train', exulted the General-Secretary of Saddam's parent party), paving the way for the eventual personal dictatorship of Saddam Hussein who remained a close US ally throughout the 1980s when he fought a US-assisted war against Iran. 'Regime change' is what the CIA brought to Iran in 1953 and the US military to Grenada and Panama more recently. And the history of the US coming as 'liberators' and staying as occupiers goes back to the Philippines at the end of the nineteenth century.

What is specific to the Bush regime is the combination of an intensification of such long-standing trends as well as a cluster of novelties which, taken together, amount to something of a historic break. Intensification of trends is obvious enough. What are the novelties internal to Bush Jr's Presidency? First, the manner of his election: he was elevated to the Presidency by a judicial decision of dubious merit, combined with widely suspected disenfranchisement of a considerable section of the black electorate in the state of Florida which *happened* to be run by his brother, Jeb. Jeb Bush's other major contribution to Bush Jr's campaign was that he was the one who assembled that cabal of the neo-conservatives, drawn from the think-tanks of the far right and supervised by Dick Cheney, who came to define the domestic as well as foreign policies, the civilian as well as military structures, of the United States after the elections: they captured the Pentagon, hence the US military machine, just as the Bush brothers captured the White House.

The second novelty of this Presidency, which distinguishes it from the preceding ones, is the will to radically re-make the United States itself as it sets out to re-map the globe. Dick Cheney's bland prediction that the war against terrorism may last for fifty years or more, and General Tommy Frank's prediction even before the invasion of Iraq that US troops may have to be stationed there fairly indefinitely, on the model of Korea, is matched by a politics of permanent hysteria at home, invoking a mixture of extreme insecurity and atavistic patriotism. The general populace is being persuaded to surrender many of its own fundamental rights, and to endorse distinctions between those born on US soil and the naturalized citizens, between immigrants from one part of the world and another, between 'good' and 'bad' members of one faith, Islam – all this buttressed by a historically new and now very extensive alliance between extreme zionism and Christian fundamentalism. The assault on American liberties is itself being coded as Patriot Act I & II. This tie between hysterical patriotism and a docile populace whose own rights are being abridged is itself something of a quasi-fascist move. Meanwhile, the already existing policies of shifting incomes upward and offering tax bonanzas to corporations and the rich while bankrupting the social state have been accelerated to a degree that a successor government may not even have the resources to save such things as Social Security in its present form even if it had the desire to do so.

What is being reversed, thus, is not only the so-called 'Vietnam syndrome' but even aspects of American social life dating back to the New Deal. In 'Re-Building America's Defenses: Strategy, Forces and Resources For a New Century', a report prepared by an impressive cross-section of the neo–conservative elite including Paul Wolfowitz, and issued by The Project for a New American Century in September 2000, the authors remarked that the kind of sweeping changes they are proposing may take some time unless some catastrophic and catalyzing event, like a new Pearl Harbour, were to occur. 11th September 2001 was the event they were waiting for. Condoleeza Rice urged her colleagues the next morning that ways be found to 'capitalize on these opportunities', while Donald Rumsfeld urged immediate invasion of Iraq.

How does one comprehend this peculiar mix of continuities and discontinuities as a whole? One way of putting it is that the rightwing backlash which began in the United States in the late 1960s (in response to the military defeats it was facing in Indochina, on the one hand, and, on the other, the immense successes at home of the Anti-Vietnam War movement, the radicalization of Afro-American politics, and the rise of the women's movement) has finally grown and matured to the point where it has actually captured state power. This offensive was prepared over a quarter century or more and Bush Jr's Presidency represents something of a historic break in the sense that these trends had remained scattered and subordinated to other exigencies of power, and its representatives, even as they began occupying positions in the Reagan and Bush Sr.'s administrations, were not in charge of all the key institutions of state, as they now are. One notable feature of this counteroffensive has been the role that think tanks and foundations of the far right have played in funding, training and delivering the requisite personnel transforming the intellectual climate in the US, and now the state apparatus. Another notable feature is the role quasi-messianic evangelical Christianity has played in preparing popular sensibilities receptive to all these changes.

A group of New York intellectuals had begun arguing as far back as the Nixon Presidency that the New Left, the anti-war movement, black nationalism, women's liberation movements *et al* collectively comprised a disruptive but highly vocal minority and the real task was to organize and mobilize the 'Silent Majority' which was opposed to all that. Milton Friedman at Chicago University formulated an assault on the social state and advanced the ideology of the market as the final arbiter of the social good. His colleague Alan Bloom wrote best-selling books on 'the destruction of the American Mind' by the reforms that leftwing/black/feminist pressures had forced upon the educational system, including the formidable elite universities. Bloom's teacher, Leo Straus, himself trained some of those who were to emerge within the last decade as members of the neo-conservative intellectual elite. Hundreds of large and small, inter-locking, neoliberal organizations now dotted the American landscape, and a rash of not very widely known rightwing foundations started appearing – the Carthage Foundation, the Henry M. Olin Foundation, the Phillip M. McKenna Foundation, the Henry Salvatori Foundation etc, etc. – which then helped to fund the more prestigious and influential ones: the American Enterprise Institute, the Heritage Foundation, the Cato Institute, and the elite of all neo-conservative think-tanks, The Project for the New American Century, whose founders include the core of the Bush Administration: Vice President Dick Cheney, Defence Secretary Donald Rumsfeld, Deputy Defence Secretary Paul Wolfowitz, Cheney's Chief Staff Lewis I. Libby, Reagan's Education Secretary William Bennet, and Zalmay Khalilzad, Bush's shadowy representative first in Afghanistan and then in Iraq.

A word about evangelical Christianity. When Reagan was re-elected with the largest electoral sweep in history, losing only one state, it was revealed that only 27 per cent of the potential voters had actually voted in his favour; the majority had stayed home. At the same time, a Gallup poll showed that 27 per cent of Americans subscribes to some variety of evangelical Christianity, and commen-tators noted that if all of them were to be mobilized as a voting bloc the US could have a permanent government of the far right. Not *all* of them have been mobi-lized yet – but that kind of government has now arrived. While Reagan gifted us supply-side economics and Star Wars, and the Left thought that he was as bad it could get, the rightwing of the Republican party thought of him as a Roosevelt democrat. That rightwing is now in power.

We may be witnessing an imperial overreach. Overdetermined by their own ideological delusions, Bush's neocons may be pursuing policies that far exceed the logic of global capitalism or the requirements of the imperial US state; even George Soros seems to think so. Two former Presidents, including the current President's father, opposed the invasion of Iraq before it happened. Ever the mildly Presbyterian Trilaterist, Bush Sr. emphasized that the US needed alliance with Europe and the war on Iraq would undermine it. As we have seen, the Franco-German alliance has accepted the consequences, however resentfully. But Iraq may yet prove to be a quagmire that cures the US populace of any appetite for the real wars that are fought on the other side of their TV screens. They may yet come to comprehend what a menace this Administration is for their own security, especially as old age sets in, and to the security of their children. At the same time, the global revolt against imperial America that we witnessed on the eve of the Iraq invasion may regain momentum. This moment of neo-conservative extremity may yet pass as one of many murderous episodes in imperial history.

THE 'NEW' IMPERIALISM: ACCUMULATION BY DISPOSSESSION

DAVID HARVEY

The survival of capitalism for so long in the face of multiple crises and reorganizations accompanied by dire predictions, from both the left and the right, of its imminent demise, is a mystery that requires illumination. Lefebvre, for one, thought he had found the key in his celebrated comment that capitalism survives through the production of space, but he did not explain exactly how this might be so.[1] Both Lenin and Luxemburg, for quite different reasons and utilizing quite different forms of argument, considered that imperialism – a certain form of the production of space – was the answer to the riddle, though both argued that this solution was finite because of its own terminal contradictions.

The way I sought to look at this problem in the 1970s was to examine the role of 'spatio-temporal fixes' to the inner contradictions of capital accumulation.[2] This argument makes sense only in relation to a pervasive tendency of capitalism, understood theoretically by way of Marx's theory of the falling rate of profit, to produce crises of overaccumulation.[3] Such crises are registered as surpluses of capital and of labour power side by side without there apparently being any means to bring them profitably together to accomplish socially useful tasks. If system-wide devaluations (and even destruction) of capital and of labour power are not to follow, then ways must be found to absorb these surpluses. Geographical expansion and spatial reorganization provide one such option. But this cannot be divorced from temporal fixes either, since geographical expansion often entails investment in long-lived physical and social infrastructures (in transport and communications networks and education and research, for example) that take many years to return their value to circulation through the productive activity they support.

Global capitalism has experienced a chronic and enduring problem of over-accumulation since the 1970s. I find the empirical materials Brenner assembles to document this point generally convincing.[4] I interpret the volatility of inter-national capitalism during these years, however, as a series of temporary spatio-temporal fixes that failed even in the medium run to deal with problems of overaccumulation. It was, as Gowan argues, through the orchestration of such volatility that the United States sought to preserve its hegemonic position within global capitalism.[5] The recent apparent shift towards an open imperialism backed by military force on the part of the US may then be seen as a sign of the weak-ening of that hegemony before the serious threat of recession and widespread devaluation at home, as opposed to the various bouts of devaluation formerly inflicted elsewhere (Latin America in the 1980s and early 1990s, and, even more seriously, the crisis that consumed East and South-East Asia in 1997 and then engulfed Russia and much of Latin America). But I also want to argue that the inability to accumulate through expanded reproduction on a sustained basis has been paralleled by a rise in attempts to accumulate by dispossession.[6] This, I then conclude, is the hallmark of what some like to call ' the new imperialism' is about.[7]

THE SPATIO-TEMPORAL FIX AND ITS CONTRADICTIONS

The basic idea of the spatio-temporal fix is simple enough. Overaccumulation within a given territorial system means a condition of surpluses of labour (rising unemployment) and surpluses of capital (registered as a glut of commodities on the market that cannot be disposed of without a loss, as idle productive capacity, and/or as surpluses of money capital lacking outlets for productive and profitable investment). Such surpluses may be absorbed by: (a) temporal displacement through investment in long-term capital projects or social expenditures (such as education and research) that defer the re-entry of current excess capital values into circulation well into the future, (b) spatial displacements through opening up new markets, new production capacities and new resource, social and labour possibilities elsewhere, or (c) some combination of (a) and (b).

The combination of (a) and (b) is particularly important when we focus on fixed capital of an independent kind embedded in the built environment. This provides the necessary physical infrastructures for production and consumption to proceed over space and time (everything from industrial parks, ports and airports, transport and communications systems, to sewage and water provision, housing, hospitals, schools). Plainly, this is not a minor sector of the economy and it is capable of absorbing massive amounts of capital and labour, particularly under conditions of rapid geographical expansion and intensification.

The reallocation of capital and labour surpluses to such investments requires the mediating help of financial and/or state institutions. These have the capacity to generate credit. A quantity of 'fictitious capital' is created that can be allocated away from current consumption to future-oriented projects in, say, highway construction or education, thereby re-invigorating the economy (including, perhaps, augmenting the demand for surplus commodities like shirts and shoes by teachers and construction workers).[8] If the expenditures on built environments or social improvements prove productive (i.e. facilitative of more efficient forms of capital accumulation later on) then the fictitious values are redeemed (either directly by retirement of debt or indirectly in the form of, say, higher tax returns to pay off state debt). If not, overaccumulations of values in built environments or education can become evident with attendant devaluations of these assets (housing, offices, industrial parks, airports, etc.) or difficulties in paying off state debts on physical and social infrastructures (a fiscal crisis of the state).

The role of such investments in stabilizing and destabilizing capitalism has been significant. I note, for example, that the starting point of the crisis of 1973 was a world-wide collapse of property markets (beginning with the Herstatt Bank in Germany which brought down the Franklin National in the United States), followed shortly thereafter by the virtual bankruptcy of New York City in 1975 (a classic case of social expenditures outrunning tax revenues); that the beginning of the decade-long stagnation in Japan in 1990 was a collapse of the speculative bubble in land, property and other asset prices, putting the whole banking system in jeopardy; that the beginning of the Asian collapse in 1997 was the bursting of the property bubbles in Thailand and Indonesia; and that the most important prop to the US and British economies after the onset of general recession in all other sectors from mid-2001 onwards has been the continued speculative vigour in property markets. Since 1998, the Chinese have kept their economy growing and sought to absorb their labour surpluses (and curb the threat of social unrest) by debt-financed investment in huge mega-projects that dwarf the already huge Three Gorges Dam (8,500 miles of new railroads, superhighways and urbanization projects, massive engineering works to divert water from the Yangtze to Yellow Rivers, new airports, etc.). It is, I think, passing strange that most accounts of capital accumulation (including Brenner's) either ignore these matters entirely or treat them as epiphenomenal.

The term 'fix' has, however, a double meaning. A certain portion of the total capital becomes literally fixed in some physical form for a relatively long period of time (depending on its economic and physical lifetime). There is a sense in which social expenditures also become territorialized and rendered geographically immobile through state commitments. (In what follows, however, I will exclude social infrastructures from explicit consideration since the matter is complicated and would take too much text to elucidate). Some fixed capital is geographically mobile (such as machinery that can easily be unbolted from its moorings and taken elsewhere) but the rest is so fixed in the land that it cannot be moved without being destroyed. Aircraft are mobile but the airports to which they fly are not.

The spatio-temporal 'fix', on the other hand, is a metaphor for solutions to capitalist crises through temporal deferment and geographical expansion. The production of space, the organization of wholly new territorial divisions of labour, the opening up of new and cheaper resource complexes, of new dynamic spaces of capital accumulation, and the penetration of pre-existing social formations by capitalist social relations and institutional arrangements (such as rules of contract and private property arrangements) provide multiple ways to absorb existing capital and labour surpluses. Such geographical expansions, reorganizations and reconstructions often threaten, however, the values fixed in place but not yet realized. Vast quantities of capital fixed in place act as a drag upon the search for a spatial fix elsewhere. The values of the fixed assets that constitute New York City were and are not trivial and the threat of their massive devaluation in 1975 (and now again in 2003) was (and is) viewed by many as a major threat to the future of capitalism. If capital does move out, it leaves behind a trail of devastation (the de-industrialization experienced in the 1970s and 1980s in the heartlands of capitalism, like Pittsburgh and Sheffield, as well as in many other parts of the world, such as Bombay illustrates the point). If overaccumulated capital does not or cannot move, on the other hand, then it stands to be devalued directly. The summary statement of this process I usually offer is this: capital necessarily creates a physical landscape in its own image at one point in time only to have to destroy it at some later point in time as it pursues geographical expansions and temporal displacements as solutions to the crises of overaccumulation to which it is regularly prone. Thus is the history of creative destruction (with all manner of deleterious social and environmental consequences) written into the evolution of the physical and social landscape of capitalism.

Another series of contradictions arises within the dynamics of spatio-temporal transformations more generally. If the surpluses of capital and labour power exist within a given territory (such as a nation state) and cannot be absorbed internally (either by geographical adjustments or social expenditures) then they must be sent elsewhere to find a fresh terrain for their profitable realization if they are not to be devalued. This can happen in a number of ways. Markets for commodity surpluses can be found elsewhere. But the spaces to which the surpluses are sent must possess means of payment such as gold or currency (e.g. dollar) reserves or tradable commodities. Surpluses of commodities are sent out and money or commodities flow back. The problem of overaccumulation is alleviated only in the short term; it merely switches the surplus from commodities to money or into different commodity forms, though if the latter turn out, as is often the case, to be cheaper raw materials or other inputs they can relieve the downward pressure on the profit rate at home temporarily. If the territory does not possess reserves or commodities to trade back, it must either find them (as Britain forced India to do by opening up the opium trade with China in the nineteenth century and thus extracting Chinese gold via Indian trade) or be given credit or aid. In the latter case a territory is lent or donated the money with which to buy back the surplus commodities generated at home. The British did this with Argentina in the nineteenth century and Japanese trade surpluses during the 1990s were largely absorbed by lending to the United States to support the consumerism that purchased Japanese goods. Plainly, market and credit transactions of this sort can alleviate problems of overaccumulation at least in the short term. They function very well under conditions of uneven geographical development in which surpluses available in one territory are matched by lack of supply elsewhere. But resort to the credit system simultaneously makes territories vulnerable to flows of speculative and fictitious capitals that can both stimulate and undermine capitalist development and even, as in recent years, be used to impose savage devaluations upon vulnerable territories.

The export of capital, particularly when accompanied by the export of labour power, works rather differently and typically has longer term effects. In this case, surpluses of (usually money) capital and labour are sent elsewhere to set capital accumulation in motion in the new space. Surpluses generated in Britain in the nineteenth century found their way to the United States and to the settler colonies like South Africa, Australia and Canada, creating new and dynamic centers of accumulation in these territories which generated a demand for goods from Britain. Since it may take many years for capitalism to mature in these new territories (if it ever does) to the point where they, too, begin to produce over-accumulations of capital, the originating country can hope to benefit from this process for a considerable period of time. This is particularly the case when the goods demanded elsewhere are fixed physical infrastructures (such as railroads and dams) required as a basis for future capital accumulation. But the rate of return on these long-term investments in the built environment eventually depends upon the evolution of a strong dynamic of accumulation in the receiving country. Britain lent to Argentina in this way during the last part of the nineteenth century. The United States, via the Marshall Plan for Europe (Germany in particular) and Japan, clearly saw that its own economic security (leaving aside the military aspect dependent on the Cold War) rested on the active revival of capitalist activity in these spaces.

Contradictions arise, because new dynamic spaces of capital accumulation ultimately generate surpluses and have to absorb them through geographical expansions. Japan and Germany became competitors with US capital from the late 1960s onwards, much as the US overwhelmed British capital (and helped pull down the British Empire) as the twentieth century dragged on. It is always interesting to note the point at which strong internal development spills over into a search for a spatio-temporal fix. Japan did so during the 1960s, first through trade, then through the export of capital as direct investment first to Europe and the United States and more recently through massive investments (both direct and portfolio) in East and South East Asia, and finally through lending abroad (particularly to the United States). South Korea suddenly switched outwards in the 1980s, shortly followed by Taiwan in the 1990s, in both cases exporting not only financial capital but some of the most vicious labour management practices imaginable as subcontractors to multinational capital throughout the world (in Central America, in Africa, as well as throughout the rest of South and East Asia). Even recently successful adherents to capitalist development have, therefore, quickly found themselves in need of a spatio-temporal fix for their overaccumulated capital. The rapidity with which certain territories, like South Korea, Singapore, Taiwan and now even China moved from being net receiving to net exporting territories has been quite startling relative to the slower rhythms characteristic of former periods. But by the same token these successful territories have to adjust fast to the blowbacks from their own spatio-temporal fixes. China, absorbing surpluses in the form of foreign direct investments from Japan, Korea and Taiwan, is rapidly supplanting those countries in many lines of production and export (particularly of the lower value-added and labour intensive sort, but it is quickly moving up to the higher value-added commodities as well). The generalized overcapacity that Brenner identifies can in this way be disaggregated into a cascading and proliferating series of spatio-temporal fixes primarily throughout South and East Asia but with additional elements within Latin America – Brazil, Mexico and Chile in particular – supplemented now by Eastern Europe. And in an interesting reversal, explicable in large part by the role of the dollar as a secure global reserve currency which confers the power of seigniorage, the US has in recent years with its huge increase in indebtedness absorbed surplus capitals chiefly from East and South East Asia but also from elsewhere.[9]

The aggregate result, however, is increasingly fierce international competition as multiple dynamic centers of capital accumulation emerge to compete on the world stage in the face of strong currents of overaccumulation. Since they cannot all succeed in the long run, either the weakest succumb and fall into serious crises of devaluation, or geopolitical confrontations erupt in the form of trade wars, currency wars and even military confrontations (of the sort that gave us two world wars between capitalist powers in the twentieth century). In this case it is devaluation and destruction (of the sort that the US financial institutions visited on East and South East Asia in 1997-8) that is being exported, and the spatio-temporal fix takes on much more sinister forms. There are, however, some further points to make about this process in order to better understand how it actually occurs.

INNER CONTRADICTIONS

In *The Philosophy of Right*, Hegel notes how the inner dialectic of bourgeois society, producing an overaccumulation of wealth at one pole and a rabble of paupers at the other, drives it to seek solutions through external trade and colonial/imperial practices. He rejects the idea that there might be ways to solve the problem of social inequality and instability through internal mechanisms of redistribution.[10] Lenin quotes Cecil Rhodes as saying that colonialism and imperialism abroad were the only possible way to avoid civil war at home.[11] Class relations and struggles within a territorially bounded social formation drive impulses to seek a spatio-temporal fix elsewhere.

The evidence from the end of the nineteenth century is here of interest. Joseph Chamberlain ('Radical Joe' as he was known) was closely identified with the liberal manufacturing interests of Birmingham, and was initially opposed to

imperialism (in the Afghan Wars of the 1850s, for example). He devoted himself
to educational reform and improvements in the social and physical infrastructures
for production and consumption in his home city of Birmingham. This
provided, he thought, a productive outlet for surpluses that would be repaid in
the long run. An important figure within the liberal conservative movement, he
saw the rising tide of class struggle in Britain at first hand and in 1885 made a
celebrated speech in which he called for the propertied classes to take cognizance
of their responsibilities to society (i.e. to better the conditions of life of the least
well off and invest in social and physical infrastructures in the national interest)
rather than solely to promote their individual rights as property owners. The
uproar that followed on the part of the propertied classes forced him to recant
and from that moment on he turned to be the most ardent advocate for imperialism (ultimately, as Colonial Secretary, leading Britain into the disaster of the
Boer War). This career trajectory was quite common for the period. Jules Ferry
in France, an ardent supporter of internal reform, particularly education, in the
1860s, took to colonial advocacy after the Commune of 1871 (leading France
into the mire of Southeast Asia that culminated in defeat at Dien Bien-Phu in
1954); Crispi sought to solve the land problem in the Italian south through colonization in Africa; and even Theodore Roosevelt in the United States turned,
after Frederic Jackson Turner declared, erroneously, at least as far as investment
opportunities were concerned, that the American Frontier was closed, to support
imperial policies rather than internal reforms.[12]

In all of these cases, the turn to a liberal form of imperialism (and one that had
attached to it an ideology of progress and of a civilizing mission) resulted not
from absolute economic imperatives but from the political unwillingness of the
bourgeoisie to give up any of its class privileges, thus blocking the possibility of
absorbing overaccumulation through social reform at home. The fierce opposition by the owners of capital to any politics of redistribution or internal social
amelioration in the United States today likewise leaves the country no option but
to look outwards for solutions to its economic difficulties. Internal class politics
of this sort forced many European powers to look outwards to solve their problems from 1884 to 1945, and this gave a specific coloration to the forms that
European imperialism then took. Many liberal and even radical figures became
proud imperialists during these years and much of the working-class movement
was persuaded to support the imperial project as essential to their well-being.
This required, however, that bourgeois interests should thoroughly command
state policy, ideological apparatuses and military power. Arendt therefore inter-
prets this Euro-centric imperialism, correctly in my view, as 'the first stage in
political rule of the bourgeoisie rather than the last stage of capitalism' as Lenin
depicted it.[13] I will consider this idea further in the conclusion.

MEDIATING INSTITUTIONAL ARRANGEMENTS FOR THE PROJECTION OF POWER OVER SPACE

In a recent article Henderson shows that the difference in 1997-8 between Taiwan and Singapore (which both escaped the crisis relatively unscathed except for currency devaluation) and Thailand and Indonesia (which suffered almost total economic and political collapse), turned on differences in state and financial policies.[14] The former territories were insulated from speculative flows into property markets by strong state controls and protected financial markets, whereas the latter were not. Differences of this sort plainly matter. The forms taken by the mediating institutions are productive of, as well as products of, the dynamics of capital accumulation.

Clearly, the whole pattern of turbulence in the relations between state, supra-state, and financial powers on the one hand, and the more general dynamics of capital accumulation (through production and selective devaluations) on the other, has been one of the most signal, and most complex, elements in the narrative of uneven geographical development and imperialist politics to be told of the period since 1973.[15] I think Gowan is correct to see the radical restructuring of international capitalism after 1973 as a series of gambles on the part of the United States to try to maintain its hegemonic position in world economic affairs against Europe, Japan and later East and South East Asia.[16] This began during the crisis of 1973 with Nixon's double strategy of high oil pricing and financial deregulation. The US banks were then given the exclusive right to recycle the vast quantities of petro-dollars being accumulated in the Gulf region. This re-centered global financial activity in the US and incidentally helped, along with the deregulation of the financial sector within the US, to rescue New York from its own local economic crisis. A powerful Wall Street/US Treasury financial regime[17] was created, with controlling powers over global financial institutions (such as the IMF) and able to make or break many weaker foreign economies through credit manipulations and debt management practices. This monetary and financial regime was used, Gowan argues, by successive US administrations 'as a formidable instrument of economic statecraft to drive forward both the globalization process and the associated neo-liberal domestic transformations.' The regime thrived on crises. 'The IMF covers the risks and ensures that the US banks don't lose (countries pay up through structural adjustments etc.) and flight of capital from localized crises elsewhere ends up boosting the strength of Wall Street …'.[18] The effect was to project US economic power outwards (in alliance with others wherever possible), to force open markets, particularly for capital and financial flows (now a requirement for membership in the IMF), and impose other neoliberal practices (culminating in the WTO) upon much of the rest of the world.

There are two major points to be made about this system. First, free trade in commodities is often depicted as opening up the world to free and open competition. But this whole argument fails, as Lenin long ago pointed out, in the face of monopoly or oligopoly power (either in production or consumption). The US, for example, has repeatedly used the weapon of denial of access to the huge

US market to force other nations to comply with its wishes. The most recent (and crass) example of this line of argument comes from the US Trade Representative Robert Zoellick to the effect that if Lula, the newly elected Workers Party President of Brazil, does not go along with US plans for free markets in the Americas, he would find himself having 'to export to Antarctica'.[19] Taiwan and Singapore were forced to sign on to the WTO, and thereby open their financial markets to speculative capital, in the face of US threats to deny them access to the US market. At US Treasury insistence, South Korea was forced to do the same as a condition for an IMF bail-out in 1998. The US now plans to attach a condition of financial institutional compatibility to the foreign aid it offers as 'challenge grants' to poor countries. On the production side, oligopolies largely based in the core capitalist regions, effectively control the production of seeds, fertilizers, electronics, computer software, pharmaceutical products, petroleum products and much more. Under these conditions, the creation of new market openings does not open up competition but merely creates opportunities to proliferate monopoly powers with all manner of social, ecological, economic and political consequences. The fact that nearly two-thirds of foreign trade is now accounted for by transactions within and between the main transnational corporations is indicative of the situation. Even something as seemingly benevolent as the Green Revolution has, most commentators agree, paralleled the increased agricultural outputs with considerable concentrations of wealth in the agrarian sector and higher levels of dependency upon monopolized inputs throughout South and East Asia. The penetration of the China market by US tobacco companies is set fair to compensate for their losses in the US market at the same time as it will surely generate a public health crisis in China for decades to come. In all of these respects, the claims generally made that neoliberalism is about open competition rather than monopoly control or limited competition within oligopolistic structures, turn out to be fraudulent, masked as usual by the fetishism of market freedoms. Free trade does not mean fair trade.

There is also, as even advocates of free trade readily acknowledge, a huge difference between freedom of trade in commodities and freedom of movement for finance capital.[20] This immediately poses the problem of what kind of market freedom is being talked about. Some, like Bhagwati, fiercely defend free trade in commodities but resist the idea that this necessarily holds good for financial flows. The difficulty here is this. On the one hand credit flows are vital to productive investments and reallocations of capital from one line of production or location to another. They also play an important role in bringing consumption needs – for housing, for example – into a potentially balanced relationship with productive activities in a spatially disaggregated world marked by surpluses in one space and deficits in another. In all of these respects the financial system, with or without state involvement, is critical to coordinate the dynamics of capital accumulation through uneven geographical development. But finance capital also embraces a lot of unproductive activity in which money is simply used to make more money through speculation on commodity futures, currency values, debt, and the like. When huge quantities of capital become available for such purposes, then open capital markets become vehicles for speculative activity some of which, as we saw during the 1990s with both the 'dot.com' and the stock market 'bubbles', become self-fulfilling prophecies, just as the hedge funds, armed with trillions of dollars of leveraged money, could force Indonesia and even South Korea into bankruptcy no matter what the strength of their under-lying economies. Much of what happens on Wall Street has nothing to do with facilitating investment in productive activities. It is purely speculative (hence the descriptions of it as 'casino', 'predatory' or even 'vulture' capitalism – with the debacle of Long Term Capital Management needing a $2.3 billion bail-out reminding us that speculations can easily go awry). This activity has, however, deep impacts upon the overall dynamics of capital accumulation. Above all, it facilitated the re-centering of political-economic power primarily in the United States but also within the financial markets of other core countries (Tokyo, London, Frankfurt).

How this occurs depends on the dominant form of the class alliances arrived at within the core countries, the balance of power between them in negotiating international arrangements (such as the new international financial architecture put in place after 1997-8 to replace the so-called Washington Consensus of the mid-1990s) and the political-economic strategies set in motion by dominant agents with respect to surplus capital. The emergence of a 'Wall Street-Treasury-IMF' complex within the United States, able to control global institutions and to project vast financial power across the world through a network of other financial and governmental institutions, has played a determinant and problem-atic role in the dynamics of global capitalism in recent years. But this power center can only operate the way it does because the rest of the world is networked and successfully hooked into (and effectively 'hooked on') a struc-tured framework of interlocking financial and governmental (including supra-national) institutions. Hence the significance of collaborations between, for example, central bankers of the G7 nations and the various international accords (temporary in the case of currency strategies and more permanent with respect to the WTO) designed to deal with particular difficulties.[21] And if market power is not sufficient to accomplish particular objectives and to bring recalcitrant elements or 'rogue states' into line, then unchallengeable US military power (covert or overt) is available to force the issue.

This complex of institutional arrangements should in the best of all possible capitalist worlds be geared to sustain and support expanded reproduction (growth). But, like war in relation to diplomacy, finance capital intervention backed by state power can frequently become accumulation by other means. An unholy alliance between state powers and the predatory aspects of finance capital forms the cutting edge of a 'vulture capitalism' dedicated to the appropriation and devaluation of assets, rather than to building them up through productive invest-ments. But how are we to interpret these 'other means' to accumulation or devaluation?

ACCUMULATION BY DISPOSSESSION

In *The Accumulation of Capital*, Luxemburg focuses attention on the dual aspects of capitalist accumulation:

> One concerns the commodity market and the place where surplus value is produced – the factory, the mine, the agricultural estate. Regarded in this light accumulation is a purely economic process, with its most important phase a transaction between the capitalist and the wage labourer.... Here, in form at any rate, peace, property and equality prevail, and the keen dialectics of scientific analysis were required to reveal how the right of ownership changes in the course of accumulation into appropriation of other people's property, how commodity exchange turns into exploitation and equality becomes class rule. The other aspect of the accumulation of capital concerns the relations between capitalism and the non-capitalist modes of production which start making their appearance on the international stage. Its predominant methods are colonial policy, an international loan system – a policy of spheres of interest – and war. Force, fraud, oppression, looting are openly displayed without any attempt at concealment, and it requires an effort to discover within this tangle of political violence and contests of power the stern laws of the economic process.

These two aspects of accumulation, she argues, are 'organically linked' and 'the historical career of capitalism can only be appreciated by taking them together'.[22]

Marx's general theory of capital accumulation is constructed under certain crucial initial assumptions which broadly match those of classical political economy and which exclude primitive accumulation processes. These assumptions are: freely functioning competitive markets with institutional arrangements of private property, juridical individualism, freedom of contract and appropriate structures of law and governance guaranteed by a 'facilitative' state which also secures the integrity of money as a store of value and as a medium of circulation. The role of the capitalist as a commodity producer and exchanger is already well-established and labour power has become a commodity that trades generally at its value. 'Primitive' or 'original' accumulation has already occurred and accumulation now proceeds as expanded reproduction (albeit through the exploitation of living labour in production) within a closed economy working under conditions of 'peace, property and equality'. These assumptions allow us to see what will happen if the liberal project of the classical political economists or, in our times, the neo-liberal project of the neo-classical economists, is realized. The brilliance of Marx's dialectical method is to show that market liberalization – the credo of the liberals and the neo-liberals – will not produce a harmonious state in which everyone is better off. It will instead produce ever greater levels of social inequality, as indeed has been the global trend over the last thirty years of neoliberalism, particularly within those countries such as

Britain and the United States that have most closely hewed to such a political line. It will also, Marx predicts, produce serious and growing instabilities culminating in chronic crises of overaccumulation of the sort we are now witnessing.

The disadvantage of these assumptions is that they relegate accumulation based upon predation, fraud, and violence to an 'original stage' that is considered no longer relevant or, as with Luxemburg, as being somehow 'outside of' the capitalist system. A general re-evaluation of the continuous role and persistence of the predatory practices of 'primitive' or 'original' accumulation within the long historical geography of capital accumulation is, therefore, very much in order, as several commentators have recently observed.[23] Since it seems peculiar to call an ongoing process 'primitive' or 'original' I shall, in what follows, substitute these terms by the concept of 'accumulation by dispossession'.

A closer look at Marx's description of primitive accumulation reveals a wide range of processes. These include the commodification and privatization of land and the forceful expulsion of peasant populations; conversion of various forms of property rights – common, collective, state, etc. – into exclusive private property rights; suppression of rights to the commons; commodification of labour power and the suppression of alternative, indigenous, forms of production and consumption; colonial, neo-colonial and imperial processes of appropriation of assets, including natural resources; monetization of exchange and taxation, particularly of land; slave trade; and usury, the national debt and ultimately the credit system. The state, with its monopoly of violence and definitions of legality, plays a crucial role in both backing and promoting these processes and there is considerable evidence, which Marx suggests and Braudel confirms, that the transition to capitalist development was vitally contingent upon the stance of the state – broadly supportive in Britain, weakly so in France and highly negative, until very recently, in China.[24] The invocation of the recent shift towards primitive accumulation in the case of China indicates that this is an on-going issue and the evidence is strong, particularly throughout East and South East Asia, that state policies and politics (consider the case of Singapore) have played a critical role in defining both the intensity and the paths of new forms of capital accumulation. The role of the 'developmental state' in recent phases of capital accumulation has therefore been the subject of intense scrutiny.[25] One only has to look back at Bismarck's Germany or Meiji Japan to recognize that this has long been the case.

All the features that Marx mentions have remained powerfully present within capitalism's historical geography. Some of them have been fine-tuned to play an even stronger role now than in the past. The credit system and finance capital have, as Lenin, Hilferding and Luxemburg all remarked, been major levers of predation, fraud and thievery. Stock promotions, ponzi schemes, structured asset destruction through inflation, asset stripping through mergers and acquisitions, the promotion of levels of debt encumbrancy that reduce whole populations, even in the advanced capitalist countries, to debt peonage, to say nothing of corporate fraud, dispossession of assets (the raiding of pension funds and their decimation by stock and corporate collapses) by credit and stock manipulations – all of these are central features of what contemporary capitalism is about. The collapse of Enron dispossessed many people of their livelihoods and their pension rights. But above all we have to look at the speculative raiding carried out by hedge funds and other major institutions of finance capital as the cutting edge of accumulation by dispossession in recent times. By creating a liquidity crisis throughout South East Asia, the hedge funds forced profitable businesses into bankruptcy. These businesses could be purchased at fire-sale prices by surplus capitals in the core countries, thus engineering what Wade and Veneroso refer to as 'the biggest peacetime transfer of assets from domestic (i.e. South East Asian) to foreign (i.e. US, Japanese and European) owners in the past fifty years anywhere in the world.'[26]

Wholly new mechanisms of accumulation by dispossession have also opened up. The emphasis upon intellectual property rights in the WTO negotiations (the so-called TRIPS agreement) points to ways in which the patenting and licensing of genetic materials, seed plasmas, and all manner of other products, can now be used against whole populations whose environmental management practices have played a crucial role in the development of those materials. Biopiracy is rampant and the pillaging of the world's stockpile of genetic resources is well under way, to the benefit of a few large multinational companies. The escalating depletion of the global environmental commons (land, air, water) and proliferating habitat degradations that preclude anything but capital-intensive modes of agricultural production have likewise resulted from the wholesale commodification of nature in all its forms. The commodification of cultural forms, histories and intellectual creativity entails wholesale dispossessions – the music industry is notorious for the appropriation and exploitation of grassroots culture and creativity. The corporatization and privatization of hitherto public assets (like universities) to say nothing of the wave of privatization of water and other public utilities that has swept the world, constitute a new wave of 'enclosing the commons'. As in the past, the power of the state is frequently used to force such processes through even against the popular will. As also happened in the past, these processes of dispossession are provoking widespread resistance and this now forms the core of what the anti-globalization movement is about.[27] The reversion to the private domain of common property rights won through past class struggles (the right to a state pension, to welfare, or to national health care) has been one of the most egregious of all policies of dispossession pursued in the name of neo-liberal orthodoxy. The Bush administration's plan to privatize social security (and make pensions subject to the vagaries of the stock market) is a clear case in point. Small wonder that much of the emphasis within the anti-globalization movement in recent times has been focused on the theme of reclaiming the commons and attacking the joint role of the state and capital in their appropriation.

Capitalism internalizes cannibalistic as well as predatory and fraudulent practices. But it is, as Luxemburg cogently observed, 'often hard to determine, within the tangle of violence and contests of power, the stern laws of the economic process.' Accumulation by dispossession can occur in a variety of ways and there is much that is both contingent and haphazard about its modus operandi. Yet it is omnipresent in no matter what historical period and picks up strongly when crises of overaccumulation occur in expanded reproduction, when there seems to be no other exit except devaluation. Arendt suggests, for example, that for Britain of the nineteenth century, the depressions of the sixties and seventies initiated the push into a new form of imperialism in which the bourgeoisie realized 'for the first time that the original sin of simple robbery, which centuries ago had made possible "the original accumulation of capital" (Marx) and had started all further accumulation, had eventually to be repeated lest the motor of accumulation suddenly die down'.[28] This brings us back to relations between the drive for spatio-temporal fixes, state powers, accumulation by dispossession and the forms of contemporary imperialism.

THE 'NEW' IMPERIALISM

Capitalist social formations, often arranged in particular territorial or regional configurations and usually dominated by some hegemonic center, have long engaged in quasi-imperialist practices in search of spatio-temporal fixes to their overaccumulation problems. It is possible, however, to periodize the historical geography of these processes by taking Arendt seriously when she argues that the European-centered imperialism of the period 1884 to 1945 constituted the first stab at global political rule by the bourgeoisie. Individual nation-states engaged in their own imperialist projects to deal with problems of overaccumulation and class conflict within their orbit. Initially stabilized under British hegemony and constructed around open flows of capital and commodities on the world market, this first system broke down at the turn of the century into geopolitical conflicts between major powers pursuing autarky within increasingly closed systems. It erupted in two world wars in much the way that Lenin foresaw. Much of the rest of the world was pillaged for resources during this period (just look at the history of what Japan did to Taiwan or Britain did to the Witwatersrand in South Africa) in the hope that accumulation by dispossession would compensate for a chronic inability, which came to a head in the 1930s, to sustain capitalism through expanded reproduction.

This system was displaced in 1945 by a US led system that sought to establish a global compact among all the major capitalist powers to avoid internecine wars and find a rational way to deal collectively with the overaccumulation that had plagued the 1930s. For this to happen they had to share in the benefits of an intensification of an integrated capitalism in the core regions (hence US support for moves towards European Union) and engage in systematic geographical expansion of the system (hence the US insistence upon de-colonization and 'developmentalism' as a generalized goal for the rest of the world). This second phase of global bourgeois rule was largely held together by the contingency of the Cold War. This entailed US military and economic leadership as the sole capitalist superpower. The effect was to construct a hegemonic US 'superimperialism' that was more political and military than it was a manifestation of economic necessity. The US was not itself highly dependent upon external outlets or even inputs. It could even afford to open its market to others and thereby absorb through internal spatio-temporal fixes, such as the interstate highway system, sprawling suburbanization, and the development of its South and West, part of the surplus capacity that began to emerge strongly in Germany and Japan during the 1960s. Strong growth through expanded reproduction occurred throughout the capitalist world. Accumulation by dispossession was relatively muted, though countries with capital surpluses, like Japan and West Germany, increasingly needed to look outwards for markets, including by competing for control of post-colonial developing markets.[29] Strong controls over capital export (as opposed to commodities) were, however, kept in place in much of Europe and capital imports into East Asia remained restricted. Class struggles within individual nation states over expanded reproduction (how it would occur and who would benefit) dominated. The main geopolitical struggles that arose were either those of the Cold War (with that other empire constructed by the Soviets) or residual struggles (more often than not cross-cut by Cold War politics that pushed the US to support many reactionary post-colonial regimes) which resulted from the reluctance of European powers to disengage from their colonial possessions (the invasion of Suez by the British and French in 1956, not supported at all by the US, was emblematic). Growing resentments of being locked into a spatio-temporal situation of perpetual subservience to the center did, however, spark anti-dependency and national liberation movements. Third world socialism sought modernization but on an entirely different class and political basis.

This system broke down around 1970. Capital controls became hard to enforce as surplus US dollars flooded the world market. Inflationary pressures resulting from the US trying to have both guns and butter in the midst of the Vietnam War became very strong while the level of class struggle in many of the core countries began to erode profits. The US then sought to construct a different kind of system, that rested upon a mix of new international and financial institutional arrangements to counter economic threats from Germany and Japan and to re-center economic power as finance capital operating out of Wall Street. The collusion between the Nixon administration and the Saudis to push oil prices sky-high in 1973 did far more damage to the European and Japanese economies than it did to the US, which at that time was little dependent upon Middle Eastern supplies.[30] US banks gained the privilege of re-cycling the petro-dollars into the world economy. Threatened in the realm of production, the US countered by asserting its hegemony through finance. But for this system to work effectively, markets in general and capital markets in particular had to be forced open to international trade – a slow process that required fierce US pressure backed by use of international levers such as the IMF and an equally fierce commitment to neo-liberalism as the new economic orthodoxy. It also entailed shifting the balance of power and interests within the bourgeoisie from production activities to institutions of finance capital. This could be used to attack the power of working class movements within expanded reproduction either directly, by exerting disciplinary oversight on production, or indirectly by facilitating greater geographical mobility for all forms of capital. Finance capital was therefore central to this third phase of bourgeois global rule.

This system was much more volatile and predatory and visited various bouts of accumulation by dispossession – usually as structural adjustment programs administered by the IMF – as an antidote to difficulties in the realm of expanded reproduction. In some instances, such as Latin America in the 1980s, whole economies were raided and their assets recovered by US finance capital. The hedge funds' attack upon the Thai and Indonesian currencies in 1997, backed up by the savage deflationary policies demanded by the IMF, drove even viable concerns into bankruptcy and reversed the remarkable social and economic progress that had been made in much of East and South East Asia. Millions of people fell victim to unemployment and impoverishment as a result. The crisis also conveniently sparked a flight to the dollar, confirming Wall Street's domi-nance and generating an amazing boom in asset values for the affluent in the United States. Class struggles began to coalesce around issues such as IMF-imposed structural adjustment, the predatory activities of finance capital and the loss of rights through privatization.

Debt crises could be used to reorganize internal social relations of production in each country on a case-by-case basis in such a way as to favour the penetration of external capitals. Domestic financial regimes, domestic product markets and thriving domestic firms were, in this way, prized open for takeover by American, Japanese or European companies. Low profits in the core regions could thereby be supplemented by taking a cut out of the higher profits being earned abroad. Accumulation by dispossession became a much more central feature within global capitalism (with privatization as one its key mantras). Resistance to this became more central within the anti-capitalist and anti-imperialist movement.[31] But the system, while centered on the Wall Street-Treasury complex, had many multi-lateral aspects with the financial centers of Tokyo, London, Frankfurt and many other financial centers participating. It was associated with the emergence of transnational capitalist corporations which, though they may have a basis in one or other nation state, spread themselves across the map of the world in ways that were unthinkable in the earlier phases of imperialism (the trusts and cartels that Lenin described were all tied very closely to particular nation states). This was the world that the Clinton White House, with an all-powerful Treasury Secretary, Robert Rubin, drawn from the speculator side of Wall Street, sought to manage by a centralized multilateralism (epitomized by the so-called 'Washington Consensus' of the mid 1990s). It seemed, for a brief moment, that Lenin was wrong and that Kautsky might be right – an ultraimperialism based on a 'peaceful' collaboration between all the major capitalist powers – now symbolized by the grouping known as the G7 and the so-called 'new international financial archi-tecture', albeit under the hegemony of US leadership – was possible.[32]

But this system has now run into serious difficulties. The sheer volatility and chaotic fragmentation of power conflicts makes it hard, as Luxemburg earlier noted, to discern how the stern laws of economics are working behind all the smoke and mirrors (particularly those of the financial sector). But insofar as the crisis of 1997-8 revealed that the main center of surplus productive capacity lay in East and South East Asia (so that the US targeted that region specifically for devaluation), the rapid recovery of some parts of East and South East Asian capitalism has forced the general problem of overaccumulation back into the forefront of global affairs.[33] This poses the question of how a new form of the spatio-temporal fix (into China?) might be organized, or who will bear the brunt of a new round of devaluation. The gathering recession within the United States after a decade or more of spectacular (even if 'irrational') exuberance indicates that the US may not be immune. A major fault line of instability lies in the rapid deterioration in the balance of payments of the United States. 'The same exploding imports that drove the world economy' during the 1990s, writes Brenner, 'brought US trade and current account deficits to record levels, leading to the historically unprecedented growth of liabilities to overseas owners' and 'the historically unprecedented vulnerability of the US economy to the flight of capital and a collapse of the dollar'.[34] But this vulnerability exists on both sides. If the US market collapses then the economies that look to that market as a sink for their excess productive capacity will go down with it. The alacrity with which the central bankers of countries like Japan and Taiwan lend funds to cover US deficits, has a strong element of self-interest. They thereby fund the US consumerism that forms the market for their products. They may now even find themselves funding the US war effort.

But the hegemony and dominance of the US is, once more, under threat and this time the danger seems more acute. If, for example, Braudel (followed by Arrighi) is correct, and a powerful wave of financialization is a likely prelude to a transfer of dominant power from one hegemon to another then the US turn towards financialization in the 1970s would appear to exemplify a self-destructive historical pattern.[35] The deficits, both internal and external, cannot continue to spiral out of control indefinitely and the ability and willingness of others, primarily in Asia, to fund them, to the tune of $2.3 billion a day at current rates, is not inexhaustible. Any other country in the world that exhibited the macro-economic condition of the US economy would by now have been subjected to ruthless austerity and structural adjustment procedures by the IMF. But, as Gowan remarks: 'Washington's capacity to manipulate the dollar price and to exploit Wall Street's international financial dominance enabled the US authorities to avoid doing what other states have had to do; watch the balance of payments; adjust the domestic economy to ensure high levels of domestic savings and investment; watch levels of public and private indebtedness; ensure an effective domestic system of financial intermediation to ensure the strong development of the domestic productive sector.' The US economy has had 'an escape route from all these tasks' and has become 'deeply distorted and unstable' as a result.[36] Furthermore, the successive waves of accumulation by dispossession, the hallmark of the new US-centered imperialism, are sparking resistance and resentments wherever they happen to break, generating not only an active worldwide anti-globalization movement (quite different in form from class struggles embedded in processes of expanded reproduction) but also active resistance to US hegemony by formerly pliant subordinate powers, particularly in Asia (South Korea is a case in point), and now even in Europe.

The options for the United States are limited. The US could turn away from its current form of imperialism by engaging in a massive redistribution of wealth within its borders and seek paths to surplus absorption through temporal fixes internally (dramatic improvements in public education and repair of aging infrastructures would be good places to start). An industrial strategy to revitalize manufacturing would also help. But this would require even more deficit financing or higher taxation as well as heavy state direction and this is precisely what the bourgeoisie will refuse to contemplate, as was the case in Chamberlain's day; any politician who proposes such a package will almost certainly be howled down by the capitalist press and their ideologists and lose any election in the face of overwhelming money power. Yet, ironically, a massive counter-attack within the US as well as within other core countries of capitalism (particularly in Europe) against the politics of neo-liberalism and the cutting of state and social expenditures might be one of the only ways to protect Western capitalism internally from its self-destructive tendencies.

Even more suicidal politically, within the US, would be to try to enforce by self-discipline the kind of austerity program that the IMF typically visits on others. Any attempt by external powers to do so (by capital flight and collapse of the dollar, for example) would surely elicit a savage US political, economic and even military response. It is hard to imagine that the US would peacefully accept and adapt to the phenomenal growth of East Asia and recognize, as Arrighi suggests it should, that we are in the midst of a major transition towards Asia as the hegemonic center of global power.[37] It is unlikely that the US will go quietly and peacefully into that good night. It would, in any case, entail a reorientation – some signs of which already exist – of East Asian capitalism away from dependency on the US market to the cultivation of an internal market within Asia itself. This is where the huge modernization program within China – an internal version of a spatio-temporal fix that is equivalent to what the US did internally in the 1950s and 1960s – may have a critical role to play in gradually siphoning off the surplus capitals of Japan, Taiwan and South Korea and thereby diminishing the flows into the United States. Taiwan, for example, now exports more to China than to North America. The consequent diminution of the flow of funds for the US could have calamitous consequences.

And it is in this context that we see elements within the US political establishment looking to flex military muscle as the only clear absolute power they have left, talking openly of Empire as a political option (presumably to extract tribute from the rest of the world) and looking to control oil supplies as a means to counter the power shifts threatened within the global economy. The attempts by the US to gain better control of Iraqi and Venezuelan oil supplies – in the former case by purportedly seeking to establish democracy and in the latter by overthrowing it – make a lot of sense. They reek of a re-run of what happened in 1973, since Europe and Japan, as well as East and South East Asia, now crucially including China, are even more heavily dependent on Gulf oil than is the United States. If the US engineers the overthrow of Chavez as well as Saddam, if it can stabilize or reform an armed-to-the-teeth Saudi regime that is currently based on the shifting sands of authoritarian rule (and in imminent danger of falling into the hands of radicalized Islam – this was, after all, Osama bin Laden's primary objective), if it can move on, as seems likely, from Iraq to Iran and consolidate its position in Turkey and Uzbekistan as a strategic presence in relation to Caspian basin oil reserves, then the US, through firm control of the global oil spigot, might hope to keep effective control over the global economy and secure its own hegemonic position for the next fifty years.[38]

The dangers of such a strategy are immense. Resistance will be formidable, not least from Europe and Asia, with Russia not far behind. The reluctance to sanction US military invasion of Iraq in the United Nations, particularly by France and Russia who already have strong connections to Iraqi oil exploitation, was a case in point. And the Europeans in particular are far more attracted to a Kautskyian vision of ultra-imperialism in which all the major capitalist powers will supposedly collaborate on an equal basis. An unstable US hegemony that rests on permanent militarization and adventurism of a sort that could seriously threaten global peace is not an attractive prospect for the rest of the world. This is not to say that the European model is much more progressive. If Robert Cooper, a Blair consultant, is to be believed, it resurrects nineteenth century distinctions between civilized, barbarian and savage states in the guise of post-modern, modern and pre-modern states with the postmoderns, as guardians of decentred civilized behaviour, expected to induce by direct or indirect means obeisance to universal (read 'Western' and 'bourgeois') norms and humanistic (read 'capitalistic') practices across the globe.[39] This was exactly the way that nineteenth century liberals, like John Stuart Mill, justified keeping India in tutelage and exacting tribute from abroad while praising the principles of representative government at home. In the absence of any strong revival of sustained accumulation through expanded reproduction, this will entail a deepening politics of accumulation by dispossession throughout the world in order to keep the motor of accumulation from stalling entirely.

This alternative form of imperialism will hardly be acceptable to wide swathes of the world's population who have lived through (and in some instances begun to fight back against) accumulation by dispossession and the predatory forms of capitalism they have had to confront over the last few decades. The liberal ruse that someone like Cooper proposes is far too familiar to postcolonial writers to have much traction.[40] And the blatant militarism that the US is increasingly proposing on the grounds that this is the only possible response to global terrorism is not only fraught with danger (including dangerous precedents for 'pre-emptive strikes'); it is increasingly recognized as a mask for trying to sustain a threatened hegemony within the global system.

But perhaps the most interesting question concerns the internal response within the United States itself. On this point Hannah Arendt again makes a telling argument: imperialism abroad cannot for long be sustained without active repressions, even tyranny, at home.[41] The damage done to democratic institutions domestically can be substantial (as the French learned during the Algerian struggle for independence). The popular tradition within the United States is anti-colonial and anti-imperial and it has taken a very substantive conjuring trick, if not outright deception, to mask the imperial role of the US in world affairs or at least to clothe it in grand humanitarian intentions over the past few decades. It is not clear that the US population will generally support an overt turn to any long-term militarized Empire (any more than it ended up supporting the Vietnam War). Nor will it likely accept for long the price, already substantial given the repressive clauses inserted into the Patriot and the Homeland Security Acts, that has to be paid at home in terms of civil liberties, rights and general freedoms. If Empire entails tearing up the Bill of Rights then it is not clear that this trade off will easily be accepted. But the other side of the difficulty is that in the absence of any dramatic revival of sustained accumulation through expanded reproduction and with limited possibilities to accumulate by dispossession, the US economy will likely sink into a deflationary depression that will make the last decade or so in Japan fade into insignificance by comparison. And if there is a serious flight from the dollar, then the austerity will have to be intense – unless, that is, there emerges an entirely different politics of redistribution of wealth and assets (a prospect the bourgeoisie will contemplate with utter horror) which focuses on the complete reorganization of the social and physical infrastructures of the nation to absorb idle capital and labour into socially useful, as opposed to purely speculative, tasks.

The shape and form any new imperialism will take is therefore up for grabs. The only thing that is certain is that we are in the midst of a major transition in how the global system works and that there is a variety of forces in motion which could easily tip the balance in one or another direction. The balance between accumulation by dispossession and expanded reproduction has already shifted towards the former and it is hard to see this trend doing anything other than deepening, making this the hallmark of what the new imperialism is all about (and making overt claims about the new imperialism and the necessity of empire of great ideological significance). We also know that the economic trajectory taken by Asia is key, but that military dominance still lies with the United States. This, as Arrighi remarks, is a unique configuration and we may well be seeing in Iraq the first stage of how it might play out geopolitically on the world stage under conditions of generalized recession. The United States, whose hegemony was based on production, finance and military power in the immediate post-war period lost its superiority in production after 1970 and may well now be losing financial dominance leaving it with military might alone. What happens within the United States is therefore a vitally important determinant of how the new imperialism might be articulated. And there is, to boot, a gathering storm of opposition to the deepening of accumulation by dispossession. But the forms of class struggle which this provokes are of a radically different nature from the classic proletarian struggles within expanded reproduction (which continue though in somewhat more muted forms) upon which the future of socialism was traditionally supposed to rest. The unities beginning to emerge around these different vectors of struggle are vital to nurture, for within them we can discern the lineaments of an entirely different, non-imperialistic, form of globalization that emphasizes social well-being and humanitarian goals coupled with creative forms of uneven geographical development, rather than the glorification of money power, stock market values and the incessant accumulation of capital across the variegated spaces of the global economy by whatever means, but always ending up heavily concentrated in a few spaces of extraordinary wealth. The moment may be full of volatility and uncertainties; but that means it is also a moment of the unexpected and full of potential.

NOTES

1   H. Lefebvre, *The Survival of Capitalism: Reproduction of the Relations of Production*, St Martin's Press, New York: 1976.

2   Most of these essays from the 1970s and 1980s have been republished in David Harvey, *Spaces of Capital: Towards a Critical Geography*, New York: Routledge 2001. The main line of argument can also be found in Harvey, *The Limits to Capital*, Oxford: Basil Blackwell, 1982 (reprint version, London: Verso Press, 1999).

3   My own version of this theoretical argument is detailed in Harvey, *Limits*, chapters 6 and 7.

4   R. Brenner, *The Boom and the Bubble: The US in the World Economy*, London: Verso, 2002. The theory of overaccumulation in Brenner is very different from mine but I find his empirical evidence, so far as it goes, useful and for the most part convincing.

5   P. Gowan, *The Global Gamble: Washington's Bid for World Dominance*, London: Verso, 1999.

6   Since this is a lot to argue for in a short piece, I will proceed in a schematic and simplified way, leaving more detailed elaborations for a later publication. D. Harvey, *The New Imperialism*, Oxford: Oxford University Press, forthcoming.

7   The topic of the 'new imperialism' has been broached on the left by L. Panitch, 'The New Imperial State', *New Left Review*, 11(1), 2000; see also P. Gowan, L. Panitch and M. Shaw, 'The State, Globalization and the New Imperialism: A Round Table Discussion', *Historical Materialism*, 9, 2001.

Other commentaries of interest are J. Petras and J. Veltmeyer, *Globalization Unmasked: Imperialism in the 21st Century*, London: Zed Books, 2001; R. Went, 'Globalization in the Perspective of Imperialism', *Science and Society*, 66(4), 2002-3; S. Amin, 'Imperialism and Globalization', *Monthly Review*, 53(2), 2001; conservative and liberal perspectives are laid out in M. Ignatieff, 'The Burden', *New York Times Magazine*, January 5th, 2003 and R. Cooper, 'The New Liberal Imperialism', *The Observer*, April 7, 2002.

8   Marx's concepts of 'fixed capital of an independent kind' and 'fictitious capital' are elaborated in Harvey, *Limits*, chapters 8 and 10 respectively and their geopolitical significance is taken up in Harvey, *Spaces*, chapter 15, 'The Geopolitics of Capitalism'.

9   The importance of siegnorage is examined in G. Carchedi, 'Imperialism, Dollarization and the Euro', *Socialist Register 2002*, London: Merlin Press, 2002.

10   G.W. Hegel, *The Philosophy of Right*, New York: Oxford University Press, 1967.

11   V.I. Lenin, 'Imperialism: The Highest Stage of Capitalism', in *Selected Works*, Volume 1, Moscow: Progress Publishers.

12   This whole common history of a radical shift from internal to external solutions to political-economic problems in response to the dynamics of class struggle across many capitalist states is told in a little known but quite fascinating collection by C.-A. Julien, J. Bruhat, C. Bourgin, M. Crouzet and P. Renouvin, *Les Politiques d'Expansion Imperialiste*, Paris: Presses Universitaires de France, 1949, in which the cases of Ferry, Chamberlain, Roosevelt, Crispi and others are all examined in comparative detail.

13   H. Arendt, *Imperialism*, New York: Harcourt Brace, 1968. There are many eerie resemblances between Arendt's analysis of the situation in the nineteenth century and our contemporary condition. Consider, for example, the following extract: 'Imperialist expansion had been touched off by a curious kind of economic crisis, the overproduction of capital and the emergence of 'superfluous' money, the result of oversaving, which could no longer find productive investment within the national borders. For the first time, investment of power did not pave the way for investment of money, but export of power followed meekly in the train of exported money, since uncontrolled investments in distant countries threatened to transform large strata of society into gamblers, to change the whole capitalist economy from a system of production into a system of financial speculation, and to replace the profits of production with profits in commissions. The decade immediately before the imperialist era, the seventies of the last century, witnessed an unparalleled increase in swindles, financial scandals and gambling in the stock market' (p. 15).

14   J. Henderson, 'Uneven Crises: Institutional Foundations of East Asian Economic Turmoil', *Economy and Society*, 28(3), 1999.

15   Brenner, *The Boom*, attempts the most general and synthetic account of this

turbulence. Details of the East Asian meltdown can be found in R. Wade and F. Veneroso, 'The Asian Crisis: The High Debt Model versus the Wall Street-Treasury-IMF Complex', *New Left Review*, 228, 1998; Henderson, 'Uneven Crises'; C. Johnson, *Blowback: The Costs and Consequences of American Empire*, New York: Henry Holt, 2000, chapter 9; the special issue of *Historical Materialism*, 8, 2001, 'Focus on East Asia after the Crisis' (particularly P. Burkett and M. Hart-Landsberg, 'Crisis and Recovery in East Asia: The Limits of Capitalist Development').

16 Gowan, *Global Gamble*.

17 Various names have been proposed for this. Gowan prefers the Dollar Wall Street Regime but I prefer the Wall-Street-Treasury-IMF complex suggested by Wade and Veneroso, 'The Asian Crisis'.

18 Gowan, *Global Gamble*, pp. 23, 35.

19 Editorial, *The Buenos Aires Herald*, December 31st, 2002, p. 4.

20 J. Bhagwati, 'The Capital Myth: The Difference Between Trade in Widgets and Dollars', *Foreign Affairs*, 77(3), 1998, pp. 7-12.

21 Gowan, *Global Gamble* and Brenner, *The Boom* offer interesting parallel accounts without, however, ever referring to each other.

22 R. Luxemburg, *The Accumulation of Capital*, New York: Monthly Review Press, 1968, pp. 452-3. Luxemburg bases her account on a theory of underconsumption (lack of effective demand) which has rather different implications from theories of overaccumulation (lack of opportunities for profitable activity) with which I work. A full exploration of the concept of accumulation by dispossession and its relation to overaccumulation is given in Part Three of Harvey, *The New Imperialism*.

23 M. Perelman, *The Invention of Capitalism: Classical Political Economy and the Secret History of Primitive Accumulation*, Durham: Duke University Press, 2000. There is also an extensive debate in *The Commoner* (www.thecommoner.org) on the new enclosures and on whether primitive accumulation should be understood as a purely historical or a continuing process. DeAngelis (http://homepages.uel.ac.uk/M.DeAngelis/PRIMACCA.htm) provides a good summary.

24 K. Marx, *Capital*, Volume 1, New York: International Publishers, 1967, Part 8; F. Braudel, *Afterthoughts on Material Civilization and Capitalism*, Baltimore: Johns Hopkins University Press, 1977.

25 Wade and Veneroso, 'The Asian Crisis', p. 7 propose the following definition: 'high household savings, plus high corporate debt/equity ratios, plus bank-firm-state collaboration, plus national industrial strategy, plus investment incentives conditional on international competitiveness, equals the developmental state.' The classic study is C. Johnson, *MITI and the Japanese Miracle: The Growth of Industrial Policy, 1925-75*, Stanford: Stanford University Press, 1982; while the empirical impact of state policies upon relative rates of economic growth has been well-documented in M. Webber and D. Rigby, *The Golden Age Illusion: Rethinking Post-war*

Capitalism, New York: Guilford Press, 1996.

26 Wade and Veneroso, 'The Asian Crisis'.

27 The extent of resistance is indicated in B. Gills, ed., *Globalization and the Politics of Resistance*, New York: Palgrave, 2000; see also J. Brecher and T. Costello, *Global Village or Global Pillage? Economic Reconstruction from the Bottom Up*, Boston: South End Press, 1994. A crisp recent guide to the resistance is given in W. Bello, *Deglobalization: Ideas for a New World Economy*, London: Zed Books, 2002. The idea of globalization from below is presented most succinctly in R. Falk, *Predatory Globalization: A Critique*, Cambridge: Polity Press, 2000.

28 Arendt, *Imperialism*, p. 28.

29 By far the best account is given in P. Armstrong, A. Glyn and J. Harrison, *Capitalism Since World War II: The Making and Break Up of the Great Boom*, Oxford: Basil Blackwell, 1991.

30 Gowan, *Global Gamble*, pp. 21-2, cites the evidence for collusion between Nixon and the Saudis.

31 The left, embedded as it was (and still in many respect is) in the politics of expanded reproduction, was slow to recognize the significance of anti-IMF riots and other movements against dispossession. Walton's pioneering study on the pattern of anti-IMF riots stands out in retrospect. See J. Walton, *Reluctant Rebels: Comparative Studies on Revolution and Underdevelopment*, New York: Columbia University Press, 1984. But it also seems right that we do a far more sophisticated analysis to determine which of the myriad movements against dispossession are regressive and anti-modernizing in any socialist sense and which can be progressive or at least be pulled in a progressive direction by alliance formation. As ever, the way in which Gramsci analyzed the Southern question seems to be a pioneering study of this sort. Petras has recently emphasized this point in his critique of Hardt and Negri: see J. Petras, 'A Rose by Any Other Name? The Fragrance of Imperialism', *The Journal of Peasant Studies*, 29(2), 2002. Affluent peasants fighting against land reform are not the same as landless peasants fighting for the right to subsist.

32 P. Anderson, 'Internationalism: A Breviary', *New Left Review*, 14, 2002, p. 20, notes how 'something like Kautsky's vision' had come to pass and that liberal theorists, like Robert Keohane, also noticed the connection. On the new international financial architecture, see S. Soederberg, 'The New International Financial Architecture: Imposed Leadership and "Emerging Markets"', *Socialist Register 2002*, London: Merlin, 2002.

33 See Burkett and Hart-Landsberg, 'Crisis and Recovery'.

34 Brenner, *The Boom*, p. 3.

35 G. Arrighi and B. Silver, eds., *Chaos and Governance in the Modern World System*, Minneapolis: University of Minnesota Press, 1999, pp. 31-3.

36 Gowan, *Global Gamble*, p. 123.

37 Arrighi does not envisage any serious external challenge but he and his

colleagues do conclude that the US 'has even greater capabilities than Britain did a century ago to convert its declining hegemony into exploitative domination. If the system eventually breaks down, it will be primarily because of US resistance to adjustment and accommodation. And conversely, US adjustment and accommodation to the rising economic power of the East Asian region is an essential condition for a non-catastrophic transition to a new world order.' See Arrighi and Silver, *Chaos and Governance*, pp. 288-9.

38 M. Klare, *Resource Wars: The New Landscape of Global Conflict*, New York: Henry Holt, 2002.

39 Cooper, 'New Liberal Imperialism'.

40 The critique mounted by U. Mehta, *Liberalism and Empire*, Chicago: Chicago University Press, 1999, is simply devastating when put up against Cooper's formulations.

41 Arendt, *Imperialism*, pp. 6-9; This has, interestingly, been a persistent internal source of concern against imperial ventures on the part of the United States, as William Appleman Williams points out in his *Empire as a Way of Life*, Oxford: New York, 1980.

THE OLD AND NEW ECONOMICS OF IMPERIALISM

Gregory Albo

Writing forty years ago in the first volume of the *Socialist Register*, Hamza Alavi argued that it was necessary to turn to an analysis of a 'new imperialism', because the 'end of direct colonial rule ... [had] not yet precipitated that final crisis which was to see the end of monopoly capitalism and to herald the age of socialism.' Insisting that the key dynamic in the world economy could no longer be captured by the classic theories of imperialism of territorial expansionism in the search for economic outlets, he concluded that

> the principal aim of ... the new imperialism is not the export of capital as a means of exploiting cheap labour overseas. It is rather that of concentrating investment at home to expand production in the metropolitan country and of seeking to dominate world markets on which it establishes its grasp by a variety of means ...[1]

This insight, at once theoretical and political, remains central to the analysis of the new imperialism today in terms of the systemic reproduction of uneven development and the hierarchical organizational arrangement of the world market through formally equal economic exchanges and political relations between states.[2] By locating imperialism in terms of the law of value and the rule of law, 'consent' can be seen as important as 'coercion' in understanding modern imperialism.

The internationalisation of capital during the long period of neoliberalism since the 1980s has given rise to new patterns and contradictions in the world market and has had profound effects on the institutionalization of state power, the organization of state apparatuses and the relations between states. This has raised three sets of issues with respect to the theory of imperialism: (1) the patterns of competition and the distribution of power in the centres of capital accumulation, i.e., inter-imperial relations; (2) the mechanisms and patterns of uneven development that reproduce hierarchical relations between dominant and dominated social formations; and (3) the political and cultural relations between, and oppression of, different peoples; or to put it another way, the question of political sovereignty vis-à-vis the development of supra-national institutions of governance. While all three issues remain fundamental to the political economy of the world market today, it is the first that is of chief concern here.

A characteristic of this period of neoliberalism is that political alternatives outside the advanced capitalist bloc have been marginalized. The new imperialism has intensified the relations of domination, in terms of both economic marginalization and geo-political subordination, within the imperialist chain. The emergence of three political-economic zones – albeit zones with great variation of organizational arrangements, from the deep integration of the European Union (EU) to the preferential trading arrangements of North America and the trade linkages formed by subcontracting networks in East Asia – is a key development. But how does the internationalisation of capital affect the organizational forms, competitive rivalries and interdependencies of these three blocs, and, in particular, what are the effects of this on the place of the US as the dominant imperialist pole?

There are today, broadly speaking, two seemingly contradictory views on this, each implying a distinct position on the nature of the new imperialism. The first sees the US as being in economic decline and faced with mounting political rivalry, recalling the classic Leninist theories of imperialism according to which processes of capital valorization and internationalisation soon find expression in geo-political conflicts.[3] The American defeat in Vietnam, the economic turmoil of the 1970s and the end of the postwar international monetary system of Bretton Woods, which had been built on the strength of the American dollar, have all been seen as indications that the limits of American power have been reached. On this view US relative decline continued through the 1980s, as witnessed in faltering per capita economic growth, low productivity advance, 'impatient' capital markets, mounting debt levels across all sectors, and languishing competitive capacity, taking the form of enormous structural current account deficits. The 'rival capitalisms' of Japan and Germany, anchoring the trade blocs of East Asia and Europe respectively, have been seen as zones of ascendant production and organizational innovation – post-Fordist, highly-engineered, flexible technologies and networked conglomerates superseding American mass production and vertically-integrated corporations. European, and at times Japanese, opposition to American unilateralism in recent years (military intervention in the Middle East, assertiveness in trade relations and neglect of the Doha Round, recklessness in managing the dollar) has been taken as a sign of mounting political antagonisms between contesting centres of world capitalism.

The other, opposing, view focuses on US economic dynamism (coinciding with the rise of the 'new economy') and contrasts this with a decade of Japanese deflation and the incoherence of EU, and especially German, economic policy (trapped in the straightjacket of the Stability and Growth Pact and disciplined by the European Central Bank). The relative strength of the US, in this view, is related, as the *Financial Times* puts it, to 'a combination of flexible capital markets and an economic climate conducive to risk-taking [which has] been at least as important as [real] investments themselves... [F]inancial markets should get a lot of credit for forcing money out of traditional management and entrenched corporations.'[4] Financialization and neoliberalism together, in this view, broke the back of US workers' organization and improved the conditions for extracting and realizing surplus value. And the 'Dollar-Wall Street regime' has not only successfully exported the US model to the US-dominated zones, but has also re-established conditions for international accumulation favourable to the advanced capitalist bloc as a whole, and pushed the EU and East Asia along necessary paths of restructuring.

A somewhat parallel division of interpretation has similarly occurred over the form of interdependence in the new 'empire'. One view is that transnational capitalist classes have now fundamentally transcended national interests, so that political sovereignty and economic co-ordination are now effectively global, an 'ultra-imperialism';[5] the other is that the new empire is predominantly a reassertion of US hegemony, a 'super-imperialism'.[6]

These theorisations of the present world economic order have at least cleared away the fog created by the 'globalization debate', with its talk of an equalizing world market and nascent cosmopolitan democracy. Attention has been re-focused on material interests and the economic processes underlying the hierarchical arrangements of the world market. But they have left unresolved the opposition between these alternative interpretations of the trajectory of US power and the juxtaposition of rivalry and unity that characterises the new imperialism. As a result the persistent underlying contradictions of the world capitalist economy, and the US role in these contradictions, continue to be taken as signs of either the terminal decline of US power, or its opposite. In reality, however, economic internationalisation during this period of neoliberalism has been marked both by continuing competitive rivalry among the leading capitalist powers, and by growing economic interpenetration among capitalist firms and political interdependence between capitalist states. Contemporary imperialism, then, is an expression of the expansionist tendencies of capital to internationalize and constitute a world market for its valorization, while simultaneously differentiating itself into units located in states where class power and the production of value are materialized. There can be neither capital accumulation nor imperialism without states, or without the uneven development and relations of domination between states within the world market. Capitalist imperialism, on this reading, inherently involves contradictions between conflict and co-operation – what Harry Magdoff referred to in the 1990s as the 'centrifugal and centripetal forces ... at the very core of the capitalist process'[7] – and between competitive economic rivalry and interdependency in the world market.

CAPITALIST EXPANSION AND THEORIES OF
IMPERIALISM

Capitalism is defined, in its simplest determinations, by a continual process of transformation of commodities and social relations in time and space in the pursuit of surplus value. In oft-cited comments in the *Grundrisse* Marx notes that 'while capital must on one side strive to tear down every spatial barrier to inter-course, i.e., to exchange, and conquer the whole earth for its market, it strives on the other side to annihilate this space with time … The result is: the tenden-tially and potentially general development of the forces of production … as a basis; likewise, the universality of intercourse, hence the world market as a basis.'[8] For Marx, the appropriation and production of value and commodities through the exploitation of labour takes place in spatially specific places of production, yet the circulation of commodities and the distribution of value in exchange flows is potentially not bound to any particular place. These two simple propositions have two important consequences. First, capitalism is inherently expansionary in a double sense: competition continuously compels firms to increase the produc-tivity of labour by technologically developing the means of production and reorganizing work, and to seek out new markets and new sectors for the produc-tion and realization of the new value added. Second, particular places of production – as both class relations and state forms – are always implicated in a wider set of social relations, exchange flows and competitive imperatives.

Marx insisted that the extended reproduction of capital was not the conse-quence of the harmonious interaction of autonomous individuals and firms acting upon an inherent human nature of self-interest as market opportunities emerge. Rather, the patterns of reproduction of social relations are always specific, conflictual and transitory: they arise from the exploitation of workers and the competition over the extraction of value at the point of production, and in the competitive struggle between 'many capitals' over the realization and distribu-tion of value in circulation. This competition drives a continual revolution in the forces of production and the circulation of capital. This is what Marx meant when he wrote that 'the tendency to create the world market is directly given in the concept of capital itself.'[9] As David Harvey has pointed out in excavating this aspect of Marx's thought, the tendency to expansionism raises an important real contradiction.[10] The extended reproduction of capital must attain a certain 'coherence' and 'materialization' in time and space if capital is to valorize itself and accumulate, but the space of capital is continuously altering across time by shifting production processes, 'condensing' distances from new transportation and communication methods and ceaselessly seeking out new markets. There is a continual process of valorization and devalorization of the fixed capital complexes and social relations in different social spaces as productive capacities, competitive position and exchange relations evolve. An inescapable contradiction exists in capitalist social relations between the fixity necessary for the production of value and the fluidity of circulation of commodities and money-capital in the pursuit of augmented exchange-value.

In Marx's theoretical abstraction, the competitive imperative to accumulate by 'capital as a whole' is registered in the circulation of commodities in the world market. The transformations within and between places of production as a consequence of competition between 'many capitals' are, however, sources of emergent interdependencies and competitive tensions – and even potential chaos – in the world market only in specific historical contexts. So, for example, Marx argued that international trade and the export of capital counteract downward pressure on the profit rate by lowering the costs of the materials for constant capital, cheapening the necessities of life and thus enabling the lowering of wages, and by increasing the scale of production. Thus competitive imperatives compel the internationalisation of the circuits of money, productive and commodity capital. The international circulation of capital, in turn, 'dissolves' pre-capitalist societies and leads to differentiated forms of colonialism, varying in their forms of coercion and settlement but integrated into a world market increasingly governed by capitalist imperatives.[11] Marx looked at this process as the 'historical mission of the bourgeoisie', but one not without ambiguities, for what unfolds is 'a new and international division of labour, a division suited to the requirements of the chief centres of modern industry springs up, and converts one part of the globe into a chiefly agricultural field of production, for supplying the other part which remains a chiefly industrial field.'[12] Moreover, 'unequal exchange' within this emergent division labour might accentuate geographical differentiation, since trade between countries of different productivities of labour and compositions of capital would entail transfers of value and surplus profits.[13]

In this context the nation-state appears, on the one hand, as a historically-specific institutionalization of class relations and, on the other, as a mediator of the wider set of relations of differentiated accumulation established by the world market. This is the sense in which, for Marx, the state is 'the form of organization which the bourgeois necessarily adopt for internal and external purposes, for the mutual guarantee of their property and interests.'[14] But if the extended reproduction of capital implicates the state in establishing the framework of property relations for competition, the valorisation, devaluation and internationalisation of capital also draws the state in more directly as the effects of competition are partly displaced into politics. As a result the state necessarily defends the capital that has been invested in its territorial domain so that this capital, and its attendant social relations, can be valorized. It does so not so much to defend an enclosed 'national space' as to safeguard particular capitalist interests in both their local and global dimensions. Thus, for Marx, the competitive imperatives that tend to equalization and the internationalisation of capital in the world market also constitute a differentiated network of concrete labour processes, competing capitals and hierarchically-organized nation-states.

But while Marx identified the competitive imperatives of capital accumulation that form the basis for the economic divisions of the world market, he did not propose any theory of imperialism to explain the competitive processes or the forms of interdependence and rivalry between states that the divisions of the world market generates. The classic theories of the economics of imperialism that emerged during the Second International, however, could not avoid trying to frame such a theory.[15] They started with two key guiding theses: that competition compels monopolisation and the internationalisation of specific circuits of capital; and that the territorial bases of inter-firm competition are transposed into inter-state rivalry and conflict amongst the imperial powers. Luxemburg, for example, argued that capitalist social relations restricted the basis for realization and thus necessitated the search for external trade outlets in pre-capitalist societies. In contrast, Hilferding contended that competition in 'organized capitalism' was characterized by banks fusing with industry to form finance capital which, in turn, exported capital in search of markets for investment and trade. For Lenin, the export of capital defined imperialism as the monopoly stage of capitalism, wherein competition between rival monopolistic firms is transformed into inter-state conflict over control of markets and territory. In opposition to Kautsky, who had suggested that the cartels and national states might co-operate in a policy of ultra-imperialism, Lenin insisted that uneven development compelled continual monopolistic competition and inter-state conflict. It was only Bukharin, however, who saw that the 'world economy as a system of production relations and, correspondingly, of exchange relations on a world scale' produced not one but two tendencies forming imperialism. As he put it, 'together with ... the internationalisation of capital, there is going on a process of "national" intertwining of capital, a process of "nationalising" capital.'[16]

Whereas the classical theories centred on excess competition leading to the export of capital and imperialist rivalry, a 'new imperialism' debate in the late 1960s and early 1970s focused on the circulation of capital internal to the imperialist bloc changing relative competitive capacities and reinforcing new patterns of uneven development.[17] For Mandel, the US predominance during the postwar period was being challenged as Japan and Germany (with the latter aided by the broader fusing of European capital through an emerging supra-national European state) re-established their productive capacities to contest the US share of the world market and its capital exports.[18] For Petras and Rhodes, on the other hand, US hegemony was re-consolidating through its dominance in international finance, superior access to natural resources, military power and the weakness of US labour.[19] But as others engaged in this debate pointed out, the issues at hand could not be left in terms of competitive capacities as determined by indices of capital export and the classical conceptions of inter-state competition. The new characteristics of the internationalisation of capital – multinational corporations (MNCs) and the international expansion of the total circuit of capital – also posed the limits and conflicts over the organization and allocation of state functions in the new phase of imperialism.[20] Indeed, this underlay Poulantzas's insistence that the internationalisation of capital should not be understood, as in the classical theories, as a quantitative relationship between two external entities – an integral state and an externally-imposed foreign capital seeking to exploit it. Rather, starting from his understanding that the state is not a set of institutions apart from capital, Poulantzas saw the internationalization of capital in terms of the changing nature of the power bloc and 'the internalized transformations of the state itself.'[21]

These contesting theorisations of the internationalisation of capital, which have again come to the fore with the consolidation of neoliberalism and the re-assertion of an explicit American imperialism, explain why there is no single Marxian theory of imperialism. To at least avoid talking past each other, it may help to focus on the following seven dimensions in attempting to conceptualise the economics of the new imperialism.

(1) *Interdependence and differentiation.* The tendencies toward equalization and differentiation identified by Marx mean that competition between geograph-ical spaces of accumulation and hence uneven development are inherent to the capitalist world market. These processes, while creating global interde-pendence, simultaneously partition the imperialist bloc from the dominated bloc, and also make differentiation an attribute of inter-imperial relations.

(2) *International competition.* The competitive struggle between firms in particular places of production as a consequence of the intensification, concentration and centralisation of production and the internationalisation of circulation is a constitutive aspect of capitalism. The local and particular forms of value production are connected with the abstract and universal flows of money in the world market. International competition, therefore, as a central, and historically specific, aspect of inter-imperialist relations, is likely to increase as capitalism develops.

(3) *Competition through states.* The competition between 'many capitals' makes for multiple power centres and their materialization in a state system. This was Bukharin's fundamental insight: capitalist expansionism is characterized by processes of both internationalisation and nationalisation (i.e., state-building). In this sense, international competition does not occur apart from or against states, but through states.

(4) *The 'internalisation' of foreign capital.* The tendencies to intensification, concentration and centralisation of capital all increase the scale of operations, the technical division of labour and the territorial complexity of capitalist firms. MNCs have a 'home' base in that the dominant agents who possess and allocate these assets have a specific location, but they also become impor-tant agents of accumulation in the places they invest in. This process of internationalisation tends to deepen international competition as places of production must compete for funds internally allocated by firms. Moreover each state gains an interest in protecting and attracting fixed capital invest-ments while advancing an interest in inter-state co-ordination to sustain the international circulation of capital. It was Poulantzas's point that foreign

capital should not be thought of as an external imposition, for at certain points it forms an 'internal bourgeoisie' within the power bloc. In this case, as opposed to a 'national bourgeoisie' organizing a national economic space for itself, the state actively reproduces, ideologically, politically and through competitive supports, both domestic and foreign capital.

(5) *Internationalisation and the circuits of capital.* The internationalisation of capital takes the form of the expansion of the circuits of productive, commodity, speculative and money capital, each entailing different modalities of uneven development, competition and interdependence. Different phases of internationalisation will be dominated by different circuits and hence uniquely configure the patterns of international competition.

(6) *The internal reorganisation of states.* As the state ensures the extra-economic conditions necessary for accumulation and social reproduction, the internationalisation of capital will affect the social form and organization of the state. Internal economic policy apparatuses will become increasingly subordinate to those dealing with the internationalisation of capital, particularly to ensure the stability of the currency and its role in international circulation. Thus the entire state will be conditioned by international competition, what Leo Panitch has referred to as the internalisation and mediation of international accumulation by the state.[22] The capacities of each state to mediate international competition will be determined by its administrative and diplomatic capacities, its place in the imperialist chain and internal class relations.

(7) *Contradictions in inter-imperial relations.* The unity and contradictions in the international circulation of capital mean that conflict and co-operation, competitive rivalry and interdependency, are equally embedded in the world market. To the extent that the circuits of capital in states are internationalised, and thus dependent on the world market for their self-expansion and realization, both increased international competition and interdependency will be present. Inter-imperial relations will register this contradiction. But only in particular historical moments will inter-firm and inter-state competitive rivalries spill over into imperial rivalry in the sense of conflict over political leadership of the imperialist bloc.

INTER-IMPERIALIST RELATIONS AND THE WORLD MARKET TODAY

One implication of what has just been said is that while general competitive imperatives always operate, the particular determinants and configuration of inter-imperialist relations vary with specific periods of capitalism. To see some of the particularities of the economics of the new imperialism, three broad aspects of the relations within the advanced capitalist bloc since the end of the postwar boom need to be considered: the uneven development that has taken place during the 'long downturn' (or more accurately the long slowdown) since 1973; the internationalisation of capital, and especially financial capital; and the emergence of particular patterns of international competition between the three main capitalist zones.

We have to start out by remembering that the advanced capitalist countries are still in the midst of a long phase of slower accumulation relative to the postwar boom.[23] Annual growth rates in the advanced capitalist countries fell from about 4 per cent over the period 1950 to 1973 to less than 2 per cent through the 1980s and they have stagnated further since, with the exception of the US in the second half of the 1990s. This exception did much, of course, to encourage the view of a resurgent US economic colossus able to extend its imperial reach via the neoliberal model. The US has, indeed, been at the heart of the world economy over both phases – thanks to its capacity to extend rapidly the use of 'leading edge' means of production, and to the flexibility of its labour markets, allowing the extraction of longer hours from its workers. Yet both the 'postwar boom' and the 'long downturn' have been periods of economic 'catch-up' with the US for Europe and Japan, in terms of both average productivity levels and per capita incomes. The degree of income closure has been less pronounced and more uneven due to increased hours of work in the US and falling hours elsewhere, but measures such as the various human development indexes that are less reliant on incomes show an even clearer process of sustained catch-up.[24] Whereas after postwar reconstruction the US had a productive capacity and technological capabilities unmatched by either Europe or Japan, today each of the three major zones of capitalist production leads in some sectors in terms of technology, productivity and market shares. This long-term development is indicated in many ways: market capitalization, total sales revenues, export shares, peripheral regions of sub-contracting networks and economic dependency, the consolidation of currency and trade zones, and trade tensions in a host of sectors over the division of production and ownership between the three imperial blocs. The competitive context and the configuration of the world market today is vastly different from the one-sided American economic dominance that defined the postwar Bretton Woods system.

The developments in productive capacity in the key zones of advanced capitalism have also been registered in shifts in the circulation of commodities and money in the world market. In the postwar period, the US supplied liquidity to the world trading system, first through capital exports to finance the trade imbalances of the reconstructing economies of Europe and North-East Asia, and then by printing dollars and borrowing as its own trade balance began to move from surplus to deficit in the late 1960s. The process of catch-up and the resulting dollar overhang meant that the American dollar eventually became unsustainable as a singular hub currency, and the Bretton Woods system came to an end. The world market moved into a quite distinct era: a pure credit money system (in place of the gold exchange system), floating exchange rates (instead of fixed rates), a range of currencies held alongside gold in central banks to clear trade balances (instead of the dollar alone), liberalization of capital movements (replacing limited controls), and negotiation of adjustment of major currencies between the three emerging economic zones (after a phase of unilateral action).

The economic impasse of the 1970s generated an additional set of concerns: many developing countries ran into trade problems, and credit issued to cover foreign exchange shortfalls soon became an equally large problem of meeting debt obligations and managing capital outflows. Slower growth rates and higher interest rates strengthened financial interests and made it systematically more difficult for governments to maintain fiscal balances; and the American current account deficit, alongside the Asian and European surpluses, proved to be chronic, representing a structural shift in relative trade and competitive capacities between the three blocs. Printing money or issuing either government or corporate bonds to keep trade imbalances liquid became a critical aspect of the flows of the world market: initially to recycle petro-dollars, subsequently to prop up Third World payments deficits and finally to cover the massive current account deficit of the US, and the mounting private and government sector debt. The increasing competition for world market shares for commodities and to attract money-capital, in a context of slower growth, was paralleled by the interdependence of the different zones seeking outlets for commodities in each others' markets, the internationalization of credit flows and claims, and G7 inter-state co-ordination of their policies in managing the international economy.

By the mid-1980s, then, exchange rate adjustments and capital flows had proven to be both arenas of co-operation and sources of tension, uncertainty and instability as a consequence of structural trade asymmetries and relative shifts in the underlying capacities of the three zones to produce value (this contradiction in turn spurring an explosion in secondary financial markets to hedge risks). The IMF, the World Bank and the G7 – with the US state playing the leading role in each – promoted financial and capital account liberalization as the mechanism to finance trade adjustments and to have foreign exchange markets impose discipline on national economies. The floating exchange rate system arose out of economic asymmetries in the world market and weakness in the dollar during the 1970s. But in the 1980s, while the American trade deficit soared to new heights, the dollar appreciated by some 40 per cent as capital poured in. The Plaza and Louvre accords of 1985 and 1987 attempted to manage the resulting tensions and to bring the dollar down in value against the yen and European currencies. But the subsequent major dollar depreciation amid slow growth left American trade problems no closer to being resolved; and the corresponding appreciation of the yen and European currencies set the conditions for the Japanese asset bubble followed by deflation, and for European stagnation. Nor could these realignments and tensions be contained within just the 'anchor' economies. The bond market swings of 1993–94 and the currency troubles of Spain, Italy, Portugal, Mexico and a host of Third World states were all 'spillover effects', acting directly on their economies and their competitiveness and drastically reducing working class and peasant incomes.

The devaluations of the early 1990s and the slowdown that ensued began a new phase of intensification of international competition, as the dollar hit record lows against the deutschemark and the yen in 1994. The Japanese began attempting competitive devaluations to revive their economy in the face of an asset meltdown; and to offset the EU Stability and Growth Pact in preparation for the single currency, the EU, too, sought room for manoeuvre through currency realignment, while European capital sought foreign assets to diversify risk. From 1995 to 2000 the dollar rose by about 40 per cent on a trade-weighted basis, although this did not restore high growth in either Europe or Japan. Moreover, the resulting inflow of capital and the economic stimulus it gave to the US economy set off a growth spurt from 1995 to 2000, when US growth averaged about 4 per cent a year (much of this was extensive growth in the size of the work force and hours worked, but productivity also moved above the average of 2.6 per cent achieved in the US from 1975-1995, and well above the sluggish productivity growth in Europe and Japan). The 'new economy' euphoria peaked in 2000 with growth at about 5 per cent and stock markets at astronomical record highs across the board.

Despite increases in productivity, however, US capital spending was not exceptional in levels or duration over the upswing, and increases in productive capacity were not registered in the trade accounts, which continued to show record deficits, making the position of the dollar vulnerable, especially with high consumption and corporate mergers being ultimately financed by external debt. Hence the fragility of the 'virtuous circle' of asset inflation, capital spending, productivity increase, and stronger dollar without improved trade performance. Moreover, without supportive growth in Europe or Japan, maintaining such a finance-led virtuous circle of growth in the US proved elusive. Even as Federal Reserve Chairman Alan Greenspan warned of the 'irrational exuberance' of the equity markets while, without seeming irony, also celebrating the 'new economy', the American response to every economic shock, and particularly that of the Fed, added to the structural imbalances. Each market crisis – the Asian and Russian crises of 1997-8, the collapse of the international hedge fund, Long Term Capital Management, and the collapse of internet stocks – was met with additional injections of liquidity to prevent further implosion of interdependent credit markets. This sustained the other affected economies as well as US growth, but at the ever-steepening cost of irrational asset levels, soaring debt loads and an increasingly unsustainable current account balance. With growth turning flat in the US after 2001 a reversal of these processes got under way. But the impact of the US shifting away from stimulating effective demand through tax cuts and credit, in a world market facing deflationary tendencies already entrenched in Japan and taking hold in Germany, has already forced a dramatic about-face from the Bush Administration.

There are, then, many continuing tensions in the 'uneven interdependence' of inter-imperial relations in the era of neoliberalism which can be briefly summarized here under the seven dimensions outlined earlier:

(1) *Interdependence and differentiation.* Since 2000, the alternation of growth and setback between the three blocs over the period of neoliberalism has given way to an 'equalization' of 'differentiated' conditions for slow growth in all three.[25] For the first time since the early 1980s, the advanced capitalist countries, and a good part of the rest of the world, have entered a synchronized recession, with both inflation rates and real GDP growth rates within the advanced capitalist countries tending to 2 per cent or less for 2003. Germany has been growing at less than one per cent since 2001 (the high growth in Europe as a whole in 2000 was largely spurred by the sharp drop in the Euro – this aided exports, but only temporarily). The ECB has cut interest rates from 4.75 per cent to 2 per cent over this period, but its firm commitment to the Stability and Growth Pact has meant that the EU continues to rely disproportionately on new external demand to sustain its sluggish growth. A soaring Euro will further trim growth prospects, and push Germany – which has been growing slower than Japan since 2000 – closer to deflation. Meanwhile, Japan's deflating asset bubble of the 1990s has spilled over into general economic deflation (with its central short-term interest rates at zero). With its growth expected to fall below 1 per cent for 2003, it would face even more difficulties with any strengthening of the yen and weakening of its exports. Although there are signals that East Asia is developing an internal dynamic of growth and trade that is deepening the interdependencies of the region as an economic bloc, it remains export dependent on zones outside the region.

The key sustaining force to the world market has been the US, but it is clearly not out of the recession that began in late 2000, and it has its own deflationary fears as unemployment rates rise to decade level highs and inflation continues to drop. With capital spending never fully recovering through the 1990s, American consumption growing faster than incomes has been critical to US growth. US consumption continues to be resilient, albeit slowing in the amount of additional debt and spending that consumers are willing to take on (although it should be recalled that Japanese consumption also held up in the first years of its asset deflation – but then Japan never had the equivalent of a Federal Reserve Chairman blithely telling people to borrow more against their rising housing values). A correction in personal expenditures in the US seems unavoidable: net worth is down; net debt is up; national savings are down; unemployment is up. Moreover, the Federal Reserve's cutting of interest rates thirteen times since the end of 2000 to a forty-five year low, with the Fed short-term rate dropping from 6.5 per cent to just 1.0 per cent by June 2003, has had no clear impact in stimulating capital spending (although it explains a great deal of the resiliency of personal consumption levels, and the housing market). The deflationary worries have been such that the Fed has been pushing down long term interest rates on Treasuries as well to put as much liquidity as possible into the market. The shift in the US government fiscal position over this period from a surplus of 1.4 per cent of GDP to a projected budgetary deficit of 4.5 per cent is also adding to the stimulus measures. But currency realignment as a result of the dollar's decline and the weaknesses in

Europe and Japan makes prospective sources of world demand outside of the US hard to foresee. The outlook in fact looks awfully gloomy: recession in all three, fiscal weakness and the threat of deflation in all three zones. This is what lies behind the IMF warning that, as with the Asia crisis of 1997, 'the risks of generalized deflation have come to the fore ... the global economic situation is now particularly uncertain, with widespread vulnerabilities.'[26]

(2) *International competition.* Rather than being a 'new economy' phase of fundamental transformation of corporate earnings, productivity and accumulation, the late 1990s US recovery followed the path already laid out by neoliberalism, albeit one with even more considerable financial excesses than the standard already set. The late 1990s phase reinforced the uneven interdependence of the world market on the US economy and American power, as the rest of the world relied on the US to be the 'locomotive' of world accumulation. This period may now be exhausted as realignment at some level now seems unavoidable between the three major zones of capitalism, with the peripheral zones of the world market compelled to line up behind one or another of them. This realignment will increase competition between the zones borne out of conditions of economic weakness. The US bloc (including Canada and Mexico) has a deflating asset base, huge capital needs and competitiveness problems at current exchange rates; the EU bloc has a relatively poor productivity performance, high unemployment, stagnant internal demand and external competitiveness sustained by a Euro that used to be weaker than it is now or likely will be in the future; and Japan has deflationary problems, weak internal demand and current account surpluses that would be damaged by any currency appreciation, and thus it has little room for manoeuvre (although there are important strengths in other parts of East Asia, notably China, that may yet offer a different trajectory to the wider zone if dependence upon export surpluses with the US can be lessened, and internal trade linkages deepened.)

Apart from the Japanese deflation, the most visible symptom of the intensified competition so far has been corporate restructuring and governance scandals, particularly in the US.[27] The weakness in the corporate sector is quite extraordinary in its breadth. The telecoms bankruptcies in the centre economies alone have totalled over $100 billion since 2000, the largest portion of this occurring in the US, surely one of the greatest episodes in the failure of market co-ordination ever. The US recorded over $382 billion of assets falling into bankruptcy in 2002, including the astonishing $104 billion collapse of Worldcom, the largest bankruptcy in history. The record levels in the numbers of bankruptcies of public companies that began in 2001 is expected to continue and cut across all sectors beyond the IT disasters. The bloating of balance sheet debt through the 1990s, especially in the US, has left, according to the OECD, a 'capital overhang' of too much capacity from over-investment relative to the growth of demand – 'too much capital had been put in place too soon.'[28] Corporate earnings are clearly down, and further threatened by increasing exposure to bad debt and risk. Thus the reduction of interest rates to stimulate economic activity has had only limited success in bringing down yields on corporate bonds. Similarly, IPOs (initial public offerings) in the US in 2002 recorded the worst year since 1991, and new stock issues by existing companies have done no better. The interdependence of the world market is reinforcing the slowdown between its different zones and, in turn, fuelling international competition in more slowly growing markets.

(3) *Competition through states.* Unbalanced patterns of commodity trade between countries and structural asymmetries in national current account balances are becoming the key symbols of the impasse in the world market. The US net debtor position arising from its cumulative current account deficits since the 1970s is estimated at some $2.7 trillion for 2002; its deficit for 2002 alone is estimated to come in at between $450-500 billion (approaching the 5 per cent of GDP level that has often triggered payments crises in other countries, a constraint which the US is released from, in part, thanks to the dollar being the main reserve currency). This is mirrored by a build-up of surpluses in the other two key zones, and in particular in East Asia. Even after falling some 30 per cent against the Euro since 2000, the US dollar may still need to fall further to improve the competitiveness of US industry (although this would not necessarily clear the current account, as a low dollar did not do so in the past, and an expansion in the US while Japan and Europe stagnate will compound the dilemmas all around).[29]

These imbalances give rise to two major tensions. First, the US must import capital to the tune of $2.7 billion a day to cover the balance of payments deficit. The rest of the world's creditors must accept the issuance of dollars to cover the debt (which is dollar-denominated) in the hope to eventually purchase, in turn, US goods or assets with the accumulated dollars (i.e., in the hope that the dollars will still purchase equivalent value, an increasingly unlikely prospect). It is not clear, however, that creditors will continue to sustain this process to the same degree. Indeed, with the dollar's slide there are already signs of less capital moving into the US, and of diversification out of US dollars. The US dollar is unlikely, in these circumstances, to maintain its exceptional position as an international means of payment and is likely therefore to lose some of its capacity to earn seigniorage (the capacity to appropriate value without producing value). The economic processes differentiating the three key advanced zones will continue, therefore, to be reflected in the increasing use of regional or 'hub' currencies as well. Second, the political pressures of trade are moving in two directions at the same time as a result of the imbalances: on the one hand, the WTO Doha round, numerous bilateral trade agreements, the FTAA and the US fast track trade authority are deepening free trade; on the other, trade protectionism is systematically surfacing, especially on the part of the US, in steel, agricultural goods, lumber, automobiles and other sectors. Continued trade liberalization can contain these tensions by deepening the interdependencies of the world market but only by realigning the existing rivalries and imbalances that promoted free trade in the first place. The path of adjustment remains clouded, however, because of the hierarchy of power within the world market.[30]

(4) *The 'internalisation' of foreign capital.* MNCs are the dominant agencies organizing the internationalisation of capital. They internalise co-operation and competition in their operational structures through the increasing specialisation and intensification of capital through technological development and intra-firm trade. Through the 1990s, some 75 per cent of the stock of foreign direct investment (FDI) was located in the advanced capitalist countries, and these countries also accounted for about 80 per cent of all outflows of FDI and about half of all inflows.[31] The capitalist alliances that MNCs embody take many forms including direct investment, mergers and acquisitions, joint investments, sub-contracting relations and the internationalisation of share ownership. And FDI is now generalised across all sectors and not limited to banking or manufacturing corporations. In other words, the export of capital is in the first instance an issue of inter-imperial relations.

The period of neoliberalism has significantly transformed the nature of the interpenetration of capital. Notably, after recording over half of all FDI globally over the postwar period, the US now accounts for only about a quarter of FDI stocks, and has an equal amount of FDI resident in the US. By 2002 the US stood as the world's largest recipient of FDI as well as its largest investor.[32] In contrast, Japanese and German FDI has grown significantly, from about 1 per cent of world FDI in 1960 to about 11 and 9 per cent respectively by 2000. Although increasing, inflows remain much lower in both countries (with Japan still receiving less than 1 per cent of world FDI). Inward FDI is now becoming as relatively important to the US as it is to the EU as a whole.

The need to finance the ballooning US current account deficit has meant, moreover, that funds have flowed in to purchase US financial assets of all kinds. During the new economy boom of 1995-2000, this was partly due to high yields on US assets of all kinds, the view of the US as a 'safe haven' and the use of mounting dollar holdings to purchase US assets. These developments pushed US net foreign assets even further into deficit (a process which began in the late 1980s), to about $-1.5 trillion and approaching a fifth of GDP.[33] With the slowdown, US assets have become less attractive and FDI has slipped, although portfolio investments have continued to flood in to cover the payments deficit. The internalisation of foreign capital within national states is plainly no longer limited to US penetration of European states, but encompasses the imperialist bloc as a whole.

(5) *Internationalisation and the circuits of capital.* The economic slowdown and neoliberalism led to a significant financialization of the economy from the 1970s onwards. Money-capital now takes many forms relatively disembedded from the real economy: foreign direct investment in the form of acquisitions rather than building new plant; vast credit markets; interconnected equities markets; a

massive turnover in currency markets, far outstripping the requirements of commodity trade; and secondary financial markets spreading risks. These developments have, at the same time, tightened the interdependencies of the world market as money and speculative capital moves more freely between different zones of the world, and sharpened rivalries as different production zones compete for financial flows and face competitive disciplines that carry the potential to amplify economic disturbances into major shocks. Slow economic growth has meant that returns to the financial sector have been higher than in the productive sector and thus have drawn capital into the financial sector and made financial capital (rather than governments, even in a minor sense) the central allocator of credit. In the countries of the centre, these processes have meant a transfer of income flows to financial asset holders. In the US, the rise in household and corporate debt and the return of the government to fiscal deficits have vastly increased this transfer.[34]

The contradictions are even sharper for peripheral countries in the world market, particularly the emerging markets that have been blessed by financial capital inflows. To take one of the major economies of the 'south', Brazil maintains exchange reserves of only $20-30 billion, owes some $250 billion in accumulated debt (denominated largely in dollars), and exhibits spreads on Brazilian bonds of over 20 per cent above US Treasury bonds (parallel to Argentinian levels before Argentina's further collapse in December 2001). This requires enormous efforts on Brazil's part to produce the exports needed to service this debt, and threatens the collapse of the *real* caused by a flight of 'hot money' at any sign of economic disorder. Latin America as a whole is in a similar situation, and it has proven quite difficult to contain the spread of 'contagion' from Argentina. The UN Economic Commission on Latin America and the Caribbean concludes from recent studies that the region has gone through yet another 'lost decade' as capital outflows from debt, interest and dividends have exceeded capital inflows in the order of $7 billion a year (about 0.4 per cent of regional GDP) in recent years.[35] This can only worsen as regional GDP is expected to decline with the world slowdown, and the difficulty of penetrating the US with exports mounts as the dollar declines in value.

The deflation of the asset bubble adds another tension between the US and other zones that complicates any path of adjustment in the world market. An estimated $7 trillion and 1000 companies were lost in market valuations in the US alone from 2000 to mid-2002, and $11 trillion world-wide).[36] This is about half the entire market valuation; narrower market indexes are down by similar amounts, with the NASDAQ tech-heavy index down by close to 80 per cent. With the drop in bond yields from interest rate cuts and the major injections of liquidity, the major stock indexes went up by about 25 per cent in the first half of 2003, fuelled more by expectations rather than economic recovery itself.[37] With the price/earnings ratios used to assess market capitalization values again well above long-run average levels (after a boom one would normally expect a longer period of under-valuations), a financial bubble may again be inflating. It is difficult to find any theoretical or empirical basis for concluding that these levels can be sustained, or that the asset bubble deflation and consequent 'bear market' will not affect the real economy.

There are in fact several reasons to suggest that the unwinding of the asset bubble will take some time and add to sluggish accumulation and deflationary tendencies. First, the financial claims made while bubble was growing are typically based on projections of continued asset growth that are hard to meet after the bubble bursts. Bankruptcies ensue, as the destruction of capital values is required to restore the profitable basis for accumulation. Capital spending is likely to be sluggish until this process is complete (unless the bubble can somehow be reflated, which simply pushes today's problems into tomorrow). Second, the shift that occurred through the 1990s as pensions moved from defined-benefit to self-directed and defined-contribution plans, so as to plough funds into equities, has seriously hurt projected future pension fund returns. Both firms and individuals will have to increase savings to meet future pensions needs. Third, the debt load of households will also have to be addressed, whatever the precise impact of the 'wealth effect' of using inflated asset values to leverage credit, at least to restore savings balances to traditional levels. In the US for 2002, redemptions of mutual funds and other risk-bearing asset classes were outstripping new inflows by billions each month to pay down debt, or to adding to 'cash hoards', although some of these funds are returning to the stock market to catch the latest bubble.

(6) *The internal reorganisation of states.* The internationalisation of capital depends upon constant state intervention. Over the period of neoliberalism the state has internalised international competitiveness as a central objective to mediate between the territorialization of value production and increased dependence upon international circulation. A key parameter in state reorganisation, therefore, has been managing the national economy in a way that exchange rates and balance of payments sustain the internationalisation of the circuits of money-capital. This has placed 'independent' central banks at the apex of the state apparatuses. Even with serious financial imbalances, the Federal Reserve, European Central Bank and the Bank of Japan continue to rely upon interest rate cuts, expansion of private net lending, international capital flows, and an asymmetrical devaluation of the dollar against the Euro (but not the Yen) to spur recovery.[38]

A second dimension has been the state's provision of a hospitable fiscal and social environment to attract new fixed capital investments and protect existing ones, in a context of monetary policy guaranteeing international capital flows. Thus even while allowing fiscal deficits to increase, states have continued to pursue a redistributive strategy of competitive austerity, which makes workers, the poor and the public services they depend on bear the entire brunt of ongoing public expenditure cuts amidst simultaneous and regressive tax cuts. The Bush Administration's 2003 budget proposal, for example, projects a deficit of $400 billion, while further cutting taxes by $350 billion, notably on dividends and marginal tax rates, and reducing spending on health, education and infrastructure; Germany, in turn, while it will likely breach the stability and growth pact deficit limit of 3 per cent of GDP in 2003, is cutting income and inheritance taxes, and curbing unemployment benefits, job protections and pensions; and Japan is planning a budget deficit of 7 per cent of GDP, while cutting income and inheritance taxes and current expenditures, and continuing with the trimming of labour market protections.[39]

Finally, the internationalisation of state apparatuses to mediate the extension and intensification of the world market is also continuing.[40] On the one side, the processes of regionalisation around the three trade blocs is pushing ahead through EU enlargement, the varied trade negotiations around the Free Trade Area of the Americas, and new co-operation linkages in East Asia. On the other side, new areas of trade liberalization, notably in agriculture and services, remain on the WTO's agenda; and both the IMF and the Bank of International Settlements continue to sponsor new measures to liberalize capital accounts and reform capital adequacy requirements of national banking systems. The reorganisation of the state, then, points to intensification of international competition between states while inter-state co-ordination continues to deepen the world market.

(7) *Contradictions of inter-imperial relations.* The 'uneven interdependence' that has characterised inter-imperial relations over the period of neoliberalism makes these relations quite different from what they were during both the postwar boom period and the crisis of the 1970s. While the US remains at the competitive centre of the world market in terms of productive capacity, command over financial flows, centrality to neoliberal modalities of governance and in its role as 'importer of last resort', it has become dependent upon supportive policies of states in the other key zones for sustaining the internationalisation of capital and the US's unprecedented absorption of the world savings. This uneven interdependence lies behind all the oscillations between inter-state competition and co-operation amongst the imperialist bloc. It has produced – and continues to reproduce – specifically neoliberal patterns of international competition and internationalisation of capital, as well as of domestic and international social relations, that have unified the world market in a way that has prevented the differentiation among the zones spilling over into political conflict over exclusive access to markets. Through the 1990s, the interactions between trade imbalances, financialization and slowdown were resolved 'positively' as the US 'new economy' provided sources of world demand to move accumulation ahead. The adjustment to 'private sector excesses' now threatens to impact 'negatively' on the world market as a whole, without the other imperialist centres being capable of filling the breach.[41] In a context of relative stagnation, neoliberalism is more likely to tighten its hold over the imperialist bloc.

NEOLIBERALISM, IMPERIALISM AND
AMERICAN POWER

The internationalisation of capital over the last two decades is not, then, an endless 'spatial fix' for a permanent economic crisis of either the imperialist bloc as a whole or US capitalism in particular. To think in that way recalls the old classical theory of imperialism's focus on outlets for surplus as an external relation. This is misconceived because, on the one hand, it treats the particularity of value production and class relations as distinct from the circulation of capital in the world market; and because, on the other hand, it sees the contradictory relations between the two as symptoms of crisis, rather than as constitutive of the new forms of international competition that have emerged under neoliberalism. This misconception then leads either to a search for more 'coherent' national models of development to oppose the 'American model', or to dire predictions of mounting inter-imperial conflict and crisis over the processes of devaluation that the US is attempting to impose on others.

In fact, neoliberalism has been consolidated as an institutionalised global regime, encompassing particular forms of development, international competition and state 'reform'. The 'internal bourgeoisie' that has become central to the organization of the power bloc of each of the imperialist countries has an interest in sustaining neoliberalism. They have a stake in the 'American model', which needs to be seen not as a foreign import or imposition undermining a defenceless 'national bourgeoisie' (as many opponents of neoliberalism would have it), but rather as a policy matrix that meets the internal class interests of the power bloc within each state in this phase of imperialism. This is partly a matter of their interest in suppressing wage-earners' incomes, to meet international competition; partly a question of the individual stakes of some of the key members of the power bloc in the privatization of the public sector; and partly a matter of the necessity of sustaining the international circuits of capital that have made both the re-investment of capital and its realization more dependent on the world market.

Neither does the internationalisation of capital mean a supercession of contradictions in inter-imperial relations due to the transnationalization of capitalist interests, nor a one-sided economic dependence on US power. International competition today takes the form of the inter-penetration of capital and the securing of extra-national economic space both through the extension of the nation-state system and the formation of multinational economic blocs. Internationalized capital has access to its own 'home' state (and, of course, the supranational institutions that are the product of states), and to the states it invests in as well, with both the 'home' and the 'host' states actively ensuring the extended reproduction of capital, not by opposing international competition but through actively promoting it. The 'uneven interdependence' that characterises the world market in this phase of imperialism means that competitive rivalry does not culminate in geo-military conflict (as Lenin thought), or in particular expansionist policies upon which the interests of all global capitalists can be unified (as Kautsky envisaged). Nor is the world market facing imminent international crisis from deepening competitive rivalries that can no longer be politically contained.

On the other hand, international competition and economic contradictions between the imperialist centres persists. The period of neoliberalism has, in other words, produced particular forms of 'unity and contradiction in the international circuits of capital' that need to be examined on their own terms. In the old economics of imperialism, the contradictions in inter-imperial relations became concentrated on territorial conflicts to meet expansionist needs for economic outlets for commodities or capital. In the new economics of imperialism, the interdependence and competitive rivalries between the imperialist centres are concentrated in the uneven development of the conditions for the international circulation of capital. As we have seen, the US has supplied the global demand necessary for international circulation, while the rest of the imperialist bloc runs trade surpluses and exports capital back to the US (while the dominated bloc, with some exceptions in East Asia, is squeezed to run trade surpluses to meet credit obligations but not development needs). This reflects, we have argued, the decline in the relative superiority of US capital from what it was in the postwar period (although it remains dominant in both size and capacity); the asymmetrical formation of the continental blocs; and the inter-penetrations of the three blocs through the internationalisation of capital. It is not at all clear how these contradictions in the world market will be resolved, especially given the progressively synchronized economic slowdown in the three blocs.

It is possible, of course, that the US economy will be successfully reflated and again provide the necessary demand for international accumulation. The US has actively used such reflations not just to spur growth, but also to bolster its hegemony. It has used other zones' export dependence on the US to make them deepen their adherence to neoliberalism, which has strengthened the internationalisation of US capital by giving it access to new markets and the purchase of foreign assets. The capital inflows into the US covering financial deficits have, in turn, allowed some measure of restructuring of the US capital stock, especially as accumulation in Germany and Japan has floundered. But without parallel reflations in Europe and Japan the US is likely generate even greater imbalances in personal and corporate debt and international payments, and to reflate asset prices. It is quite unclear how future re-balancing could occur without significant disturbances in the world market, and some re-alignment of inter-imperial relations, including the position of the dollar as almost the sole international currency.

Alternatively, recalling the early 1990s, an adjustment of the US dollar to new levels could continue, with slower growth allowing corrections to internal balances, and the rest of the imperial bloc playing a larger role in establishing world demand, and absorbing net exports from the US accordingly. This is what the US recession in progress since 2001 should be encouraging. But the shift toward reflation and away from export dependency that would be required from the EU and East Asia for this path of adjustment has not been forthcoming. Japan is still in the grip of an asset-driven deflation that a decade of Keynesian fiscal measures has not compensated for; much of Asia is still underdeveloped and export-dependent; and the Asian currencies (notably, the Chinese renminbi) have all been kept pegged at low values relative to the dollar to maintain export competitiveness. All this has, in turn, left the Japanese spending some 6 trillion yen (over $50 billion) in the first of half 2003 to keep the yen from appreciating and further undermining Japanese hopes of recovery.[42] It therefore effectively depends on Europe becoming capable of absorbing much more of the world's – including the US's – exports, the rise in the Euro reflecting these pressures. It is not at all clear that the EU is politically, organizationally or economically capable of undertaking such a project. The Stability and Growth Pact and the independence and restrictiveness of the European Central Bank have blocked both fiscal activism and any credit-driven reflation. European paralysis in these areas of economic policy-making, while pushing ahead with measures for market flexibility and competitiveness, is likely to endure.

In neither of these two scenarios, however, is there any reason to expect that the modulation in inter-imperial relations they would entail would constitute a break with neoliberalism or the centrality of US power. A stronger Euro, a new EU constitution with an enlarged membership, and moves toward a common security and defence policy may well already be registering these modulations. But it is difficult to see that the EU is proposing any strategic departures, as opposed to mere tactical ones, outside the confines of existing institutions and neoliberal mechanisms for co-ordinating inter-imperial relations.

There is a third more dramatic scenario that cannot be written off as impossible. The recession enveloping the US might simply continue for some time with the correction of US imbalances spilling over into a deflationary cycle from further asset meltdowns and debt hangovers. This would reinforce the already existing deflationary problems of both Japan and Germany. If brutal enough, such a process of radical devaluation might correct US imbalances, although where that might end and how is impossible to foresee. In an earlier phase of imperialism, these processes unleashed the economic disasters of the interwar period as competitive rivalries choked and then broke off the international circulation of capital. But today an attempt at a co-ordinated response would surely be attempted by the imperialist bloc through existing international institutions to cut such an economic death spiral short, and restore some measure of stability, if not full conditions for rapid accumulation.

The uneven interdependence of the world market during this period of neoliberalism has precisely served to avert 'beggar-thy-neighbour' trade wars and sharp devaluations. Instead, policy co-ordination has been pursued within the imperialist bloc to re-align currencies or to inject liquidity at crucial junctures, to reproduce the existing patterns of international competition at the cost of placing ever more fictitious and speculative capital into circulation. If Leo Panitch and Sam Gindin are correct in suggesting that inter-imperial relations today prevent inherent economic contradictions from repeating the past violent clashes of imperial rivals, they are also correct to point to 'the limits that the American empire ruling through states poses to a strategy of co-ordinated neoliberal growth even among the advanced capitalist countries.'[43] This is because the new economics of imperialism does not eliminate competition: there remains competition as well as unity in the international circuits of capital. Moreover, in conditions of slow economic growth and unused capacity in the world market, competitive rivalry compels each zone of the world to engage in a continual process of innovation, cost-cutting and to internationalise its capital so as to seek out new markets and cheapen production.

Indeed, the reorganisation of states and social relations to foster international competition, in all these forms, has been an integral feature of this phase of imperialism in all three imperialist blocs. State apparatuses are being systematically re-organized around a strategy of 'competitive austerity' – strengthening the economic apparatuses that sponsor the internationalisation of capital while restructuring labour policies to enforce wage compression, pursuing fiscal austerity for social policies while cutting taxes to attract international capital, and so forth. However apparently 'Keynesian' are measures to reflate the economy and hold up conditions for realization through extending private credit and returning to government deficits (while still sacking public workers), it is the redistributional dynamic of working class austerity to enhance international competitiveness that above all governs state policy. The intensification of exploitation in the class relations of the differentiated spaces of the world market is the other face of the internationalisation of capital and the expansion of the world market in this phase of imperialism.

As Alavi pointed out, the new imperialism mandates the incorporation of all zones of the world into a universalized economic system – the formally 'equal' rules of exchange of the capitalist world market and the norms of the nation-state system. The internationalisation of capital has solidified in the imperialist bloc a material interest in sustaining the forms of uneven development and hierarchical organizational arrangements of the world market today. Neoliberalism as a social form of power and class relations, and international competitiveness as its externalized expression, is reproduced in national capitalisms, not against a more 'rational' organization of the world market or as an imposition of the 'American model' on 'European' or 'East Asian models', but as part and parcel of contemporary imperialism. Indeed, even the ruling classes in the dominated bloc can see their interests – both in terms of capital accumulation and the desire to move up the rungs of the imperialist chain – represented in the international circulation of capital, just as colonial and comprador elites of the past did in the old imperialism. This is despite the abhorrent inequities produced by neoliberal structural adjustment policies of cutting consumption for the poor and workers in these countries to improve external competitiveness, while the world's savings flows to finance the profligacy of US consumers and the imperialist bloc as a whole.

How is this sustained? Here lies the importance of Dick Bryan's insight that today 'the contradiction between the internationality of accumulation and the nationality of state regulation is not solved by the subordination of the latter to the former, but by the role of state policy being recast so that the dominance of global calculation is presented as beneficial for all nationals. In particular, the working class in each nation must be convinced that the pursuit of international competitiveness is an agenda of labor as well as capital.'[44] Whereas the old economics of imperialism politically combined a 'labour aristocracy' with 'imperial projects' through nationalism, the new economics of imperialism internalizes a logic of international competitiveness between workers, firms and states in constructing 'local' and 'national projects' to sustain 'their' space in a globalized world. To undermine that logic, it will be crucial for anti-imperialist struggles today to challenge the ideology and practice of international competition, as universalized in institutions like the WTO and IMF and as particularised in national states and local workplaces. Anti-globalization struggles against the international economic institutions fostering the internationalisation of capital have been an important step taken by the Left in this context. New struggles for 'democratic sovereignty' over the empires of capital, entailing appropriate visions and practices for 'a different kind of state' are necessary next steps. These are the only democratic exit strategies out of neoliberalism and its endless pursuit of competitiveness, that is, out of the economics of the new imperialism.

NOTES

1   'Imperialism Old and New' in *Socialist Register 1964*, New York: Monthly Review Press, 1964, pp. 104 and 123-4.

2   This insight has been developed most by Harry Magdoff in terms of his 'imperialism without colonies' (see his *Imperialism: From the Colonial Age to the Present*, New York: Monthly Review Press, 1978), and by Leo Panitch and Sam Gindin in terms of their conception of 'informal empire' (see their essay in this volume), both writing with respect especially to US imperialism.

3   See: David Gordon, 'The Global Economy: New Edifice or Crumbling Foundations?', *New Left Review*, 168, 1988; Giovanni Arrighi, *The Long Twentieth Century*, London: Verso, 1994; and Robert Brenner, 'The Economics of Global Turbulence', *New Left Review*, 229, 1998. Weberian analyses have been even more insistent about growing economic rivalry, but not nearly as attuned to the power dynamics involved or the contradictory processes of uneven development. See: Jeffrey Hart, *Rival Capitalists: International Competitiveness in the United States, Japan, and Western Europe*, Ithaca: Cornell, 1992; and Robert Boyer and Jean-Pierre Durand, *After Fordism*, London: Macmillan, 1997.

4   'New US Economy Part 2: Winning Ways: Ready Bucks and a Flair for Risk', *Financial Times*, 14 December 1999.

5   Michael Hardt and Antonio Negri, *Empire*, Cambridge: Harvard University Press, 2000; Leslie Sklair, *The Transnational Capitalist Class*, Oxford: Blackwell, 2001; and Stephen Gill, *Power and Resistance in the New World*

Order, New York: Macmillan, 2003.

6   Peter Gowan, *The Global Gamble*, London: Verso, 1999; Leo Panitch, 'The New Imperial State', *New Left Review*, 2, 2000; and Michael Hudson, *Super Imperialism: The Origin and Fundamentals of US World Dominance*, London: Pluto, 2003.

7   'Comments on Imperialism', *Radical History Review*, 57, 1993, p. 77.

8   Karl Marx, *Grundrisse*, New York: Vintage, 1973, pp. 539, 542.

9   Marx, *Grundrisse*, p. 408.

10   David Harvey, *The Limits to Capital*, Chicago: University of Chicago Press 1982.

11   See Aijaz Ahmad, ed., *On the National and Colonial Questions: Selected Writings of Marx and Engels*, New Delhi: Leftwords Books, 2001.

12   Karl Marx, *Capital, Volume 1*, New York, International Publishers, 1967, p. 451.

13   Karl Marx, *Capital, Volume 3*, New York, International Publishers, 1967, pp. 237-40.

14   Karl Marx, *A Contribution to the Critique of Political Economy*, New York: International Publishers, 1970, p. 80.

15   For assessments see: Anthony Brewer, *Marxist Theories of Imperialism*, London: Routledge, 1980; Charles Barone, *Marxist Thought on Imperialism*, Armonk: M.E. Sharpe, 1985; and Alex Callinicos, 'Marxism and Global Governance' in David Held and Anthony McGrew, eds., *Governing Globalization*, Oxford: Polity, 2002.

16   Nikolai Bukharin, *Imperialism and World Economy*, London: Merlin, 1972, pp. 25-6 and 80. Also see: Rosa Luxemburg, *Accumulation of Capital*, London: Routledge and Kegan Paul, 1951; Rudolf Hilferding, *Finance Capital*, London: Routledge, 1981; V.I. Lenin, *Imperialism: The Highest Stage of Capitalism*, Peking: People's Publishing House, 1964; and Karl Kautsky, 'Ultra-Imperialism', *New Left Review*, 59, 1970.

17   This was taken up by dependency theorists as well as by new Marxist theorists of imperialism who focused on the peripheral countries.

18   Ernest Mandel, *Europe versus America: Contradictions of Imperialism*, New York: Monthly Review Press, 1970; Robert Rowthorn, 'Imperialism in the 1970s – Unity or Rivalry?' *New Left Review*, 69, 1971; and Jon Halliday and Gavan McCormack, *Japanese Imperialism Today*, New York: Monthly Review Press, 1973.

19   James Petras and Robert Rhodes, 'The Reconsolidation of US Hegemony', *New Left Review*, 97, 1976; and Martin Nicolaus, 'The Universal Contradiction', *New Left Review*, 59, 1970.

20   See Alavi, 'Imperialism Old and New' as well as the essays by Stephen Hymer, Christian Palloix and Robin Murray in Hugo Radice, ed., *International Firms and Modern Imperialism*, New York: Penguin, 1975.

21   Nicos Poulantzas, *Classes in Contemporary Capitalism*, London: New Left Books, 1974, p. 81.

22 Leo Panitch, 'Globalisation and the State' in *Socialist Register 1994*, London: Merlin Press, 1994.

23 This section draws upon: Michel Beaud, *A History of Capitalism, 1500-2000*, New York: Monthly Review Press, 2001; Robert Brenner, *The Boom and the Bubble*, London: Verso, 2002; and Robert Albritton, Makoto Itoh, Richard Westra and Alan Zuege, eds., *Phases of Capitalist Development*, New York: Palgrave, 2002.

24 Angus Maddison, *The World Economy: A Millennial Perspective*, Paris: OECD, 2001, pp. 131ff.

25 IMF, *World Economic Outlook*, April 2003, Washington: IMF, 2003, ch. 1; Stephen Roach, *Deflation in the World Economy*, New York: Morgan Stanley, November 2002; and 'Breaking the Deflationary Spell', *The Economist*, 28 June 2003.

26 *World Economic Outlook*, p. 11.

27 See: 'Bankruptcies Forecast to Stay Near Record', *Financial Times*, 27 February 2003; Robert Brenner, 'Towards the Precipice', *London Review of Books*, 25(3), 2003; and Wynne Godley, 'The US Economy: A Changing Strategic Predicament', Levy Economics Institute, 2003.

28 OECD, *Economic Outlook*, 73, Paris: OECD, 2003, pp. 10-16.

29 Fred Bergsten and John Williamson, eds., *Dollar Overvaluation and the World Economy*, Washington: Institute for International Economics, 2003; and 'Washington's Weak Dollar Policy', *Financial Times*, 20 May 2003.

30 This is exactly what the Bank of International Settlements puzzles over in its *Annual Report 2003*, Basel: BIS, 2003, ch. 8.

31 UNCTAD, *World Investment Report 2002*, New York: United Nations, 2002; Peter Dicken, *Global Shift*, New York: Guilford, 1998, pp. 42-9; and Richard Kozul-Wright and Robert Rowthorn, eds., *Transnational Corporations and the Global Economy*, London: Macmillan, 1998.

32 UNCTAD, *World Investment Report* 2002, p. 37.

33 Maddison, *The World Economy*, pp. 135-7. In contrast, Germany and especially Japan have surpluses on their net assets.

34 See: 'The Debt Bomb', *Barron's*, 20 January 2003; and 'The True Cost of Hegemony: Huge Debts', *New York Times*, 20 April 2003.

35 ECLAC, *Latin America and the Caribbean in the World Economy, 2000-1*, Santiago: ECLAC, 2002.

36 Based on the Wiltshire 5000 index of all publicly traded companies: see 'Hold on for a Wild Ride', *New York Times*, 21 July 2002.

37 'Market Bubble Being Inflated?', *Toronto Globe and Mail*, 20 June 2003; and 'On a Wing and a Prayer', *Financial Times*, 3 July 2003.

38 BIS, *Annual Report 2003*, ch. 4.

39 OECD, *Economic Outlook*, pp. 71-80; Paul Krugman, 'Jobs, Jobs, Jobs', *New York Times*, 22 April 2003; and 'Schroder Urges Party to Grasp Need for Reform', *Financial Times*, 24 May 2003.

40 WTO, *Annual Report 2003*, Geneva: WTO, 2003, ch. 1.

41 See: 'The World Economy Adjusts to a Disappointing Decade', *Financial Times*, 2 July 2003; and Alex Izuurieta, 'Economic Slowdown in the US, Rehabilitation of Fiscal Policy and the Case for Co-ordinated Global Reflation', Cambridge University, CERF Paper Working Paper N. 6, 2003.

42 'Investors Place Bets on Asia Foreshadowing US Recovery', *Financial Times*, 27 June 2003.

43 Leo Panitch and Sam Gindin, 'Global Capitalism and American Empire', in this volume.

44 Dick Bryan, *The Chase Across the Globe*, Boulder: Westview Press, 1995, p. 186.

TRUTHS AND MYTHS ABOUT
THE INVASION OF IRAQ *

Noam Chomsky

The invasion of Iraq cannot seriously be described as a war with Iraq, any more than the Nazi invasion of Belgium in 1940 was a war with Belgium. Iraq's capacity to resist was so limited that it cannot even be described as an uneven war. The declaration by President Bush, wearing a combat suit and standing on the deck of the aircraft carrier Abraham Lincoln, that 'the United States and our allies have prevailed', completed a carefully constructed myth.[1] It is important to remind ourselves of some salient facts.

THE OFFICIAL REASONS WERE SPECIOUS

Bush and Powell and the rest went out of their way to make sure we understood this, by a steady dose of self-contradiction from September 2002 when the war drums began to beat. One day the 'single question' was whether Iraq would disarm: 'We have high confidence that they have weapons of mass destruction – that is what this war was about and is about', said White House spokesperson Ari Fleischer. That was the pretext throughout the whole UN–disarmament farce. In reality UNMOVIC was doing a good job of carrying forward the disarmament of Iraq, and could have continued if that had been the goal. But after Colin Powell and others had stated solemnly that this was the 'single question', President Bush went on at once both to affirm that claim, and also to reject it by announcing that it wasn't the goal at all: even if there wasn't a pocket knife anywhere in Iraq, the US would invade anyway, because it was committed to

* This essay is partly based on interviews with V. K. Ramachandran on April 3, 2003, in *Frontline* (India), and with Michael Albert on April 13, 2003, both posted at Znet (www.zmag.org).

'regime change'. Then we heard that there was nothing to that either: at the Azores summit, where Bush and Blair issued their ultimatum to the UN – do what we say or render yourselves 'irrelevant' – they made it clear that they would invade even if Saddam and his gang left the country. So 'regime change' was not enough: it has to be the right regime, one that provides the US rulers with an 'Arab façade', to borrow Britain's terminology as it ruled the region during its day in the sun. On other days we heard that the goal was 'democracy' in the world. Pretexts depended on audience and circumstances. No thinking person could take this charade seriously.

Iraq was not much of a military force to begin with, and had been largely disarmed through the 1990s, while much of Iraqi society was driven to the edge of survival by the US-UK sanctions, using the UN as a cover. Its military expenditures and economy were about one-third those of Kuwait, with 10 per cent of Iraq's population, far below others in the region, and even farther below the regional superpower, Israel (by now virtually an offshore military base of the US). And the invading force not only had utterly overwhelming military power, but also extensive information to guide its actions from satellite observation and over-flights for many years, and more recently U-2 flights on the pretext of disarmament, surely sending data directly back to Washington.

'DEMOCRACY' WAS ANYTHING BUT THE GOAL

The US has consistently opposed democracy inside Iraq, as elsewhere, unless it remains within narrow bounds. Their nature emerges with great clarity from the historical and documentary record. One prominent scholar, who also served in the Reagan administration's 'democracy enhancement' programs, accurately describes the goal as 'limited, top-down forms of democratic change that did not risk upsetting the traditional structures of power with which the United States has long been allied'.[2]

In 1991 Saddam Hussein was authorized to suppress, brutally, an uprising that might have overthrown him, but would have left the country in the hands of Iraqis who might not have subordinated themselves sufficiently to Washington. That was understood very well by those who now pretend to be appalled by the mass graves they always knew existed, and who now choose to suppress the explanation they gave at the time, that it was right for Washington to authorize the slaughter because Saddam 'offered the West and the region a better hope for his country's stability than did those who have suffered his repression'.[3] The chief diplomatic correspondent of the *New York Times*, who now writes that the mass graves justify his moral argument for the invasion, told a rather different story when the decision was made not to permit Iraqis to overthrow Saddam in 1991: 'the best of all worlds' for Washington, he explained, would be 'an iron-fisted Iraqi junta without Saddam Hussein' that would rule as Saddam did. But since this wasn't available, we would just have to settle for Saddam, Washington's friend and ally, who had fallen from favour when he disobeyed (or maybe misunderstood) orders by invading Kuwait in August 1990 but was nevertheless a better choice than an Iraq run by the Iraqi people.[4] The Azores summit merely reiterated this position twelve years later: Iraqis can run Iraq as Washington's Latin American friends could run the USA's 'backyard', or as Iraqis ran their country under Britain's supervision after World War I.

The murderous US–UK sanctions regime of the following years devastated Iraqi society but strengthened the tyrant, compelling the population to rely for survival on his (highly efficient) system for distributing basic goods. The sanctions thus undercut the possibility of the kind of popular revolt that had overthrown an impressive series of other monsters who had been strongly supported by the current incumbents in Washington: Marcos, Duvalier and Ceausescu up to the end of their bloody rule, along with Mobutu, Suharto and a long list of others, some of them easily as tyrannical and barbaric as Saddam. Had it not been for the sanctions, Saddam might well have gone the same way, as has been pointed out for years by the westerners who know Iraq best, Denis Halliday and Hans van Sponeck, who were the chief UN humanitarian coordinators in Iraq, with an international staff of hundreds of investigators travelling daily through the country.[5]

In the early days of the invasion, Leith Kubba, one of the most respected secular Iraqi opposition voices abroad, who is connected with the congressional National Endowment for Democracy, demanded that the UN play a vital role after the end of the fighting and rejected US control of reconstruction or government. And one of the leading Shi'ite opposition figures, Sayed Muhamed Baqer al-Hakim, the leader of the Supreme Council for Islamic Revolution in Iraq (SCIRI), in exile in Iran, informed the press that 'we understand this war to be about imposing US hegemony over Iraq', adding that they perceived the US as 'an occupying rather than a liberating force'. He stressed that the UN must supervise elections, and called on 'foreign troops to withdraw from Iraq' and leave Iraqis in charge. He reiterated this stance on his return to Iraq on May 10, 2003.

Speaking generally, the Shi'ite majority is likely to join the rest of the region in seeking closer relations with Iran, the last thing the Bushites want; and the next largest component of the population, the Kurds, are likely to seek some kind of autonomy within a federal structure that would be anathema to Turkey, a major regional base for the US. Throughout the region genuine democracy would have outcomes that are inconsistent with the goal of US hegemony. Recent studies indicate that from Morocco to Lebanon to the Gulf, a large majority of the population want a greater role in government for Islamic religious figures, and about 95 percent believe that the sole US interest in the region is to control its oil and strengthen Israel.

It was always fanciful to imagine that Washington would tolerate truly democratic elections in Iraq, and respect the outcome. What US policy-makers wanted was a client regime, following practice elsewhere in the region, and most instructively in the regions that have been under US domination for a century, Central America and the Caribbean. Brent Scowcroft, National Security Adviser to Bush I, just repeated the obvious: 'What's going to happen the first time we hold an election in Iraq and it turns out the radicals win? What do you do? We're surely not going to let them take over.'[6]

The Bush administration's contempt for democracy was even more blatant in relation to the states which declined to join the invasion. The failure of its so-called 'diplomatic efforts' to gain their support – in fact, a failure of coercion, by bribes and threats – was due to the massive opposition of the vast majority of their populations. The most dramatic case was Turkey. Turkey was very vulnerable to US punishment and inducements. Nevertheless, to everyone's surprise the new government was unable to get the Turkish parliament to endorse the role the US wanted Turkey to play, which was opposed by 95 per cent of the population. Turkey was bitterly condemned for that in the US, just as France and Germany were bitterly condemned because the governments also took the position of the overwhelming majority of their populations. The countries that were praised were countries like Italy and Spain (and of course the UK), whose leaders agreed to follow Washington over the opposition of an even larger majority of their electorates than in the reviled Old Europe. The criterion distinguishing Old Europe (denounced and punished) and New Europe (praised and rewarded) was quite sharp: if a government took the same position as the vast majority of the population, it belonged to Old Europe; if it followed the marching orders from Crawford, Texas, and dismissed the views of the vast majority of its population, it joined the exciting and promising New Europe, the wave of the future in the crusade for democracy.

All of this proceeded along with much media acclaim for the dedication to democracy of these leaders who were actually expressing their hatred of it with such dramatic clarity. It might have been amusing if it had been happening in Andorra, but not when it was happening in front of our eyes in the most powerful state in history, which had just proclaimed its intention to rule the world, by force if necessary.

Fear and hatred of substantive democracy among elites is neither new nor surprising. But I do not recall any precedent for such open and brazen contempt for the belief that in a 'democracy' the voice of the people should have some role. It was not just government officials who reacted in this way, with remarkable uniformity, but also many commentators. That includes liberals like Thomas Friedman who informed us that 'France, as they say in kindergarten, does not play well with others', and should therefore be replaced on the Security Council by India, which is 'serious' now that it is governed by an ultra–right nationalist party which, he believes, is more willing to 'play well' with the righteous in Washington. The populations of Europe must be in pre-kindergarten, then, by his standards, since according to an international Gallup poll at the time, which was not reported, most were even more opposed than the French to the Bush-Blair war. A whole literature was spawned to explain why France, Germany, Turkey and others were trying to undermine the United States. It appeared to be inconceivable to these commentators that when the overwhelming majority of a population has an opinion, a government might want to pay some attention to them.

This contempt for democracy on the part of the Bush administration and its supporters was matched by contempt for the international system. There were even calls to disband the United Nations, which was widely described as having 'failed' – i.e. having failed to endorse US policy. The US will not try to dismantle the UN but will aim to ensure that its role is diminished even further, because if it won't follow orders, of what use is it? As the official administration moderate Colin Powell put it, the UN can authorize the US to do what it intends to do, or it can 'go off and have other discussions', but those are its choices: follow orders, or be a debating society. There's nothing particular novel about that, as the record of vetoes reveals since the UN achieved a limited measure of independence in the 1960s (the US far in the lead, UK second, no one else close). But the extremism of recent stands is, nevertheless, of no slight significance.

THE PRIME MOTIVE WAS TO TAKE 'EXEMPLARY ACTION'

In September 2002 the Bush administration released its National Security Strategy, sending many shudders around the world, including within the US foreign policy elite. The Strategy had many precedents, but did break new ground: for the first time in the post-war world a powerful state announced, loud and clear, that it intended to rule the world forever, crushing by force any potential challenge it might perceive. This is often called a doctrine of 'pre-emptive war'. That is wrong; it goes vastly beyond pre-emption. Sometimes it is called, more accurately, a doctrine of 'preventive war', but that too understates the doctrine. No military threat, however remote, need be 'prevented'; challenges can be concocted at will, and may not involve any threat other than 'defiance'. Those who pay attention to history and the documentary record will be aware that 'successful defiance' has often been taken to be justification for resort to force in the past, sometimes called 'maintaining credibility', in the style of a Mafia Don.

At the outset, the doctrine was interpreted as authorizing the US government to resort to war against a country that has or is developing weapons of mass destruction (WMD). Perhaps the most important consequence of the collapse of US-UK claims with regard to WMD in Iraq is that the doctrine has been re-interpreted. As Bush and others have made clear, for a country to be selected as a target for attack, it suffices that it have the 'potential' to develop WMD. The President announced that the search for WMD was successful, because two trailers were found that might be usable for production of WMD. By these criteria, virtually every country is a legitimate target of attack, now and in the indefinite future. The new doctrine therefore becomes quite impressive in its scope.

When a new doctrine is announced, action must be taken to demonstrate that it is seriously intended, so that it can become a new 'norm in international relations', as legal and academic commentators will soberly explain, and it is important to establish such a norm if you expect to rule the world by force for the foreseeable future. The action needed in this case was a war with an 'exemplary nature', as Harvard Middle East historian Roger Owen pointed out, discussing the reasons for the invasion of Iraq.[7] Exemplary action teaches a lesson that others must heed, or else.

The target must have certain crucial qualities: it must be important – there's no point illustrating the doctrine by invading Burundi – and it must be defenceless. Iraq qualified perfectly in both respects. Its importance is obvious, and so was the required weakness. It was therefore a perfect choice for an exemplary action to establish the doctrine of global rule by force as a new 'norm'. This was recognized as soon as the test case was declared a success. Publication of the National Security Strategy 'was the signal that Iraq would be the first test, not the last', the *New York Times* reported: 'Iraq became the petri dish in which this experiment in pre-emptive policy grew.' A high official added that 'We will not hesitate to act alone, if necessary, to exercise our right of self-defence by acting pre-emptively' – now that the norm had been established. Throughout, the concept of pre-emption has been redesigned to refer to what the Nuremberg Tribunal called the 'supreme crime' of waging unprovoked war – which the Bush administration now undertakes to do whenever it sees fit.[8]

It was plausibly assumed that Iraqi society would collapse, that the soldiers would go in, and that the US would be able to establish a regime of its choice, and military bases. The US would then be in a better position to take on harder cases, some already named: North Korea, Iran and Syria. But there are other possible targets too. The Andean region qualifies, for example. It has very substantial resources, including oil. It is in turmoil, with dangerous independent popular movements. It is surrounded by US military bases, with US forces already on the ground.

THE ATTACK ON IRAQ BELONGS TO ESTABLISHED REPUBLICAN ELECTORAL STRATEGY

The declaration of the new National Security Strategy and the propaganda drive to prepare American public opinion for the invasion coincided with the opening of the mid-term election campaign, all in September 2002. Karl Rove, the administration's campaign manager, had already explained that Republicans have to 'go to the country on the issue of national security [because voters] trust the Republican Party [for] protecting America.'[9] One didn't have to be a political genius to realize that if social and economic issues had dominated the election the Bush administration would not have a chance. Accordingly it was necessary to concoct a threat to national survival which the President would brilliantly overcome. For the mid-term elections the strategy worked, if only just barely. Polls reveal that voters maintained their preferences, but suppressed concerns over jobs, pensions, benefits, etc., in favour of security. Something similar will be needed for the presidential campaign in 2004, as Rove has also been kind enough to explain. The *Wall Street Journal* was quite accurate in reporting that the PR operation on the USS Abraham Lincoln was not a declaration of the end of the war, but of the opening of the presidential campaign of 2004 – which, merely by coincidence, was being delayed by several weeks so as to open in New York right after September 11.

All of this was second nature for the Bush administration. They were mostly recycled from the more reactionary sectors of the Reagan-Bush I administrations, and knew that they had been able to run the country for twelve years, carrying out domestic programmes the public largely opposed, by periodically pushing the panic button: Libyans attempting to 'expel us from the world' (in Reagan's words); an air base in Grenada from which the Russians would bomb the USA; Nicaraguans (only 'two-days driving time from Harlingen Texas', Reagan again) planning to take over the hemisphere; black criminals about to rape your sister (Willie Horton in the 1988 presidential campaign); Hispanic narco-traffickers about to destroy us; and on and on. It was one such thing after another, every year. The Reagan Administration actually declared a National Emergency in 1985 because of the threat to the security of the United States posed by the government of Nicaragua. Virtually the same words were used in the congressional authorization for invading Iraq in October 2002, shortly after the propaganda campaign began.

If the narrow – and unusually corrupt – sectors of private power and privilege represented by the Bush administration are to carry out their reactionary domestic program over strong popular opposition, and ensure that what they are dismantling will be very hard to reconstruct, the American public has to be made to feel under constant threat. Bush's declaration that Americans 'refuse to live in fear' was precisely the opposite of the aim and consequence of the propaganda and domestic 'security' policies instituted by his administration.[10]

THE MEDIA PLAYED A CRUCIAL PROPAGANDA ROLE

The drumbeat for war began in September 2002, and the government-media propaganda campaign achieved spectacular success. The media relayed government propaganda about the threat to US security posed by Iraq, its involvement in 9-11 and other terrorism, etc., sometimes embellishing it on their own. A majority of the population quickly became convinced that Iraq was an imminent threat to US security. Soon, almost half were convinced that Iraq was responsible for the 9-11 attacks (as compared with 3 per cent after the attacks). Not surprisingly, these carefully manufactured beliefs correlated closely with support for the war. These beliefs were unique to the US. After September 2002, the US became the only country in the world where 60 per cent of the adult population believed that Iraq presented an imminent threat to its security. Even in Kuwait and Iran, which Saddam Hussein had invaded, he was not feared, though he was despised. Kuwaitis and Iranians knew perfectly well that Iraq had become the weakest state in the region. But a highly effective propaganda assault drove the American public far off the spectrum of world opinion. These were impressive successes of what Anatol Lieven called 'a propaganda programme which for systematic mendacity has few parallels in peacetime democracies' – though in fact it is not that unusual. The achievement is surely understood by the perpetrators, and should not be ignored by those who care about the fate of the world.

As a result of these successes, Bush was even able to proclaim in his USS Abraham Lincoln extravaganza that the conquest of Iraq was a victory in the 'war on terror'. His advisers and speech-writers were surely aware that the only known relation between Iraq and al Qaeda-style terror was that the invasion led to a sharp 'spike in recruitment'[11] for al Qaeda and was 'a huge setback in the "war on terror"'[12], as high officials and other specialists observed, and as had been widely predicted before by intelligence agencies and others. But in a well-managed doctrinal system, even as outlandish a proclamation as this can be produced with little fear of meaningful contradiction in the mainstream.

Pre-invasion discussion was overwhelmingly restricted to 'pragmatic grounds': would the US government get away with its plans at a cost acceptable at home. Once the attack on Iraq began, reporting it became to a large extent a shameful exercise in cheering for the home team, appalling much of the rest of the world, and many at home as well. But the effect of the panic induced by government-media propaganda persisted. Studies released in June revealed that 34 per cent of the population believed that the US had found WMD in Iraq (an additional 7 per cent were unsure), and 22 per cent believed that Iraq had used chemical or biological weapons during the war (an additional 9 per cent were unsure).

GLOBAL ELITES ARE DIVIDED

Planners expect their version of globalization to proceed on course. US intelligence predicts that it will lead to a 'widening economic divide' and 'chronic financial volatility', extending the generally poor economic record associated with adherence to 'neoliberal reforms'. Intelligence also predicts that 'deepening economic stagnation, political instability, and cultural alienation [will] foster ethnic, ideological and religious extremism, along with the violence that often accompanies it', much of it directed against the United States.[13] Military planners make similar predictions; this has been part of the motivation for militarization of space since the Clinton years.

It is well understood that the Bush administration is aggravating these problems by telling the world: if you are defenceless, we will feel free to attack you when we want, but if you have a deterrent, we will back off, because we only attack defenceless targets. Compare North Korea and Iraq. Iraq was defenceless and weak. While there was a horrible monster running it, it did not pose a threat to anyone else. North Korea, however, was not attacked because it has a deterrent. It has massed artillery aimed at Seoul, and if the United States attacks, it can wipe out a large part of South Korea, and cause substantial casualties among US forces near the border – now to be withdrawn to the south, a decision causing considerable concern in Korea because of fears of what it implies.

So the US is telling the countries of the world that they had better develop a terrorist network or weapons of mass destruction or some other credible deterrent. The CIA and other intelligence agencies, along with many prominent specialists in international affairs and terrorism, have warned that the new US doctrine of 'preventive war' carries serious risks, and some have warned specifically of the likely stimulus to terrorism and the proliferation of weapons of mass destruction.[14]

This is surely a large part of the reason why the invasion of Iraq was strongly opposed in the main centres of corporate capitalism. At the World Economic Forum in Davos, in January 2003, opposition was so strong that Powell was practically shouted down when he tried to present a case for the war. With the last remnants of a functioning system of world order being torn to shreds, the Bush administration is telling the world that nothing matters but force – but economic and foreign policy elites are concerned that others are not likely to tolerate that for long. They fear that the Bush administration's militarism may prove very costly to their own interests, or even to their survival.

US military planners realize the dangers very well. This forms a good part of their rationale for increasing military spending, and for the militarization of space that the entire rest of the world has been trying to block – without much hope as long as the matter is kept from the sight of Americans, who have the prime responsibility to stop it. And can stop it, if they know about it. That is perhaps why some major events that occurred in October 2002 were not even reported, among them US refusal, alone with Israel, to support UN resolutions reaffirming the 1925 Geneva Protocol banning biological weapons and strengthening the 1967 Outer Space Treaty, which prohibits the use of space for military purposes, including offensive weapons that may well bring biology's experiment with human intelligence to an inglorious end.

THE STRENGTH OF WORLD-WIDE OPPOSITION WAS UNPRECEDENTED

Opposition to the invasion throughout the world was enormous and unprecedented, much of it motivated not just by the attack itself but by the overarching strategy for which it was a test case, establishing the 'new norm'. Pre-war polls indicate less opposition in the US than elsewhere (wartime and post-war polls have completely different significance), but that is misleading. It is necessary to take into account the panic factor, unique to the US. When that is extracted, US opposition was probably not much different from the global norm, which was overwhelming.

Comparisons are often drawn to Vietnam, in revealing ways. Article after article asks 'where are the Vietnam-era protestors?' The comparison reveals that the remarkably low level of elite opposition to the Vietnam war at the time still persists, so much so that the facts are not even recognized. In fact, for several years there was very little protest in any circles. The US attacked South Vietnam in 1962, when the Kennedy administration announced that the US air force was bombing South Vietnam, and also initiated use of napalm, chemical warfare to destroy food supplies and ground cover for the indigenous resistance, and programs that drove millions of people into what amounted to concentration camps. That is what we call the war crime of aggression when carried out by enemies. Protest was virtually non-existent.

It did not begin on any substantial scale until several years later. By then South Vietnam had been devastated, hundreds of thousands of US troops were on the ground, and Washington had extended the war to the rest of Indochina. As late as 1965, in liberal Boston, years after the aggression began, peaceful demonstrations were broken up by force with the support of the liberal press and radio which denounced people who dared to protest against an American war. In 1966 even meetings in churches were attacked by counter-demonstrators.

The reaction to the invasion of Iraq was dramatically different. There were enormous protests well before the attack began, and again on the day it was launched – with no counter-demonstrators. That is a radical difference. And had it not been for the spectacular government-media propaganda campaign that frightened much of the population, there would have been be much more opposition.

We should not underestimate the significance of this change in public attitudes. Protest against the wars in Indochina was slow in developing, but once it began, as part of much more wide-ranging activism, it had substantial effects. By 1968, the Joint Chiefs of Staff were unwilling to send more troops to Vietnam because they feared they would need them for control of the population in the United States. The Reagan administration at first adopted the Kennedy model for the 'war on terror' it declared in Central America, but drew back as a result of unanticipated popular protest, and turned instead to 'clandestine terror' – meaning that the American population is kept in the dark, though everyone else knows. A leaked document of the first Bush Administration in 1989 described how the U.S. would have to fight wars in the future. It said that in conflicts with 'much weaker enemies' – the only kind it is sensible to fight – US military forces must 'defeat them decisively and rapidly' or popular support will erode. It is no longer like the 1960s, when a war could be fought for years with no opposition at all. The government knows that it cannot carry out long-term aggression and destruction as in Vietnam because the population will not tolerate it. The doctrinal system has invented a 'Vietnam syndrome', based on fear of casualties, but that is just a device to conceal the real reasons, which are doctrinally unacceptable: far less public tolerance for aggression and violence.

The anti-war movement's agenda now should be to work to ensure that Iraq is run by Iraqis who are genuinely representative and independent, and that the US and Britain provide massive reparations for what they have done to Iraq for 20 years (by supporting Saddam Hussein, by two wars, and by brutal sanctions which probably caused a great deal more damage and deaths than the wars); and if that is too much to expect, then at least massive aid, to be used by Iraqis, as they decide, aid which will be something other than US taxpayer subsidies to Halliburton and Bechtel. Also high on the agenda must be ending the extremely dangerous policies announced in the National Security Strategy, and carried out in the 'petri dish'. And related to that, there should be serious efforts to block the bonanza of arms sales that is happily anticipated as a consequence of the war, which will also contribute to making the world a more awful and dangerous place. But that's only the beginning. The anti-war movement is indissolubly linked to the global justice movements, which, properly, have much more far-reaching goals.

NOTES

1   Reported in the *Guardian*, May 2, 2003.
2   Thomas Carothers, 'The Reagan Years', in Abraham Lowenthal, ed., *Exporting Democracy*, Baltimore: Johns Hopkins University Press, 1991, and *In the Name of Democracy*, Berkeley: University of California Press, 1991): referring to the 'backyard' in Central America and the Caribbean, which teaches the richest lessons over a century.
3   *New York Times*, April 11, 1991.
4   Thomas Friedman, *New York Times*, June 4, 1991.
5   For some recent comment, see van Sponeck, 'Too Much Collateral Damage', Toronto *Globe and Mail*, July 2, 2002; Denis Halliday, 'Scylla and Charybdis', and Hans van Sponeck, 'The Policy of Punishment', *Al-Ahram Weekly*, 26 December 2002.
6   Quoted by Bob Herbert, 'Spoils of War', *New York Times*, Op-Ed, April 10, 2003.
7   In *Al-Ahram Weekly*, 3-9 April, 2003.
8   David Sanger and Steven Weisman, 'Bush's Aides Envision New Influence in Region', *New York Times*, April 10, 2003.
9   Adam Nagourney and Richard Stevenson, 'Pushing an Agenda, Far From Iraq', *New York Times*, April 5, 2003.
10 Address by President Bush in Cincinnati, October 7 2002.
11 David Johnston and Don Van Natta, 'U.S. Officials See Signs of Revived Al Qaeda in Several Nations,' *New York Times*, May 17, 2003. On the sharp rise, see also Don Van Natta and Desmond Butler, 'Anger on Iraq Seen as Al Qaeda Recruiting Tool,' *New York Times*, March 16, 2003; Scott Atran, 'Who Wants to Be a Martyr,' *New York Times* op-ed, May 5, 2003.
12 Jason Burke, 'Terror's Myriad Faces,' *Sunday Observer*, May 18, 2003.
13 National Intelligence Council, *Global Trends 2015: A Dialogue About the Future With Nongovernment Experts*, Washington, December, 2000.
14 See, among others, articles in the two leading foreign policy journals, *Foreign Affairs* and *Foreign Policy*; an unusual study by the American Academy of Arts and Sciences, *War in Iraq*; Kenneth Waltz in Ken Booth and Tim Dunne, eds., *World in Collision*, London: Palgrave, 2002; and the Hart-Rudman Commission report on terrorist threats to the United States.

HUMAN RIGHTS AS SWORDS OF EMPIRE

AMY BARTHOLOMEW AND JENNIFER BREAKSPEAR

[T]he transition from a nation-state world order to a cosmopolitan world order brings about a very significant priority shift from international law to human rights. The principle that *international law precedes human rights* which held during the (nation-state) first age of modernity is being replaced by the principle of the (world society) second age of modernity, that *human rights precede international law*. As yet, the consequences have not been thought through, but they will be revolutionary.

Ulrich Beck[1]

It is the very universalistic core of democracy and human rights itself which forbids its universal propagation by fire and sword.

Jürgen Habermas[2]

The US-led war of aggression against Iraq displays, for at least the fourth time since 1990 (the first three occasions being the Gulf War, the NATO intervention in Kosovo and the American attack on Afghanistan), the 'revolutionary' nature of the developments afoot in the transition from the 'first' to the 'second age of modernity'. Yet any transition that may be underway is neither an historical necessity nor a clean break with the past. Rather, it is shaping up to be a contradictory and contested set of processes, since the politics of the 'first age of modernity' are intertwined with those emerging in its 'second age'. In emphasizing that cosmopolitanism has brought with it the 'military humanism of the West', Beck saw it as 'founded on an uninterrogated world monopoly of power and morality'. But in making this argument he seemed to run together three distinct stances toward the relationship between international law and human rights: noninterventionism, cosmopolitanism, and what can only be called imperialism (however 'benign') – i.e. a situation where a self-appointed hegemonic power 'defends' human rights abroad by engaging in 'military humanism'.

We wish to suggest that justifications for the most recent Gulf war fall predominantly into the third category, resting on a predatory *rhetorical* commitment to a cosmopolitan conception of human rights that is, in fact, wielded in the service of an imperialist project, rather than what Jürgen Habermas calls an 'egalitarian universalism'.[3] The dangers people face under these conditions are, of course, 'asymmetrical' – *who* faces *what* dangers is deeply important. Yet reliance on a cosmopolitan conception of human rights as ideological cover for imperialist world politics also poses universalistic risks, undermining not only the norm of nonintervention so central to the international legal architecture of the 'first age of modernity', but also the nascent development of cosmopolitan conceptions of law and human rights of the 'second age'.

It is remarkable in this respect that it is not just the neo-conservative hawks in the Bush administration and right-wing think tanks who justified this war against Iraq partly with reference to liberty, democracy and human rights for all, but also liberals like Jean Bethke Elstain, Christopher Hitchens and Paul Berman among many others.[4] These 'liberal hawks' have argued that 'pre-emptive' war and 'regime change' are legitimate insofar as the war is aimed at countering real threats to human life and liberty, and that even forceful, unilaterally pursued 'regime change' may be a duty for those who enjoy freedom. But they have also seen this cosmopolitan aim as a duty falling pre-eminently on the United States.

This essay asks how is it that liberals justify military humanism in the name of protecting freedom, human rights and democracy, even when it is pursued unilaterally by a self-appointed imperialist power. We will focus on the justifications put forward by Michael Ignatieff, the Director of the Carr Center for Human Rights Policy at Harvard University, whose prominent writings in the *New York Times Magazine* in the run-up to the war and during it exemplify the 'military humanism' that Beck diagnosed.[5] In self-consciously embracing both the 'military humanism' currently espoused by many advocates of human rights *and* American imperialist politics, Ignatieff starkly reveals the dangers that reside in *liberal nationalist* conceptions of world politics and human rights when these are articulated by a self-appointed hegemonic power. While cosmopolitan justifications of military intervention may have played a prominent role elsewhere (pre-eminently in Europe during the war on Kosovo, and perhaps more generally in human rights organizations), in the USA liberals have been wont to appeal to a cosmopolitan military humanism in support of an imperialist republican nationalism. This point is important, because the implications of the liberal hawks' justification for the American-led war on Iraq, like their neo-conservative counterparts, are deeply *inconsistent* with cosmopolitan principles in the crucial dimensions of morality, legality and politics; because they threaten to erode multilateral institutions like the UN, and to legitimize 'regime change' and 'pre-emptive war' by an imperial power. We will argue that *even if* the US could accurately be viewed as a republican Empire morally motivated to spread democracy and human rights abroad *it could not do so morally, without undermining the development of international law in a cosmopolitan direction, and without further entrenching imperialism*, which stands as one of the greatest impediments to human rights and democracy today.

Our analysis is premised on a 'critical cosmopolitanism' that we think is required to underpin any genuinely universal respect for, and protection of, human rights and popular sovereignty. But this position is deeply suspect in the eyes of many on the Marxist Left, as seen for example in the recent writings of Tariq Ali, Perry Anderson and Peter Gowan. We endorse their criticisms of 'military humanism' undertaken by imperialist powers but in the second part of this essay we shall suggest that to develop anti-imperialist, pro-human rights and democratic politics today requires us not to dismiss international law and institutions. And in order to develop a critical cosmopolitanism of this kind we also need to avoid the 'instrumentalism' that is evident in Left critiques of the UN and of human rights. Rather, human rights and transnational institutions like the UN can be crucial arenas of struggle – as Marxists used to say – made more, not less, pertinent by the emergence of an imperialist power bent on self-legitimation and unilateral assertion in every instance that suits it.

INTERROGATING IGNATIEFF'S 'I DON'T KNOW'

The United Nations lay dozing like a dog before the fire, happy to ignore Saddam, until an American president seized it by the scruff of the neck and made it bark. Multilateral solutions to the world's problems are all very well, but they have no teeth unless America bares its fangs .... The 21st century imperium is a new invention in the annals of political science, an empire lite, a global hegemony whose grace notes are free markets, human rights and democracy, enforced by the most awesome military power the world has ever known.[6]

Who wants to live in a world where there are no stable rules for the use of force by states? Not me. Who wants to live in a world ruled by the military power of the strong? Not me. How will we oblige American military hegemony to pay 'decent respect to the opinions of mankind'? *I don't know*. When the smoke of battle lifts, those who support the war will survey a battle zone that will include the ruins of the multilateral political order created in 1945 .... To support the war entails a commitment to rebuild that order on new foundations.[7]

Long seen as a principled left-liberal, Michael Ignatieff 'plumped' – a term he has borrowed from Isaiah Berlin – in favour of the attack on Iraq just prior to its commencement. Coming out in support of the war after due anguish, and against his friends (including those 'left-wingers who regard American imperialism as the root of all evil'),[8] he insisted that support for the war did not make him or anyone else an 'apologist for American imperialism', and stated what was, for him, the key principle: 'The problem is not that overthrowing Saddam by force is "morally unjustified". Who seriously believes 25 million Iraqis would not be better off if Saddam were overthrown?' The 'consequential' justification that 25 million Iraqis will be liberated clearly overrides, he argued, the 'deontological' one that 'good consequences cannot justify killing people.' This is how Ignatieff believes the moral issue should be answered – regime change undertaken, in effect unilaterally by the US and British administrations, is morally justified by the cosmopolitan aim of liberating the Iraqi people.[9] But as if recognizing that the moral justification for the war was not as straightforward as he initially asserted, he went on to argue that while it was unfortunate that the debate about Iraq became a debate about American power, rather than about the human rights of oppressed peoples, the events of September 11, 2001 had fundamentally altered the security threats to which the world must respond; and that those who failed to recognize this were blindly 'wishing they could still live in the safety and collective security of the world that existed before 9/11.'[10] Arguing against the world-wide anti-war movement and world public opinion, he suggested that while the fact that the world did not support the US-led war posed a problem, a principle is not wrong because people disagree with it (nor right because they agree).[11] Having asserted, then, the moral rightness of this war, the only remaining question, he suggested, is whether the risks are worth it; whether it is a prudent move. By implication, since he supported the war, the answer must be yes.

Much of this echoed Ignatieff's long-standing position that human rights considerations in the contemporary period have made judgments about war and the use of force complicated, as seen in his support for the military interventions in Bosnia and Kosovo, and his insistence that these interventions demanded radical rethinking along cosmopolitan lines. In repeating many times the banal phrase that Saddam Hussein 'really is awful', and in later asserting that his regime not only had 'just about the worst human rights record on Earth' but was also 'in possession of weapons of mass destruction',[12] he also posed the cosmopolitan question: by what moral authority does a brutal regime claim unfettered sovereignty? He reiterated the case for American Empire as the best hope for installing stability, nation-building, and encouraging human rights, free markets and democracy around the world. Yet from another point of view his candid admission that the war would be fought at the price of leaving the multilateral political order in ruins did seem to fly in the face of his prewar support for military humanism on the basis of multilateralism. In 2000 he had claimed unconditionally that the Security Council 'should remain the ultimate source of legitimacy for the use of military force' – although this might require 'crushing force' by 'combat capable warriors under robust rules of engagement' directed by 'a single line of command to a national government or regional alliance';[13] and as late as 2002 he had argued that the US must respect international legal norms with regard to any military actions and 'should accept international accountability for its actions'.[14] But Ignatieff's 'muscular' conception of human rights[15] seemed to prepare the way for his unequivocal support for the war and his insistence that

Iraq's continuing violations of UN Security Council resolutions meant that the whole international community should 'walk the walk' with the American Empire.[16]

Ignatieff admitted well before the war that the idea of an Empire's burden, American imperial power at work under what he views as the 'official moral ideology of Empire – i.e. human rights', was far removed from that which had been sought by liberal cosmopolitan human rights activists and lawyers 'who had hoped to see American power integrated into a transnational legal and economic order organized around the UN .... [Rather] a new international order is emerging, but it is being crafted to suit American imperial objectives.'[17] He also recognized that while Europe was more inclined toward a multilateral order that might hope to limit American power, 'the Empire will not be tied down like Gulliver by a thousand legal strings'.[18] And yet he 'plumped' in favour of American Empire, showing, with each new article, greater confidence in the American imperial project, since it is, as Ignatieff put it, quoting Melville, an Empire that views itself as bearing 'the ark of the liberties of the world'.[19]

This admittedly 'imperial project' will require bringing actual stability to the 'frontier zones' – and this must be done, Ignatieff insists, 'without denying local peoples their rights to *some degree* of self-determination'.[20] Thus Ignatieff's realist acknowledgement that 'empire lite' is still empire (i.e., that 'the real power in these [frontier] zones ... will remain in Washington' and will involve protecting 'vital American interests') is married to his insistence that achieving human rights rests on republican duty which itself requires the Empire as midwife: 'The case for empire is that it has become, in a place like Iraq, the last hope for democracy and stability alike.'[21]

How should we evaluate this position? On the one hand, Ignatieff recognizes the realpolitik of the situation – the horrors visited on the Iraqi people under Saddam Hussein, the fumbling, the weaknesses and the complicity of the UN system, the enormous power that the US wields, *and* the fact that the American invasion would be oriented to American interests. On the other hand, he has shown a stunning disregard for the lack of evidence, even before the war, of weapons of mass destruction or of any link between the Iraqi regime and Al Qaeda before he 'plumped' for war. He did not discuss, so far as we can find, the human rights issues implicit in civilian casualties. Nor did he address issues having to do with environmental contamination and the other ruthless 'side' effects that war was sure to produce. Surely a liberal human rights scholar favouring the war should have addressed these issues. The most that can be said is that he relied on his emerging philosophical position that we must act on the 'lesser evil'.[22] But even here, he did not soberly address questions crucial to calibrating this equation, nor the requirement of 'proportionality' in the use of force in 'just war' theory, nor the enormous normative problems posed by asymmetric warfare (by which we mean the responsibility that must attend the power to produce 'shock and awe' or, as Ignatieff puts it, using 'crushing force' against an 'enemy' with far inferior military might).

Even months after the officially declared end of war, no weapons of mass destruction and no links with Al Qaeda have emerged. But insecurity and instability in the world have surely been increased, as clear-headed commentators across the political spectrum acknowledge, not just by increased hatred for Western (and particularly American) power and arrogance, but also by cluster bombs left over for Iraqi children to find, the pollution of Iraqi towns and drinking water, ongoing guerrilla warfare, and so on. Add to this that civilian casualties produced during the 'official' war have been estimated by a British and US group of independent experts to range between five and ten thousand, while the US Defence Department spokesperson says the Pentagon has not looked into the question of civilian deaths because it was focused on 'defeating enemy forces rather than aiming at civilians.'[23] And now, Paul Wolfowitz admits that the WMD justification for war was 'settled on' by the American administration 'for bureaucratic reasons', while Donald Rumsfeld concedes that WMD may never be found.[24] Finally, in a remarkable breach of his usual diplomatic demeanour, Hans Blix has admitted that the 'bastards' in the US administration viewed the UN as an 'alien power'[25] and 'leaned on' the weapons inspectors to produce more damning reports while initiating a smear campaign against him.[26]

But beyond all of this, which hardly needs rehearsal for any critical observer of the war and its aftermath, we need to consider the implications of the liberal hawks' justification for war in terms of the categories of morality and legality. What are we to make of a liberal intellectual of Ignatieff's stature recommending bypassing and potentially undermining fundamental norms of international law and resting his support so squarely on the moral case for war waged by a 'moral' republican Empire? Even if we were to assume that the US actions were genuinely motivated by and aimed at achieving the liberation of the Iraqi people from oppression, the purported moral argument for unilateral intervention fails on two crucial counts.

First, as Ignatieff recognizes, imperialism threatens republicanism. As an imperial power takes on the role of GloboCop, emphasizing military, police and secret spying power, the more does it risk, as Habermas points out, 'endangering its own mission of improving the world according to liberal ideas.'[27] This is obvious from such facts as the illegal detention of 'enemy combatants' at Guantanamo Bay (and the US Supreme Court's refusal to consider its unconstitutionality), the detention of 'illegal aliens', the ill-treatment of US citizens suspected of ties to terrorist groups, and the treatment of prisoners in Afghanistan and outside Baghdad Airport. Second, as Ignatieff acknowledges, following Thomas Jefferson and the Declaration of Independence, morality requires that we pay 'decent respect to the opinions of mankind'. Ignatieff's moral argument – who can believe that 25 million Iraqis would not be better off without Saddam Hussein? – implies a universal right to be free from oppression, and some version of this may indeed be defensible as a universal moral principle.[28] But the problem is not just that imperialism violates it, which it does by undercutting the republic's commitment to the rule of law both at home and abroad, but also that the basic moral principle and the universalistic core of human rights should not be 'confused', as it is here, with the 'imperial demand that the political life-form and culture of a *particular* democracy …is to be exemplary for all other societies'.[29] Again, while Ignatieff is careful to call for an avoidance of the 'narcissism' of earlier empires – i.e. the delusion of earlier empires that their colonized aspired only to be 'versions of themselves'[30] – his support for *this* war under *these* unilateralist conditions cannot avoid 'narcissism' or, more forthrightly put, an imperialist imposition of a false universalism.[31]

Paying 'decent respect to the opinions of mankind' requires an egalitarian universalism that breaks with a liberal nationalist conception of republicanism and an imperial vehicle for its expansion. This is so for many reasons, but the core moral reason is that no 'republican' imperialism – even that of the American 'republic' – can break from its provincial, particular perspective. An egalitarian universalism, on the other hand, as Habermas says, 'insists on the de-centering of each specific perspective; it requires the relativization of one's own interpretive perspective from the point of view of the autonomous Other.'[32] It is only in this way that even a 'good hegemon' could know whether the actions it justifies as in the best interest of others is in fact equally 'good for all'.

We may summarize the moral problem as follows: The problem is that one party, even a 'good hegemon', cannot *morally* assume a moral duty unilaterally. 'Plumping' for war without taking into account the voices of all those others who also have interests at stake is immoral. Assuming a moral duty *morally* requires that those affected are genuinely involved in shaping the contours of the response to oppression, mutually and reciprocally. To do so would require, at a minimum, global political public spheres aimed at formulating a response that takes into account everyone's point of view. Second, and consequently, even a 'good hegemon' bases its justification (as Ignatieff admits) on the ethnocentric ground of liberal nationalism – aimed at securing US safety, possibly at the expense of others and, very importantly, spreading the US's *particular* interpretation of human rights and democracy abroad. This is why unilateralism is morally unacceptable. This is also why, as Habermas says, the 'multilateral formulation of a common purpose is not one option amongst others – especially not in international relations.'[33]

This suggests why Ignatieff's 'liberal hawk' position in support of unilateralism poses a moral danger. But it also poses grave dangers to international law and the future of human rights. Ignatieff implied that the war might be legal when he suggested that Iraq's continuing violations of Security Council resolutions might legitimate war. This runs contrary to the views of the great preponderance of respected legal scholars, including the International Commission of Jurists which has condemned the invasion of Iraq as an illegal war of aggression, finding there is no 'plausible legal basis for this attack.'[34] The most recent war on Iraq has illustrated, once again, the ease with which an illegal war can be waged while threatening the legal norms by which nations previously agreed to abide. This poses significant dangers for international law, both in its noninterventionist orientation, characteristic of the 'first age of modernity', and in its development toward a cosmopolitan order in the 'second age'.

In supporting this war Ignatieff also seemed to suggest that the international legal norms of nonintervention and national sovereignty of the post-World War II era, the 'first age of modernity', have run their course, when he acknowledged that the war would be waged on the 'ruins of the multilateral political order'.[35] This is a dangerous derogation from the nonintervention principle because it violates the rule that the legitimate authority to decide whether Iraq was in violation of agreements to such an extent that intervention was warranted is the Security Council, not the hegemonic power. Dispensing with the legitimating authority of the UN, Ignatieff seems to see no reasonable alternative to the sovereign power of an imperial hegemon pursuing, as he admits, liberal nationalism, self-interest and an American conception of human rights. Such a shift not only violates the principle of nonintervention, but also endorses the Bush Doctrine of the right to wage 'pre-emptive war' against any entity the US deems hostile to its interests – a doctrine that threatens to undermine not just the norms of nonintervention but also the further development of norms of egalitarian universalism.

Ignatieff clearly sees the path stretched out before us but shows little concern for its perils: '[a] new international [legal] order is emerging, but it is being crafted to suit American imperial objectives. The empire signs on to those pieces of the transnational legal order that suit its purposes ... while ignoring or even sabotaging those parts ... that do not.'[36] He claims he is neither apologizing nor rationalising but rather stating the reality of international law in an age of empire. The American Empire is not to be constrained by multilateral concerns. International institutions that can be controlled and commandeered are to be retained, those that would require an egalitarian framework and fail to guarantee American dominance are to be discarded. Ignatieff offers essentially no juridical foundations for military humanism but merely approves as obvious the burden America is said to carry – a duty to breach bothersome legal trivialities in defence of human rights and freedoms. 'Americans are multilateral when it is to the advantage of the United States, unilateral when they can get away with it. It is a vision in which world order is guaranteed by the power and might and influence of the superpower, as opposed to the spreading influence of international law.'[37] This serves as an apt description of American foreign policy, but if Ignatieff is critical of this vision the reader may be forgiven for failing to notice.

International law failed in the lead-up to the invasion of Iraq. It failed the American imperial leadership that attempted to use international legal norms to frame their intent in legally justifiable rationales. It failed the leaders of France, Germany and Russia who played by the old rules while others rewrote the rulebook. It failed the people of Iraq who were powerless to face aggressors from within and without. And it failed the international rallying cry of concerned world citizens that defiantly and peacefully marched in numbers never before seen in opposition to an unjust war. All this because the international legal norms of the 'first age of modernity' were unable to constrain an imperial power determined and strong enough, in Habermas's words, to 'break the civilizing bounds which the Charter of the United Nations placed with good reason upon the process of goal-realization.'[38]

Habermas maintains that the neo-conservatives associated with the Bush Doctrine confront international law 'with a quite revolutionary perspective [asserting that] ... when international law fails then the politically successful hegemonic enforcement of a liberal world order is morally justifiable ...' even when it is formally illegal.[39] What is remarkable, as we have emphasized, is that this is at least as characteristic of liberal hawks like Ignatieff as it is of the American neo-conservatives. Still, this seems perplexing. For why would one committed to human rights and democracy, as Ignatieff surely is, but as Bush and Co. clearly are not, recognize yet fail to undertake a consideration of the 'revolutionary consequences' attendant to this war aimed at pre-emption and 'regime change' and threatening the sole, however flawed, international institution available today to deal with such challenges? With the ratification of the UN Charter after World War II, states formally agreed to 'give up their sovereign right to go to war'.[40] Since this war is premised on re-establishing that right perhaps it would be better to call this a 'restoration' rather than a 'revolution'. The liberal hawks, not unlike the neo-conservatives, have thus supported a war that is not only unjust and illegal but one that threatens to imbricate regressive norms in international law. Michael Glenndon has stated, regarding the Kosovo intervention by NATO, that if 'power is used to do justice, law will follow.'[41] But this logic works equally in reverse: if power is used to do injustice, unjust law will follow.

And need we even say that this was not likely a 'one off' war? Plenty of commentators have made it clear that it is the *first* in a series of such wars – as Ignatieff implies when he claims that '[i]mperial ruthlessness requires optimism as a continued act of will.'[42] The empire must remain vigilant against all that would stand in the way of its advance. Imperial ruthlessness, however, seems also to require an elusive villain (Osama Bin Laden, Saddam Hussein, take your pick) that can be stalked across borders. A well-oiled public relations machine, replete with politicians to add accountability, embedded journalists to add 'integrity' and public intellectuals to add weight, lays the groundwork for war without end.

We do not mean to suggest that Security Council approval for multilateral military force would have wholly addressed the lack of legitimacy of the ensuing intervention. We recognize the undemocratic, not to mention the undeliberative, nature of the Security Council and see that the bullying and bribery of the Bush administration further undermined any possibility of achieving a legitimate decision taken by equals. But in 'plumping' for unilateral war, Ignatieff was also plumping *for* future forms of unilateralism, and plumping *against* multilateralism under international law and international institutions, pre-eminently the UN. A hegemonic unilateralism is primed to step into the void between the discarded norms of the 'first age of modernity' and the (still to be conceived) cosmopolitan norms and institutions of the 'second age'. The key question is whether an international law justification for war should be replaced with 'empire's law', provided by the 'unilateral global politics of a self-empowering hegemon'.[43] We think the answer is clear: it should not. As Eric Hobsbawm notes: 'few things are more dangerous than empires pushing their own interest in the belief that they are doing humanity a favour.'[44]

THE CASE FOR CRITICAL COSMOPOLITANISM

Habermas, then, is right – there is no acceptable alternative to the further development of a cosmopolitan legal order where all voices receive equal and reciprocal recognition.[45] He is also right that the countries of the 'Old Europe' and others that held out against overwhelming American pressure before the war did not – as so many American commentators contended – undermine the UN or relegate it to insignificance.[46] On the contrary, it is that sort of resistance that may save the international legal architecture. Of course, resisting American domination, and saving and then transforming international institutions like the UN, will be no mean feat under conditions of American imperialism. The Security Council's unanimous capitulation to the US in the 'reconstruction' era reveals this all too starkly.[47]

There are obviously no clear or easy answers to offer to the question of how to resist American domination, how to maintain international institutions and how to resist the perversion of nascent cosmopolitan norms and transnational institutions capable of fulfilling them. Can Europe help offset a determined American imperialism? Can the emerging global public sphere as witnessed, for example, in the World Social Forum and the massive anti-war movement, do so? *We don't know.* Clearly these are all sites for anti-imperialist struggle. But we also believe that we need to develop a critical cosmopolitanism as well, and this requires that we confront a crucial question: How can we even think, let alone enact, cosmopolitan commitments and institutions under imperialist conditions? To put it in Habermasian terms, how can we mediate in a democratic and progressive way between 'facts and norms' – between the facts of imperial power and the normative demand for a cosmopolitan system of governance, including a commitment to human rights, that may allow the development of an egalitarian, rather than an imperialist, universalism?

One thing is clear. This cannot be achieved through positions like Ignatieff's or the complicity of intellectuals and officials in Europe and elsewhere who, after resisting the war, have turned their minds to 'transatlantic relations' after the war and have begun to speak in terms of attempting to influence the US from a position within the empire. Rather, we must undertake at least a preliminary defence of the sort of critical cosmopolitan orientation that we believe should be developed in the face of the pointed criticisms that cosmopolitanism and international legal institutions have received from some of the strongest voices on the Left. Cosmopolitanism is, of course, very contested territory – internally as well as externally – and we do not claim to speak for most versions of it. We view the project of developing a *critical* cosmopolitanism as a significant departure from other versions, particularly that which Peter Gowan has termed the 'new liberal cosmopolitanism', let alone analyses like Ignatieff's.[48] Rather than enter into a discussion of the protracted debates over cosmopolitanism, we wish to focus on these critics' treatment of the UN, the international legal norm of nonintervention, and human rights.

Tariq Ali is one of the main authors who raises questions about the sorts of institutions, pre-eminently the UN, that cosmopolitans tend to believe should not be razed but rather reformed. Ali views the UN as the 'United Nations of America', a 'disposable instrument' of American power and policy.[49] Citing with stinging, if over-generalized, accuracy the delivery of the UN in the post-Cold War period into 'American hands', he suggests that appealing to the UN to constrain the US is 'like expecting the butler to sack the master'. Recognizing the deep division between the US and many of its usual allies over the latest war on Iraq, Ali still sees no reason to appeal to the UN. He argues that any anti-imperialist project must look elsewhere – to struggles within the Middle East itself, to resistance in Iraq and in the heart of American Empire, and to global anti-imperialist struggle – citing the World Social Forum as one space for developing campaigns, for example, to close down American military bases.[50] Since the war, Ali argues, the UN Security Council has recognized the occupation of Iraq, approved its 're-colonization' by the US, and 'provided retrospective sanction to a pre-emptive strike'. We agree with this final point. But we are dismayed at the implication of his argument that at least the League of Nations 'had the decency to collapse after its charter was serially raped'.[51]

Perry Anderson presents a similar analysis. He argues that opponents of the war require principles for opposition to the war, not just prudential reasons, but he suggests that the standard principled reasons offered for valuing the UN and international law will not do since they treat these as if they were 'a salve against the Bush Administration'. Anderson argues that this is ineffective, that we require an alternative position that, among other things, recognizes that the UN is not impartial (thereby echoing Ali's line that it is a mere 'butler'), that its structure is 'politically indefensible' and that, since the end of the Cold War at least, it has functioned primarily as 'a screen for American will',[52] 'as much an arm of the State Department as the IMF is of the Treasury'.[53] Anderson does recognize that some elements of the UN – its 'secondary affiliates' – 'do good work', while the General Assembly 'does little harm'. Still, he argues that the Security Council bears no prospect of reform and suggests that 'the world would be better off – a more honest and equal arena of states – without it.'[54] Finally, and very importantly, he suggests that human rights are the 'jemmy in the door of national sovereignty'.[55]

Much of this is echoed by Peter Gowan, but he goes further to critically assess cosmopolitan justifications for interventionism as well. Gowan characterizes the global governance institutions as 'lightly disguised instruments of US policy' and cites the UN as 'striking' in this regard.[56] He also provides a compelling critique of the 'new liberal cosmopolitans' who refuse to attend to US global dominance, and who applaud the US as the party in the 'international community' with the capacity to pursue global justice, insisting that it has shed its 'egoistic national interest'.[57] He criticizes them for supporting military intervention in the interest of human rights as a step toward the realization of liberal principles over power. On balance, Gowan argues that the humanitarian interventions that have so inspired the liberal cosmopolitans, and have in turn been inspired by their arguments for cosmopolitan justice, provide instead 'a model of power-projection that virtually inverts this description'. And he correctly observes that the new liberal cosmopolitanism is fixed within a 'liberal-individualist corset [that] does not fit the world as it is: it fails to strap American power into its prognosis of a supra-state order.'[58] Finally, Gowan argues that with humanitarian interventions, as well as other forms of globalization, we are witnessing an 'asymmetrical pattern of change in the field of state sovereignty' with the erosion of most states' sovereignty in favour of 'exceptional prerogatives' for the US.[59]

We agree with much of this analysis, starting with the recognition that the UN Security Council is no impartial arbiter. As we have also argued, it functions in a context of American hegemony and imperialism that has enormous consequences for its ability to function independently. We also agree with the critique of the 'new liberal cosmopolitans' who fail to distinguish between an imperialist and an egalitarian universalism. But we want to raise three questions. What about the norms of international law and nonintervention? What about human rights? And why not consider developing norms of cosmopolitan law and justice viewed as part of a long-term anti-imperialist struggle against American power and domination and in favour of addressing the problems of the UN, multilateralism and human rights, rather than either relegating them to the 'dustbin of history' or side-stepping them, as these analyses appear to do?

The norm of nonintervention, so central to the international juridical architecture of the 'first age of modernity', receives conflicting treatments in these analyses. On the one hand, Anderson and Ali agree that this is the pre-eminent norm to be adhered to in the hopes of resisting the asymmetrical and imperial sovereignty associated with the military missions justified by cosmopolitan conceptions of human rights.[60] On the other hand, they also argue that given the instrumental character of the Security Council, in particular, and perhaps of the UN in general, we would be better off without it. But to endorse its collapse in the name of being 'more honest' is a serious mistake. The problem with it is revealed by Alan Dershowitz's cynical use of this kind of argument to support the creation of 'judicial torture warrants' in the US. His reasoning is not that we should encourage torture but rather, if states are going to engage in it, which being a realist he recognizes states will, it should be done 'honestly' and openly. Anderson and Ali are no doubt disgusted by this, but their notion that without the Security Council international politics might offer a more 'equal arena of states' clearly threatens to slip us into a Hobbesian war of all against all, sending us back prior to the 'first age of modernity'. The collapse of the Security Council would mean the collapse of the only institution that is formally oriented to enforcing the rules of the UN Charter, which pre-eminently embodies, to date, the norm of nonintervention and the principle of equal state sovereignty.

When Tony Blair's policy advisor, Robert Cooper, and Michael Ignatieff agree that we must accept a new imperialism based on unilateralism, in which hegemonic states are now free to ignore international law, deciding upon the need for military force and wielding it in the name of security, nation-building and human rights outside the UN system when it suits their purposes;[61] and when this appears to reiterate the major themes in the US's National Security Strategy;[62] then it is time, we suggest, to reconsider the Left critique of cosmopolitanism. Its disregard for the institutional embodiment of the international law of the 'first age of modernity' effectively condones erasing the legal limits against intervention. Not only is this unwise in the extreme, but it also contradicts these critics' commitment to nonintervention.

Nonintervention is advanced by these authors as an antidote to the imperialist manipulation of human rights; they want to stave off the assault on the sovereign equality of states that they see being perpetrated by those who make the case for military intervention in the name of human rights. So, for Anderson, the war on terrorism is seen as merely a 'temporary bypass on the royal road leading to "human rights and liberty" around the world'. The latter provide the 'permanent possible ideals that a hegemony requires'. Human rights are not, then, *just* a 'jemmy in the door of national sovereignty', but also an ideology that masks force, providing a basis for consent to and direction of an imperialist project. Thus does Anderson condemn human rights, under these conditions, as part of the 'arrogance of the "international community"'.[63] We agree that dangers come with abandoning the principle of nonintervention in the name of human rights. We agree that human rights can be mobilized ideologically as part of a hegemonic project. But the position adopted by Anderson and Ali goes so far as to threaten the very core of human rights themselves.[64]

It is crucial to maintain the norm of nonintervention, that seeks to protect not just peace, but also the equal sovereignty of nation-states, while also acknowledging the protection of human rights as another key norm emerging in the 'second age of modernity'. A critical cosmopolitanism should develop a position that links a commitment to nonintervention to a commitment to human rights and makes an exception to the nonintervention principle to the extent that systematic human rights abusers would forfeit the right to sovereign equality. Of course, we agree that sovereign equality is violated by empowering a hegemonic state to intervene. This lies at the heart of our critique of the 'liberal hawks'. But, if the judgment were made under procedurally just, multilateral conditions aiming at egalitarian universalism, the 'expansion of international justice' would not abolish international law. Those who think it would are making the mistake of rejecting the principle of egalitarian universalism, and equating international law with a faulty conception, *a merely formal conception*, of sovereign equality. In other words, respect for equal sovereignty should not be extended to states that are judged, by fair processes, to be massive human rights abusers. For that merely formal conception of sovereign equality, while having the virtue of avoiding the real problems of 'apparently' cosmopolitan politics ('military humanism' underwritten by and in the interest of imperial power chief among them), would ride roughshod not only over human rights but also over *popular sovereignty*. It would mean that any state, simply by virtue of being a state, deserves equal recognition. This is a position that must be rejected by a democratic Left. Furthermore, it violates the principle of the 'self-determination of peoples'. And, ultimately, a merely formal view of equal sovereignty would violate the normative meaning of international law, which refers back to the 'law of the people'.

As against the Left critics of cosmopolitanism, then, we would go this far with the cosmopolitans: the nonintervention principle cannot be upheld as unassail-able. But we reject the position of the 'liberal hawks' who really rely on a republican imperialism, and also that of the 'new liberal cosmopolitans' who, ulti-mately, would do the same. And we also want to resist, therefore, the sort of cosmopolitan position that suggests that humanitarian intervention should not be the prerogative of the UN since it is unreliable – or stated more directly, that it is a 'prerogative of the West'.[65] We reject this, as should be clear by now, because the determination to follow a moral principle cannot be made morally by a single set of interests, because it not only breaches international law but threatens to develop regressive new principles in international law, and because it fuels impe-rialism. It is not moral or legal. It is, rather, an imperialist universalism.

Cosmopolitans are regularly accused of being either dangerously utopian or militaristic. We have agreed that some analyses that travel under the banner of, or close to, cosmopolitanism are dangerous and we agree that many are utopian. But this is not a characteristic of cosmopolitans alone. While we, too, are deeply troubled by the descriptions of the necessity for 'combat capable warriors' and 'lethality' in the name of human rights (descriptions that call up images of Arnold Schwarzenegger far more than Lady Liberty), and while we share the Left critics' position that military humanism as it is now practised expands rather than constrains imperialism (always one of the chief enemies of human rights), do the critics really think that international judgments should not be made, and that multilateral forces should never be deployed, say, in Rwanda or in the Congo today? Is it clear headed anti-utopianism and anti-militarism, or is it just negli-gence to avoid discussing what to do about situations in which literally millions are dying? It is not enough to stand back and criticize the West's, and particu-larly the USA's, complicity and responsibility for fuelling these wars. Civil wars and ethnic violence are also major enemies of human rights today and, as Daniele Archibugi says, asserting sovereignty and noninterference alone 'does nothing to protect the victims of violence inside states.'[66] Human rights-based intervention must be considered a legitimate, and pressing, topic for the Left where it might aim at preventing massive human rights abuses on the scale of genocide and prepare the way for a future in which more peaceful and deliberative problem solving procedures are possible.[67]

But a critical cosmopolitanism would, of course, engage other alternatives as well – ones that are aimed at *avoiding* military intervention, including the devel-opment of international policing, international tribunals and the like and, as with intervention, the aim behind these would be an egalitarian universalism rather than an imperialist project of extending 'Western justice'. To even imagine these, however, requires a different orientation on the part of the Left than that discussed above.

All of this makes crucial the final question we have posed regarding the possibility of pursuing the development of cosmopolitan norms and institutions as part of an anti-imperialist strategy, in part by addressing the problems of the UN, multilateralism and human rights instead of rejecting them. We have no intention of falling into a naive utopianism by failing to take power into account. We fully recognize the importance of the distinction Peter Gowan makes between two types of cosmopolitanism, the 'new liberal cosmopolitanism' (of which he is rightly unremittingly critical) and 'democratic cosmopolitanism' (as found in Daniele Archibugi's work) which has the virtue of attempting to envisage a 'global polity' that would be capable of bringing under global majority control the 'rich minority of states and social groups'. And we also recognize, with Gowan, that even 'democratic cosmopolitan' positions will always suffer from crucial weaknesses if they limit their attention to the institutions of politics, and principles for their reform, without attending to the 'Herculean popular agency' that would be necessary in order to realize even these goals. Gowan is right: any attempt to constitute cosmopolitan solidarity would have to 'confront the social and economic relations of actually existing capitalism', particularly when a 'complacent cosmopolitanism' fails to grapple with the real, imperialist project of which US hegemony is a core part.[68]

This is where a critical cosmopolitanism should begin. But to address the problem of agency means *avoiding instrumentalist conceptions of the political architecture of international governance.* Treating the UN (as a key feature of global governance) as an 'instrument' – as 'butler' to 'master' (Ali), an 'arm of the US State Department' (Anderson), or a 'lightly disguised instrument of US policy' (Gowan) – may suffice for polemical purposes, but not for political analysis. It betrays an inadequate and largely un-theorized conception of power, with international institutions treated as so captured by capitalist and military power that they function merely as brittle, compliant and 'disposable instruments'. To be sure, democratic cosmopolitan analyses often display a kind of instrumentalism as well, insofar as they treat international institutions as 'neutral instruments' that may be readily reformed this way or that, and fail to take into account the obstacles to that project that exist both within and without those institutions.[69]

We suggest that in order to avoid these instrumentalist pitfalls we should develop a *relational* cosmopolitan analysis of international organizations and the global public sphere, employing concepts that draw on the lessons learned in the earlier Marxist debates on the theory of the state to analyze the limits and possibilities of transformative struggles under conditions of the new imperialism.[70] Such theories will need to be reworked to account better for the relations of gender and race, and the changed context of globalization and imperialism – and the ways in which international institutions differ from capitalist state institutions.

But to be able to address the gap between the 'facts' of imperial power and the conditions for the generation of legitimate 'norms' we might do well to begin by developing a more nuanced analysis of international institutions, global political public spheres and cosmopolitan principles like human rights. The analysis needs to be advanced in relational terms because only in this way can we see them appropriately as 'arenas of struggle' – expressing an institutional materiality premised on the unequal balance of class forces as well as a wide array of popular and progressive movements. Such an analytical reorientation may be capable of revealing, in addition to the sedimented materiality of imperialist and state interest inside these institutions and public spheres, the fissures that may represent openings for democratic and transformative transnational political struggles. In this way we may also be able to begin to address the conditions for that 'Herculean popular agency' whose necessity Gowan properly emphasizes, while opening analyses up to confront the obstacles that both capitalist social relations and imperialism pose.

Such an analysis will need to assess the possibilities for struggles to democratize the international institutions like the UN,[71] and attend to the struggles that would be required to change national states – including the imperial state – so as to link up these struggles with an emerging global public sphere in order to bring about transformative change at the international level. This analytical reorientation may allow us, finally, to *value* international law at the same time as we criticize and struggle against its shortcomings, to *critically*, and not just rhetorically, express outrage at imperialist violations of it. The point is to *recuperate* human rights politics as part of a critical cosmopolitan project aimed explicitly against imperialism, but also in favour of strengthening the relationship between human rights and popular sovereignty. It is only in this way that we may begin to counterpoise human rights against Empire.

NOTES

1   Ulrich Beck, 'The Cosmopolitan Perspective: Sociology of the Second Age of Modernity', *British Journal of Sociology*, 51(1), p. 83.

2   Jürgen Habermas, 'What Does the Felling of the Monument Mean?', http://slash.autonomedia.org/analysis/03/05/12/1342259.shtm. This is a translation of 'Was bedeutet der Denkmalsturz?' in Frankfurter Allgemeine Zeitung, 17 April 2003, p. 33.

3   On egalitarian universalism, see Habermas, 'What Does the Felling of the Monument Mean?' Here we develop the distinction between an imperialist liberal nationalism and cosmopolitanism that Habermas has proposed and apply it to the liberal hawks' analysis. See ibid., and Habermas, 'Letter to America', *The Nation*, 16 December 2002, http://www.thenation.com/doc.mhtml?i=20021216&s=habermas.

4   See Jean Bethke Elstain, *Just War Against Terror: The Burden of American power*

in a Violent World, New York: Basic Books, 2003; Paul Berman, *Terror and Liberalism,* New York: WW Norton, 2003; and more generally, Kate Zernike, 'Liberals for War: Some of the Intellectual Left's Longtime Doves Taking on Role of Hawks', *New York Times,* 14 March 2003, and George Packer, 'The Liberal Quandary over Iraq', *The New York Times Magazine,* 8 December 2002.

5   See especially Michael Ignatieff, 'The Burden', *The New York Times Magazine,* 5 January 2003 and 'I am Iraq', *The New York Times Magazine,* 23 March 2003.

6   Ignatieff, 'The Burden', p. 24.

7   Ignatieff, 'Friends Disunited', *Guardian,* 24 March 2003, emphasis added.

8   Ignatieff, 'The Burden', p. 26.

9   Ignatieff, 'I am Iraq'.

10   Ignatieff, 'Friends Disunited'.

11   'A Debate on American Power and the Crisis in Iraq', moderated by Steve Wasserman, with: Christopher Hitchens, Michael Ignatieff, Mark Danner, and Robert Scheer. Broadcast on Radio Nation, March 19-25 2003, http://archive.webactive.com/radionation/rn20030319.html (accessed June 10, 2003).

12   See Michael Ignatieff, 'Time to Walk the Walk', *National Post,* 14 February, 2003; and the quotation of him in Zernike, 'Liberals for War'.

13   Michael Ignatieff, 'A Bungling UN Undermines Itself', *The New York Times,* 15 May 2000.

14   Michael Ignatieff, 'Human Rights, the Laws of War, and Terrorism', *Social Research,* 69(4), pp. 1145, 2002.

15   This was the term Doris Buss coined to characterize the hawks' position at a Carleton University Anti-War Roundtable on 24 March 2003.

16   Ignatieff, 'Time to Walk the Walk'.

17   Michael Ignatieff, 'Barbarians at the Gate?', *The New York Review of Books,* 49(3), 28 February 2002.

18   Ignatieff, 'The Burden', p. 50.

19   Ibid., p. 24.

20   Ibid., p. 50, emphasis added. Note as well how this analysis of 'frontier zones' echoes that of the neo-conservative Thomas Barnett of the Naval War College who emphasizes the dangers to the US of countries that are 'disconnected' from economic globalization and the need to address this 'gap'. See Thomas P.M. Barnett, 'The Pentagon's New Map: It Explains Why We're Going to War and Why We'll Keep Going to War', *Esquire,* March 2003. http://www.nwc.navy.mil/newrules/ThePentagons NewMap.htm. Also see, Jim Lobe, 'Pentagon Moving Swiftly to Become 'GloboCop' *Inter Press Service,* 11 June 2003.

21   Ignatieff, 'The Burden', p. 54.

22   Michael Ignatieff, 'Mission Possible', *The New York Review of Books,* 19 December 2002.

23   Simon Jeffrey, 'The War May have Killed 10,000 Civilians, Researchers Say', *Guardian,* 13 June 2003.

24   David Usborne, 'WMD Just a Convenient Excuse for War, Admits Wolfowitz', *Independent*, 30 May 2003. Also see Paul Krugman who suggested in the New York Times that if the claim that Saddam 'posed an immanent threat …was fraudulent, the selling of the war is arguably the worst scandal in American political history…'. 'Standard Operating Procedure', *New York Times*, 3 June 2003. The only surprising thing about Senator Robert Byrd's argument that '[w]e were treated to a heavy dose of over-statement concerning Saddam Hussein's direct threat to our freedoms' is how few in Congress seem to have been scandalized. 'The Truth Will Emerge', http://byrd.senate.gov/byrd_speeches/byrd_speeches_2003may/2.html.

25   John O'Farrell, 'Hans off the UN', *Guardian*, Friday June 13, 2003.

26   Helena Smith, 'Blix: I was Smeared by the Pentagon', *Guardian*, 11 June 2003.

27   Habermas, 'What does the Felling of the Monument Mean?' para. 36.

28   For a brilliant, and narrower articulation of this idea as a basic moral right to justification see Rainer Forst, 'The Basic Right to Justification: Toward a Constructivist Conception of Human Rights', *Constellations* 6(1), 1999, pp. 35-60 and for an extension to transnationalism see Forst, 'Towards a Critical Theory of Transnational Justice', in Thomas W. Pogge, ed., *Global Justice*, Oxford: Blackwell Publishers, 2001, pp. 169-87.

29   Habermas, 'What does the Felling of the Monument Mean?', para. 41, emphasis added.

30   Ignatieff, 'The Burden', p. 53.

31   On this see Amy Bartholomew 'Human Rights and Post-Imperialism', *Buffalo Human Rights Law Review*, forthcoming 2003, and 'Toward a Deliberative Legitimation of Human Rights', *Warwick-Sussex Papers in Social Theory*, 6, 2001.

32   Habermas, 'What Does the Felling of the Monument Mean?', para. 43.

33   *Ibid.*, para 47.

34   See International Commission of Jurists, 'Iraq – This War Must be Conducted Lawfully', http://www.icj.org/news.php3?id_article=2774&lang=en (accessed June 9, 2003). Also see The Center for Economic and Social Rights Emergency Campaign on Iraq, 'Tearing up the Rules: The Illegality of Invading Iraq', March 2003. www.cesr.org/iraq/docs/tearinguptherules.pdf (accessed May 31, 2003), Michael Ratner, 'War Crime Not Self-Defense: The Unlawful War Against Iraq', http://www.ccr-ny.org/v2/print_page.asp?ObjID=BMreedARu7&Content=107 (accessed June 12, 2003) and Phyliss Bennis, 'Understanding the U.S.-Iraq Crisis: The World's Response, the UN and International Law', pamphlet of the Institute for Policy Studies, January 2003.

35   Ignatieff, 'Friends Disunited'.

36   Ignatieff, 'Barbarians at the Gate?'.

37 Ignatieff, 'Time to Walk the Walk'.
38 Habermas, 'What Does the Felling of the Monument Mean?', para. 10.
39 Ibid., para. 8. Habermas addresses his view of the differences between NATO intervention in Kosovo and the 1991 Gulf war, both of which he supported, and the US's most recent war against Iraq, of which he is deeply critical, in 'Letter to America'. On Kosovo, also see Habermas, 'Bestiality and Humanity: A War on the Border between Legality and Morality', *Constellations*, 6(3), 1999.
40 David Chandler cites Louis Henkin on this point. See 'International Justice', *New Left Review*, 6, p. 59.
41 Quoted in Danilo Zolo, *Invoking Humanity: War, Law and Global Order*, London: Continuum Press, 2002, p. 67.
42 Ignatieff, 'Barbarians at the Gate?', p. 6.
43 Habermas, 'What Does the Felling of the Monument Mean?', para. 34. We borrow the characterization of this as 'empire's law' from Trevor Purvis's comments at the Carleton University Anti-War Roundtable on 24 March 2003.
44 Eric Hobsbawm, 'America's Imperial Delusion', *Guardian*, 14 June 2003.
45 This does not imply a necessity for 'world government' or the end of state sovereignty. See Jürgen Habermas, *The Postnational Constellation: Political Essays*, Translated by Max Pensky, Cambridge, MA: MIT Press, 2001; John S. Dryzek, *Deliberative Democracy and Beyond*, Oxford: Oxford University Press, 2000; and Daniele Archibugi, 'Cosmopolitical Democracy', *New left Review*, 4, 2000.
46 And, note here the much better analysis of this in Habermas, 'What Does the Felling of the Monument Mean' and Marc Lynch, 'Irrelevance Lost', *Middle East Report Online*, 20 March 2003, www.merip.org/mero/mero032003.html, (accessed May 29, 2003) than in Arundhati Roy, 'Instant-Mix Imperial Democracy (Buy One, Get One Free)' who emphasizes how the 'resisting' nations rolled over for the Americans. http://www.wagingpeace.org/articles/03.05/0513roy_instantmix.htm, (accessed May 20, 2003).
47 Both in terms of the failure to pass something like a 'Uniting for Peace' declaration and in terms of the capitulation of the Security Council to the US demand for a US post-war administration. See Tariq Ali, 'Business As Usual: The UN has Capitulated. Now let the North's Plunder of the South Begin', *Guardian*, 24 May, 2003.
48 Peter Gowan, 'Neoliberal Cosmopolitanism', *New Left Review*, 11, 2001, p. 84. Some would place Ignatieff in this category but we believe that Ignatieff's position is better described as a republican imperialism, even if it does exhibit many of the features that Gowan ascribes to the 'new liberal cosmopolitans'.
49 Ali, 'Re-colonizing Iraq', *New Left Review*, 21, p. 15.
50 Ibid., pp. 16-18.

51 Ali, 'Business As Usual'.
52 Perry Anderson, 'Casuistries of Peace and War', *London Review of Books*, 25(5), 6 March 2003.
53 Perry Anderson, 'Force and Consent', *New Left Review*, 17, p. 8.
54 Anderson, 'Casuistries of Peace and War'.
55 Anderson, 'Force and Consent', p. 9.
56 Peter Gowan, 'Neoliberal Cosmopolitanism', *New Left Review*, 11, p. 84.
57 Ibid., p. 81.
58 Ibid., p. 91.
59 Ibid., p. 85. David Chandler's 'International Justice' develops the theme of the erosion of sovereign equality and presents an extended critique of the assault that human rights cosmopolitanism has perpetrated on norms of nonintervention and the sovereign equality of states that provided the juridical, if seldom the substantive, anchor for the 'first age of modernity'.
60 In this they echo Chandler in 'International Justice'.
61 For this analysis of Blair, see David Chandler, 'Imperialism May be Out, But Aggressive Wars and Colonial Protectorates are Back', *Observer,* 14 April 2002 www.observer.co.uk/worldview/story/0,11581,684308,00.html (accessed April 18, 2003).
62 'The National Security Strategy of the United States of America', 'The U.S. national security strategy will be based on a distinctly American internationalism that reflects the union of our values and our national interests. The aim of this strategy is to help make the world not just safer but better'. September 2002, p. 1. http://www.whitehouse.gov/nsc/nss.pdf (accessed May 30, 2003).
63 Anderson, 'Force and Consent', pp. 29-30.
64 It also threatens to return us to the sterile debates over rights and human rights between Leftists in the 1970s and 1980s over whether the Left should be 'for' or 'against' constitutional and human rights and the rule of law. See Amy Bartholomew, 'Should A Marxist believe in Marx on Rights?', *Socialist Register 1990*, London: Merlin, 1990.
65 Chandler, 'International Justice', p. 61. And, see Gowan, 'Neoliberal Cosmopolitanism', p. 91.
66 Daniele Archibugi, 'Demos and Cosmopolis', *New Left Review,* 13, 2002, p. 35.
67 See Karl-Otto Apel 'On the Relationship Between Ethics, International Law and Politico-Military Strategy in Our Time: A Philosophical Retrospective on the Kosovo Conflict', *European Journal of Social Theory* 4(1). This also signals our disagreement with Gopal Balakrishnan's assessment that the 'new Habermas' is 'an essentially establishment philosopher' and that the 'turn towards discourse ethics allows a curtain of mystifying euphemism to be drawn across the enormity of contemporary imperialism'. 'Overcoming Emancipation', *New Left Review*, 19, 2003, p. 124.
68 Gowan, 'Neoliberal Cosmopolitanism', p. 93. The idea of 'complacent

cosmopolitanism' is attributed to Timothy Brennan, 'Cosmopolitanism and Internationalism', *New Left Review*, 7, 2001.

69   These analytical shortcomings are mirrored, as well, in the respective positions around human rights.

70   See for example, Nicos Poulantzas, *State, Power, Socialism*, Translated by Patrick Camiller, London: Verso, 1978; Stuart Hall, *Drifting into a Law and Order Society*, Amersham: The Cobden Trust, 1980; Stuart Hall, 'Nicos Poulantzas: State, Power, Socialism', *New Left Review*, 119, 1980; Ralph Miliband, 'Poulantzas and the Capitalist State', *New Left Review*, 82, 1973; Leo Panitch, 'The New Imperial State', *New Left Review*, 2, 2000 and 'The Role and Nature of the Canadian State', in Leo Panitch, ed., *The Canadian State: Political Economy and Political Power*, Toronto: University of Toronto Press, 1977.

71   Dryzek, *Deliberative Democracy and Beyond*.

THE US MILITARY POSTURE: 'A UNIQUELY BENIGN IMPERIALISM'?

PAUL ROGERS

Before his appointment as President Clinton's first Director of Central Intelligence in 1993, James Woolsey was asked at a Senate hearing to characterize the nature of the changed post-Cold War world. He replied that the United States had slain the dragon but now lived in a jungle full of poisonous snakes.[1] Woolsey has gone on to become one of the leading neo-conservative security advocates of the Bush era, and his early remarks encapsulated the changing US military posture of the 1990s. This posture was sufficiently robust by the end of that decade to enable the Bush administration to underpin its new foreign and security policy with military power that gives the United States an almost unchallenged ability to dominate the global security environment.

This essay examines the changes in the US military posture during the 1990s, analyzes its status at the end of the decade and explores its potential and its crucial limitations under the Bush administration. It surveys the transformation of the US armed forces to fit them for a posture of comprehensive international control, bearing in mind the effects of the 1991 Gulf War and the experiences in Somalia and former Yugoslavia. The essay also examines the relevance of NATO, relations with Russia and China and the impact of missile defence, before assessing the impact of the September 11 attacks and the subsequent war in Afghanistan and the invasion of Iraq.[2]

THE END OF THE COLD WAR AND
THE 1991 GULF WAR

The rapid collapse of the Soviet bloc after 1989 resulted in the United States finding itself in a position of unparalleled power, with the intention of seeking a 'new world order' based on a western-dominated global market.

Almost immediately, the Iraqi occupation of Kuwait in August 1990 resulted in the development of a powerful coalition that put some 600,000 troops into the region and ended with the forcible eviction of Iraqi troops from Kuwait. The war had come barely two years after a period in which the United States had been closely allied to the Saddam Hussein regime. Indeed, only one month after the regime had killed some 5,000 people in a chemical attack on the Kurdish town of Hallabjah in March 1988, US Navy units had been active in destroying Iranian Navy warships, at the end of the 'tanker war', in an action that helped end the Iran/Iraq war on terms satisfactory to Baghdad when it had previously been facing a potential Iranian ascendancy. This was largely forgotten at the time of the 1991 Gulf War, which was hailed as an extraordinary success for the United States and its coalition allies.

Even so, there were four aspects of that war that remain relevant today. The first relates to oil security, an underlying theme of the US military posture that has become much more significant under the Bush administration. After the success of the Arab members of OPEC in putting up oil prices at the time of the Yom Kippur/Ramadan War of October 1973, the oil market entered a remarkable 'bull' period in which crude oil prices rose by over 400 per cent in less than a year. With the United States already becoming dependent on oil imports, the significance of Persian Gulf security was apparent, as Gulf States controlled over 50 per cent of global oil reserves. The US response was to establish a Joint Rapid Deployment Task Force at the end of the 1970s, upgraded in the mid-1980s to a unified military command, Central Command (CENTCOM). CENTCOM was responsible for US security in an arc of nineteen countries across South West Asia and North East Africa.[3]

Although it had been established in the context of Cold War perceptions of a possible Soviet intervention in the region, CENTCOM's development was sufficient to ensure that adequate basing and logistical support facilities were available in the Gulf region to enable the coalition to assemble forces and evict the Iraqis from Kuwait. Following the 1991 war CENTCOM developed a permanent presence in the region, including bases in Kuwait, Saudi Arabia and Bahrain, backed up by a large air base and logistical centre on the British colonial territory of Diego Garcia in the Indian Ocean. As oil security has become an increasingly significant element in the US military posture, so CENTCOM has become a core part of that posture.

A second aspect of the 1991 Gulf War was the early but incorrect assumption that the Saddam Hussein regime had been damaged beyond the point at which it could retain power, an assumption that was based in part on gross overestimates of the damage done to the Iraqi Army. In practice, there had been two quite different war aims for the two parties to the conflict. For the US-led coalition, the aim was the eviction of Iraqi forces from Kuwait, whereas the Iraqi war aim was simply regime survival. To ensure this, the regime kept almost all of its elite forces away from the immediate war zone, including most of the Republican Guard divisions. These were then available to consolidate post-war survival, including the suppression of Kurdish and Shi-ite revolts, and to support a leadership that was to last for a further twelve years.

The third aspect of the 1991 war was that Iraq had developed, by the start of the war, a deployable deterrent made of up missiles and bombs containing chemical and biological weapons. The broad details of this capability were known to US intelligence agencies and it was also known that such systems would only be used if the regime itself was threatened with destruction.[4] At the time of the war, there had been indications that the United States would be prepared to use nuclear weapons in response to the use of chemical and biological weapons by Iraq. This appeared to be an asymmetric deterrent, but the significant fact is that Iraq was also demonstrating a deterrent capability with its own capacity to respond with chemical and biological weapons to any attempt to destroy the regime. As one US analyst put it a short time afterwards, what was actually happening in the 'new world order' was the development of the ability of the weak to deter the strong.[5]

A fourth aspect of the war that had a profound effect on US military thinking related to the Iraqi attacks on Israel and Saudi Arabia with crude and inaccurate ballistic missiles based on the Soviet Scud system. During the war itself, the Scud attacks, especially those on Israel, resulted in the coalition having to divert much of its effort to destroying the launchers. The missiles may have been crude and obsolete but they still had a substantial political effect.

There was a further legacy of the war that did not become apparent until some years later. The most damaging single incident for the US during the war was a Scud attack on a storage and billeting area in Saudi Arabia that killed twenty-eight people. While this was widely reported at the time, it was not reported that nine days earlier another missile had narrowly missed a large munitions and fuel depot at a major pier complex at the Saudi port of al Jubayl, alongside which were several US Navy ships including the large amphibious warfare ship the *Tarawa*. If the crude, 1960s vintage missile had hit its target, the results would have been catastrophic.[6]

The effect of the Scud missile attacks and the knowledge of Iraqi biological and chemical weapons capabilities was to have a major impact on US military thinking over the next decade; there was now a clear need to control the proliferation of weapons of mass destruction, a need for missile defence, and a need to minimize US casualties in overseas military operations – the last of these being strongly reinforced when a number of US Rangers were killed and injured in Mogadishu in Somalia in March 1994.

One result was that the NATO-backed US intervention in former Yugoslavia later in 1999 was restricted almost entirely to the use of airpower, with strike aircraft operating at altitudes of more than 15,000 feet to avoid anti-aircraft fire. This made it exceedingly difficult for NATO forces to destroy Serbian armed forces that were camouflaged and concealed in Kosovo, and led the United States to concentrate heavily on attacking the economic infrastructure of Serbia itself.

While this helped result in the withdrawal of Serbian forces from Kosovo and the subsequent fall of the Milosevic regime, the human costs, both direct and indirect, were considerable. Over 1,000 civilians were killed in the air attacks, and substantial economic damage was done through the targeting of power plants, refineries, bridges, roads, railways, tunnels, factories and transmission lines. Overall, the air attacks did over $60 billions' worth of damage to the Serbian economy, reducing that already weakened country to the poorest in Europe.[7]

THE TRANSFORMATION OF THE US MILITARY

The experiences in the Gulf in 1991, and in Somalia and former-Yugoslavia later in the decade, together with numerous rebellions and uprisings and the development of 'rogue states', all gave the US military planners a mind-set or paradigm of a fractured world in which diverse threats to US interests were present, if often unpredictable, and had to be countered.

As a result of this, and during the course of the 1990s, US military forces underwent a substantial transformation even at a time of budget cuts, so that with the advent of the Bush administration in 2001, and in the aftermath of 9/11, the US was in an extraordinarily strong position to be the dominant player in international security.

The transition was incremental and was essentially a case of cutting back on those forces that had been designed primarily to limit Soviet power, while maintaining and even enhancing those that served to 'keep the violent peace' in the post-Cold War world. There were also some significant developments in military technology in which the United States had international pre-eminence that seemed likely to enable it to maintain a unique level of global military superiority.

For the United States Air Force (USAF), the Cold War era had placed the greatest emphasis on strategic nuclear forces in the form of intercontinental ballistic missiles and long-range bombers, together with the forward basing of large numbers of strike aircraft and interceptors, especially in Western Europe and East Asia. The change in the decade after the Cold War took two main forms.

The first was a substantial cutback in strategic and forward-based forces, balanced by a move towards 'global reach' – the ability to project power around the world. Part of this involved the ability to deploy long-range aircraft from bases in the United States supported by aerial refuelling, and the development of 'air expeditionary wings' that were akin to self-contained air forces of a hundred aircraft or more that could be deployed to overseas bases in response to regional crises.

The second main change was the development of precision-guided weapons, based usually on satellite or laser guidance, that could hit targets with great accuracy. Moreover, while many of these weapons were launched from aircraft they could fly considerable distances. One such 'stand-off' weapon was the conventionally armed air-launched cruise missile (CALCM) that was itself a modification of a nuclear missile of the Cold War era.

A remarkable example of the early use of such a system was seen on the opening night of the Gulf War in January 1991, when a number of B-52 strategic bombers were deployed from their base in the United States and flew over the Atlantic and Western Europe to the Middle East, firing a number of cruise missiles at targets in Iraq before returning to their base. This was by far the longest-range air raid in military history and was a powerful demonstration of global reach.[8]

A more recent USAF development, also used by other branches of the US armed forces, has been the deployment of pilot-less aircraft for reconnaissance purposes and also for the automatic deployment of bombs and missiles. In the latter form they are known as uninhabited combat aerial vehicles (UCAVs). They are operated from bases far away from their area of use, and therefore involve no risk to US personnel. UCAVs have been used in recent conflicts including Afghanistan and Iraq, and are likely to become much more common instruments of war.

For the US Navy (USN), a similar transformation has taken place since the end of the Cold War. This has involved the scaling down of naval nuclear forces, both strategic and tactical, together with substantial reductions in the total numbers of warships, especially those formerly deployed in an anti-submarine role against the Soviet Navy. At the same time, the types of naval forces required for long-distance operations against regional threats have been maintained and often enhanced. Central to this process has been the further development of the carrier battle group, based on a single large aircraft carrier, often nuclear powered, accompanied by a large flotilla including cruisers, destroyers, submarines and support vessels.

The largest class of US aircraft carrier, the *Nimitz* class, is by far the largest warship ever built. A single carrier battle group based on such a warship has more firepower than the combined strength of the aircraft carriers in service in the five European navies that have them – Britain, France, Spain, Italy and Russia. During the course of the 1990s, the US Navy reduced its numbers of aircraft carriers by only two, from fourteen to twelve, even though the main supposed enemy, the Soviet Union, had collapsed. Moreover, new ships were launched and the number of nuclear-powered carriers actually increased from five to nine, giving the overall carrier fleet substantially increased endurance.

In addition to maintaining these very large aircraft carriers the US Navy has also invested heavily in sea-launched cruise missiles (SLCM). Scores of such missiles can be deployed on a single cruiser and they can strike targets over 1,000 km from the launch point. Their primary function is land attack and they have been used against targets in former-Yugoslavia, Iraq, Sudan and Afghanistan.

One variant of the SLCM that illustrates the range of tactics available to the United States is a version that is intended specifically to disrupt electricity supplies. Instead of being armed with a high explosive charge, the missile disperses large number of highly conductive carbon fibre filaments that are deposited on electricity transmission lines and switching centres, short-circuiting the systems. Such a weapon may be described as non-lethal in that it does not directly kill or injure anyone, but its indirect impact, on hospitals and water purification or sewage treatment plants, can still be disastrous.

The end result of the transformation of the US Navy is that it has the capability to project substantial military force anywhere in the world, principally with its carrier battle groups. As a result there is considerable inter-service rivalry between the navy and air force. The navy points to its carriers as functioning like massive mobile air bases, able to take up station anywhere in the world to meet a threat to US interests, whereas the air force has to have forward-basing facilities or else may have to fly its bombers over global distances. The air force counters this by pointing out that the navy may take three weeks or more to get its carriers into position, whereas the air force can strike any point on the earth's surface in a matter of hours.

An illustration of this rivalry was the B-52 raid on Iraq at the start of the 1991 war, cited earlier. That raid, conducted over intercontinental distances, involved the use of air-launched cruise missiles almost identical to the sea-launched variants deployed at the time on US warships in the Persian Gulf and used extensively during that war. The navy missiles could have been used with much greater economy, but the air force raid was essentially an experiment in rapid global power projection.

This inter-service rivalry extends to the US Army, the branch of the armed forces that experienced the greatest cuts during the 1990s. This was largely because the army was primarily configured for an East-West conflict in Europe during the Cold War era, and had consequently developed heavily armoured forces that were less relevant to the new era.

Even so, the army has been able to adapt by altering the balance of its forces and producing equipment appropriate to the new era. The overall trend has been to cut back on the heavily armoured divisions while preserving and enhancing those geared to rapid deployment such as the 82nd and 101st Airborne Divisions. The army has also developed a policy of forward-basing equipment for key units in zones of long-term security interest such as the Middle East.

The army has also played a leading role in the development of special operations forces, especially those concerned with counter-insurgency. In this respect it works with the navy, air force and marines in an inter-service Special Operations Command (SOCOM).[9] Although relatively small by US standards, SOCOM still has 50,000 personnel, about half the size of the entire British army, and operates its own aircraft, ships and a range of specialist equipment. SOCOM is seen as having a particularly important function in supporting the elites of allied states in the South, and a feature of the last five years has been a substantial involvement in counter-insurgency training. This was a common feature of the Cold War era, especially in the 1950s and 1960s, where many right-wing governments in Latin America and elsewhere were supported forcefully in their actions against left-wing insurgents, the latter often backed directly or indirectly by the Soviet bloc.

Much of the recent expansion appears to be directed at countering aspects of the drugs trade, but controlling anti-elite insurgencies is also a key purpose. The extent of SOCOM's involvement is substantial, with US training units operating in over fifty countries worldwide. In 1998, some 2,700 special operations troops were involved in training the armed forces of nineteen Latin American and nine Caribbean states, including the armies of Guatemala, Colombia and Suriname which have been widely criticized for human rights abuses.[10]

As significant as is the work of SOCOM, perhaps most interesting of all is the fourth branch of the US armed forces, the Marine Corps. Unlike most countries, the United States maintains four rather than three branches of its armed forces, an army, a navy, an air force and a marine corps, the latter being structured particularly for amphibious operations and sustainable global deployments. Moreover, the US Marine Corps is larger than the entire armies of most other countries, including Britain. And whereas the air force, navy and army all had their personnel strengths reduced by 30-40 per cent during the 1990s, the reduction in the Marine Corps strength, from 195,000 to 171,000, was barely a tenth. Although the marines have played significant roles in major wars such as the Pacific War against Japan, they have been traditionally seen as relatively lightly armed but highly mobile forces that can be used most effectively in regional conflicts.

Historically, the marines were particularly active in protecting US interests in Central and South America, and their particular strengths, such as their amphibious capabilities, mean that they now have a much more global role. A Marine Expeditionary Force made up a large component of the US invasion force in Iraq in March 2003 and this was, in turn, a result of the longer-term commitment to the Persian Gulf region undertaken more than a decade previously.

Overall, then, the four branches of the US armed forces were able to adapt effectively to the changing world order of the 1990s, but this also applied to three other aspects of US military power, nuclear forces, missile defence and the development of new generations of very powerful conventional weapons.

WEAPONS OF MASS DESTRUCTION, MISSILE DEFENCE AND THE CONTROL OF SPACE

Although the United States and the Soviet Union cut their nuclear forces substantially after the end of the Cold War, they and other nuclear powers such as Britain and China showed no interest in moving away from maintaining nuclear forces. In the case of the United States, in particular, there were a number of changes in nuclear policy in the 1990s, which set the scene for more radical changes by the incoming Bush administration in 2001.

Clinton's election in 1992 resulted in a significant number of arms control specialists joining the administration, forcing a change in nuclear policy. Under the presidency of Bush senior, there had been cuts in arsenals, but these were accompanied by a strong belief in the utility of nuclear weapons in the newly disorderly world. An example was some work done for the Strategic Air Command, known as the Strategic Deterrence Study, whose terms of reference included the belief that 'the growing wealth of petro-nations and newly hegemonic powers is available to bullies and crazies, if they gain control, to wreak havoc on world tranquillity'. The study itself called for a new nuclear targeting strategy that would include the ability to assemble a 'Nuclear Expeditionary Force... primarily for use against China or Third World targets.'[11]

This extreme view was somewhat modified at the start of the Clinton era, including a congressional ban on research and development of new small nuclear weapons and a policy of transparency at the Department of Energy, the federal department responsible for the nuclear stockpile. Under the Energy Secretary, Hazel O'Leary, there was a concerted programme to clear up the serious contamination at many nuclear weapons manufacturing sites, but the overall inclination of the Clinton administration to limit the further development of nuclear weapons was undermined when the Republicans took control of Congress in 1994.

From then on the Clinton administration showed little interest in nuclear arms control and even allowed the modification of one tactical nuclear bomb into an earth-penetrating warhead suitable for attacking underground facilities.[12] In the Senate there was clear opposition to ratifying the Comprehensive Test Ban Treaty and the Democrats did not even attempt to take it to a vote.

The significance of these changes was heightened after the second Bush administration came to power, as evidence surfaced of a renewed interest in nuclear weapons modernization, as well as a much clearer linkage between nuclear weapons on the one hand, and chemical and biological weapons on the other. The point about this connection is that there is now a clear trend towards seeing nuclear weapons as useful in countering the less dangerous chemical and biological weapons that are being developed and deployed by substantially more countries than are seeking nuclear status.

At a more general level, this represents a further move away from controlling proliferation through multilateral action and a greater interest in pre-empting the acquisition of nuclear, biological and chemical systems by states that may act against US interests.

This trend, in turn, relates to the renewed interest in missile defence, again being promoted vigorously by the Bush administration following prevarication by Clinton. In the current US view, it is essential to develop a missile defence system that provides some protection for the entire continental United States, in addition to developing other systems designed specifically to protect US military forces and other security interests in other regions of the world.

In an ideal world, at least from a neo-conservative perspective, the United States would be able to mount regional missile protection systems together with a national missile defence while at the same time maintaining the world's most powerful set of offensive nuclear forces, including a range of tactical nuclear weapons that could be used in circumstances that fall short of a global conflict.

Furthermore, one particular aspect of the missile defence programme has much wider military implications, and may even be capable of setting off an entirely new arms race. This concerns the development of high-power lasers and other directed energy weapons, an aspect of military technology that is currently receiving substantial funding.[13] Since the first development of lasers in the 1960s, their military potential has attracted particular attention. If a weapon is defined as a means of delivering energy from a source to a target, then an 'ideal' weapon would be able to do so with great accuracy, at a very long range and at close to the speed of light. A directed energy weapon could theoretically have such properties and one of the most significant of the current programmes is the development of the Airborne Laser (ABL) a high-power chemical laser mounted on a Boeing 747 and expected to be capable of destroying a ballistic missile shortly after it has been launched at a range of up to 650 km.

The ABL could be deployed as soon as 2010, but there is greater interest in a much larger system of Space-Based Lasers (SBLs) that would be used primarily for destroying missiles but might also be capable of targeting any point on the Earth's surface with impunity. The SBL may still be fifteen or more years in the future, but it and other systems have already attracted much attention because of their potential for other military uses.

In June 1998, the USAF sat up a programme to investigate the wider military applications of directed energy. Termed the Directed Energy Applications for Tactical Air Combat (DEATAC) and headed by the former USAF Chief of Staff, General Ronald Fogelman, one of its main aims is to study how directed energy weapons could be used from aircraft in a variety of tactical roles. It is concerned with generic directed energy systems, not just the application of the ABL to tasks other than missile defence. As Fogelman put it: 'I believe that directed energy weapons will be fundamental to the way the Air Force fights future wars. This study, which I am pleased to be part of, will help prepare us for the changing face of warfare, It is an important step in pursuing the potential of directed-energy technologies.'[14] The leader of the study, William Thompson, indicated the wide scope of the programme:

> We'll be looking exclusively at directed-energy concepts at a range of power levels, to address weapon and mission-support applications. We'll also be considering a variety of airborne mediums, from manned aircraft to remotely piloted vehicles.[15]

What this means is that the US military is already fully alert to the implications of directed energy weapons as a potential military revolution, giving the possessor the ability to destroy targets at extreme ranges with almost instantaneous effect. Such weapons would further aid the ability of the United States armed forces to achieve what is commonly termed 'full spectrum dominance', the ability to win any conflict at any level at any time.

Such dominance also extends to the control of space, the widespread view across the US military being that it is essential for the United States to be the world's dominant space power. New weapons systems such as the planned Space Based Laser are seen as having an impressive potential in this regard, allowing the development of systems that could destroy any other state's satellites and other space-based systems as well as being able to attack targets on the Earth's surface.

The US Space Command has developed a Long Range Plan for the period through to the year 2020 that is predicated on the principle that the United States must have clear and unequivocal control of space, including what is termed 'worldwide situational awareness'. This would form the basis for an ability to counter any threat, ensuring that US military dominance is as near complete as can be achieved.

AREA IMPACT WEAPONS

There is one further military development that has had a substantial effect in recent conflicts – the area-impact munition (AIM). Much has been made of the development of precision-guided munitions that can hit targets with great accuracy, avoiding collateral damage, but there has been a parallel development of weapons that are designed specifically to cause the maximum number of casualties over as wide an area as possible.

Early examples were napalm and fragmentation shells, but the more recent emphasis has been on cluster bombs, multiple-rocket systems and very large blast bombs. Modern cluster bombs are actually canisters that disperse 150 to 200 grenade-sized 'bomblets' that detonate, collectively releasing several hundred thousand high velocity shrapnel fragments against 'soft' targets such as people. Each cluster bomb may disperse over an area of half a hectare, and satellite-guided cluster bombs can be set to spread over a much wider area. A B-52 bomber can deliver twelve such bombs over six hectares in a single sortie.

The Multiple Launch Rocket System is a ground-based area impact weapon that is even more devastating. A salvo of twelve MLRS missiles can disperse the power of forty cluster bombs over an area of twenty hectares at a range of over thirty kilometres. The most recent large blast bomb is the Massive Ordnance Air Burst (MOAB), a 9.5 tonne bomb that would be capable of killing an entire battalion of troops, up to 600 people, if they were caught in the open.

Many of these area impact weapons were originally developed for use by the US in Vietnam or by the Soviets in Afghanistan, but they have been used in several conflicts since the end of the Cold War including former-Yugoslavia, Afghanistan and both the wars with Iraq. In all of these more recent cases there has been a persistent use of such weapons and the effects on military and civilians have been substantial, with the added problem that many of the individual bomblets fail to detonate and act like anti-personnel land mines, particularly dangerous to children.

THREATS AND RESPONSES

This essay has so far reviewed developments in US military forces and technologies from the end of the Cold War through to the end of the twentieth century, including an indication of current trends. To summarize, an incremental transition in the US armed forces during the 1990s transformed them into forces that were considered to be well-suited to the disparate regional threats to the United States and its economic and political interests. These included a transition to a much stronger global 'reach' for the US Air Force and the US Navy, the maintenance and re-equipping of the US Marine Corps and the re-orientation of the US Army to more mobile forces. Power projection was aided by the development of long-range stand-off weapons such as the air-launched and sea-launched cruise missiles and specialized munitions for causing major economic damage through, for example, disrupting electricity supplies.

More recent trends include the extensive use of pilot-less aircraft, concentrated levels of intelligence-gathering, often space-based, and the early development of directed energy weapons that may have the capacity to cause a further revolution in military power.

What is now required is to place these changes in military technologies and tactics in their political and strategic context. This is best considered in three stages – the state of US strategic thinking prior to the Bush administration, the changes brought about by that administration after January 2001, and the subsequent impact of 9/11.

The decade after the end of the Cold War was characterized by the evolution of a world view within US security circles that was reasonably homogeneous and appeared relatively stable. On this view, there was no global challenger to US military hegemony but there were two states – Russia and China – that might present a challenge at some time in the future. In addition, there were two regions of the world that were considered to be endemically unstable, and where US security might be indirectly threatened – the Middle East and North East Asia – and there were areas of sporadic conflict such as the Balkans and Central Africa that might impinge on US interests. In addition, there were four issues that were more generic than geographical: the proliferation of nuclear, chemical and biological weapons and ballistic missiles, terrorism and the narcotics trade.[16]

North East Asia was seen as an area of threat because of the perceived antagonistic behaviour of North Korea, although that had partly been eased by diplomatic moves in the mid-1990s. By contrast, Iraq and Iran represented continuing problems, along with anti-US paramilitary actions in western Gulf states and wider anti-American sentiment in the region stemming from US support for Israel. Elsewhere, the United States would intervene in pursuit of its own security interests, sometimes in coalition with other states, but its armed forces had little interest in peace-keeping, not least after the experience of Mogadishu.

Russia was not seen as a major near-term threat, and there was some ambivalence over the extent to which it was appropriate to incorporate Russia into the NATO group. Although Russia retained some core strategic nuclear forces, and maintained tactical nuclear forces, partly because its conventional forces were so weak, that very weakness meant that Russia was of little direct military concern. The dubious security of its stocks of old nuclear weapons and fissile material was a cause for concern, as were the determined efforts of near-bankrupt Russian arms companies to export weapons systems, but the Russian military threat was essentially minimal.

China was a different matter. Even though its GDP per capita was barely one thirtieth of that of the United States, China's economic growth, at up to 10 per cent a year, combined with a population more than four times that of the United States, were indicators of substantial potential as a possible superpower within two decades. China raised, and still raises, conflicting views on the American right. Those whose main interests lay with business tended to see China primarily as a state with immense potential as a market, whereas neo-conservative thinking, even before the Bush administration, was far more concerned with China as a rival great power. In this line of thinking, indeed, one motive for national missile defence was the probability that it would get a highly negative reaction from China.

Historically, China has developed and maintained fairly robust and survivable nuclear forces that have been oriented primarily towards the immediate region, including Russia. In spite of having the technical and manufacturing capability to develop substantial strategic nuclear forces that could readily target the continental United States, China declined to do so, instead maintaining an arsenal of barely twenty missiles of intercontinental range.

From an American neo-conservative perspective, it could well be feasible to develop a national missile defence programme that would counter such a small force. Furthermore, the effect on China would be that it would see itself as having no effective deterrent in any kind of future Sino-American crisis, leading to a likely decision to expand massively its own strategic nuclear forces in order to swamp US missile defences, given that it would not have the technical competence to develop its own missile defence system. Such a Chinese nuclear expansion would have, from a neo-conservative perspective, two advantages. Firstly, it would encourage China to divert public spending from the civil economy to the military, limiting its potential for economic growth. Secondly, it would establish China as a clear threat across a wider swathe of the US political spectrum than just the neo-conservative right.

From this same perspective, the role of NATO is seen to be one of assisting with the stability of Europe and its immediate environs, with appropriate increases in defence spending to enable this to be possible. At the same time, there would be a deep reluctance to see NATO member states develop capabilities that could any substantial way infringe US military power.

THE BUSH ADMINISTRATION AND THE NEW AMERICAN CENTURY

Prior to the formation of the Bush administration, the threats and possibilities outlined above represented mainstream centre-right opinion in the United States, and this included a tolerable commitment to international cooperation and even to multilateral arms control processes such as the Chemical Weapons Convention and the Biological and Toxic Weapons Convention.

The bio-weapons commitment was actually quite significant. The convention dates back to 1972, but has no provision for inspection and verification. Given the risks of new kinds of bio-weapons, utilizing developments in genetic engineering, there is a widespread belief in the arms control community that strengthening the treaty should be a priority. As a consequence, negotiations started in Geneva in the mid–1990s to develop a protocol that built a rigorous verification regime into the treaty. The United States was key to this, as acceptance by the US of the need to inspect its advanced biotechnology industries would greatly increase the chance of world-wide acceptance. Under Clinton, the US was an active participant in the negotiations.

It is true that such multilateralism was not universally supported, especially where the Republican-controlled Congress was concerned, and this was reflected in caution on such issues as the proposed ban on anti-personnel land mines and United Nations proposals on the control of arms transfers, and outright opposition to the ratification of the Comprehensive Test Ban Treaty.

One other significant feature of the 1990s was the consolidation of US defence companies into a handful of very large enterprises, and this meant that there were singularly powerful and well-financed pro-defence lobbies, operating especially in Washington. One area of considerable emphasis was the threatened proliferation of ballistic missiles, so that the need for a national missile defence programme was promoted with great vigour.

More generally, the years immediately before the election of George W. Bush witnessed a degree of political activity on international security issues that was reminiscent of the final three years of the Carter presidency twenty years previously. Then, there had been a very powerful conservative campaign to 're-arm America' in the face of a perceived Soviet threat, with interest groups such as the Heritage Foundation, the Committee on the Present Danger and High Frontier all vigorous in their pursuit of higher defence spending. Many of the people involved in these interest groups went on to be influential members of the first Reagan administration, and some were involved in broadly similar campaigns in the late 1990s.

In the more recent experience, though, there was a fundamental difference in general outlook. In the late 1970s US foreign policy was seen, somewhat crudely, as a matter of an ideological conflict between American free enterprise capitalism and communism. In the late 1990s, communism was considered to be defeated and the neo-conservative view was that there was now an historic mission for the United States to consolidate this victory by creating a world economic environment built on American principles. Indeed, the mission was to create an 'American Century', one of the key neo-conservative groups promoting this view being the Project for the New American Century, established in 1997.

The Project had as its initial supporters people such as Richard Cheney and Donald Rumsfeld, in addition to many other luminaries who now feature in the Bush administration, particularly in defence and foreign affairs. In its statement of principles, the Project asks 'Does the United States have the resolve to shape a new century favourable to American principles and interests?' It believes that this is essential and that it is necessary 'to accept responsibility for America's unique role in preserving and extending an international order friendly to our security, our prosperity, and our principles.'[17]

The neo-conservative right does not accept that there can be any legitimate alternative. It is an article of faith that this is the appropriate way for the United States and the whole world. To accept the possibility of alternatives would mean that the dominant model may not be fully valid. Therefore any other approach must at least be deeply wrong-headed if not malign.

Although Bush was elected with the narrowest of margins, failing to get even the largest share of the actual vote, any idea that his administration would seek consensus was ruled out at once, especially on issues of international security. It was clear from the start that a unilateralist approach would dominate security thinking, both in the narrow sense of cooperative arms control and in more broadly based arenas. This extended to opposition to the proposed International Criminal Court, withdrawal from the Anti-Ballistic Missile Treaty as a national missile defence programme was accelerated, and strong opposition to planned talks to control the weaponization of space, and also to the strengthening of the bio-weapons treaty. As a result of this last issue, over six years of negotiations in Geneva were lost. To the dismay of European states that considered themselves allied to the US, the Bush administration even took the decision to withdraw from the Kyoto Protocols on the control of climate change, a modest agreement that had had strong European support.

This is not to suggest that the United States was unilateralist on all issues. On the contrary, the North American Free Trade Area was supported as were other trade agreements favourable to the US economy, but the policies of the new administration were highly selective and were predicated in the belief that what was good for America was necessarily good for the world. It was a view put effectively by Charles Krauthammer, writing just three months before 9/11:

> Multipolarity, yes, when there is no alternative. But not when there is. Not when we have the unique imbalance of power that we enjoy today – and that has given the international system a stability and essential tranquillity it had not known for at least a century.
> The international environment is far more likely to enjoy peace under a single hegemon. Moreover, we are not just any hegemon. We run a uniquely benign imperium.[18]

THE IMPACT OF 11 SEPTEMBER

The attacks on the World Trade Centre and the Pentagon on 11 September 2001 had a profound impact on the US as a whole and on the military and the neo-conservatives in particular. The twin towers were culturally the very symbols of post-war American success and their destruction, watched live on television by tens of millions of Americans, was visceral in its effect. Although far less prominent, the attack on the Pentagon had a similar effect within the US military and the Washington security community. The ability of a small paramilitary group to attack the centre of global military power was a deep shock to the military leadership, both attacks demonstrating a vulnerability that had hardly been recognized.

This came at a time when the neo-conservative security agenda was really getting into its stride, with a near universal perception that the United States had a commanding authority in terms of global security. 9/11 might have caused a re-think. It might even have suggested that maintaining international stability through economic dominance backed up, where necessary, by military force, would lead not to stability but an indefinite state of conflict.

An astute Southern perspective, published in the immediate aftermath of 9/11, was that of Walden Bello. Condemning the 9/11 attacks as horrific, despicable and unpardonable, he went on to caution against an 'iron fist' response that ignores the underlying context. He pointed to the frequent use of indiscriminate force by the United States, not least in Korea and Vietnam, and to the bitter mood throughout much of the Middle East and South West Asia, directed partly against the United States because of its perceived dominance of these regions, but also against autocratic states dependent on continuing US support. He concluded:

> The only response that will really contribute to global security and peace is for Washington to address not the symptoms but the roots of terrorism. It is for the United States to re-examine and substantially change its policies in the Middle East and the Third World, supporting for a change arrangements that will not stand in the way of the achievement of equity, justice and genuine national sovereignty for currently marginalized peoples. Any other way leads to endless war.[19]

In practice, the reverse was the case, and in the eighteen months following 9/11 there were four major developments in the US security posture, all of them signalling a reinforcement of the neo-conservative security agenda.

The first was the vigorous pursuit and destruction of the Taliban regime and al-Qaida elements in Afghanistan, using a combination of air power, special forces and the large scale recruitment and arming of Northern Alliance ground troops. The Taliban regime was destroyed and al-Qaida dispersed, at a cost of the lives of at least 3,000 civilians, a similar number to those who died in the 9/11 attacks. The US subsequently resisted attempts by a number of states to establish a countrywide stabilization force to add civil redevelopment, not least because this would involve a much greater involvement of other states and a loss of control for the US itself.

While some of the larger cities such as Kabul underwent a successful transition to a more peaceful environment, much of the country remained in the hands of warlords, with continuing US military action against Taliban and other militia. Moreover, few of the Taliban or al-Qaida leadership were killed or taken into custody and al-Qaida and its associates continued paramilitary actions across the world, including attacks in Indonesia, the Philippines, Kenya, Morocco and Pakistan.

A second response was a marked curtailing of human rights through many actions of the US government, often in concert with other states. The latter included more marked control of opposition groups in many states in the guise of the 'war on terror', as well as the US policy of detaining presumed terrorists without trial at the Guatanamo base in Cuba.

A third response was the declaration of a number of 'rogue' states as part of an 'axis of evil', with Iran, Iraq and North Korea being primary candidates for evil status, followed by Syria, Libya and Cuba. This was combined with the development of a new international security strategy that was notably open about pre-empting possible future threats to US interests.

Finally, the Bush administration proved determined to execute a comprehensive change of regime in Iraq. While this was initially predicated on the need to eliminate Iraqi chemical and biological weapons, the war proved deeply controversial and resulted in worldwide protests and a clash with some European states, most notably France. The war itself was costly in human terms, with at least 5,000 civilians and well over 10,000 Iraqi soldiers killed and many tens of thousands injured.

IMPLICATIONS AND CONSEQUENCES

United States military capabilities are pre-eminent. The US has a degree of military superiority that is unparalleled even by Britain at the height of its imperial capabilities in the late nineteenth century. Furthermore, these capabilities are present in a state pursuing a wider global agenda of a single economic paradigm, and one that is readily prepared to use military force when it perceives its interests to be at risk. The impact of the 9/11 attacks has powerfully reinforced the existing neo-conservative mindset, making their security agenda more widely acceptable to US public opinion.

At the same time, this powerful unilateralism is not accepted as appropriate by many states such as France and Germany that would otherwise share many aspects of the economic agenda. Even stronger is the opposition to US power in much of the rest of the world, especially outside the ruling elites. And as a result, one trend that is already evident, as the sheer power of US military capabilities becomes apparent, is a move towards asymmetric warfare.

Currently this takes two main forms. One is a greater imperative for potential oppositional states such as Iran and North Korea to develop their own deterrent capabilities, primarily to forestall US intervention. The other is a pronounced tendency for oppositional paramilitary groups to develop the capability to attack US and other interests at weak points in their power structures. While 9/11 was the most notable example of such action, it represents only one part of the potential capabilities of oppositional paramilitaries.

It is probable that this will become one of the major responses to US power, and that further attacks such as those of 9/11 will further reinforce the neo-conservative security paradigm, leading progressively to Bello's 'endless war'. Given the confluence of oil reserves, US support for Israel, the occupation of Iraq and continuing instability in Afghanistan, it is likely that the core region for such developments will be the Middle East and South West Asia.

Such a prognosis is daunting. It implies the prospect of further major paramilitary attacks on the United States and its overseas interests, followed by even more forceful responses. It might be the case that the political system in the United States would eventually see that such policies were self-defeating and would accept the need for an alternative security paradigm. The problem is that such a development might take some years and would follow much suffering and violence.

A more positive analysis relates to the evidence that a more general political antagonism to the 'New American Century' is developing, centred on two elements: the attitudes of political elites in Southern states, and a more global movement encompassing individuals, non-government organizations and a wide range of groups often labelled as part of an 'anti-globalization' movement.

A perceptive analysis from the Geneva-based South Centre, published soon after the 9/11 attacks, argued that the 'war on terror' was already being seen in the context of Northern dominance of the international financial institutions such as the IMF, the World Bank and the WTO, as well as attitudes to climate change and the tardy and thoroughly limited progress on debt relief.

> Increasing numbers in the South perceive the evolving situation as no less than modern imperialism, using the full panoply of mechanisms to bend the will and shape the global order to suit the preferences and needs of the major advanced industrial nations. Moreover, this new imperialism is largely unhindered, in fact it is even aided and abetted, by the multilateral mechanisms developed over the past five decades.
>
> Growing resentment in the South at the sense of powerlessness in the face of Northern arrogance and impunity breeds frustration, which hardly provides fertile ground for development or peace or building the international community. Now, the fear of speaking up in defence of one's own interests has been further exacerbated by the new dictum 'You are either with us or against us'.[20]

Prior to the 9/11 attacks, one of the most significant global developments was the rise of a broad movement that was critical of the adverse effects of globalization. This was expressed in many individual campaigns on issues such as trade reform, labour rights and debt relief, but also coalesced into much bigger oppositional gatherings around meetings of international financial institutions in Seattle, Genoa and Washington, as well as being expressed through a series of alternative 'peoples' summits'.

In the immediate aftermath of the attacks, such opposition was muted, but it had re-emerged with renewed vigour by the time of the G8 Summit at Evian in France in May 2003. By then the movement of global opposition was no longer constrained by a fear of criticizing the military responses to 9/11. Moreover, it was actually strengthened by the parallel opposition that had developed to the war in Iraq, producing, in the early part of 2003, the largest ever anti-war protests across the world.

A consensus may therefore be emerging composed of several elements. The first is the view that the 'war on terror' has evolved from what would have been acceptable as a legitimate attempt to bring to justice those responsible for 9/11 to a much wider process of curbing opposition to US policies. The 'war on terror' therefore continues with decreasing legitimacy. The second is that the destruction of the Saddam Hussein regime in Iraq was primarily about the control of an immensely resource-rich region, as part of a wider policy of international control by the United States and some coalition partners.

These views coalesce with a third element, a much more broadly based opposition to global economic trends. As such, western economic policies, dominated by the United States, form an integral part of a wider hegemony into which the security paradigm is incorporated.

One complication is that a number of western governments may share some of the first two elements of the analysis, but are deeply reluctant to accept the radical critique of the global economic system. Because of this, it would make little sense to rely on such governments to seek to curb current US policies beyond the more narrow aspects of counter-terrorism and Middle East policy.

It follows that the main focus in promoting an alternative security paradigm must be on non-government organizations, citizen groups and independent analysts. Following the attacks of 9/11, there has been a marked hardening of the old paradigm that may well have set us back a decade, but there is every chance of further analysis, and the demonstration of alternatives, that will help to show the futility of that approach. The next decade will be crucial in this regard and it follows that activists and engaged intellectuals of all kinds have an immensely important role to play and a considerable responsibility to use all their efforts to do so.

NOTES

1   Statement by James Woolsey at Senate Hearings, Washington DC, February 1993.

2   This contribution concentrates almost entirely on US military developments rather than the wider socio-economic context. For the latter see the lead essay by Peter Gowan, 'The American Campaign for Global Sovereignty', in *Socialist Register 2003*, London: Merlin, 2003.

3   One of the clearest expositions of the increasing strategic significance of the Persian Gulf oil supplies was in the Military Posture Statement of the US Joint Chiefs of Staff, Fiscal Year 1982, published in Washington DC in February 1981.

4   The most detailed account of the development of the Iraqi chemical and biological weapons programmes prior to the 1991 Gulf War, including the actual deployment of offensive systems during the war, is to be found in a 1995 report of the UN Special Commission on Iraq (UNSCOM), to the Security Council: 'Report of the Secretary-General on the status of the implementation of the Special Commission's plan for ongoing monitoring

and verification of Iraq's compliance with relevant parts of Section C of Security Council resolution 687 (1991)', New York: UN Security Council report S/1995/684, 11 October 1995. The fact that US intelligence agencies were aware of an Iraqi willingness to use such systems came to light in 1996 when the US Department of Defense made available on the Internet a large number of reports and studies relating to the Gulf War. These included, by mistake, a classified report relating to a National Intelligence Estimate of November 1990, two months before the start of the war. The report was quickly removed from the website but not before it had been read by a number of analysts.

5   One of the threats said to be facing the United States was listed by Roger Barnett, a military analyst and former US Navy submarine captain as the 'Impact of high technology weapons and weapons of mass destruction on the ability – and therefore the willingness – of the weak to take up arms against the strong. Roger W. Barnett, 'Regional Conflict: Requires Naval Forces', *Proceedings of the United States Naval Institute*, June 1992.

6   This incident only came to light almost eight years after the event: John D. Gresham, 'Navy Area Ballistic Missile Defense Coming On Fast', *Proceedings of the US Naval Institute*, January 1999.

7   Economist Intelligence Unit report, 21 August 1999.

8   Details of the development of the conventionally-armed air-launched cruise missiles (known as the 'secret squirrels' after a cartoon character) were not published until three years after the 1991 Gulf War: John Tirpal, 'The Secret Squirrels', *Air Force Magazine*, April 1994.

9   Mark Hewish and Rupert Pengelly, 'Special Solutions for Special Forces', *International Defense Review*, May 1995.

10   Douglas Farah, 'Shadowy U.S. Troop Training Operation Spreads Across Latin America', *International Herald Tribune*, 14 July 1998.

11   Strategic Advisory Group of the Joint Strategic Target Planning Staff, US Strategic Air Command, 'The Role of Nuclear Weapons in the New World Order', reported in *Navy News and Undersea Technology*, Washington, D.C., 3 January 1992.

12   Greg Milo, 'New Bomb, No Mission', *The Bulletin of the Atomic Scientists*, March/April 1997.

13   Paul Rogers, 'Towards and Ideal Weapon? Military and Political Implications of the Airborne and Space-based Lasers', *Defense Analysis*, 17(1), 2001, pp. 73-88.

14   'Directed Energy Study Kicks Off', Air Force Research Laboratory Office of Public Affairs DE Release No. 98-32, Kirtland Air Force Base, New Mexico, 26 June 1998.

15   *Ibid.*

16   Of the numerous sources on the military view in the latter part of the 1990s, the following are indicative: Hans Binnendijk, 'America's Military Priorities', *Strategic Forum Number 20*, Institute for National Security

Studies, National Defense University, February 1995; Paul Mann, 'Fathoming a Strategic World of "No Bear, But Many Snakes"', *Aviation Week and Space Technology*, 6 December 1999; Prepared Statement by Lieutenant General Patrick M. Hughes USA, Director, Defense Intelligence Agency, before the Senate Armed Services Committee, 'Global Threats and Challenges: The Decades Ahead', Tuesday, 2 February 1999; Prepared Statement of George J. Tenet, Director of Central Intelligence, before the Senate Armed Services Committee, 'Current and Projected National Security Threats', Tuesday, 2 February, 1999.

17   See a perceptive article on this outlook published just three weeks before the 9/11 attacks: Thomas E. Ricks, 'U.S. Urged to Embrace An "Imperialist" Role', *International Herald Tribune*, 22 August 2001. For details of the Project for the New American Century, see www.newamericancentury.org/.

18   Charles Krauthammer, 'The Bush Doctrine: ABM, Kyoto and the New American Unilateralism', *The Weekly Standard*, 4 June 2001, Washington, D.C. *The Weekly Standard* is probably the best source of thinking on the neo-conservative agenda and is available at www.weeklystandard.com/.

19   Walden Bello, 'Endless War', *Focus on the Global South*, Manila, September 2001. For analyses of global issues by FGS, see www.focusweb.org/.

20   'Autumn 2001: A Watershed in North-South Relations?', *South Letter*, Volumes 3 and 4, 2001, Geneva: The South Centre.

BLOOD FOR OIL:
THE BUSH-CHENEY ENERGY STRATEGY

Michael T. Klare

Oil had nothing to do with Washington's motives for America's March 2003 invasion of Iraq – or so we were told. 'The only interest the United States has in the region is furthering the cause of peace and stability, not in [Iraq's] ability to generate oil,' said Ari Fleischer, the White House spokesperson, in late 2002.[1] But a close look at the Administration's planning for the war reveals a very different picture. In a January briefing by an unnamed 'senior Defense official' on US plans for protecting Iraqi oil fields in the event of war, the Pentagon leadership revealed that General Tommy Franks and his staff 'have crafted strategies that will allow us to secure and protect those fields as rapidly as possible in order to preserve those prior to destruction, as opposed to having to go in and clean them up after.'[2] If these assumptions prove accurate, and if the new regime in Baghdad opens its territory to exploitation by outside firms, Iraq could become one of America's leading oil suppliers in the decades ahead.[3]

To fully appreciate America's strategic interests in Iraq, it is useful to go back in time to the first few months of the Bush Administration. On first assuming office as President in early 2001, George W. Bush's top foreign policy priority was not to prevent terrorism or to curb the spread of weapons of mass destruction (or any of the other foreign policy goals he espoused after 9/11); rather, it was to increase the flow of petroleum from foreign suppliers to markets in the United States. The preceding year had witnessed severe oil and natural gas shortages in many parts of the United States, along with periodic electric-power blackouts in California. In addition, US oil imports had just risen to over 50 per cent of total US consumption for the first time in American history, provoking great anxiety about the security of America's long-term energy supply. For these and other reasons, Bush asserted at the time that addressing the nation's 'energy crisis' was to be his most important task as President.[4]

Addressing the energy crisis was seen by Bush and his advisers as a critical matter for several reasons. To begin with, energy abundance is essential to the health and profitability of many of America's leading industries, including automobiles, airlines, construction, petrochemicals and agriculture, and so any shortages of energy can have severe and pervasive economic repercussions. Petroleum is especially critical to the US economy because it is the source of two-fifths of America's total energy supply – more than any other source – and because it provides most of the nation's transportation fuel. In addition to this, petroleum is absolutely essential to US national security, in that it powers the vast array of tanks, planes, helicopters, and ships that constitute the backbone of the American war machine.[5]

Given these realities, it is hardly surprising that the incoming Bush Administration viewed the energy scarcities of 2000-2001 as a matter of great concern. 'America faces a major energy supply crisis over the next two decades,' Secretary of Energy Spencer Abraham told a National Energy Summit on March 19, 2001. 'The failure to meet this challenge will threaten our nation's economic prosperity, compromise our national security, and literally alter the way we lead our lives.'[6]

To address this challenge, President Bush established a National Energy Policy Development Group (NEPDG) composed of senior government officials and charged it with the task of developing a long-range plan for meeting the nation's energy requirements. 'One thing is for certain', Bush told the group in March 2001. 'There are no short-term fixes ... the solution for our energy shortage requires long-term thinking and a plan that we'll implement that will take time to bring to fruition.'[7] To head the NEPDG and to oversee this long-term process, Bush picked his closest political adviser, Vice President Dick Cheney. A Republican Party stalwart and a former Secretary of Defense, Cheney had served as Chairman and Chief Executive Officer of the Halliburton Co., an oilfield services firm, before joining the Bush campaign in 2000. Cheney, in turn, relied on top officials of US energy firms, including the Enron Corporation, to provide advice and recommendations on major issues.[8]

As the NEPDG began its review of US energy policy, it quickly became apparent that the United States faced a critical choice between two widely diverging energy paths: it could continue down the road it had long been travelling, consuming ever-increasing amounts of petroleum and, given the irreversible decline in domestic oil production, becoming ever more dependent on imported supplies; or it could choose an alternative route, entailing vastly increased reliance on renewable sources of energy and a gradual reduction in petroleum use. The existence of these two competing routes and the need for a decision on which to follow had long been known to experts in the field; it was only now, with the creation of the NEPDG, that this critical choice was being addressed at the very highest level.

Clearly, the outcome of this decision would have profound consequences for American society, the economy, and the nation's security. A decision to continue down the existing path of rising petroleum consumption would bind the United States ever more tightly to the Persian Gulf suppliers and to other oil-producing countries, with a corresponding impact on American security policy; a decision to pursue an alternative strategy, on the other hand, would require a huge investment in new energy-generation and transportation technologies, resulting in the rise or fall of entire industries. Either way, Americans would experience the impact of this choice in their everyday life and in the dynamics of the economy as a whole. No one, in the United States or elsewhere, would be left entirely untouched by the decision on which energy path to follow.[9]

The National Energy Policy Development Group wrestled with these choices over the early months of 2001 and completed its report by early May. After careful vetting by the White House, the report was anointed as the National Energy Policy (NEP) and released to the public by President Bush on May 17, 2001.[10] At first glance, the NEP – or the 'Cheney Report', as it is widely known – appeared to reject the path of increased reliance on imported oil and to embrace the path of conservation, renewable energy, and improved fuel efficiency. The new plan 'reduces demand by promoting innovation and technology to make us the world leader in efficiency and conservation,' the President declared on May 17. 'It will underwrite research and development into energy-saving technology. It will require manufacturers to build more energy-efficient appliances.'[11] But despite all of the rhetoric about conservation, the NEP does not propose a reduction in America's overall consumption of oil. Instead, it proposes to slow the growth in US dependence on imported petroleum by increasing production at home through the use of more efficient drilling methods and by exploiting untapped reserves in protected wilderness areas.

As is widely known, the single most important step toward increased domestic oil production proposed by the NEP was the initiation of drilling on the Arctic National Wildlife Refuge (ANWR), a vast, untouched wilderness area in northeastern Alaska. This proposal has won great praise from many Republicans and from private interests that favour the increased use of federal lands for energy development, but has been roundly condemned by environmentalists who deplore the destruction of a pristine wilderness area. So sharp has the disagreement between these two camps become that debate over ANWR has wholly monopolized public discussion of the NEP. But while debate over ANWR has allowed the White House to suggest that the Administration is fully committed to a policy of energy independence, careful examination of the Cheney report leads to an entirely different conclusion. Aside from the ANWR proposal, there is virtually *nothing* in the NEP that would contribute to a significant decline in American dependence on imported petroleum. In fact, the very opposite is true: the basic goal of the Cheney plan is to increase the flow of oil from foreign suppliers to the United States.

In the end, therefore, President Bush did make a clear decision regarding America's future energy behaviour. But the choice he made was not that of diminished dependence on imported oil – as suggested by White House rhetoric – but rather the opposite. Knowing that nothing can reverse the long-term decline in domestic oil production, and seeking to quench America's ever-growing thirst for petroleum products, the Administration chose to continue down the existing path of increased dependence on foreign oil.

The fact that the Bush energy plan envisions increased rather than diminished reliance on imported petroleum is not immediately apparent from the President's public comments on the NEP or from the first seven chapters of the Cheney report itself. It is only in the eighth and final chapter, 'Strengthening Global Alliances', that the true intent of the Administration's policy – increased dependence on imported oil – becomes fully apparent. Here, the tone of the report changes markedly, from a professed concern with conservation and energy efficiency to an explicit emphasis on securing more oil from foreign sources. 'US national energy security depends on sufficient energy supplies to support US and global economic growth,' Chapter 8 begins. Because the United States cannot generate the required supplies of oil from domestic reserves, it must rely on foreign sources. 'We can strengthen our own energy security and the shared prosperity of the global economy' by working with other countries to increase the global production of energy. To this end, the President and his senior associates are enjoined by the Cheney report to 'make energy security a priority of our trade and foreign policy.'[12]

But while acknowledging the need for increased supplies of imported petroleum, the Cheney report is very circumspect about the *amount* of foreign oil that will be required. The only clue provided by the report is a chart of America's net oil consumption and production over time. According to this chart, domestic US oil field production will decline from about 8.5 million barrels per day (mbd) in 2002 to 7.0 mbd in 2020 while consumption will jump from 19.5 mbd to 25.5 mbd, meaning that total imports will have to rise from 11 mbd to 18.5 mbd.[13] It is to procure this *increment* in imported petroleum – approximately 7.5 mbd, or the equivalent of total current oil consumption by China and India combined – that most of the recommendations in Chapter 8 are aimed.

To facilitate American access to overseas sources of petroleum, the Cheney report makes 35 foreign policy recommendations – exactly one-third of all of the recommendations in the report. Although many of these proposals are region- or country-specific, the overall emphasis is on removing obstacles – political, economic, legal, and logistical – to the increased procurement of foreign oil by the United States. To give just one example, the NEP calls on the Secretaries of Energy, Commerce, and State 'to deepen their commercial dialogue with Kazakhstan, Azerbaijan, and other Caspian states to provide a strong, transparent, and stable business climate for energy and related infrastructure projects.'[14] Similar recommendations are applied to other regions of the world that are seen as major future sources of oil for the United States.

The Cheney report's emphasis on procuring ever-increasing supplies of imported energy to satisfy America's growing demand will have a profound impact on American foreign policy in the years ahead. Not only will American officials have to negotiate access to these overseas supplies and arrange for the sorts of investments that will make increased production and export possible, but they must also take steps to make certain that foreign deliveries of oil to the United States are not impeded by war, revolution, or civil disorder. These imperatives will govern US policy toward all significant energy-supplying regions, especially the Persian Gulf area, the Caspian Sea basin, Africa, and Latin America.

As will become evident from the discussion that follows, moreover, implementation of the Cheney energy plan was also bound to have significant implications for US security policy and for the actual deployment and utilization of American military forces. This is so because most of the countries that are expected to supply the United States with increased petroleum in the years ahead are riven by internal conflicts, harbour strong anti-American sentiments, are located in dangerous neighbourhoods, or exhibit some combination of all three of these characteristics. This means that American efforts to procure additional oil from foreign sources are almost certain to encounter violent disorder and resistance in key producing areas. And while American officials might prefer to avoid the use of force in such situations, they have every reason to conclude that the only way to ensure the continued flow of energy is to guard the oil fields and pipelines with American soldiers.

To add to Washington's dilemma, the very deployment of American forces in the oil-producing areas is likely to stir up resentment from inhabitants of these areas who fear the revival of colonialism or who object to particular American policies (such as, for example, US support for Israel). As a result, American efforts to safeguard the flow of oil could well result in the intensification rather than the diminution of local disorder and violence. Clearly, this has something of a built-in escalatory character: the more that the United States relies on imported oil, the greater the likelihood that this will lead to American military involvement in key producing areas and the bigger the risk that this will lead to anti-American violence.[15]

To fully appreciate the manifold consequences of the Bush Administration's energy plan for American foreign and military policy, it is useful to examine US interests and behaviour in each of the regions that are seen in Washington as a major source of imported petroleum in the years ahead. Our survey of these areas begins with the Persian Gulf – the world's leading supplier of petroleum – and looks in succession at the Caspian Sea basin, the West coast of Africa, and Latin America.

THE PERSIAN GULF

The Persian Gulf area has long been and will remain a major focus of concern for American foreign and military policy because it sits atop the world's largest reservoir of untapped petroleum. According to BP, the major Gulf oil producers jointly possess some 680 billion barrels of petroleum, or about two-thirds of known world reserves. The Gulf countries are also the world's leading producers on a day-to-day basis, jointly accounting for approximately 22 mbd in 2000, about 30 per cent of worldwide production.[16] Most analysts assume, moreover, that the Gulf's share of total world petroleum output will rise significantly in the years ahead as production in other areas, including the United States, Mexico, the North Sea, China, and Indonesia, experiences irreversible decline.[17]

Although the United States currently obtains only about 18 per cent of its imported petroleum from the Persian Gulf area, Washington perceives a significant strategic interest in the stability of Gulf energy production because its major allies, including Japan and the Western European countries, rely on imports from the region and because the Gulf's high export volume has helped to keep world oil prices relatively low, thus benefiting the petroleum-dependent US economy. With domestic production in decline, moreover, the United States will become ever more dependent on imports from the Gulf. For this reason, the NEP observes, 'this region will remain vital to U.S. interests.'[18]

The United States has, of course, played a significant role in Persian Gulf affairs for a very long time. During World War II, President Franklin D. Roosevelt met with Abdul-Aziz ibn Saud, the founder of the modern Saudi dynasty, and concluded an agreement with him under which the United States agreed to protect the royal family against its internal and external enemies in return for privileged access to Saudi oil. In subsequent years, the United States also agreed to provide security assistance to the Shah of Iran and to the leaders of Kuwait, Bahrain, and the United Arab Emirates (UAE). These agreements have led to the delivery of vast quantities of US arms and ammunition to these countries and, in some cases, to the deployment of American combat forces.[19] (The US security link with Iran, however, was severed in January 1980, when the Shah was overthrown by militant Islamic forces.)

American policy with regard to the protection of Persian Gulf energy supplies is unambiguous: when a threat arises, the United States will use whatever means are necessary, including military force, to ensure the continued flow of oil. This principle was first articulated by President Jimmy Carter in January 1980, following the Soviet invasion of Afghanistan and the fall of the Shah, and has remained American policy ever since. In accordance with this principle – known since 1980 as the 'Carter Doctrine' – the United States has used force on several occasions: first, in 1987-88, to protect Kuwaiti oil tankers from Iranian missile and gunboat attacks (Operation Earnest Will), and then in 1990-91, to drive Iraqi forces out of Kuwait (Operation Desert Storm).[20]

In explaining the need to use force on these occasions, US officials have repeatedly stressed the importance of Persian Gulf oil to American economic stability and prosperity. 'Our strategic interests in the Persian Gulf region, I think, are well known, but bear repeating,' then Secretary of Defense Dick Cheney told the Senate Armed Services Committee on September 11, 1990, five weeks after the Iraqi invasion of Kuwait. In addition to America's security ties to Saudi

Arabia and other states in the area, he continued, 'We obviously also have a significant interest because of the energy that is at stake in the Gulf.' Iraq already possessed 10 per cent of the world's oil reserves and, by seizing Kuwait, acquired another 10 per cent; the occupation of Kuwait also placed Iraqi forces within a few hundred miles of another 25 per cent, in the Eastern Province of Saudi Arabia. 'Once [Hussein] acquired Kuwait and deployed an army as large as the one he possesses, he was clearly in a position to be able to dictate the future of worldwide energy policy, and that gave him a stranglehold on our economy and on that of most of the other nations of the world as well.' It was for this reason, Cheney insisted, that the United States had no choice but to employ military force in the defence of Saudi Arabia and other friendly states in the area.[21]

Once Iraqi forces were driven from Kuwait, the United States adopted a policy of 'containment' of Iraq, employing severe economic sanctions and the enforcement of a 'no-fly zone' over northern and Southern Iraq to weaken the Hussein regime and to prevent any new attacks on Kuwait and Saudi Arabia. At the same time, Washington substantially expanded its military presence and basing structure in the Persian Gulf area in order to facilitate future US military operations in the region. Most importantly, the Department of Defense 'pre-positioned' vast quantities of arms and ammunition in Kuwait and Qatar so that American troops could be sent to the region and rushed into combat without having to wait weeks or months for the delivery of their heavy equipment from the United States.[22]

By the early spring of 2002, the Bush Administration had concluded that the policy of containment was not sufficient to eliminate the threat posed to American interests in the Gulf by Saddam Hussein, and that more aggressive action was required. Although Iraq's alleged possessed of weapons of mass destruction (WMD) was cited as the main reason for acting in this manner, it is instructive to note that Dick Cheney – now Vice President – employed virtually the same arguments that he had in September 1990 to justify the use of force. 'Should [Hussein's] ambitions [to acquire WMD] be realized, the implications would be enormous for the Middle East and the United States,' Cheney told the annual convention of the Veterans of Foreign Wars on August 26, 2002. 'Armed with an arsenal of these weapons of terror and a seat at the top of ten per cent of the world's oil reserves, Saddam Hussein could then be expected to seek domination of the entire Middle East, take control of a great portion of world's energy supplies, [and] directly threaten America's friends throughout the region.'[23]

With the successful US invasion of Iraq, it now appears that the United States is in firm control of the Persian Gulf area and its critical oil supplies. But a realistic assessment of the situation in the Gulf would suggest that long-term stability cannot be assured. Looking into the future, it is evident that American policy-makers face two critical challenges: first, to ensure that Saudi Arabia and other Gulf producers increase oil production to the extent required by growing US (and international) demand; and second, to protect the Saudi regime against internal unrest and insurrection.

The need to increase Saudi production is particularly acute. Possessing one fourth of the world's known oil reserves – an estimated 265 billion barrels – Saudi Arabia is the only country with the capacity to satisfy ever-increasing US and international demand for petroleum. According to the Department of Energy, Saudi Arabia's net petroleum output must increase by 133 per cent over the next twenty-five years, from 10.2 mbd in 2001 to 23.8 mbd in 2025, in order to satisfy anticipated world requirements (estimated at 119 mbd) at the end of that period.[24] But expanding capacity by 13.6 mbd – the equivalent of total current production by the United States and Mexico – will cost hundreds of billions of dollars and produce enormous technical and logistical challenges. The best way to achieve this increase, American analysts believe, is to persuade Saudi Arabia to open up its petroleum sector to substantial US oil-company investment. Indeed, this is exactly what the Cheney report calls for. However, any effort by Washington to apply pressure on Riyadh to allow greater American oil invest-ment in the kingdom is likely to meet with significant resistance from the royal family, which nationalized US oil holdings in the 1970s and is fearful of being seen as overly subservient to American bidding.

The Administration faces yet another problem in Saudi Arabia: America's long-term security relationship with the Saudi regime has become a major source of tension in the country, as growing numbers of young Saudis turn against the United States because of its close ties to Israel and what is seen as Washington's anti-Islamic bias. It was from this anti-American milieu that Osama bin Laden recruited many of his followers in the late 1990s and obtained much of his finan-cial support. After September 11, the Saudi government cracked down on some of these forces, but underground opposition to the regime's military and economic cooperation with Washington persists. Just ten days after President Bush declared 'victory' in Iraq, a series of massive explosions rocked the north-eastern suburbs of Riyadh, destroying several compounds occupied by Western firms and residents.[25] Finding a way to eradicate this opposition while at the same time persuading Riyadh to increase its oil deliveries to the United States will be one of the most difficult challenges facing American policymakers in the years ahead.[26]

The United States also faces a continuing standoff with Iran. Although Iranian leaders expressed sympathy with the United States following 9/11 and provided modest assistance to US forces during the campaign in Afghanistan, relations between the two countries remain strained. Iran was, of course, included among the three members of the 'axis of evil' in President Bush's January 2002 State of the Union address, leading many in Tehran to fear that the American victory in Iraq will be followed by a US invasion of Iran. Such fears are compounded by American charges that Iran is proceeding with the development of nuclear weapons. And while these concerns may not lead to the early outbreak of war between the two countries, it is likely that tensions between Iran and the United States will remain high for the foreseeable future.[27]

Although the United States will remain dependent on oil from the Persian

Gulf area for a long time to come, American officials seek to minimize this dependency to the greatest degree possible by diversifying the nation's sources of imported energy. 'Diversity is important, not only for energy security but also for national security,' President Bush declared on May 17, 2001. 'Over-dependence on any one source of energy, especially a foreign source, leaves us vulnerable to price shocks, supply interruptions, and in the worst case, black-mail.'[28] To prevent this, the Administration's energy plan calls for a substantial US effort to boost production in a number of non-Gulf areas, including the Caspian Sea basin, the West coast of Africa, and Latin America.

THE CASPIAN SEA BASIN

Among these areas, the one that is likely to receive greatest attention from American policy-makers is the Caspian Sea basin, consisting of Azerbaijan, Georgia, Kazakhstan, Kyrgyzstan, Turkmenistan, Tajikistan, and Uzbekistan, along with adjacent areas of Iran and Russia. According to the Department of Energy, this area houses proven reserves (defined as 90 per cent probable) of 17 to 33 billion barrels of oil, and possible reserves (defined as 50 per cent probable) of 233 billion barrels – an amount that, if confirmed, would make it the second largest site of untapped reserves after the Persian Gulf area.[29] To ensure that much of this oil will eventually flow to consumers in the West, the US government has made a strenuous effort to develop the area's petroleum infrastructure and distri-bution system. Because the Caspian Sea is land-locked, oil and natural gas from the region must travel by pipeline to other areas; any efforts to tap into the Caspian's vast energy reserves must, therefore, entail the construction of long-distance export lines.

The United States first sought to gain access to the Caspian's vast oil supplies during the Clinton Administration. Until that time, the Caspian states (except for Iran) had been part of the Soviet Union, and so outside access to their energy reserves was tightly constricted. Once these states became independent, however, Washington waged an intensive diplomatic campaign to open their fields to Western oil company investment and to allow the construction of new export pipelines. President Clinton himself played a key role in this effort, repeatedly telephoning leaders of the Caspian Sea countries and inviting them to the White House for periodic visits.[30] These efforts were essential, Clinton told President Heydar Aliyev of Azerbaijan in 1997, to 'diversify our energy supply and strengthen our nation's security.'[31]

The Clinton Administration's principal objective during this period was to secure approval for new export routes from the Caspian to markets in the West. Because the Administration was reluctant to see Caspian oil flow through Russia on its way to Western Europe (thereby giving Moscow a degree of control over Western energy supplies), and because transport through Iran was prohibited by US law (because of its pursuit of weapons of mass destruction), President Clinton threw his support behind a plan to transport oil and gas from Baku in Azerbaijan to Ceyhan in Turkey via Tbilisi in the former Soviet republic of Georgia. Before leaving office, Clinton flew to Turkey to preside at the signing ceremony for a regional agreement permitting construction of the $3 billion Baku-Tbilisi-Ceyhan (BTC) pipeline.[32]

While concentrating on the legal and logistical aspects of procuring Caspian energy, the Clinton Administration also sought to address the threat to future oil deliveries posed by instability and conflict in the region. Many of the states on which the United States hoped to rely for increased oil supplies or for the transport of Caspian energy were wracked by ethnic and separatist conflicts. With this in mind, the Administration initiated a number of military assistance programs aimed at strengthening the internal security capabilities of friendly states in the region. This entailed, inter alia, the provision of arms and military training to their forces, along with the conduct of joint military exercises. In the most noteworthy of these exercises, Operation CENTRAZBAT '97, some 500 paratroopers from the Army's 82nd Airborne Division were flown 7,700 miles from Fort Bragg in North Carolina to Shymkent in Kazakhstan to participate in joint military manoeuvres with troops from that country plus Kyrgyzstan and Uzbekistan.[33]

Building on the efforts of President Clinton, the Bush Administration seeks to accelerate the expansion of Caspian production facilities and pipelines. 'Foreign investors and technology are critical to rapid development of new commercially viable export routes,' the Cheney report affirms. 'Such development will ensure that rising Caspian oil production is effectively integrated into world oil trade.' Particular emphasis is placed on completion of the BTC pipeline and on increasing the participation of US companies in Caspian energy projects. Looking further ahead, the Administration also seeks to build an oil and gas pipeline from Kazakhstan and Turkmenistan on the east shore of the Caspian to Baku on the west shore, thus permitting energy from Central Asia to flow to the West via the BTC pipeline system.[34]

Until September 11, US involvement in the Caspian Sea basin and Central Asia had largely been restricted to economic and diplomatic efforts, accompanied by a number of military aid agreements. To combat the Taliban and Al Qaeda in Afghanistan, however, the Department of Defense deployed tens of thousands of combat troops in the region and established military bases in Kyrgyzstan and Uzbekistan. Some of these troops have now been recalled to the United States, but it appears that the Department of Defense plans to retain its bases in Central Asia. Indeed, there is every indication that the United States plans to maintain a permanent military presence and to strengthen its ties with friendly regimes in the area.[35] This presence is supposedly intended to assist in the war against terrorism, but it is clear that it is also intended to safeguard the flow of petroleum. Most noteworthy, in this regard, is the US decision to deploy US military instructors in Georgia in order to provide counter-insurgency training to the special units that will eventually guard the Georgian segment of the BTC pipeline.[36]

Although the Bush Administration has high hopes for the development of Caspian Sea energy supplies, it is evident that many obstacles stand in the way of increased petroleum exports from this region. Some of these are logistical: until new pipelines can be built, it will be difficult to transport large quantities of Caspian oil to the West. Other obstacles are political and legal: the largely authoritarian regimes now in control of most of the former Soviet republics are riddled with corruption and reluctant to adopt the legal and tax reforms needed to attract large-scale Western investment. In effect, the major problem facing the United States in seeking to rely on the Caspian basin as an alternative to the Persian Gulf is the fact that the Caspian is no more stable than the Gulf, and so any effort to ensure the safety of energy deliveries will entail the same sort of military commitments that the United States has long made to its principal energy suppliers in the Gulf.[37]

WEST AFRICA

Another area that is viewed by the Bush Administration as a promising source of oil is West Africa. Although African states accounted for only about 10 per cent of global oil production in 2000, the Department of Energy predicts that their share will rise to 13 per cent by 2020 – adding, in the process, another 8.3 mbd to global supplies.[38] This is welcome news in Washington. 'West Africa is expected to be one of the fastest-growing sources of oil and gas for the American market,' the Cheney report observes. Furthermore, 'African oil tends to be of high quality and low in sulphur,' making it especially attractive for American refiners.[39]

The Administration expects to concentrate its efforts in two countries: Nigeria and Angola. Nigeria now produces about 2.2 mbd, and is expected to double its capacity by 2020 – with much of this additional oil going to the United States. But Nigeria lacks the wherewithal to finance this expansion on its own, and its existing legal system – not to mention widespread corruption and ethnic unrest – tends to discourage investment by outside firms.[40] The Cheney report thus calls upon the Secretaries of Energy, Commerce, and Energy to work with Nigerian officials 'to improve the climate for U.S. oil and gas trade, investment, and operations.' A similar outlook governs the Administration's stance toward Angola. With sufficient external investment, the Cheney report notes, Angola 'is thought to have the potential to double its exports over the next ten years.'[41] But here, too, endemic corruption and an uninviting legal climate have discouraged substantial investment by foreign firms.[42]

Much as in the Caspian region, moreover, American efforts to obtain additional oil from Africa could be frustrated by political unrest and ethnic warfare. Indeed, much of Nigeria's production was shut down during the spring of 2003 because of ethnic violence in the Delta region, the site of much of Nigeria's onshore oil. In addition, local activists – many of them women – have occupied offshore oil facilities in an effort to obtain additional funds for community projects. Crime and vandalism have also hampered Nigeria's efforts to increase oil production.[43]

The United States is not likely to respond to these challenges by deploying

American troops in the area – that undoubtedly would conjure up images of colonialism and so would provoke strong opposition at home and abroad. But Washington is willing to increase its military aid to friendly regimes in the region. Total US assistance to Angola and Nigeria – the two countries of greatest interest to Washington – amounted to some $300 million in Fiscal Years 2002-2004, a significant increase over the previous three-year period. Angola and Nigeria also become eligible in the US budget for fiscal year 2004 to receive surplus American arms under the Pentagon's Excess Defense Articles (EDA) program.[44] (Several other oil-producing countries in Africa, including Cameroon, Chad, Gabon, and Congo-Brazzaville, will also receive US arms under this program.) And while the deployment of American troops in the region is not a likely prospect in the short term, the Department of Defense has begun to look at potential basing sites there – most notably in the islands of São Tomé e Principe – in the expectation that such a deployment may someday be deemed necessary.[45]

LATIN AMERICA

Finally, the Cheney plan calls for a significant increase in US oil imports from Latin America. The United States already obtains a large share of its imported oil from these countries – Venezuela is now the third largest supplier of oil to the United States (after Canada and Saudi Arabia), Mexico is the fourth largest, and Columbia is the seventh – and Washington hopes to rely even more heavily on this region in the future. As indicated by Secretary of Energy Spencer Abraham, 'President Bush recognizes not only the need for an increased supply of energy, but also the critical role the hemisphere will play in the Administration's energy policy.'[46]

In presenting these aspirations to governments in the region, US officials stress their desire to establish a common, cooperative framework for energy development. 'We intend to stress the enormous potential of greater regional energy cooperation as we look to the future,' Abraham told the Fifth Hemispheric Energy Initiative Ministerial Conference in Mexico City on March 8, 2001. 'Our goal [is] to build relationships among our neighbors that will contribute to our shared energy security; to an adequate, reliable, environmentally sound, and affordable access to energy.'[47] But however sincere, these comments overlook the fundamental reality: all of this 'cooperation' is essentially aimed at channelling more and more of the region's oil supplies to the United States.

The Bush energy plan places particular emphasis on the acquisition of additional oil from Mexico and Venezuela. 'Mexico is a leading and reliable source of imported oil', the Cheney report observes. 'Its large reserve base, approximately 25 per cent larger than our own proven reserves, makes Mexico a likely source of increased oil production over the next decade.'[48] Venezuela is considered vital to US energy plans because it possesses large reserves of conventional oil, and because it houses vast supplies of so-called heavy oil – a sludge-like material that can be converted to conventional oil through a costly refining process. According to the NEP, 'Venezuelan success in making heavy oil deposits commercially viable suggests that they will contribute substantially to the diversity of global energy supply, and to our own energy supply mix over the medium to long term.'[49]

But US efforts to tap into abundant Mexican and Venezuelan energy supplies will run into a major difficulty: because of a long history of colonial and imperial predation, these two countries have placed their energy reserves under state control and have established strong legal and constitutional barriers to foreign involvement in domestic oil production. Thus, while they may seek to capitalize from the economic benefits of increased oil exports to the United States, they are likely to resist both increased US participation in their energy industries and also any significant increase in oil extraction. Such resistance will no doubt prove frustrating to American officials, who seek exactly these outcomes. The NEP thus calls on the Secretaries of Commerce, Energy, and State to lobby their Latin American counterparts to eliminate or soften barriers to increased American oil investment.

These endeavours are likely to meet particularly strong resistance in Venezuela, where oil production has long been under state control. A new Constitution adopted in 1999 bans foreign investment in the oil sector, and President Hugo Chávez has taken other steps to impede such investment. Following a prolonged general strike organized by opponents of the President in late 2002 and early 2003, Chávez effectively seized control of the state-owned oil company, Petróleos de Venezuela, S.A. (PdVSA), and fired those managers considered most amenable to links with foreign firms.[50] (Although the United States is not known to have played a direct role in the strike, many of its leaders had been received warmly in Washington and given signals of the Administration's sympathy for their cause.) So long as Chávez remains in power, then, it is unlikely that Washington will make much headway in its efforts to increase US investment in Venezuela's oil industry.

Energy considerations are also likely to figure prominently in US relations with Colombia. Although known primarily for its role as a supplier of illegal drugs, Colombia is also a major oil supplier to the United States. Efforts to increase Colombian oil production have been hampered, however, by frequent attacks on oil installations and pipelines mounted by anti-government guerrilla groups.[51] Claiming that these groups also provide protection to the drug traffickers, the United States is assisting the Colombian military and police in their efforts to suppress the guerrillas. Furthermore, under a special $94 appropriation awarded by Congress in 2002, American military instructors are providing counter-insurgency training to the Colombian forces assigned to the protection of the 500-mile-long Caño Límon pipeline, connecting oilfields in the interior to refineries and export facilities on the Caribbean coast.[52] In seeking additional supplies of energy, therefore, the United States is likely to become increasingly embroiled in the civil war in Colombia.

THE ENERGY-SECURITY NEXUS: LINKING THE BUSH
ENERGY PLAN TO THE BUSH MILITARY PLAN

The implications of all of the above are unmistakable: in its pursuit of ever-growing supplies of imported petroleum, the United States is intruding ever more assertively into the internal affairs of the oil-supplying nations and, in the process, exposing itself to an ever-increasing risk of involvement in local and regional conflict situations. This reality has already influenced US relations with the major oil-producing nations and is sure to have an even greater impact in the future. And, as we have seen, growing American dependence on these countries is likely to be accompanied by the expanded presence of US military forces in their midst.

At no point, however, does the NEP acknowledge this fundamental reality. Instead, the Cheney plan focuses on the economic and diplomatic dimensions of US energy policy – suggesting thereby that America's energy dilemmas can somehow be overcome in this fashion. But the architects of the Bush/Cheney policy know better: an energy plan that calls for increased reliance on the Persian Gulf countries and on other suppliers located in areas of recurring turmoil will not be able to overcome every conceivable threat to American energy interests through economic and diplomatic efforts alone. At some point, it may prove impossible to ensure access to a particular source of oil without the use of military force.

It is in this regard that one cannot help but be struck by the clear parallels between the Administration's energy policy and its preferred military strategy. To fully appreciate the extent of overlap between the energy and security policies of the Bush Administration, it is first necessary to know something about the types of capabilities the United States might need to ensure access to foreign sources of oil at a time of crisis or conflict. Essentially, such action would require the possession of well-equipped and versatile forces that could be sent to distant areas in order to protect a vital supplier against enemy attack or internal disorder, or to reestablish control over an oil-producing area that has fallen under the control of a hostile power. These forces might also be required to protect pipelines, ports, refineries, and other such facilities against sabotage or attack.

In American military parlance, the formations that are earmarked for these sorts of activities are generally identified as 'power projection' forces, meaning forces that can be transported from established bases in the United States and Europe to distant combat zones, and then fight their way into the area (if no friendly bases are available) or otherwise come to the assistance of a beleaguered ally. Typically, power projection forces are said to include both the ground and air combat units intended for penetration of enemy territory plus the ships and planes used to carry these units into the battle zone. Power projection forces also include long-range bombers and the naval platforms – aircraft carriers, surface combatants, and submarines – used to launch planes or missiles against onshore targets.

It is precisely these sorts of forces that have been accorded top priority in the military plans of the Bush Administration. During his first presidential campaign,

George W. Bush promised to conduct a sweeping reassessment of US military policy when assuming office and to commence the 'transformation' of American forces, so as to render them better equipped to confront the perils of the 21st century. Because these perils might arise at any point on the earth's surface, Bush explained in an important speech at The Citadel military academy on September 23, 1999, 'Our forces in the next century must be agile, lethal, readily deployable, and require a minimum of logistical support.' In particular, our land forces 'must be lighter [and] more lethal'; our naval forces must be able 'to destroy targets from great distances'; and our air forces 'must be able to strike from across the world with pinpoint accuracy.'[53]

These priorities dominated US military planning during the early months of the Bush Administration and established the baseline for future military budget requests. From a strategic perspective, the most significant expression of this outlook was contained in the report of the Quadrennial Defense Review (QDR), released in September 2001. Many aspects of US military policy are covered in the QDR, including homeland security, national missile defence, information warfare, and anti-terrorism. As in Bush's Citadel speech, however, heavy emphasis is placed on bolstering America's capacity to project military power to distant battlefields. 'The United States must retain the capability to send well-armed and logistically supported forces to critical points around the globe, even in the face of enemy opposition,' the report notes.[54]

By the end of the Administration's second year in office, therefore, the White House had succeeded in incorporating many of its basic strategic objectives into formal military doctrine. As we have seen, these objectives stress the steady enhancement of America's capacity to project military power into areas of turmoil – that is, to strengthen precisely those capabilities that would be used to protect or gain access to overseas sources of petroleum. Whether this was the product of a conscious linkage between energy and security policy is not something that can be ascertained at this time; what is undeniable, however, is that President Bush gave top priority to the enhancement of America's power projection capabilities at exactly the same time that he endorsed an energy strategy that entails increased US dependence on oil derived from areas of recurring crisis and conflict.

What we have, therefore, is a two-pronged strategy that effectively governs US policy toward much of the world. Although arising from different sets of concerns – one energy-driven, the other security-driven – these two strategic principles have merged into a single, integrated design for American world dominance in the 21st Century. One or the other of these policy concerns may play the lead role in any particular situation, but it is the combination of the two that increasingly will set the tone for America's international behaviour in the decades ahead.

Clearly, this is not a reactive strategy, but one that requires assertive action on the part of the United States to satisfy its growing energy requirements. As America's reliance on oil from the Persian Gulf, the Caspian Sea basin, West

Africa, and Latin America grows, Washington will become more deeply involved in the political and economic affairs of key producing states in these regions. This will entail, at the very least, close ties with friendly regimes in these areas and the conspicuous presence of American oil companies. In many cases, it will also involve the delivery of arms and military assistance to friendly regimes. And, in those cases where there is a direct threat to the flow of oil, we can expect outright military intervention.

This pattern has long been evident in the Persian Gulf area. The United States first declared its intent to employ force in the protection of Persian Gulf oil in 1980, in the Carter Doctrine, and first applied this principle in 1987, with the 'reflagging' of Kuwaiti oil tankers (equipping them with American flags so as to permit their defence by US naval forces). The 1990-91 Gulf War was another application of this principle, and, in effect, so was the 2003 US invasion of Iraq. Now, what we are seeing is the extension of this principle to other areas of the world upon which the United States has become dependent for its petroleum supplies, including the Caspian Sea area and Colombia. If America's experience in the Gulf is any indication, this will ultimately result in the deployment and use of American military forces in these areas.

Where and when this principle will next be put to the test cannot be foreseen. What can be stated, however, is that the two-pronged strategy adopted by the Bush Administration in 2001-2002 will almost certainly lead to further US military intervention in the major oil-producing areas. Such intervention may not be described as a 'war for oil', but the underlying logic of the Bush strategy will be evident to all those who have followed its development over the past few years. 'Blood for oil' has, in fact, become a dominant feature of the Bush Administration's military policy.

NOTES

1   As quoted in Serge Schmemann, 'Controlling Iraq's Oil Wouldn't Be Simple', *The New York Times*, November 3, 2002.

2   From the transcript of a Department of Defense news briefing, The Pentagon, January 24, 2003, electronic document accessed at www.defenselink.mil on January 27, 2003.

3   US Department of Energy, Energy Information Administration, 'Iraq', Country Analysis Brief, electronic document accessed at www.eia.doe/gov/cabs/iraq.html on October 23, 2002.

4   For background on the 2000-2001 energy crisis and the remedies being considered by the Bush administration at the time, seeRobert L. Bamberger, *Energy Policy: Setting the Stage for the Current Debate*, CRS Issue Brief for Congress (Washington, D.C.: Congressional Research Service, U.S. Library of Congress, August 13, 2001).

5   For background on the 2000-2001 energy crisis and its implications for the

US economy and security, see Robert L. Bamberger, *Energy Policy: Setting the Stage for the Current Debate, Issue Brief for Congress*, Washington, D.C.: Congressional Research Service, US Library of Congress, August 13, 2001.

6   Spencer Abraham, 'A National Report on America's Energy Crisis', remarks before the National Energy Summit, March 19, 2001, electronic document accessed at www.energy.gov on April 24, 2001.

7   'Remarks by the President in Photo Opportunity after Meeting with National Energy Policy Development Group', the White House, March 19, 2001, electronic document accessed at www.whitehouse.gov on March 5, 2003.

8   See Richard A. Oppel, Jr., 'White House Acknowledges More Contacts with Enron', *The New York Times*, May 23, 2003.

9   For background and discussion of these choices, see *Strategic Energy Policy Challenges for the 21st Century*, Report of an Independent Task Force Sponsored by the James A. Baker III Institute for Public Policy of Rice University and the Council on Foreign Relations, Edward L. Morse, Chair, April 2001, electronic document accessed at www.bakerinstitute.org on October 21, 2002.

10   National Energy Policy Development Group, *National Energy Policy*, Washington, D.C.: The White House, May 2001. (Hereinafter cited as NEPDG, NEP 2001.)

11   From the transcript of Bush' speech at River Centre Convention Center, St. Paul, Minn., May 17, 2001, as published in *The New York Times*, May 18, 2001.

12   NEPDG, NEP 2001, chap. 8, pp. 1, 3-4.

13   *Ibid.*, Figure 2, p. x.

14   *Ibid.*, chap. 8, p. 13.

15   For elaboration of this point, see Klare, 'The Deadly Nexus: Oil, Terrorism, and America's National Security', *Current History*, December 2002, pp. 414-20.

16   BP, *Statistical Review of World Energy 2002*, pp. 4, 6.

17   See projections of oil production through 2025 in US Department of Energy (DoE), Energy Information Administration (EIA), *International Energy Outlook 2003*, Table D4, p. 238. (Hereinafter cited as DoE/EIA, IEO 2003.)

18   NEPDG, NEP 2001, chap. 8, p. 4.

19   For background, see Michael A. Palmer, *Guardians of the Gulf*, New York: The Free Press, 1992. See also Michael Klare, *Resource Wars: The New Landscape of Global Conflict*, New York: Metropolitan Books, 2001, pp. 51-80.

20   See Palmer, *Guardians of the Gulf*, pp. 102-242.

21   US Congress, Senate, Committee on Armed Services, *Crisis in the Persian Gulf Region: U.S. Policy Options and Implications*, Hearings, 101st Congress, 2nd Session, Washington, D.C.: US Government Printing Office, 1990, pp. 10-13.

22 For details, see Klare, *Resource Wars*, pp. 62–68.

23 From the transcript of Cheney's speech in *The New York Times*, August 27, 2002.

24 DoE/EIA, IEO 2003, Table D1, p. 235.

25 Neil MacFarquhar, 'Explosions Rock Western Enclaves in Saudi Capital', *The New York Times*, May 13, 2003. For background on political unrest in Saudi Arabia, see Craig S. Smith, 'Saudi Arabia Seems Calm, But, Many Say, Is Seething', *The New York Times*, March 24, 2003; Douglas Jehl, 'U.S. and Saudis Sensed Attacks Were Imminent', *The New York Times,* May 14, 2003.

26 For background on these issues, see Alfred B. Prados, *Saudi Arabia: Current Issues and U.S. Relations*, Issue Brief for Congress, Washington, D.C.: Congressional Research Service, Library of Congress, April 3, 2003.

27 For background and discussion, see Kenneth Katzman, *Iran: Current Developments and U.S. Policy*, Issue Brief for Congress, Washington, D.C.: Congressional Research Service, Library of Congress, March 13, 2003. See also David S. Cloud, 'U.S., Iran, Stall on Road to Rapprochement', *Wall Street Journal*, May 12, 2003.

28 From the transcript of Bush's speech of May 17, 2001, as published in *The New York Times*, May 18, 2001.

29 US Department of Energy, Energy Information Administration, 'Caspian Sea Region', Country Analysis Brief, February 2002, electronic document accessed at http://www.eia.doe.gov/cabs/caspian.html on February 22, 2002.

30 For background, see Klare, *Resource Wars*, pp. 84–92.

31 'Visit of President Heydar Aliyev of Azerbaijan', statement by the Press Secretary, the White House, August 1, 1997, electronic document accessed at www.library.whitehouse.gov on March 2, 1998.

32 For background and discussion, see Klare, *Resource Wars*, pp. 88–92, 100–4.

33 See R. Jeffrey Smith, 'U.S. Leads Peacekeeping Drill in Kazakhstan', *Washington Post*, September 15, 1997. See also Klare, *Resource Wars*, pp. 1–5.

34 NEPDG, NEP 2001, chap. 8, pp. 12–13.

35 See 'The Yankees Are Coming', *The Economist*, January 19, 2002, p. 37; Jean-Christophe Peuch, 'Central Asia: U.S. Military Buildup Shifts Spheres of Influence', Radio Free Europe/Radio Liberty, Prague, January 11, 2002.

36 See Chip Cummins, 'U.S. Plans to Send Military Advisers to Georgia Republic', *Wall Street Journal,* February 27, 2002; *Oil and Gas Journal Online*, 'Azerbaijan, Georgia Address Security Threats to BTC Pipeline', January 23, 2003, electronic document accessed at www.ogj.pennnet.com on January 24, 2003.

37 For discussion, see Jim Nichol, *Central Asia's New States: Political Developments and Implications for U.S. Interests*, Issue Brief for Congress, Washington, D.C.: Congressional Research Service, Library of Congress, April 1, 2003. See also Martha Brill Olcott, 'The Caspian's False Promise', *Foreign Policy*, Summer 1998, pp. 95–113.

38 DoE/EIA, IEO 2002, Table D1, p. 239.

39 NEPDG, NEP 2001, chap. 8, p. 11. See also 'Black Gold', *The Economist*, October 26, 2002, pp. 59-60; James Dao, 'In Quietly Courting Africa, White House Likes Dowry', *The New York Times*, September 19, 2002.

40 See US Department of Energy, Energy Information Administration, 'Nigeria', Country Analysis Brief, January 2002, electronic document accessed at www.eia.doe.gov/emeu/cabs/nigeria.html on October 21, 2002.

41 NEPDG, NEP 2001, chap. 8, p. 11.

42 US Department of Energy, Energy Information Administration, 'Angola', Country Analysis Brief, November 2002, electronic document accessed at www.eia.doe.gov/emeu/cabs/angola.html on December 2, 2002.

43 See 'Nigerian Women, in Peaceful Protest, Shut Down Oil Plant', *The New York Times*, July 14, 2002; 'Nigerian Troops Move Into Delta to Put Down Ethnic Riots', *The New York Times*, March 20, 2003; Sarah Moore, 'Nigeria's New Challenge for Big Oil', *Wall Street Journal*, July 26, 2002; Norimitsu Onishi, 'As Oil Riches Flow, Poor Village Cries Out', *The New York Times*, December 22, 2002; Somini Sengupta, 'Nigerian Strife, Little Noted, Is Latest Threat to Flow of Oil', *The New York Times*, March 22, 2003.

44 US Department of State, *Congressional Budget Justification: Foreign Operations, Fiscal Year 2004*, February 2003, electronic document accessed at www.fas.org on February 27, 2003.

49 Ibid., Chap. 8, p. 10.

45 See Antony Goldman and James Lamont, 'Nigeria and Angola to Discuss U.S. Plan for Regional Military Base', *Financial Times*, October 4, 2001; 'U.S. Naval Base to Protect Sao Tome Oil', BBC News World Edition, August 22, 2002, electronic document accessed at news.bbc/co.uk on March 6, 2003.

46 Spencer Abraham, Remarks before the Fifth Hemispheric Energy Initiative Ministerial Conference, Mexico City, March 8, 2001, electronic document accessed at www.energy.gov/HQ/Docs/speeches/2001/marss/mexico_v.html on April 24, 2001.

47 Ibid.

48 NEPDG, NEP 2001, chap. 8, p. 9.

49 Ibid., chap. 8, p. 10.

50 See 'Venezuela Oil Woes Are Long Term', *Wall Street Journal*, February 14, 2003; Juan Forero, 'Venezuelan Oilman: Rebel with a New Cause', *The New York Times*, February 9, 2003. For background on the Venezuelan oil industry, see US Department of Energy, Energy Information Administration, 'Venezuela', Country Analysis Brief, December 2002, electronic document accessed at www.eia.doe.gov/cabs/venez.html on December 20, 2002.

51 For background on the Colombian oil industry, see US Department of

Energy, Energy Information Administration, 'Colombia', Country Analysis Brief, May 2002, electronic document accessed at www.eia.doe. gov/cabs/colombia.html on May 29, 2002.

52 See Juan Forero, 'New Role for U.S. in Colombia: Protecting a Vital Oil Pipeline', *The New York Times*, October 4, 2002.

53 Speech by Governor George W. Bush at The Citadel, Charleston, South Carolina, September 23, 1999, electronic document accessed at www.georgewbush.com on December 2, 1999.

54 US Department of Defense, *Quadrennial Defense Review Report,* Washington. D.C.: DoD, September 30, 2001, p. 43.

ECOLOGICAL IMPERIALISM: THE CURSE OF CAPITALISM

JOHN BELLAMY FOSTER AND BRETT CLARK

In the spring of 2003 the United States, backed by Britain, invaded Iraq, a country with the second largest oil reserves in the world. The United States is now working to expand Iraqi oil production, while securing for itself an increasingly dominant position in the control of this crucial resource as part of its larger economic and geopolitical strategy. Earlier, the same US administration that invaded Iraq had pulled out of the Kyoto Protocol, designed to limit the growth in the emissions of carbon dioxide and other greenhouse gases responsible for global warming – a phenomenon threatening all life as we know it. It is no wonder, then, that the last few years have seen a growth of concern about ecological imperialism, which in many eyes has become as significant as the more familiar political, economic and cultural forms of imperialism to which it is related.

In 1986 Alfred Crosby published a work entitled *Ecological Imperialism: The Biological Expansion of Europe, 900-1900,* that described the destruction wrought on indigenous environments – most often inadvertently – by the European colonization of much of the rest of the world.[1] Old World flora and fauna introduced into New World environments experienced demographic explosions with adverse effects on native species. As the subtitle of Crosby's book suggested, his historical analysis dealt mainly with 'biological expansion' and thus had no direct concern with imperialism as a political-economic phenomenon. It did not consider how ecology might relate to the domination of the periphery of the capitalist world economy by the centre, or to rivalry between different capitalist powers. Like the infectious diseases that killed tens of millions of indigenous peoples following Columbus' landing in the Americas, ecological imperialism in this view worked as a purely biological force, following 'encounters' between regions of the earth that had previously been separated geographically. Social relations of production were largely absent from this historical account.

The ecological problem under capitalism is a complex one. An analysis at the level of the entire globe is required. Ecological degradation at this universal level is related to the divisions within the world capitalist system, arising from the fact that a single world economy is nonetheless divided into numerous nation-states, competing with each other both directly and via their corporations. It is also divided hierarchically into centre and periphery, with nations occupying fundamentally different positions in the international division of labour, and in a world-system of dominance and dependency.

All of this makes the analysis of ecological imperialism complicated enough, but understanding has also been impeded by the underdevelopment of an ecological materialist analysis of capitalism within Marxist theory as a whole.[2] Nevertheless, it has long been apparent – and was stipulated in Marx's own work – that transfers in economic values are accompanied in complex ways by real 'material-ecological' flows that transform relations between city and country, and between global metropolis and periphery.[3] Control of such flows is a vital part of competition between rival industrial and financial centres. Ecological imperialism thus presents itself most obviously in the following ways: the pillage of the resources of some countries by others and the transformation of whole ecosystems upon which states and nations depend; massive movements of population and labour that are interconnected with the extraction and transfer of resources; the exploitation of ecological vulnerabilities of societies to promote imperialist control; the dumping of ecological wastes in ways that widen the chasm between centre and periphery; and overall, the creation of a global 'metabolic rift' that characterizes the relation of capitalism to the environment, and at the same time limits capitalist development.

THE 'METABOLIC RIFT'

The main ecological contradictions of capitalism, associated with ecological imperialism, were already evident to a considerable extent in the writings of Marx. The accumulation of capital is in some respects a self-propelling process; the surplus accumulated in one stage becomes the investment fund for the next. One of the crucial questions in classical political economy, therefore, was where the original capital had come from that set off the dynamic accumulation that characterized the late eighteenth and nineteenth century. This raised the issue of prior, primary or 'primitive' accumulation.

Taking Britain as the classical case, Marx saw primitive accumulation as having three aspects. First, the removal of peasants from the land by land enclosures and the abrogation of customary, common rights, so they no longer had direct access to or control over the material means of production. Second, the creation by this means of a pauperized pool of landless labourers, who became wage labourers under capitalism, and who flocked to the towns where they emerged as an industrial proletariat. Third, an enormous concentration and centralization of wealth as the means of production (initially through the control of the land) came to be monopolized by fewer and fewer individuals, and as the surplus thus made available flowed to the industrial centres. Newly proletarianized workers were available to be exploited, while 'Lazarus layers' of the unemployed kept down wages, making production more profitable.

The whole process of primitive accumulation – involving, as Marx put it, 'the forcible expropriation of the people from the soil', and the 'sweeping' of them, as Malthus expressed it, into the towns – had deep ecological implications.[4] Already land under feudal property had been converted into 'the inorganic body of its lord'. Under capitalism, with the further alienation of the land (and nature), the domination of human beings by other human beings was extended. 'Land, like man', Marx noted, was reduced 'to the level of a venal object'.[5]

Marx's concept of a 'metabolic rift' was developed in the context of the alarm raised by agricultural chemists and agronomists in Germany, Britain, France and the United States about the loss of soil nutrients – such as nitrogen, phosphorous and potassium – through the export of food and fibre to the cities. Rather than being returned to the soil, as in traditional agricultural production, these essential nutrients were being shipped hundreds or even thousands of miles away and ended up as waste polluting the cities. The most advanced form of capitalist agricultural production at the time, British 'high farming', was, the German chemist Justus von Liebig contended, nothing but a 'robbery system', due to its effects on the soil.[6]

Marx, who was a careful student of Liebig and other soil chemists, saw this antagonism between human beings and the earth as an important problem. Capitalism had, as he put it, created an 'irreparable rift' in the 'metabolic interaction' between human beings and the earth; a 'systematic restoration' of that necessary metabolic interaction as a 'regulative law of social production' was needed, but the growth under capitalism of large-scale industrial agriculture and long-distance trade intensified and extended the metabolic rift (and still does). Moreover the wastage of soil nutrients had its counterpart in pollution and waste in the towns.[7]

Marx treated both primitive accumulation and the metabolic rift as embodying global implications fundamental to the understanding of the development of capitalism as a world system. As he famously put it:

> The discovery of gold and silver in America, the extirpation, enslavement and entombment in mines of the indigenous population of that continent, the beginnings of the conquest and plunder of India, and the conversion of Africa into a preserve for the commercial hunting of blackskins, are all things which characterize the dawn of the era of capitalist production. These idyllic proceedings are the chief moments of primitive accumulation.[8]

The genocide inflicted on the indigenous populations went hand in hand with the seizure of wealth in the New World. 'The treasures captured outside Europe by undisguised looting, enslavement and murder flowed back to the mother-country and were turned into capital there.' Great fortunes were built on robbing the periphery of its natural wealth and exploiting ecological resources. In India 'the monopolies of salt, opium, betel and other commodities were inexhaustible mines of wealth.'[9] In his famous 1848 speech on free trade Marx observed, 'You believe perhaps, gentlemen, that the production of coffee and sugar is the natural destiny of the West Indies. Two centuries ago, nature, which does not trouble herself about commerce, had planted neither sugar-cane nor coffee trees there.'[10]

The creation of such monocultures for the export of cash crops to Europe – and the enslaved or semi-enslaved labouring populations that worked them – were products of the development of the capitalist world economy, with its open plunder of the periphery for the benefit of the centre. Monoculture plantations constituted, in the words of Eduardo Galeano in his *Open Veins of Latin America*,

> a sieve for the draining-off of natural wealth … Each region, once inte-grated into the world market, experiences a dynamic cycle; then decay sets in with the competition of substitute products, the exhaustion of the soil, or the development of other areas where conditions are better. The initial productive drive fades with the passing years into a culture of poverty, subsistence economy, and lethargy …. The more a product is desired by the world market, the greater the misery it brings to the Latin American peoples whose sacrifice creates it.[11]

But tropical monoculture was not the only mode of ecological imperialism in the nineteenth century. British 'high farming' – or early industrialized agricul-ture – robbed the soil of England of its nutrients, and then sought to compensate for this by robbing other countries of the means to replace them. Marx was again well aware of this. Following Liebig, he noted that British agriculture in effect imported the soil of some countries by shipping soil nutrients and natural fertilisers from these countries back to Britain. British agriculture had become dependent on imported guano.

This illustrated precisely the 'rift' in the natural metabolism that Marx iden-tified, as Jason Moore notes:

> With the transition to capitalism, a new division of labor between town and country took shape – on a world scale and within regions – whereby the products of the countryside (especially, but not only in the peripheries) flowed into the cities, which were under no obligation to return the waste products to the point of production. Nutrients were pumped out of one ecosystem in the periphery and transferred to another in the core. In essence, the land was progressively mined until its relative exhaustion fettered profitability. At this point, economic contraction forced capital to seek out and develop new ways of exploiting territories hitherto beyond the reach of the law of value.[12]

FROM THE CURSE OF NITRATES TO
THE CURSE OF OIL

British cotton textiles, as Galeano noted, were exchanged for the hides of Rio de la Plata, the copper of Chile, the sugar of Cuba, and the coffee of Brazil, but also for the guano and nitrates of Peru.[13] In 1840, the same year that Liebig first pointed to the issue of the loss of soil nutrients, a French scientist, Alexandre Cochet, discovered that valuable quantities of nitrate of soda could be extracted from guano and nitrates (saltpeter), both of which were abundant in Peru. In 1841, shortly after Cochet's laboratory results were published, an international guano rush began, as European (especially British) and US agriculturists sought the precious fertilizer to compensate for the soil nutrients that they were losing. In the early 1850s a British officer reported witnessing the simultaneous loading of guano on ships from the following countries from a single island off the coast of Peru: forty four United States ships, forty English, five French, two Dutch, one Italian, one Belgian, one Norwegian, one Swedish, one Russian, one Armenian and three Peruvian. Loading the guano into ships required digging into deep mounds of excrement that covered rocky islands. Acrid dust penetrated the eyes, the nose, the mouth of a worker, and the stench was appalling. After slavery was abolished in 1854 tens of thousands of Chinese coolies were contracted for through Macao and Hong Kong. By 1875 some 80,000 were working under conditions of virtual slavery in the desert and islands of Peru.[14]

Then in 1853 a process was discovered for efficiently mining the nitrate fields in the Tarapacá desert province of Peru, and soon afterwards rich deposits were also found in the adjacent Bolivian province of Atacama. By the 1860s these nitrate fields had become even more important as a source of fertilizer than guano, the availability of which had began to diminish. Nitrates were in high demand not only for fertilizers, but also for the recently invented TNT and other explosives, crucial to the expanding war industries of the industrial capitalist states.[15] By 1875 British investments primarily in the nitrate industry in Peru totalled £1,000,000.

The Peruvian ruling class grew enormously wealthy as a result of the guano trade and the mining of nitrates. This wealth did not, however, flow significantly into economic development, apart from the building of railways; for the rest of the population the nitrate resource soon proved to be a curse. Peru became heavily indebted, in a classic pattern, primarily to British investors, with its guano exports mortgaged well into the future. In 1875, attempting to get out of its debt trap, Peru imposed a state monopoly in its nitrate zones in Tarapacá, expropriating the holdings of private investors (many of whom were foreign, particularly British) and offering them government certificates of payment. Subsequently the Peruvian government also sought to regulate the output of guano and nitrates so that they would not compete against each other.

This led to the War of the Pacific (also sometimes called the Nitrate War), which broke out four years after the Peruvian expropriation of the nitrate industry, when Bolivia, breaking a previous treaty, attempted to raise taxes on exports by Chilean intermediaries of nitrates from its Atacama province. Chile, backed by British investors, declared war on Bolivia but also on Peru, with which Bolivia was allied. With its more modern, British-built navy and French-trained army, Chile was soon able to seize Bolivia's Atacama province and Peru's Tarapacá – never to leave. Before the war Chile had almost no nitrate fields and no guano deposits. By the end of the war in 1883 it had seized all of the nitrate zones in Bolivia and Peru and most of Peru's coastal guano deposits.[16] Before the war British controlled 13 per cent of Peru's Tarapacá nitrate industry; immediately after the war – given Chile's possession of the region – the British share rose to 34 per cent, and by 1890 it was 70 per cent.[17] As the former US Secretary of State James G. Blaine told a congressional committee investigating the US diplomatic role during the war, the war was about guano and nitrates: 'Nothing else …. It is an English war on Peru, with Chili as the instrument …. Chili would never have gone into this war one inch but for her backing by English capital, and there was never anything played out so boldly in the world as when they came to divide the loot and the spoils.'[18]

Having lost its two principal resources for export, the Peruvian economy collapsed after the war. As the great Peruvian Marxist José Carlos Mariátegui noted, defeat in the War of the Pacific increased Peruvian dependence on British capital. 'Very soon [after the war] the capitalist group that had formed during the period of guano and nitrates resumed its activity and returned to power….The Grace Contract [which they negotiated] ratified British domination in Peru by delivering the state railways to the English bankers who until then had financed the republic and its extravagances.'[19] Now that the Peruvian government no longer had the same wealth of resources to exploit it had no other way to pay off the foreign debts with which it was still encumbered except by handing its railroads over to British investors who had themselves clandestinely backed Chile in its seizing of much of Peru's territory and its most valuable natural resources. As Bruce Farcau observed, the guano and nitrate deposits in Peru turned out, 'like the Midas touch', to be 'a curse disguised as a blessing', first in creating a debt-laden economy, and then giving rise to a war and the loss of these resources.[20]

As a result of its seizure of the nitrate territories in the War of the Pacific Chile was to take on the curse of nitrates in the decades that followed. Europe still needed guano and nitrates in vast quantities to maintain its agricultural productivity and sought to control this trade imperialistically for the benefit of its own capitalists, exploiting these ecological resources to their limit while siphoning off the bulk of the economic wealth they generated. In 1888 the Chilean President José Manuel Balmaceda, who had carried out modernizing reforms including extensive public works and support for education, announced that the nitrate areas of Chile would have to be nationalized through the formation of Chilean enterprises, and blocked the sale of state-owned nitrate fields to the British. Three years later a civil war broke out, with British and other foreign investors supporting the opponents of Balmaceda with money and armaments. The press in London characterized Balmaceda (in tones very recognizable today) as a 'dictator of the worst stripe'. When the defeated Balmaceda committed suicide in 1891 the British ambassador wrote to the Foreign Office: 'The British community makes no secret of its satisfaction over the fall of Balmaceda, whose victory, it is thought, would have implied serious harm to British commercial interests.' State control of industries and economic infrastructure in Chile quickly receded after the civil war, as the British extended their investments.

In the early 1890s Chile was delivering three-quarters of all its exports to Britain while obtaining almost half of its imports from Britain, creating a trade dependence on Britain greater than that of India at that time. When the First World War broke out in Europe, two-thirds of Chile's national income was derived from nitrate exports primarily to Britain and Germany. The British monopoly of the nitrate trade through its control of the Chilean economy had put Germany at a serious disadvantage in its competition with Britain, since nitrates were necessary for explosives as well as fertilizer. Like Britain, Germany had worked to have Balmaceda ousted, but Chile remained largely under British control, creating a problem for Germany. Just prior to the First World War, however, the German chemist and nationalist Fritz Haber devised a process for producing nitrates by fixing nitrogen from the air. The result within a few years was to destroy almost completely the value of Chilean nitrates, creating a severe crisis for the Chilean economy.[21]

But the curse of nitrates (and nitrogen) did not end there; it was transferred to the world at large, including the rich countries themselves. Nitrogen fertilizers, used on an ever-increasing scale (currently around 100 million tons annually) to maintain agricultural productivity, now pollute more and more of the world's groundwater, lakes and rivers through fertilizer runoff, giving rise to one of the major ecological problems facing the world today.[22]

Outside Latin America the history of the curse of nitrates is now forgotten. But the modern history of the curse of oil, with its all too close parallels with that earlier history, is still very much ongoing. As the *New York Times* noted in its June 7, 2003 issue, in an article entitled 'Striking it Poor: Oil as a Curse', 'scholarly studies for more than a decade have consistently warned of what is known as the resource curse: that developing countries whose economies depend on exporting oil, gas or extracted materials are likely to be poor, authoritarian, corrupt and rocked by civil war.' The mainstream argument attributes this persistent 'curse' to bad governments in poor countries, which supposedly lack the capacity to utilize the enormous and potentially corrupting economic benefits provided by such resources in a productive manner.

The root explanation of the 'curse of oil', however, like that of nitrates, is to be found in ecological imperialism. As Michael Perelman has cogently stated,

> The origins of the curse of oil do not lie in the physical properties of petroleum but rather in the social structure of the world ... A rich natural resource base makes a poor country, especially a relatively powerless one, an inviting target – both politically and militarily – for dominant nations.

In the case of oil, the powerful nations will not risk letting such a valuable resource fall under the control of an independent government,
especially one that might pursue policies that do not coincide with the
economic interests of the great transnational corporations. So, governments that display excessive independence soon find themselves
overthrown, even if their successors will foster an environment of corruption and political instability.[23]

Nowadays, the curse of oil has also come back to haunt the rich countries too
– their environments and their economies – in the form of global warming, or
what might be called a planetary rift in the human relation to the global
commons – the atmosphere and oceans. This planetary ecological rift, arising
from the workings of the capitalist system and its necessary companion imperialism, while varied in its outcomes in specific regions, has led to ecological
degradation on a scale that threatens to undermine all existing ecosystems and
species (including the human species).

THE ECOLOGICAL DEBT

The mobilization of opposition to ecological imperialism is now increasingly
taking place via the concept of 'ecological debt'. Acción Ecológica, an Ecuador-
based organization that is leading the ecological debt campaign, defines ecological
debt broadly as 'the debt accumulated by Northern, industrial countries toward
Third World countries on account of resource plundering, environmental
damages, and the free occupation of environmental space to deposit wastes, such
as greenhouse gases, from the industrial countries.'[24] Accounting for ecological
debt radically alters the question: 'Who Owes Whom?'

Fundamental to this position is an analysis of the social interactions between
nature and society, as organized by ecological imperialism. The history of pillage
and super-exploitation of peoples is seen as part of a larger ecological debt. Capital
remains a central focus, since it is the production and consumption patterns of the
central capitalist countries that are held responsible for the deteriorating ecological conditions of the planet.[25] A wide range of activities contribute, Third World
critics contend, to the ecological debt: the extraction of natural resources; unequal
terms of trade; degradation of land and soil for export crops; other unrecognized
environmental damage and pollution caused by extractive and productive
processes; appropriation of ancestral knowledge; loss of biodiversity; contamination of the atmosphere and oceans; the introduction of toxic chemicals and
dangerous weapons; and the dumping of hazardous waste in the periphery.[26]

Within the discussion of ecological debt there are two major dimensions: (1)
the social-ecological destruction and exploitation that takes places within
nations under the influence of ecological imperialism; and (2) the imperialist
appropriation of global commons and the unequal use (exploitation) of the
absorption capacity of these commons.

In his *Hungry Planet*, first published in 1965, Georg Borgstrom introduced the
concept of 'ghost acres' to illustrate Britain's dependence on food and raw

materials from colonial (or neo-colonial) hinterlands in order to sustain the productive, consumption, and trade operations of that nation. The growth of capital has increased the demands placed on the world as a whole. The 'ecological footprint' of the core nations continues to expand, as they deplete their own historic stocks of material and energy, as well as those of other nations.[27] Debt cycles and military interventions maintain global inequalities, as the South continues to subsidize the North in terms of labour, commodities and natural resources. Extraction of raw materials for commodity production is organized around meeting the demands of the countries of the North, where approximately 25 per cent of the world's population lives but which consumes 75 per cent of global resources.[28] For hundreds of years, the centre has depended on cheap primary materials and labour from the periphery. The volume of material and economic value that flows out of the South increases (the volume of exports from Latin America increased by 245 per cent between 1980 and 1995),[29] yet the financial debt of these nations continues to grow, exacerbated by arbitrary increases in interest rates. At the same time monopoly capital, dominating the world market, is able to overvalue the North's industrial, high-value commodity exports, further unbalancing international trade.[30]

Imperialist forces impose socio-ecological regimes of production on the world, deepening the antagonistic division between town and country, as well as between the North and South. Agro-ecosystems (including both labour and nature) are restructured and 'rationally and systematically reshaped in order to intensify, not merely the production of food and fiber, but the accumulation of personal wealth' by comprador bourgeoisies and monopoly capital.[31] As Josué de Castro noted in a classic 1952 study, 'It was to the advantage of economic imperialism and international commerce, both controlled by profit-seeking minorities, that the production, distribution and consumption of food products be regarded as purely business matters rather than as phenomena of the highest importance to society as a whole.'[32]

At the planetary level, ecological imperialism has resulted in the appropriation of the global commons (i.e. the atmosphere and oceans) and the carbon absorption capacity of the biosphere, primarily to the benefit of a relatively small number of countries at the centre of the capitalist world economy.[33] The North rose to wealth and power in part through high fossil-fuel consumption, which is now culminating in a climate crisis due to the dumping of ecological wastes into the atmosphere. Climate change is already occurring due to the increased concentrations of carbon dioxide and other minor greenhouse gases, warming the earth 0.6°C during the last hundred years.

The ecological debt approach to the question of ecological imperialism, while addressing the larger problem in its full dimensions, nonetheless focuses tactically on the carbon debt as its most concrete, empirical basis – taking advantage of the urgent global necessity of addressing this problem. The nations of the North that cause a disproportionate amount of the emissions due to industries, automobiles, and lifestyles, are largely responsible for climate change, as the 'fossil-fuel economy creates waste emissions faster than natural systems can absorb them.'[34] The Intergovernmental Panel on Climate Change (IPCC) now expects an increase in temperature of 1.5-6.0° C during this century. 'A temperature rise of 4°C would create an earth that was warmer than at any time in the last 40 million years,' potentially undermining the ability of human civilization to survive.[35] The extreme weather patterns (hurricanes, floods, droughts, etc.) in recent decades, which disproportionately affect the nations of the South, may be partly the result of greenhouse gases accumulating in the atmosphere. Global warming leading to a rise in sea levels threatens many islands as well as some densely populated, low-lying countries such as Bangladesh with floods that would submerge them.

Given that no one owns the atmosphere or oceans, calculating the carbon debt is an attempt to measure how unsustainable the production and consumption of a given economy is, relative to all the others. Simply stated, if a nation uses fossil fuel above a set rate, then it is accumulating a carbon debt, making a disproportionate use of environmental space in the commons for the disposal of its carbon waste.

In determining how to calculate this set rate of emissions, several things must be considered. In the year 1996, already, approximately 7 billion metric tons of carbon were released into the atmosphere, more than 50 per cent of it by the United States and Europe – a massively disproportionate share. Second, current carbon emissions exceed the amount that the environment can absorb. The IPCC has estimated that at least a 60 per cent reduction in carbon emissions from 1990 levels (down to 2,800 million metric tons) is necessary to stabilize or reduce the risk of further climate change.

For all these reasons it follows that the rich industrialized nations, whose output alone already exceeds the world's total allowable amount, must – from a moral standpoint – bear the brunt of the necessary reduction in emissions. As Agarwal and Narain suggested in 1991, any just and reasonable approach for determining how much carbon a nation can emit into the global commons, without accumulating a carbon debt, must be based on emissions per head of population.[36] Andrew Simms and his colleagues have calculated that 'based on the 1990 target for climate stabilization, everyone in the world would have a per capita allowance of carbon of around 0.4 tonnes, per year.'[37] But as time passes and the release and accumulation of gases continues, that allowance decreases. Before long the per capita allowance of carbon will only be 0.2 tons, per year. Inaction creates an ever more difficult position for the future. In fact, if current trends continue, global warming could spiral out of control, seriously threatening the sustainability of life on earth. An 'ecological discontinuity' can occur with few, if any, immediate warning signs.[38]

When the North's current excess of carbon emissions (beyond what is sustainable per capita for the entire world) is translated into dollar terms, based on 'the historically close correlation between the basic measure of economic activity, Gross Domestic Product (GDP) and carbon dioxide emissions,' the ecological debt owed by the North to the South in terms of carbon emissions alone amounts to an estimated $13 trillion per year.[39] The annual ecological debt of the North, owed to the South, without even looking at the cumulative impact, is thus calculated to be at least three times the financial debt that the South currently 'owes' to the North. Paying it would cancel out the loans that have imprisoned Third World nations, and would also allow them to adopt more fuel-efficient technologies.

But payment of this debt and new technologies will not solve the carbon rift if capitalist production in the South takes place in the same way that it has in the North. Ecological debt proponents therefore advocate a process of contraction and convergence. In this scenario, the rich nations of the North would reduce their carbon (and other greenhouse gas) emissions to an appropriate level to meet the IPCC recommendations, while the poor nations of the South would be allowed to increase their emissions gradually in the interest of social and economic development. The nations of the world would thus converge towards 'equal, and low, per capita allotments'.[40] Variations in allotments may exist, given differences in climate, but per capita emissions for the world as a whole would be within acceptable standards.

Assessing the ecological degradation and conditions of international inequality as these relate to global warming is, of course, only the beginning in trying to access the ecological debt owed to the South. The ocean, another global commons, has long been used for the dumping of toxins and hazardous waste, and its ability to serve as a sink for carbon is decreasing. Furthermore, the depletion of the ocean fish stock threatens to disrupt metabolic relationships within the ocean ecosystem. The full extent of the damage caused by ecological imperialism is indeed unaccounted for, especially if we take into account the historical pillage carried out over several centuries throughout the global periphery as a result of the economic expansion of the core capitalist states.

The ecological debt movement today fights for the restoration and renewal of nature on a global basis. And as ecological sustainability is impossible without social and economic balance, ecological debt activists are increasingly confronting the forces of capitalist expansion, calling into question the legitimacy of the global order. The concentration of wealth is explicitly linked to the impoverishment and exploitation of people and nature throughout the world. A system of incessant accumulation on an ever-increasing scale – and of consumption without bounds – is recognized as one bent on suicide. Stopping the destruction caused by ecological imperialism is seen as the only solution to this global problem. A transformation of the social-ecological relationships of production is needed. If the global commons is the sink where wastes are absorbed, the sink is clogged and overflowing. To challenge ecological imperialism, Acción Ecológica insists that 'it's time to shut off the tap' to prevent the 'unjust flow of energy, natural resources, food, cheap labour and financial resources from the South to the North.'[41]

THE STRUGGLE AGAINST ECOLOGICAL IMPERIALISM TODAY

The problem with the ecological debt campaign is, clearly, that given the current balance of world forces it cannot hope to succeed. This is indicated by the level of resistance on the part of capital marked by the US withdrawal from the Kyoto Protocol, and by the declaration of victory by the Global Climate Coalition (representing many of the leading global monopolistic corporations) with the effective collapse of the protocol. As they state on their web page:

> The Global Climate Coalition has been deactivated. The industry voice on climate change has served its purpose by contributing to a new national approach to global warming.
>
> The Bush administration will soon announce a climate policy that is expected to rely on the development of new technologies to reduce greenhouse emissions, a concept strongly supported by the GCC.
>
> The coalition also opposed Senate ratification of the Kyoto Protocol that would assign such stringent targets for lowering greenhouse gas emissions that economic growth in the US would be severely hampered and energy prices for consumers would skyrocket. The GCC also opposed the treaty because it does not require the largest developing countries to make cuts in their emissions.
>
> At this point, both Congress and the Administration agree that the US should not accept the mandatory cuts in emissions required by the protocol.[42]

If global warming is a problem, the Bush administration has contended, it does not constitute an immediate threat to the United States; hence actions to address the problem that would carry high economic costs should be avoided. Better to depend on futuristic 'carbon-sequestration' technologies and similar means. For many island or low-lying nations watching sea levels rise as the arctic glaciers melt, such a stance is a particularly extreme case of ecological imperialism. While the poor nations of the periphery are expected to continue to pay financial debts to banks of the rich nations of the centre, the enormous ecological debt incurred by the latter is not even being acknowledged – and the entire planetary problem is growing worse by the year. The struggle is therefore likely to intensify.

The ecological debt struggle, organized around the degradation of the global commons – particularly the warming of the atmosphere – brought on disproportionately by the rich countries, has certainly given a new practical meaning to the concept of ecological imperialism. This age-old fight has now become associated with an organized form of resistance centred on the need to set the ecological debt of the rich countries against the financial debts of the poor countries. This immediate struggle, moreover, brings the larger ecological curse of capitalism more and more clearly into view. The economic development of capitalism has always carried with it social and ecological degradation as its other side: the degradation of work, as Marx argued, is accompanied by the degradation of the earth. Further, ecological imperialism has meant that the worst forms of ecological destruction in terms of pillage of resources, the disruption of sustainable relations to the earth, and the dumping of wastes – all fall on the periphery more than the centre. This relation has not changed at all over the centuries as witnessed by the wars over guano and nitrates of the late nineteenth century and the wars over oil (and the geopolitical power to be obtained through control of oil) of the late twentieth and early twenty-first century.

It is in the nature of this process that it continually worsens. Capital in the late twentieth and twenty-first century is running up against ecological barriers at a biospheric level that cannot be overcome, as was the case previously, through the 'spatial fix' of geographical expansion and exploitation. Ecological imperialism – the growth of the centre of the system at unsustainable rates, through the more thoroughgoing ecological degradation of the periphery – is now generating a planetary-scale set of ecological contradictions, imperiling the entire biosphere. Only a revolutionary social solution that addresses the rift in ecological relations on a planetary scale and their relation to global structures of imperialism and inequality offers any genuine hope that these contradictions can be transcended. More than ever the world needs what the early socialist thinkers, including Marx, called for: the rational organization of the human metabolism with nature by freely associated producers. The fundamental curse to be exorcised is capitalism itself.

NOTES

1   Alfred W. Crosby, *Ecological Imperialism: The Biological Expansion of Europe*, Cambridge: Cambridge University Press, 1986.

2   The importance of ecological materialism is highlighted in John Bellamy Foster, *Marx's Ecology: Materialism and Nature*, New York: Monthly Review Press, 2000.

3   For a detailed analysis of the relationship between material-ecological flows (usually expressed in terms of use values) and value flows in Marx's analysis see Paul Burkett, *Marx and Nature*, New York: St. Martin's Press, 1999.

4   Karl Marx, *Capital*, Volume 1, New York: Vintage, 1976, p. 896; Malthus to Ricardo, August 17, 1817, in David Ricardo, *Works and Correspondence*, Cambridge: Cambridge University Press, 1952, Volume 7, p. 175.

5   Karl Marx, *Early Writings*, New York: Vintage, 1974, pp. 318-19.

6   For an elaboration of Liebig's argument and its influence on Marx, see John Bellamy Foster, 'The Communist Manifesto and the Environment', *Socialist Register 1999*, London: Merlin, 1999, p. 179.

7   Based on these observations Marx developed a view of the necessity of a sustainable relation between human beings and nature (going beyond the issue of the soil) – a relation that had to be governed by the principle of maintaining (or improving) the earth for the sake of future generations. As he famously put it: 'From the standpoint of a higher socio-economic formation, the private property of particular individuals in the earth will appear just as

absurd as the private property of one man in other men. Even an entire society, a nation, or all simultaneously existing societies taken together, are not the owners of the earth. They are simply its possessors, its beneficiaries, and have to bequeath it in an improved state to succeeding generations as *boni patres familias* [good heads of the household].' (See *Capital*, Volume 1, London: Penguin Books, 1976, pp. 636-38; Volume 3, pp. 949-50 and 911).

8   Marx, *Capital*, Volume 1, p. 915.
9   Ibid., pp. 914-30.
10 Karl Marx, *The Poverty of Philosophy*, New York: International Publishers, 1963, p. 223.
11 Eduardo Galeano, *Open Veins of Latin America*, New York: Monthly Review Press, 1973, pp. 72-73.
12 Jason W. Moore, 'Environmental Crises and the Metabolic Rift in World-Historical Perspective', *Organization & Environment*, 13(2), 2000, p. 124.
13 Galeano, *Open Veins of Latin America*, pp. 191-92.
14 Bruce W. Farcau, *The Ten Cents War: Chile, Peru and Bolivia in the War of the Pacific, 1879-1884*, Westport, Connecticut: Praeger, 2000, pp. 8-10; William Jefferson Davis, *Tacna and Arica*, New Haven: Yale University Press, 1931, pp. 27, 34-37.
15 Farcau, *The Ten Cents War*, p. 10.
16 See Dennis, *Tacna and Arica*; Farcau, *The Ten Cents War*; John Mayo, *British Merchants and Chilean Development, 1851-1886*, Boulder: Westview Press, 1987, pp. 157-87; William F. Sater, *Chile and the War of the Pacific*, Lincoln: University of Nebraska Press, 1986; Dr. I. Alzamora (former Vice President of Peru), *Peru and Chile*, pamphlet (publisher unknown), no date (around 1908); Harold Blakemore, *British Nitrates and Chilean Politics, 1886-1896: Balmaceda and North*, London: University of London, 1974, pp. 14-22; Michael Montéon, *Chile in the Nitrate Era*, Madison, Wisconsin: University of Wisconsin Press, 1982, pp. 19-20, 27; Henry Clay Evans, *Chile and its Relations with the United States*, Durham, North Carolina: Duke University Press, 1927, pp. 97-119.
17 John Mayo, *British Merchants and Chilean Development*, p. 181.
18 US House of Representatives, 47th Congress, 1st Session, House Reports, Report no. 1790, *Chili-Peru*, pp. 217-18. See also Perry Belmont, *An American Democrat*, New York: Columbia University Press, 1941, pp. 255-62. Blaine's claims regarding the clandestine role of Britain in fomenting the War of the Pacific have been denied by Victor Kiernan, who, based on a careful perusal of British Foreign Office records, delivered a verdict of 'not guilty'. Kiernan's argument, however, rested on the contrary claim that no actual smoking-gun evidence had been located proving that the British Foreign Office had directly instigated the war. The support of British investors and the British government for Chile in the war itself is not in doubt, nor is the division of the loot during and after the war (so strongly emphasized by Blaine). Kiernan also indicates that the British influence was exercised more directly from Valparaiso and Santiago, rather than directly from the Foreign Office in London. The one

factual point in Kiernan's argument that is most doubtful is his insistence that there were no restrictions on Peruvian purchase of British armaments. Representatives of both the Chilean and American governments claimed otherwise. See V.G. Kiernan, 'Foreign Interests in the War of the Pacific', *Hispanic American Historical Review*, 35(1), 1955, pp. 14–36.

19   José Carlos Mariátegui, *Seven Interpretive Essays on Peruvian Reality*, Austin: University of Texas Press, 1971, pp. 9–13; Paul Gootenberg, *Imagining Development: Economic Ideas in Peru's 'Fictitious Prosperity' of Guano, 1840–1880*, Berkeley: University of California Press, 1993, pp. 183–84.

20   Farcau, *The Ten Cents War*, p. 14.

21   Galeano, *Open Veins of Latin America*, pp. 157–58; Blakemore, *British Nitrates and Chilean Politics;* Andre Gunder Frank, *The Development of Underdevelopment in Latin America*, New York: Monthly Review Press, 1969, pp. 73–93; Evans, *Chile and its Relations with the United States*; Montéon, *Chile in the Nitrate Era*; J.R. McNeill, *Something New Under the Sun*, New York: W.W. Norton, 2000, pp. 24–25. During the events leading up to the civil war in Chile US foreign policy, headed by Blaine, who was again Secretary of State, was sympathetic toward Balmaceda, whose nationalism was seen as a curb on British power.

22   See John Bellamy Foster and Fred Magdoff, 'Liebig, Marx, and the Depletion of Soil Fertility: Relevance for Today's Agriculture', in Fred Magdoff, John Bellamy Foster and Frederick H. Buttel, eds., *Hungry for Profit*, New York: Monthly Review Press, 2000, p. 54; National Public Radio, 'The Tragedy of Fritz Haber', July 11, 2002; from www.npr.org/programs/morning/features/2002/jul/fritzhaber/ (Retrieved June 17, 2003).

23   Michael Perelman, 'Myths of the Market: Economics and the Environment', *Organization & Environment*, 16(2), 2003, pp. 199–202.

24   Acción Ecológica, 'Ecological Debt: South Tells North "Time to Pay Up"' (Retrieved March 6, 2003, from www.cosmovisiones.com/DeudaEcologica/a_timetopay.html, 2003).

25   Aurora Donoso, 'Who Owes Who?: Collecting the Ecological Debt' (Retrieved March 6, 2003, from www.Brisbane.foe.org.au/eco_debt.htm, 2003).

26   Acción Ecológica, 'No More Plunder, They Owe Us the Ecological Debt!' (Retrieved March 6, 2003, from www.cosmovisiones.com/DeudaEcologica/a_averde78in.html, 1999).

27   Georg Borgstrom, *The Hungry Planet*, New York: The Macmillan Company, 1965; Mathis Wackernagel and William Rees, *Our Ecological Footprint*, Gabriola Island, British Columbia: New Society, 1996; Richard York, Eugene A. Rosa and Thomas Dietz, 'Footprints on the Earth', *American Sociological Review*, 68 (April) 2003, pp. 279–300.

28   Donoso, 'Who Owes Who?'.

29   Aurora Donoso, 'No More Looting!: Third World Owed an Ecological Debt' (Retrieved March 6, 2003, from www.cosmovisiones.com/

DeudaEcologica/a_looting.html, 2000). The increase is measured in terms of volume not price because of the tendency of the prices of goods from the South to decline.

30 Paul A. Baran and Paul Sweezy, *Monopoly Capital: An Essay on the American Economic and Social Order*, New York: Monthly Review Press, 1966.

31 Donald Worster, 'Transformations of the Earth: Toward an Agroecological Perspective in History', *The Journal of American History*, 76(4), 1990, pp. 1087-1106.

32 Josué de. Castro, *The Geography of Hunger*, Boston: Little, Brown and Company, 1952, pp. 7, 212.

33 For a discussion of the commons and struggles to maintain environmental space free from capitalist intrusion see The Ecologist, *Whose Common Future? Reclaiming the Commons*, Philadelphia: New Society Publishers, 1993.

34 Andrew Simms, Aubrey Meyer, and Nick Robins, *Who Owes Who? Climate Change, Debt, Equity and Survival* (Retrieved March 6, 2003, from www.jubilee2000uk.org/ecological_debt/Reports/Who_owes_who.htm, 1999).

35 John Bellamy Foster, *Ecology Against Capitalism*, New York: Monthly Review Press, 2002, pp. 21, 64.

36 Acción Ecológica, 'Trade, Climate Change and the Ecological Debt' (Retrieved March 6, 2003, from www.cosmovisiones.com/DeudaEcologica/a_averdetrade.html, 2000); Anil Agarwal and Sunita Narain, *Global Warming in an Unequal World: A Case of Environmental Colonialism*, New Delhi: Centre for Science and Environment, 1991. While efficiencies vary between nations, the poorest nations are the most efficient users of energy in terms of GDP. See Simms, Meyer, and Robins, *Who Owes Who?* and Tom Athanasiou and Paul Baer, *Dead Heat: Global Justice and Global Warming*, New York: Seven Stories Press, 2002.

37 Simms, Meyer, and Robins, *Who Owes Who?*

38 See Marten Scheffer, Steve Carpenter, Jonathan A. Foley, Carl Folke, and Brian Walker, 'Catastrophic Shifts in Ecosystems', *Nature*, 403, 2001, pp. 591-596 and Roldan Muradian, 'Ecological Thresholds: A Survey', *Ecological Economics*, 38, 2001, pp. 7-24.

39 A relationship has been established such that $3,000 of GDP produces on average a ton of carbon emissions. See Simms, Meyer, and Robins, *Who Owes Who?* and Acción Ecológica, 'Trade, Climate Change and the Ecological Debt'.

40 Athanasiou and Baer, *Dead Heat*, p. 84. Also see Andrew Simms, *An Environmental War Economy: The Lessons of Ecological Debt and Global Warming*, London: New Economics Foundation, 2001 and Acción Ecológica, 'Ecological Debt'.

41 Acción Ecológica, 'No More Plunder'.

42 Retrieved June 12, 2003 from www.globalclimate.org.

NGO DILEMMAS: TROJAN HORSES FOR GLOBAL NEOLIBERALISM?

TINA WALLACE

Recent critical writings on NGOs, whether stressing their role in fostering 'a new type of cultural and economic colonialism',[1] or in becoming 'an increasingly important part of the international regulatory system' of global capitalism,[2] have unfortunately painted an over-generalized picture, failing to capture the concrete mechanisms and specific effects of what is a complex and contradictory process. This process needs to be understood in terms of the way in which over the past decade development aid conditionality has moved from the strictly economic sphere into every aspect of social and political life. It is now commonly accepted for aid donors, on which development NGOs are increasingly dependent, to make demands around social policies, budget allocations, democratic structures and systems of accountability.

As a result NGOs now have to work in a context where many of their strategies and approaches are set and monitored closely by external donor agencies. It can sometimes be hard to remember the previous core aims set for development NGOs (e.g. improving the environment, developing service delivery models, 'scaling up', promoting popular participation, micro-finance, strategic planning), as new ones come on stream all the time (e.g. advocacy to change policies, rights-based approaches, 'gender mainstreaming', accountability and transparency, impact assessment).

This process is fuelled by changing foreign policy positions, along with the outputs of think-tanks and certain key individuals – often funded by the same donors that fund NGOs. Evidence-based research does not noticeably shape this analysis, which appears to be influenced more by changing macroeconomic ideologies. The roles civil society and NGOs are expected to play have shifted as the dominant paradigms have moved successively from a focus on the state as the key to economic development, to markets, to an understanding of market failures. This has been accompanied by an increased emphasis on other development players to complement the market, and most recently to monitor the 'enabling state', which (the argument now goes) needs to drive development but which has to be regulated; this job has been allocated to 'civil society' – a confused and ahistorical term deployed to promote this development model. These are largely theoretical positions, distant from the rough-and-tumble of lived experience.

This is the wider global context in which development NGOs now work and try to facilitate processes of positive social and economic change. This essay shows that as northern NGOs increasingly rely on official donor funding and goodwill, and as the conditionalities attached to that aid increase, they are inevitably drawn into supporting and even spreading many aspects of the dominant global agenda. In addition northern NGOs are rooted in their own societies, and increasingly draw trustees and even chief executives from the business sector, and so import tools and approaches drawn from business. These are based on the 'new public management' paradigm and embedded in northern principles and analyses of what count as effective interventions. The increasing use of these tools and approaches, adopted to ensure funding flows, plus the increasing professionalization of the NGO sector, pushes many NGOs into becoming carriers of these concepts, values and practices.

There is a contradiction at the heart of these processes at every level, and especially for NGOs. The current interventionism and models of control and accountability are in stark contrast to the stated commitment at all levels – from the World Bank, the UK Department for International Development (DFID) and USAID, to the NGO sector itself – to widening the real participation of 'civil society' and poor people in democratic processes. 'The people', especially the poor, are supposed to increase their inputs into policy planning and implementation processes, and to take responsibility for their own development. But current policy and practice in development aid belie this commitment, and follow a top-down approach, reflecting an agenda heavily set by a few key institutions and players. This essay argues that NGOs are, perhaps unwittingly, increasingly part of this approach, limiting their perspectives and excluding new ideas and different ways of thinking and analyzing. Doing this they destroy rather than promote the rich organizational culture that Amartya Sen[3] and many others believe is essential for democracy to flourish.

Of course many NGOs in the north, and increasingly the south, officially oppose many aspects of the dominant trends: in world trade and the role of the World Trade organization for example, and around debt (Jubilee 2000 being a notable example of co-ordinated opposition to IMF/World Bank and donor practice). They campaign for human rights, less loudly for women's rights, and for the environment. They recognize that wider processes and conditions can undermine changes achieved on the ground in development, and they campaign on specific issues that concern them most. It is noticeable, however, that few lobby around the tight conditionality governing donor aid to governments in the south, and indeed Jubilee 2000 tied debt relief to a series of conditionalities set by the NGO sector itself, concerning health and education spending.

These campaigning efforts are also often marred by the lack of co-ordination between NGOs: competition for hearts and minds as well as funds, and a desire to raise NGOs' profiles, diminish the impact of some of this work,[4] as does the fact that NGOs increasingly rely on those they are critiquing for funding and for access to the corridors of power. Most campaigns, moreover, are limited to attacking specific aspects of the neo-liberal agenda; there is almost no deep questioning of the roots of that paradigm. And despite their rhetoric most NGOs campaign on behalf of the poor as part of the global elite, rather than trying to ensure that the poor get proper opportunities to be represented and voice their concerns. The desire for a high profile often means a rush to be seen as an important voice, without a concern for the wider implications of this, or of who they may be disempowering.

This essay focuses on who is setting agendas and the relative position of NGOs within the wider development context. It concentrates especially on the larger NGOs and those heavily dependent on donor funding. It does not attempt to analyze the value and relevance of NGO work on the ground, some of which certainly has real value for poor and marginalized people. It also ignores those NGOs which receive or ask for little or no official external funding, and those radical NGOs, which certainly do exist especially in the fields of e.g. gender, sexual and reproductive health, environment, and trafficking that are exceptions to the broad trends identified. It does, however, explore the question of whether the way NGOs are now funded and run is preventing many of them from achieving their stated aims of empowering the marginalized and combating poverty. How far are they becoming – knowingly or unthinkingly – carriers of the beliefs, policies and procedures of a global agenda, which many of them overtly oppose? The material in this essay is drawn largely, but not exclusively, from research on NGOs in the UK, Uganda and South Africa.[5]

The number of northern NGOs has increased over the past twenty years. In OECD countries they grew from 1,600 to 2,500 between 1980 and 1990. The UK sector and its funding have many peculiarities, but many European countries share similar features and some indeed are now following trends started in the UK. Some features of donor-NGO relationships in the UK have been experienced even more strongly in the USA.

As in most other countries, the development NGO sector in the UK is very diverse. Many agencies have grown up within the last ten years, while a few have been in existence for over forty years. They vary in size from household names with incomes of over £30 million a year, and a few with over £200 million in annual turnover, to innumerable small and specialized NGOs. Some operate from the UK directly, others implement their work through locally-based field offices. They differ in targeting and identifying where they want to work, some tackling all aspects of poverty, while others focus on children, women, the disabled, street children, people with HIV/AIDS, or the blind. Some work on rural issues, others – far fewer – tackle the problems of the slums. They work in different countries around the world and focus on different sectors – health, water, education, environment, social welfare, transport, libraries, and so on. For the most part they share a generalized focus on poverty, but with little definition or theory to explain the relationships of exploitation that bring it about. They avoid analyzing the nature and consequences of capitalism; instead they grapple with various categories of 'the poor', identifying their heterogeneity through the lenses of gender, class, age and so on.[6]

A lot of work has been done developing typologies of NGOs.[7] In the mid-1990s, however, in spite of all their differences of ideology, focus, origin and modes of operation they shared many characteristics and ways of behaving when it came to accessing, disbursing and accounting for aid. These characteristics were being shaped increasingly by their donors and their growing interaction with management thinking in UK through trustees invited in from the business sector.[8]

One differentiating factor that does seem to be emerging as critical is financial size. The largest NGOs in the UK, and indeed globally, are now transnational players with access to significant resources, investing heavily in fundraising, marketing and increasing market share around humanitarian and advocacy work, which for many have become more important than development work. However, even the largest players do not buck the trend of growing reliance on, and closeness to, official donors and international development agencies.

FUNDING TRENDS

Figures on funding to NGOs as a percentage of overseas development assistance are notoriously difficult to collect and often unreliable. NGOs in the UK also increasingly access bilateral, and even multilateral, funding through contracts, and money can also be accessed in countries in the south as well as from the UK, so it becomes more and more difficult to be precise about how much NGOs actually get, or how important they are as users of official aid. The overall global flow of funding through NGOs, however, increased from $200 billion in 1970 to $2,600 billion in 1997.[9] Using the DFID's own figures provided to the Development Assistance Committee (DAC) of the OECD, total UK NGO income was £428 million in 1998/9. Forty-three per cent of this – a total of £182 million – came from DFID; the rest came from the public, other donors and trust funds.

The total revenues and coverage for some of the largest global NGOs help to underline their significance as players on the global development stage. The Oxfam family had a turnover of $504 million in 1999 and worked in 117 countries; World Vision had over $600 million and worked in 92 countries; Save had $368 million and worked in 121 countries. Seven of the largest NGOs had a combined income of $2.5 billion in 1999.[10] The major donors to the UK NGO sector, other than members of the public, are DFID, the European Union, Comic Relief, the Community Fund (money from the lotteries), and a large

206 SOCIALIST REGISTER 2004

number of small trusts including Nuffield and the Princess Diana Fund. DFID is the most significant institutional funder and has funded a plethora of NGOs in the UK over the years.

There have been many complaints that funding to UK NGOs has dropped recently, as DFID policy shifted away from funding through the private sector (including NGOs) towards more support for governments. DFID funding earmarked for NGOs, however, has not fallen overall, and was £184.2 million in 2000/1, including emergency allocations.[11] On the other hand while funding to NGOs has not significantly dropped, the way it is allocated to NGOs has shifted significantly. There has been a rise in 'block funding' for a number of agencies – in the past only five received block funding. Under the new partner-ship agreements (so-called PPAs) DFID is increasing the number of NGOs they allocate block funds to, but within strict frameworks. A PPA can only be signed when the work undertaken by the NGO fits tightly with DFID's agenda and policy approach. Over time these frameworks are becoming increasingly prescriptive about what DFID money can be used for and how it is to be accounted for. A new agency, the Performance Assessment Resource Centre (PARC) has been established to assist these NGOs to meet DFID demands concerning planning, monitoring and evaluation, and to find ways to measure and demonstrate effectiveness.

And DFID funding for the rest of the NGO sector has fallen. Much less funding is going through DFID's 'Civil Society Challenge Fund' (CSCF) than went through the previous 'Joint Funding Scheme' (JFS), and the conditions have changed radically. The JFS funded NGOs to work on projects they had designed and developed, in countries they selected, and major battles were fought and won to keep this fund free from constraints. It was seen as a fund supporting NGO initiatives. In contrast, the CSCF is only available for NGOs working in DFID priority countries, in areas DFID wants to focus on, and incorporating approaches DFID wants to promote.

This switch has had a profound effect on many medium and small NGOs, which focus on sectoral skills and undertake service delivery. They have found it increasingly hard to access DFID funds, as have those working in contexts where rights and asserting rights is almost impossible. A recently rejected small NGO asked why their proposal had been refused. They were told it was because they had not addressed the issue of poor people claiming their rights. However no one was able to explain how or where people living under conflict and without a government in areas of Southern Sudan could possibly go about claiming their rights. Or how a population decimated by war and lacking even basic education could begin to grapple with such a requirement without first addressing issues of education, skills and organizational development – as the project proposed.

Access to DFID funding for many UK NGOs has also been undermined by a switch of some funding to local DFID offices, to be invested directly in NGOs in that country. While the larger UK NGOs have in fact managed to access some of this funding through their southern field offices (often in competition with their local 'partners' in that country – a major ethical issue few appear to be grappling with seriously), smaller and medium-sized northern agencies have been largely excluded.

Another form of NGO funding, mentioned above, has been a rise in contracting. NGOs are now invited to compete and bid for DFID contracts. These are designed by DFID to meet its agenda through using sub-contractors, who will implement the projects and account for the funding and impact of the work. NGOs compete with both governments and the private sector for these contracts. Relatively huge sums of money are available through contracting, and while even Oxfam finds it hard at times to compete for contracts with professional consulting agencies and firms, NGOs do occasionally get access to these funds, which can carry up to £15-£20 million for the agency. It is only the largest agencies that can attempt to compete for contracts, and even they often struggle at the implementation phase because the contracts are vast compared to the scale of much traditional NGO work on the ground. It is one thing for an agency to learn how to work well in a given country on water or HIV/AIDS, alongside good local partners. It is quite another to try to manage a multi-country programme, working in countries new to the agency where relationships are not yet formed and the context is poorly understood. Or to move from working with several partners at the local level to a single service delivery model designed to cover vast areas of a country.

The broad trends of DFID funding are that they increasingly favour the larger NGOs; in 2000/1 the five agencies most funded by DFID received 59 per cent of all DFID's designated NGO funding, excluding contracts.[12] Money is also now tied to DFID's agenda and priorities much more closely than it was five or six years ago, when DFID still accepted that NGOs should be helped to work in countries where DFID itself did not work. It is tied to a range of conditionalities, shaped by DFID's analysis and understanding of the role it wants NGOs and the wider civil society to play in development. That role has changed from the one applauded in the 1990s – service delivery and how to 'scale up'[13] – towards a watchdog, advocacy and monitoring role for NGOs in countries DFID prioritizes. As DFID moves away from project funding to support for governments, it has huge anxieties about how to monitor and account for the use of its aid money and has designated NGOs as guardians of government spending and promoters of rights in contexts where democracy is often weak.

These trends are echoed in the EU, which after a period of crisis reshaped its NGO funding strategy. It moved towards a bidding process, following a call for proposals.[14] The EU develops bids in line with its development priorities and strategies, again taking the initiative away from the NGOs. There is some limited room for negotiation and discussion around the small print of contracts, and the argument of some NGOs, seeking to increase both their funding and their influence, is that taking money from the EU or DFID allows a relationship and a dialogue to develop. They rarely analyze the reverse process, and ask how this relationship shapes and influences them. The experience of many of those involved is that the room for manoeuvre is actually negligible, but quite a few of the larger NGOs choose to believe that a rise in funding means a rise in their influence with the donors.

Two other significant donors are Comic Relief (CR) and the Community Fund (CF), with allocations of £17 and £13 million respectively in 2001. They are more flexible about funding criteria. However, as CR has grown and staff are under increasing work pressure, a team of assessors has been appointed and trained, and they are often drawn from a pool of people versed in DFID assessment and reporting requirements. CR has to work hard to ensure their assessment processes remain as open and responsive as possible, and do not mirror too closely the increasingly tight funding procedures of EU and DFID. The same applies to CF, which anyway has a much more rigid assessment system based on a long questionnaire approach used by external assessors. The turnover of assessors, the length and complexity of the forms, and the fact that NGOs themselves, and many assessors, are well versed in DFID approaches, means they risk following those procedures, even though the principles of the CF are very different.

CR and CF, along with small foundations such as Barings and Nuffield, have nonetheless provided a lifeline to many small and medium NGOs hit hard by the changing focus and priorities of the EU and DFID. It remains to be researched whether small UK NGOs attempt to do their development work differently from the larger NGOs. They are certainly as constrained by donor policies and procedures, indeed probably more so. However, anecdotal evidence suggests that they are very careful with their use of every penny, and are driven by a different ideology and commitment from some of the largest, more bureaucratic NGOs. They certainly share many experiences of powerlessness and insecurity with their local partners in Africa, and may be more open to negotiation, discussion and shared decision-making with them.

The changing priorities of government have included realigning NGO roles to complement the changing focus of DFID's work with states. The shift away from supporting service delivery and NGOs' own agendas has been accompanied by a desire to broaden the notion of 'civil society' and its role well beyond the development NGO sector,[15] forcing them to compete for funding with a wide range of other players.

A final factor shaping the funding context for UK NGOs has been the growing demand within the UK generally for demonstrable impact and performance results. Targets, 'league tables', and 'performance indicators' dominate the domestic scene in education, health and social services, and even prisons and the police; and this trend is reflected in the Millennium development targets which now dominate much development funding and debate. This target-driven approach has been critiqued by many. The think-tank Demos, for example, remarks that

> The demands and expectations of central and local government – with
> their strict performance criteria, emphasis on qualitative outputs and formal

participatory structures, such as local strategic partnerships – all act against communities achieving their aim … as this report shows, a heavy audit culture often breeds an atmosphere of distrust and risk aversion, which encourages uniformity in programme design and inhibits the distinctive contribution that Community Based Organisations make.[16]

The 'audit culture' is predicated on the fear of people cheating, thus undermining their sense of being valued, and the role they feel they could creatively play in their work. It is a culture that, of course, fits very well with global concerns about corruption and the misuse of funds in both government and non-government organizations in the south.

EFFECTS OF NGO DEPENDENCY ON DONOR FUNDING

Many small and medium NGOs may be almost 100 per cent reliant on one or two donors for their work, which is funded project by project. They have no other real choices because their work is too unknown or unpopular, or because they are too small to do much in the way of independent fund-raising from the public. These agencies find themselves in a similar position to most NGOs in Africa, almost totally dependent on the goodwill and funding of other agencies for their survival. Larger NGOs, and those able to raise public funds through shops, child sponsorship, liaison with a particular industry (e.g. Wateraid, which raises money through the water industry through direct mailing to their customers, and Transport Aid, which receives funding from the transport industry) should, in theory, be less tied to or reliant on DFID, the EU and other funders' shifting priorities, policies and procedures. However, a number of other factors come into play that tie them too quite closely to these donors' agendas.

First, many NGOs want to increase their share of official funding. In the 1980s a major church agency debated whether or not to take *any* official funding, many of its personnel arguing this would compromise their independence, values and ethics; in 2002, by contrast, many UK agencies were commissioning research into how to increase their share of official funding. Discussions of the difference in values between donors and NGOs, and the possible effect on values, mission and mandate, are not heard anywhere – except perhaps in private internal NGO meetings.

The argument for growth is – to oversimplify – that more money enables the agency to do more work and so, given its aim of addressing poverty, alleviating suffering and promoting rights, growing larger is necessarily a good thing – even though many NGOs are worrying internally (and even in public forums) about the value and effectiveness of their development work, and the huge challenges they face really promoting positive social change and transformation. At a recent meeting in Oxford a journalist challenged European NGOs about the lack of profile of development in the media – 'why are you not getting your stories into the press?' He pushed them hard, resulting in the following comment (echoed by several present): 'we have few stories of development success to tell'. The crisis of development work and its relevance is reflected in the ever-growing piles of internal monitoring and evaluation manuals, the growing external clamour for impact assessment and proofs of effectiveness – tied to the 'new public management' paradigm.

Secondly, discussion around the ethics of funding is muted – so much so that, for example, very few of the agencies interviewed had any policy at all about whether or not to try and access direct 'southern' funding – even when this put them in direct competition with southern NGOs; and few appeared to have any qualms about the amounts of official funding they received. One large agency that used to have a 10 per cent rule is now happy to receive up to 50 per cent of all its funding for development work from official donors. Teams of professional fundraisers have been brought in: in some agencies several posts are designated for raising institutional funding world-wide. The drive for growth, strong in many UK NGOs, especially those with incomes of over £10 million, and certainly those with over £50 million, appears to override any serious discussions about whether official funding can subvert an NGO's values, mission, or even its advocacy work. It also overrides serious analysis of the organizational and management issues raised by rapid growth. Yet fast growth, and the need to keep up with spending the money raised, clearly has a negative impact on the ability of staff to stop and reflect, and may change patterns of recruitment and management in ways that can conflict with an NGO's founding values.

Trustees and Chief Executives certainly want to see growth and increased power, influence and significance for their NGOs. The competition between NGOs is legendary, and pushing for increased profile, funding and market share drives many boards and directors. This is perhaps inevitable, given how dependence on donor funding has increased, and the growth of such funding in the 1980s fostered the creation of many small and medium sized NGOs. Now times have changed and the new millennium is seeing the demise of a number of small and medium NGOs, while others struggle to merge, or transfer to Africa, as institutional donors tighten their agendas and seek to fund only projects and programmes that fit with their priorities.

There are also other new and increasingly important aid conditionalities that have an impact on NGOs, especially the procedures for the management of aid and constantly shifting policy foci. The current emphasis is on poverty, complemented by a rights-based approach, combined with seeking policy changes and the ability to demonstrate that all this is having a positive impact on poverty. The roles assigned to NGOs shift from service delivery to capacity building, from capacity building to facilitating networks, from facilitating networks to acting as watchdogs, from being watchdogs to lobbyists and monitors of government probity … Changing donor fashions are well known, even if few agencies have found any way to resist them. Indeed many NGOs play a part in generating the next wave of ideas, in their discussions with key players in donor and development agencies, universities and think-tanks.

THE DOMINANT TOOLS FOR ADMINISTERING
DEVELOPMENT AID

What is less discussed are the tools of aid management, yet these also play a vital role in shaping the nature and quality of aid relationships (partnerships), and in determining what capacities are needed to run NGO programmes and projects. They carry specific cultural values, definitions and understandings around change and the relative value of skills and capacities held in the north and in the south. These procedures have become so universal that the language of aid management has become universal too. Small community-based organizations (CBOs) from India to Mexico, Ghana, South Africa and Uganda all know the language of 'logframes', a tool now almost universally used in development planning and implementation, in spite of its many well-recognized shortcomings.[17] It is essentially a matrix, based on a logical analysis of the problem to be solved, the inputs needed to solve it, the time taken to achieve the required outputs, and a clear set of indicators for measuring achievements against this clearly laid-out plan. The key elements and processes of 'strategic planning' are followed in country after country, by organizations from small women's groups to large umbrella networks. Organizations at parish, district and country levels can tell you of the need for impact indicators, SMART objectives, and 'results oriented management'. Right down to the village level you will hear development discussions interspersed with the English words for goals, aims, objectives, mission and vision, outcomes and so on: 'Instead of a diverse, heterogeneous mix of projects, ideas and practices, which are locally derived and designed, we see powerful waves of global development fashions sweeping everything before them.'[18] Indeed it could be argued that northern NGOs, together with their partners – those they fund and support in the south – have become highly effective distributors of a set of approaches and procedures for development that could be said to rival Coca Cola in reaching down to the grassroots.

In spite of differences between NGOs in this respect – differences which can be important in shaping work relationships and providing more or less space for creativity – some tools are now used almost universally. Such a situation was unthinkable even seven years ago when models, approaches, procedures were very varied and reflected the ethos and approaches of different agencies. For example, one large UK NGO had very relaxed grant-making procedures, working on the maxim of providing support to organizations trying to do useful and interesting work, while another had very rigid application and assessment forms, tight reporting against a few key criteria. Church agencies particularly worked with their partners in quite collegial ways, with little emphasis on paperwork, aims and objectives, and more on building relations of trust and working to support local church agendas.

Whatever the pros and cons of that context it has now gone, and has been replaced by many elements of the 'new public management' with a focus on change as a logical process, controllable, measurable and accountable. Impact is expected quickly and has to be measured against agreed criteria, inputs have to be specified in advance and good reasons have to be given before changes can be made. The process is dominated by business plans, work plans, plans against logframes, and detailed procedures for reporting, monitoring and evaluation, and longer-term impact assessment.

These tools have been developed in the north, by special departments, consultants or agencies working to support NGOs in meeting donor requirements. They have a range of names and acronyms: ALPS, Camel, Promise, Sprouts and so on. A great deal of time is spent in training people to use them, both in the north and in the local field offices and NGOs based in the south. All development schools, training providers and capacity-building organizations in the UK specialize in teaching NGO staff how to do strategic planning, how to develop logframes, how to do monitoring and evaluation against logframes, how to do SWOT (analysis of Strengths, Weaknesses, Opportunities and Threats, usually done through brainstorming), and financial accountability, report writing and impact assessment. In turn many UK NGOs run courses for staff and partners in the south using these tools, or support their staff to attend locally-run training courses.

While other training courses are also provided – for example in participatory techniques, in gender analysis, in advocacy work – far more time is spent on aid management training than any other kind of training. These are the courses that are over-subscribed, and only one training institution in South Africa had refused to work with these tools and was working on a totally different set of understandings about what is needed to deliver good development.[19]

Research found these tools to be almost universally used, and also found several similar trends resulting from their increasing use. Examples of the kinds of relationships dominated by the disbursement and accounting for aid money within tight frameworks, were graphically presented by research teams from Uganda and South Africa to a meeting at Actionaid in London in April 2003.

One clear conclusion was that strategic planning had put the power and control of what was to be funded back into the control of agencies in the UK, where in most cases strategic planning was undertaken. Even where it was done more consultatively, many final decisions that shaped the plans were taken in the UK on the basis that only people based there could understand the global as well as the local contexts for the development work. This had disempowered local partners, who often had to ensure that their projects now fitted the global plan of a northern NGO to secure funding.

Logframes carry many cultural understandings with them. They are always written in English, and even if initially developed in a participative way between communities and the field staff of partner CBOs or NGOs, they are usually revised and rewritten as they climb the development bureaucracy. This is to ensure that by the time they are submitted for funding they meet the current priorities, language and concepts of the donor – be that a northern NGO, or DFID. While staff in NGOs and donor organizations talk of 'participatory' logframes, in fact they often treat them as blueprints which they have helped to shape. Approved logframes are often unrecognizable when compared to the original concepts developed participatively, leaving implementing staff with many problems in generating local 'ownership' of the approved project. For example, while local women may have prioritized access to better health care, or developing their local group for savings and credit, funders think this approach is no longer appropriate, and so it gets modified. The proposal may instead propose that the women will learn how to lobby their local council for the health care they have a right to – even in contexts where the local council may be corrupt, or dominated by one ethnic group, or where there is no funding available. They will be told to connect to wider institutions of micro-finance, which have their own regulations, rules on interest charges and so on, which may not serve the original needs the women identified. Groups may have to organize in new ways and develop plans, accounts and monitoring that fit the donor organization's needs, even when they have little or no literacy and have to bring in outsiders to help them with this. Thus they lose control and even understanding of the processes of development work. Groups may have prioritized health but get water, or prioritized poverty and get HIV/AIDS projects.

In fact in some cases front line staff are not able to use the logframe in implementation at all, but proceed to work in ways that make sense to local people on the ground. However, reporting and evaluations have to be against the logframe, causing real problems. Often the work on the ground is one component and reporting is done by someone else with more skills in writing and English. Many NGOs in the south hire consultants to help them write acceptable logframes, while in other cases the NGO in the north tweaks and finalizes the logframe for approval. Some NGOs live happily with these ambiguities and conflicts of rhetoric and reality, although in every organization at some level discomfort and contradiction are experienced around this approach to project planning and implementation.

When these consequences are reported back to donors and NGOs it is interesting how many people laugh them off as minor difficulties – yet would a builder use plans for building a house that were of no use in practice? Does it make for good development practice to devalue and take decision-making away from the very people and organizations you claim you are trying to empower and build up?

Moreover there is a lot of evidence that the new tools of management and accountability, which have such high costs for real development, are not in fact used by the donors. There has been an exponential growth in the demand for written reporting, financial, qualitative and quantitative. NGO staff at all levels now put hours and hours in to writing detailed reports, often in logical formats. They all say this detracts from the time they have for their fieldwork, or for reading or attending network meetings. Often reports are hugely time-consuming because they are usually required to be in English. Yet research shows that at every level right up to the top no one has the time to read, digest and comment meaningfully on these mountains of reports. Many lie unread in piles on office floors, others are read by external consultants whose feedback may be at odds with the initial purposes of the project, others are read quickly by harassed staff and filed away and rarely used. Yet the demand for more detailed reports rises inexorably.

Donors demand more and more from the NGOs they fund, calling for concrete evidence of positive change, even when tracking official aid and accounting for it, let alone measuring its impact is notoriously difficult. A recent Development Effectiveness Review for DFID, 2002, concluded that the monitoring and evaluation systems needed for tracking and assessing the impact of official aid, totalling billions of pounds, were not available. So financial reporting requirements for NGOs have been tightened, while less and less money is allotted (except by CF and CR and one or two trusts) for core costs and administration, making the running of NGOs increasingly difficult. At a time when NGOs have to promise more in order to secure funding, they receive less for their core costs and the demands on them around aid management rise year on year. Now only larger NGOs with independent funds are able to find the funding for reflection, learning, analysis and new development thinking.

While there is constant talk of downward accountability in the aid chain, the reality for most NGOs is that accountability is upward. Meeting the needs of the next level up in the chain overrides the needs of all other stakeholders. While programme approaches and partnership agreements were meant to get away from the straight-jacket of project cycle management and reporting, in practice reporting against programme and even global targets imposes even more demands on local NGOs. It forces them to see and present their work in relation to global agendas set far away. The search for global indicators and proving 'global impact' dominates much of the work of impact assessment units in the UK, in agencies that are in receipt of partnership grants from DFID.[20]

Yet within the NGO sector there appears to be an acceptance of this, and even passivity about the increasingly tight frameworks for managing development aid. Indeed many staff in British, South African and Ugandan NGOs were unaware that there were any other ways of 'doing development', so universal have these approaches become. Many argue that they can learn these tools and work with them, so why make a fuss about them when there are big issues like poverty and debt to confront. Many seem relatively unaware of the negative impact they have on relationships, which are very hierarchical; few were raising any concerns about the cultural concepts embedded in these tools, or whether or not they were relevant to promoting good development. Most talked about having relationships of 'partnership' with agencies at every level, from donors down to local NGOs, yet the way aid is working does not foster open relationships, or the equal valuing of the different skills of different parties, or respect for different cultural norms.

Indeed at the workshop mentioned above, where researchers from SA and Uganda criticized strongly certain aspects of the aid chain and the tools used up and down the chain, many aspects of these relationships which are rarely mentioned started to emerge. People talked of the colonial nature of many of them: racism was said to be a factor in the way northern agencies push their own agendas onto countries in Africa with little regard for local skills and knowledge. Issues of race, gender, religion and class were raised, suggesting that the new tools of management and accountability are used where trust does not exist or has broken down, and where people feel they are working with 'the other'.[21] This feeling was exacerbated when it was found that those NGOs in the south that had managed to break these rigid hierarchies and take different approaches had been led by white South Africans or expatriates in Uganda.

The contradiction between what donors do and what they say they want NGOs, and the wider 'civil society', to do, is starkly highlighted by recent developments in Uganda. There the World Bank and an academic institution in the UK are currently working with the Government of Uganda on how to better register, monitor and control the work of all NGOs in Uganda, and an NGO bill, seen as draconian by local NGOs, is passing through parliament. While NGOs are being encouraged through the funding criteria to work on policy issues and debates, recent research in Uganda showed that NGOs from both the north and south only participate in policy work at the invitation of northern institutions or the Ugandan government. They are not setting an independent policy agenda.[22] This is all too well illustrated by a quote from the donors' group in Uganda:

> The country's macro-economic policies are close to perfect, socio-economic policies are very much OK ... (with a few exceptions ...) Democracy, human rights, corruption, transparency, accountability and in general the regional security situation are issues that concern us very much ... (they concern) all donors and especially those putting in general budget support.[23]

CONCLUSIONS

The pressures on UK and other northern NGOs from both donors and trustees, and often chief executives drawn from the private sector, combine to push them to behave in certain ways and follow certain agendas. These are set globally by the Bretton Woods institutions, and by current management paradigms in Europe and USA, and transmitted by donors and NGOs directly to organizations in the south. Yet the rhetoric of development, especially poverty-focused development, is that it must be locally generated and 'owned', that it has to build strong local organizations and 'civil society' in order to be effective and sustainable. Countries wanting IMF/World Bank and bilateral aid flows in sub-Saharan Africa now have to complete Poverty Reduction Strategies (PRSPs), in which 'civil society' plays its designated participatory role. But the reality is different: 'The World Bank, IMF and governments (under the influence of the IMF according to critics) are not allowing debate and alternative views on fundamental questions of economic policy. The participation in economic policy-making to which civil society is being invited in the PRSP process is strictly limited'.[24]

Current ways of working in northern NGOs, adopted because of pressures to become more professional, to make complex development realities manageable, and to obtain funding – all donor requirements – increasingly follow agendas set by the multi-and bi-lateral organizations. They often appear to be only infrequently offering an alternative voice or a source of alternative values, ideology and thinking; they more often appear as extensions of the dominant aid agenda.

NGOs feel increasingly pressured to play roles and take up positions they may not feel comfortable with, and many ameliorate this with work critiquing aspects of the world economic system through their advocacy work. But this falls far short of an analysis and rejection of the relations of exploitation and the forces that lead to the growth of poverty in Africa, and seems rather a piecemeal picking away at the edges. In contrast some have adopted all the new policies and procedures with alacrity and even claim to be shaping the new global agendas through dialogue with donors. Others, especially some of the medium and smaller ones, and individuals or departments within the larger agencies, do hold to alternative analyses and worldviews, but feel increasingly disempowered; for many their very existence is threatened by the new funding priorities. Many staff have been forced to leave NGOs they felt committed to as the values they held dear appear eroded by the new incorporation of NGOs into global agendas.

In turn the northern NGOs are increasing their hold on local organizations and NGOs in the south. Some of them are competing directly with southern organizations for funding, others are passing on the tight conditionalities of their funding; a few see themselves as mediating between the demands of northern donors and the real needs of southern NGOs and populations. These processes and demands are forcing southern NGOs to learn and comply with northern agendas, creating a set of dependent organizations, not a vibrant and independent sector. This fits well with government agendas in the south, where NGOs are appreciated for their role in providing much-needed services to the poor, but not for creating independent organizations able to engage robustly with their governments and donors.

While northern donors claim they want to see such a strong civil society developing, and demand that NGOs play this role if they want to get funded, their position is highly contradictory. At the same time as donors are demanding that NGOs be independent watchdogs, monitoring weak or corrupt governments as they spend donor and debt relief money, they are moving towards funding local governments' budgets, which will require NGOs to access their funding in future via these governments. It is hard to see how NGOs can really be watchdogs and monitors of those they have to go to for funding.

Current funding trends and the influence of business sector management thinking are shaping the way development is conceptualized, analyzed and addressed by development NGOs, reflecting agendas and paradigms developed by the rich and powerful countries. While there never was a golden age of

NGOs, they are now becoming increasingly tied to global agendas and uniform ways of working. This reality threatens their role as institutions providing an alternative, as champions of the poor, as organizations working in solidarity with those marginalized by the world economy.

NOTES

1   James Petras and Henry Veltmeyer, *Globalization Unmasked: Imperialism in the 21st Century,* London: Zed Books, 2001, p. 132.

2   Joachim Hirsch, 'The State's New Clothes: NGOs and the Internationalization of States', *Rethinking Marxism,* forthcoming 2003.

3   Amartya Sen, 'Forward' in *Winning the War Against Humiliation, Report on Independent Commission on Africa,* New York: UNDP Publications, 2002.

4   These issues are well explored in Mark Lindenberg and Coralie Bryant, *Going Global: Transforming Relief and Development NGOs,* Connecticut: Kumarian Press, 2002.

5   This essay draws on my own experience as an NGO worker and a researcher of NGOs over the last 15 years in the UK, with a special focus on Africa, especially Uganda. It draws on a three-country research project started in 1999, focusing on the forces that shape the work of NGOs in the UK, Uganda and South Africa. The researchers are: in the UK, Tina Wallace and Jenny Chapman; in Uganda, Patrick Mulindwa, John de Coninck and staff of CDRN, Kampala; Martin Kaleeba and Juliet Kiguli; and in South Africa, Lisa Bornstein, Terry Smith, Isaivani Hyman and Ansilla Nyar.

6   For the kind of analysis of the World Bank's relation to 'making poverty work' for capitalism that the international development community needs, see Paul Cammack, 'Making Poverty Work', *Socialist Register 2002,* London: Merlin Press, 2002, pp. 193-210.

7   Typologies for NGOs and analysis of the wide range of organizations covered by this term are explored in many texts, including Thomas Carroll, *Intermediary NGOs: The Supporting Link in Grassroots Development,* Connecticut: Kumarian Press, 1992. Roger Riddell and Mark Robinson, *NGOs and Rural Poverty Alleviation,* London: Overseas Development Institute, 1995. Alan Fowler, *Striking a Balance: A Guide to Enhancing the Effectiveness of NGOs in International Development,* London: Earthscan, 1997.

8   Tina Wallace, Sarah Crowther and Andrew Shepherd, *Standardising Development: Influences on UK NGOs Policies and Procedures,* Oxford: Worldview Press, 1997.

9   Lindenberg and Bryant, *Going Global,* p. 4.

10 *Ibid.,* table compiled from data on pp. 36-37.

11 It may have fallen as a percentage of total ODA spending, though, as DFID's budget has risen significantly since 1999. The figures for this section are taken from a longer paper by Tina Wallace and Jenny Chapman, 'The donor landscape for UK NGOs', presented to ISTR conference in Cape Town

South Africa, July 2002.

12   These agencies are Red Cross, VSO, CARE, Save the Children and Oxfam.

13   These approaches were the subject of several NGO conferences in Manchester. Key papers are to be found in Michael Edwards and David Hulme, *Making a Difference: NGOs and Development in a Changing World*, London: Earthscan, 1992 and Michael Edwards and David Hulme, *Beyond the Magic Bullet: NGO Performance and Accountability in the Post-Cold War World*, Connecticut: Kumarian, 1996.

14   200 million Euros remain for allocation through the co-financing budget, but a minimum grant size of 50,000 Euros makes even this funding biased to either larger NGOs or consortia.

15   DFID is currently searching out new civil society players to work in development, including the Trade Union Council and the General Medical Council. They found no one outside UK NGOs could understand their jargon or complete their documentation for funding, so they are now training new public bodies in their development procedures to ensure involvement beyond NGOs.

16   *Demos Report*, London: Demos, 2003.

17   Logframes and their limitations were well discussed in papers by Das Gupta, Rosalind Eyben and others presented at a Power and Participation workshop, Sussex: IDS, May 2002. These are not yet published.

18   Emma Mawdsley, Janet Townsend, Gina Porter and Peter Oakley, *Knowledge, Power and Development Agendas: NGOs North and South*, Oxford: Intrac Publications, 2002.

19   This is Community Development Resource Association in SA. The writings of the first director (Allan Kaplan) and other staff members (e.g. James Taylor), presented especially through their annual reports, are becoming well known in development circles and provides a profound critique of current approaches to development, seeing development as interventions in life long processes for those on the ground; to be positive they have to be approached slowly, responsively and in ways that support local processes and understanding. See for example Allan Kaplan, 'Understanding Development as a Living Process' in David Lewis and Tina Wallace, ed., *New Roles and Relevance: Development NGOs and the Challenge of Change*, Connecticut: Kumarian, 2000. Few have dared to follow in their footsteps, however, and most providers find their bread and butter work in training in LFA, strategic and business planning etc.

20   The five most prestigious NGOs in UK have recently made a submission to EU (Development Assistance Committee) on how to do this kind of global impact assessment. The paper is available from the Impact Assessment Unit, Actionaid, Hamlyn House, Macdonald Road, Archway, London N 19.

21   Edward Said, 'Representing the Colonised: Anthropology's Interlocutors', *Critical Inquiry*, 15(2), 1989.

22   This is research being currently undertaken by IDS, Sussex and Community

Development Research Network in Kampala. The first publication from the research is Karen Brock, Rosemary McGee and Richard Ssewakirinyanga, *Poverty Knowledge and Policy Processes: A Case Study of Ugandan National Poverty Reduction Policy*, Research report No.53, Sussex: IDS, 2002.

23 The New Vision, Uganda, April 25th 2003.

24 Panos, *Environmental and Globalisation Programme*, Press release, 12th Sept. 2002.

GLOBALIZATION, IMPERIALISM, DEVELOPMENT: FALSE BINARIES AND RADICAL RESOLUTIONS

JOHN S. SAUL

The global expansion of European capitalism and the imperial conquest of peoples outside the western/northern centres of capital accumulation is a crucial dimension of the past several centuries of world history.[1] Moreover, the juxtaposition, in terms of power and prejudice, of 'the west and the rest of us', of 'North' versus 'South', continues to have significant implications for the fate of people, and, in particular, of the poorest of people, right into the current epoch. This essay will concern itself with the question of how best to conceive, and to act upon, the problem of contemporary global inequality that has been so closely, if complexly, linked to the world-wide history of capitalist imperialism. Amidst the complexities, however, there is one thing about which there can be no doubt: that is the fact of staggering inequality and the sheer scale of grinding poverty that marks so much of the present global scene. Indeed, in a more humane and just world it would be perceived clearly for what it is: the single most scandalous fact about the current period of human history.

Of course, we may feel slightly overwhelmed by figures indicating that 'a growing divide between the haves and have-nots has left increasing numbers in the Third World in dire poverty, living on less than a dollar a day' or that 'despite repeated promises of poverty reduction made over the last decade of the twentieth century, the ... number of people living in poverty has actually increased by almost 100 million [to an estimated 2,801 billion living on less than $2 a day in 1998].'[2] Similarly, it is difficult to register fully the import of discovering (from the WTO) that the average American earned '5,500% more than the average Ethiopian ... a gap that will double in a century and a half at the current trend.'[3]

Or (from the UN) that 'the world's richest three men have more assets than the combined GDPs of the world's 48 poorest countries' and 'the 225 richest men in the world have a combined wealth of more than $1 trillion – equal to the income of the poorest 47% of the earth's population, some 2,5-billion people.'[4] Nonetheless, on the left, we do at least know that we should be doing something dramatic both to expose and to redress such inequities.

But doing what? In order to help clear the ground and to clarify what an appropriate answer to this question might look like, this essay will seek to explore a number of relevant theoretical issues. We begin with a critical reflection on the common tendency to offer diagnoses of global inequality in terms of false binaries – 'the geographical' vs. 'the social', 'globalization' vs. 'the state' (as well as 'globalization' vs. 'imperialism'), 'development' vs. 'anti-development' – while suggesting just how unhelpful these are in establishing a target against which progressive struggle can be directed. The essay then turns to ask whether, even as we come to see more clearly what we are fighting against, we can also begin to define more pertinently just what we are fighting for in our efforts to overcome Third World poverty and exploitation. The word 'socialism' springs to mind here (not too surprisingly since what we are fighting against is indeed capitalism), but how far can this take us? For even if, as we shall see, the limited and contradictory nature of reformist alternatives presently on the global agenda encourages us to adopt a more revolutionary stance, there are real difficulties in establishing the precise meaning of 'revolution' in the contemporary world. An inventory and evaluation of world-wide resistances – already the subject of a growing literature[5] – is beyond the scope of the present essay. It must suffice here to identify some of the categories in terms of which such an inventory and evaluation might best be carried out, while seeking to suggest the ways in which greater clarity regarding issues of site, agency and appropriate imaginary could help facilitate the building and sustaining of a revolutionary project of worldwide dimensions.

I. DIAGNOSES: FALSE BINARIES

(1) 'The geographical' vs. 'the social'

To start with: how, precisely, are the fact of imperialism as an historical phenomenon on the one hand, and the fact of gross pan-global inequality as a contemporary phenomenon on the other, to be linked analytically? The commonsensical understanding of the existence of some causal connection between the coexistence of a wealthy North and an impoverished South that once structured many understandings in both left and liberal circles has come under increased critical scrutiny. There are the even more visible discrepancies of wealth and power *within* the countries of both North and South that must be accounted for, for example. Moreover, the countries of the South are now seen to be far more heterogeneous economically than was once supposed. Indeed, so much less straightforward is a North/South mapping of inequality now said to be that a leading development theorist like Hoogvelt can suggest global inequality to be now much more 'social' than 'geographical' in its coordinates: 'The familiar pyramid of the core-periphery hierarchy is no longer a geographical but a social division of the world economy', she writes.[6] As Arrighi and Silver have pointed out,[7] Hoogvelt's use of the term 'social' is misleading: the geographical hierarchy of nations that they themselves continue to emphasize is, of course, also a social relationship. Nonetheless, what Hoogvelt underscores is important: for her, a global division of labour, more centrally than ever defined along lines of class and (often) socio-economic exclusion that cut across national frontiers, has created both a dominant transnational capitalist class and vast outer circles of less privileged people, both North and South. Such a model helps, she suggests, to comprehend both the diversity to be found in the Third World (stretching from the NICs to the most impoverished zones of Africa) and growing inequalities within individual countries – these latter leading, in turn, to 'chaotic disturbances, violence and conflict in the [social] periphery.'

But can we so readily displace from centrality the geographical coordinates of inequality? As Giovanni Arrighi has tirelessly documented, there is still a great deal about the global hierarchy that remains spatially-defined, and along lines that are also 'largely a legacy of Western territorial and industrial expansion since about 1800.' Thus, in a 1992 article on 'the increasing inequality of the global distribution of incomes', he demonstrated 'a major widening of the already large income gap that fifty years ago separated the peoples of the South from the peoples of the organic core of the capitalist world-economy.' His conclusion: 'the nations of the world ... are differentially situated in a rigid hierarchy of wealth in which the occasional ascent of a nation or two leaves all the others more firmly entrenched than ever they were before',[8] thus exemplifying a 'seemingly "iron law" of a global hierarchy that stays in place no matter what governments on the lower rungs of the hierarchy do or do not do.' For in the absence of self-conscious correctives, the 'oligarchic wealth' achieved by the West always tends to draw the bulk of capitalist activity towards it, hence widening the gap. Arrighi, updating his argument in 2003,[9] also emphasizes the extent to which aggressive Northern 'neo-liberal' policies deliberately reinforced this hierarchy when, in the 1970s, things seemed set to shift slightly in the South's favour. He thus comes to precisely the same conclusion he had a decade earlier as to the persistence of a North/South hierarchy of income – and this despite (even because of) the fact that some degree of industrial convergence has indeed occurred.

It bears noting, if only in passing, that the implications of the picture Arrighi so sketches have led him to make quite different responses over the short span of a decade. Thus, writing at the beginning of the 1990s Arrighi saw the on-going geographical polarization of global wealth as also linked to 'systemic chaos', to 'the continual ... escalation of conflicts in the South and in the East', and to 'increasingly intractable problems of world-system regulation for the West.' Only the prospect that 'Western socialists will join forces with Eastern and Southern associates' to facilitate the emergence of a 'socialist world government' capable of 'promoting greater world equality and solidarity' offered any hope to Arrighi at that time.[10] By the turn of the millennium, however, any whisper of socialism as best advancing the claims of 'democratic wealth' against oligarchic wealth has vanished from his writings. Now 'for understanding the present and future of the global hierarchy [and for envisaging its "subversion"] it is the continuing economic expansion of Mainland China that may be the most important.'[11] In fact, this is the sole development, he and his co-authors suggest, that might have the potential (albeit one somewhat unspecified) to disrupt significantly the world-wide status quo. But note that this is a possible development that arises strictly from *within* the system of global capitalism.

Many will not wish to foreclose so readily the possibility of non-capitalist outcomes, of course. This is a point to which we will have to return. For the moment, it is sufficient merely to reject any implied contradiction between the 'social' (read: class, and class-related exclusion) and the geographical dimensions of global inequality that the juxtaposition of Hoogvelt and Arrighi's emphases might seem to force upon us – and to register instead their irreducible simul-taneity. Arrighi himself has no difficulty in recognizing the diversity of Southern capitalisms, for example, or the facts of income inequality internal to both North and South. But his continuing emphasis on spatial coordinates suggests the reason why notions of 'the Third World', 'the global South', 'global apartheid', and even 'the post-colonial' retain some efficacy in identifying the faultlines of global inequality. As writers like Smith and Cooper have observed, such notions can also be part of a language in terms of which global claims are staked and progres-sive mobilization is advanced in the South – even if they can also encourage a brand of 'Third-Worldism' that (especially when manipulated by local elites in their own interests) blurs the inherently capitalist/class nature of world-wide contradictions.[12] In addition, any movement that seeks to unite anti-capitalist struggles, North and South, cannot ignore the extent to which many in the North have both shared in the North's 'oligarchic wealth' and been tempted by the racist premises spawned by the Western imperial project. If the legitimate claims of Southern peoples to global income redistribution, rights of migration, and freedom from high-handed military incursions are to be grasped and supported by potential allies of the South in the North, the latter will have to understand more clearly the facts regarding both the creation and persistence of a geographical hierarchy.

(2) 'Globalization' vs. 'the state', 'globalization' vs. 'imperialism'

The temptation to falsely resolve 'the geographical' vs. 'the social' binary in favour of one pole or the other is in turn linked to another set of binaries that can with equal ease distort both the theory and the practice of challenging global inequality: the binaries of 'globalization' versus 'imperialism' (of 'Empire' versus 'empire', in effect) and of globally-focused versus nation-state-focused politics. Thus, it is no accident that Hoogvelt's 'social' rather than geographic under-standing of global inequality has been strongly influenced by the work of Manuel Castells. For Castells is amongst those who has most assertively argued the novelty of the current moment in the history of global capitalism, the epoch of 'the network society', of 'timeless time' and of the 'space of flows' (rather than of places).[13] It is a world in which capital more generally, and the most dominant of capitalists more specifically, are said to have sprung free from their erstwhile moorings in nation-states and now dictate policies to all and sundry in terms of their now more forthrightly global interests. It is the world of Hardt and Negri's 'Empire',[14] of Sklair's now predominantly *global* capitalist class,[15] and of a situation in which, in Teeple's strong statement of the argument, 'capital [has] moved decisively beyond its historic political shell, the nation state and its associated mitigating forces and influences... [as] the consequent growing loss of national sovereignty over social reform and government policy began to become displaced by the imperatives of global markets.'[16]

There is something to this model, as thousands protesting against the inhuman toll of capitalist globalization have underscored in the streets of Seattle, Quebec, Genoa and in many other parts of the world in recent years. At the same time, as numerous critics of this particular take on globalization have observed, there is also something too neat about it – too apolitical to begin with. To be sure, globalists of right and left have underscored the saliency of emergent political institutions on the world-wide stage – the IMF and the World Bank, the WTO, and the like – but critics on the left have also been quick to point out that the system of global capitalism does not work quite so straightforwardly. Although capitalists (and their politicians) might be groping towards a kind of global 'state', real states are still there to do a lot of the heavy lifting on behalf of capital. Indeed, so much is this the case for authors like James Petras that they feel confident to argue that not really much has changed: what we have is still pretty much imperialism – western imperialism – as usual[17]: in effect, the all too familiar realm of historical imperialism ('empire') rather than Hardt and Negri's centre-less 'Empire'. And certainly the recent activities of the United States (and its military) – now more active than ever, in the wake of 9/11 and with the invasions of Afghanistan and Iraq – as self-proclaimed global policeman has focused attention on that particular reality, with anti-globalization protesters on the one hand and anti-war/anti-imperialist protesters having to work overtime to find a effective common language to tie together more precisely their obviously inter-related causes.

Leo Panitch has also emphasized the role of the state, criticizing much globalization literature for its 'tendency to ignore the extent to which today's globalization both is authored by states and is primarily about reorganizing, rather than by-passing states.'[18] In so arguing Panitch seeks, he suggests, merely to preempt any 'false dichotomy between national and international struggles.' Questions can be raised about his emphasis, nonetheless, for to some extent it could be taken to be quite complementary to the strong argument for the primacy of 'globalization'. Thus, the role for the state that Panitch seems to foreground is primarily that of necessary agent for establishing the parameters of smooth integration of the countries concerned into the global capitalist economy – including, at such states' most assertive moments, acting primarily as agents for advancing the global aspirations of those of their own 'national capitals' that have chosen to go 'transnational' (cf. the Canadian case). At the same time, Panitch's argument is, with its careful balancing act, at some distance from a much more extreme form of the argument that insists upon continuing to see states as crucially active agents within the global economy – that exemplified by Hirst and Thompson.

Still, in dismissing much of the globalization literature, even the latter pair of authors depict states as being active almost solely in terms of their ability to advance the 'competitiveness', globally, of their own nation's principal economic sectors – presenting, in doing so, a 'refutation' of the globalization hypothesis that, ironically, comes close to echoing the position of the arch-globalist, Teeple, especially in its implications for the Third World. For even as they suggest the possible emergence, to frame such international competition, of various 'institutional arrangements and strategies [to] assure some minimal level of international economic governance, at least to the benefit of the major advanced industrial nations', they nonetheless argue that 'such [global] governance cannot alter the extreme inequalities between those nations and the rest, in terms of trade and investment, income and wealth.' For them, indeed, 'the issue is not whether the world's economy is governable towards ambitious goals like promoting social justice, equality between countries and greater democratic control for the bulk of the world's people, but whether it is governable at all.'[19]

So much for 'the bulk of the world's people', then. And just where does this leave states that lie beyond the pale of the 'major advanced industrial nations'? For present purposes, one can even assume, with Panitch, that states in advanced capitalist settings do indeed have more room for economic manoeuvre than the strongest versions of globalization theory might seem to imply. And we can also acknowledge the importance in the current moment of one particular state, for clearly it would be naive for anyone not to give great weight in understanding the present workings of the global hierarchy to the role of the American state. Nonetheless, the possible weakness of a state-centric emphasis becomes far more evident when one turns one's attention to the *Southern* state. In this context, there is considerable cause for scepticism about the potentially positive role of such a state as an active agent of national economic advance, a reality that has prompted so astute an observer as Leys to write, in his seminal overview of contemporary development theory, that, especially in the Third World, 'the era of national economies and national economic strategies is past'.[20]

Of course, any such statement does bring us up, once again, against the fact of Third World diversity, from Asia through Latin America to Africa: it is no accident, perhaps, that Leys' major point of reference is Africa where he can list a series of measures that might, in theory, be adopted internationally to lift the weight of an inequitable global economy off the back of Africa and facilitate development while nonetheless concluding:

> The problem with such ideas is that they have no attraction for those who currently own Africa's debt, buy Africa's exports or arrange official capital-

assistance flows. Such ideas could come to seem rational only in a world that was in the process of rejecting the currently predominant ideology of the market. While this world must come, it is not yet in place, and meantime the African tragedy will unfold.[21]

And yet, even if Africa presents a worst case scenario of marginalization and non-transformative exploitation under global capitalism, it remains true more generally that the strand of development theory once premised on the presumed viability of national capitalist strategies to realize an expansive form of development sounds, in the wake of the Asian crisis and the free-fall of much of Latin America, quite dated.[22] As the late Bill Graf has specified, 'the Third World state is diminished, and more subordinate than at any time since the colonial era. Its elites are more externalized, and its hold on national sovereignty more tenuous than ever.'[23]

And what of more left variants of the developmental state? The disappearance of most Third World socialisms (the 'recolonization' of Mozambique, for example, so well described by David Plank[24]), and the apparent ease with which Mandela and Mbeki's South Africa and Lula's Brazil have been drawn into global capitalism's web, are not promising auguries here. Does this throw us back, necessarily, on a 'global politics' as the key to unlocking the future for the South? Not everyone would so argue: there is, for example, Bienefeld's powerful claim for the continuing primacy within left practices of nation-state-centred politics. As he puts the point, it is because 'of the total inability to conceive, let alone construct, a meaningful political process at the global level' that the requisite 'global management of the competitive process, or of a socialist economy, must be built on sub global units, namely our "generic nation states."'[25] Once again, it is difficult to avoid the suspicion that this is an argument easier to make for advanced capitalist countries than it is for those lodged more firmly on the lower rungs of the global hierarchy. Still, thinking along similar lines, Graf himself manages to conclude his negative survey of the nature of the actually existing 'state in the Third World' with the argument that, nonetheless, only the state (albeit an alternative, still largely 'theoretical', state, in his phrase),

> ... can offer a feasible *agency* capable of aggregating the multifarious counter-hegemonic forces in the peripheral state. Only state-economic power in the South has any prospects of standing up to, negotiating with or countering the pervasive economic power of international capital ... no doubt too, only the state, in combinations with other states, can forge collective emancipatory projects directed against the hegemonic powers.[26]

Here he explicitly echoes Panitch whose seminal article argues not only (as we have seen) the continued saliency of the state as 'constitutive element' of global capitalism, but also emphasizes 'the Left's need to develop its own strategies for transforming the state, even as a means of developing an appropriate international strategy.'[27] It is a strong case, and all the more so when one juxtaposes it to the rather nebulous and all too unmediated politics inherent in, say, Hardt and Negri's celebration of the 'multitude' as their nominated agent to impose a humane logic on capital. Writers like Bienefeld and Graf force us to think more clearly about what are the actual mechanisms, beyond the drama of the demonstration, that might be capable on a prolonged and sustainable basis, of bringing real, effective power to bear on global capital – and on the imperial (American) state. And yet Negri and Leys are not wrong either: there is also a realm of global capitalist dictate that, through the actions of the IFIs and the WTO and international agencies and of the rampaging money marketeers and mobile investors, cannot readily be tamed by any one Third World state, however progressive, and that is not quite reducible to the actions of western states either, however important those actions may often be. The fact is that 'Empire' (the world of capitalist globalization) and 'empire' (the world of western imperialism) coexist: they structure, in not entirely coterminous ways, both the circumstances that produce global inequality (that is, the target of progressive activity for change) and the modalities of advancing such activity (that is, the most promising ways of 'naming the enemy' and crafting the struggle against it). Avoiding misleading binaries in this regard, even as we seek in real and non-rhetorical ways to link both the global and the national (not to mention 'the local', to which we will return) as appropriate sites of struggle, is one central thing that contemporary 'development theory' must be about.

(3) 'Development' vs. 'anti-development'

Development theory? Here we confront another language that has conventionally offered itself to those who would deal with such issues: the language of 'development' (as in the binary 'developed' and 'underdeveloped' countries, albeit often specified in terms of quite diverse notions of the relative importance of economic growth, the material betterment of people's lives, and more expansive definitions of possible human fulfillment). Since so much sound and fury has been thrown up on both the right and the left of the political spectrum around this term, and since so much confusion continues to reign with respect to it, it bears reflecting upon here.

Although not without historical antecedents, the 'development project' was a product of the immediate post-Second World War epoch. It sought to evoke an 'intellectual universe and ... moral community' shared by rich and poor countries alike, built around the 'conviction that the alleviation of poverty would not occur simply by self-regulating processes of economic growth or social change [but rather] required a concerted intervention by the national governments of both poor and wealthy countries in cooperation with an emerging body of international aid and development organizations.' Eminently modernist (and capitalist) in its presuppositions, this developmentalist agenda (often articulated as, precisely, 'modernization theory') for the 'emerging nations' was the Third World twin of the Keynesian agenda then ascendant in the advanced capitalist centres. The critics of this mainstream model were no less 'modernist' and developmentalist, of course, with the most articulate of them grouping under the banner of a 'dependency theory' which countered that it was actually the existing hierarchy of rich and poor countries that comprised the chief structural obstacle to realizing positive outcomes for the global poor. There were variants, too, within this latter camp, some more reformist, others more revolutionary and overtly socialist (along both populist and Marxist lines) in their orientation.[28] Still, as events would soon demonstrate, what linked together both modernization theory and dependency theory – the imperative of willed efforts to materially transform people's lives and the wisdom of utilizing the state as one key instrument in facilitating such a transformation (whether along capitalist or socialist lines) – was almost as important as what divided them.

But these shared premises would come under sharp attack from both right and left, a simultaneous assault that has created the murky terrain upon which (post-, neo-, anti-) development theory now finds itself. From the right came the neo-liberal 'counter-revolution'[29] – one still largely ascendant in establishment circles – and, it would seem, launched as much or more against the capitalist theorists of Keynesian/developmentalist provenance as against any theorists and practitioners further to the left. This 'ultra-modernist' project (as Cooper and Packard term it) was advanced in the name of the ever more extreme liberalization of markets and the attendant premise that, if only the state and the 'developmentalists' would get out of the way, optimum results would follow for all, everywhere. Meanwhile, from the 1970s on, falling prices for primary products and rising prices for oil combined with the United States' new high interest rate regime to push many Third World countries ever deeper into debt and to make them ever more vulnerable to external dictate. With such political avatars as Thatcher and Reagan to trumpet it, the new orthodoxy of 'freedom' swept through the IFIs, producing the so-called 'Washington Consensus' that became so much a part of the common-sense of capitalist globalization, especially in the Third World, in the late twentieth century. For 'free', however, read 'free-market', the latter also presented as being the essential underpinning for the kind of 'democracy' (best defined, however, as mere 'polyarchy' or 'low-intensity democracy') that such capitalist revolutionaries have also sometimes advocated. True, others have sought to wrest the discourse of 'individual freedom' away from the free-marketeers for more humane purposes (Amartya Sen, for example[30]). For many on the left, however, it is the claims of the social collectivity (these claims being freed, to be sure, from the negative and undemocratic practices too often associated with them in the past) that seem most in need of reassertion.

The reinvigorated strength of global capital and the American state, as well as the neo-liberal ideology that has now come to epitomize their project, has also placed the developmentalist left on the defensive – as has the defeat/failure of socialist alternatives as economic strategies and as vehicles for democratic self-expression. In this context an attack on the pretensions of previously-existing development theory also sprang up on the left (broadly defined), often linked to the wider claims of 'oppositional post-modernism', anarchism and environmentalism, and calling into questions the 'modernist', 'westernizing' and undemocratic premises of the former orthodoxy, right and left. This is the discursive world of 'development stinks', one that finds the development project to be an overwhelmingly modernist and Eurocentric project that also, in its emphasis on growth and participation in a wider global sphere, primarily serves Western economic interests.[31] In so arguing, many development-sceptics also underscore the extent to which the claims of women, the racially oppressed and the bearers of diverse cultures have been lost in the lofty abstractions of developmentalism,[32] and the integrity and positive potential of many local initiatives steamrollered in the name of grand theory and the disempowering centralization of many so-called 'counter-hegemonic' struggles. Meanwhile, others stress the degree to which the language of development, with its productionist biases and its alleged Enlightenment arrogance, has blurred environmental concerns that are of crucial importance to the survival of the human race as a whole.

But even granted the need for such a sensibility – in order to beat back the high-handedness of often-Western-serving development agencies and NGOs, for example, and to ground our understanding of resistance to the inequities of global capitalism more effectively in the demands of diverse localities, cultures and identities – this need not dictate the abandonment of any vision of 'development'. Sutcliffe, for example, has argued convincingly of the need to bring environmental concerns together with a keen sensitivity to the facts of inequality on a global scale: 'The conflict between the poor of today and the unborn exists to the extent that a real reduction in the negative environmental impact of the rich of today is not contemplated …. Thus, human development is in danger of being unsustainable unless there is redistribution; and sustainable development is in danger of being anti-human unless it is accompanied by redistribution.'[33] But this perspective has also carried Sutcliffe further, towards the strongest possible argument for the sustaining of an unapologetic (if circumspect) left-developmentalism. As he phrases it,

> The criticism of the standard development model seems at times too total. Because the old destination, which in the West we experience every day, seems so unsatisfactory, all aspects of it are often rejected as a whole. Along with consumerism out goes science, technology, urbanization, modern medicine and so on. And in sometimes comes a nostalgic, conservative postdevelopmentalism. In all projects, there is a danger of losing the baby when we throw out the old bath water. In this case the baby is the material, economic, productive basis of whatever satisfactory utopia can be, to echo Vincent Tucker's suggestive words, imagined and democratically negotiated among the inhabitants of earth …. One way of rephrasing all these concerns would be to say that development and globalization are experienced in practice in conditions of profound inequality of wealth and power between nations (imperialism) as well as between classes and sexes (capitalist class exploitation and patriarchy). It is necessary to distinguish

which of the rejected aspects of development and globalization are inherent in these concepts and which come about because of the unequal circumstances in which we experience them. If we reject them completely because of the form in which they arrive we will always be struggling against the wrong enemy.[34]

This is a position echoed, in my experience, by a great many Southern social justice activists themselves, and also by such theorists as Cooper and Packard who, in speaking positively of 'the marvellous ambiguity of the word development' suggest that 'what at one level seemed like a discourse of control is at another a discourse of entitlement, a way of capturing the imagination of a cross-national public around demands for decency and equity.'[35] Similarly Frans Schuurman, who professes himself to be 'not particularly sensitive to criticisms raised against the concept of emancipation because it happens to be a so-called Enlightenment notion discredited by postmodernism', argues further that 'a universal, yet context sensitive notion of justice is still far more attractive to reclaiming a normative and political progressive domain for development studies than any postmodernist-inspired attempt in that direction':

> The very essence of development studies is a normative preoccupation with the poor, marginalized and exploited people in the South. In this sense *inequality* rather than *diversity* or *difference* should be the main focus of development studies: inequality of access to power, to resources, to a human existence – in short, inequality of emancipation. There is no doubt that there is a diversity in forms, experiences and strategies for coping with inequality which deserves to be an integral part of the domain of development studies. There is also no doubt that globalization will contribute new forms of inequality and new forms of resistance. Nonetheless, it is inequality as such which should constitute the main focus within the explication of development studies.[36]

We need only complement such insights with Leys' more explicitly anti-capitalist injunctions – articulated in concluding his own impressive overview of the current state of theorizing about development, cited above – in order to reground a revolutionary left-developmentalism of great promise. As he argues, we must 'revive development theory, not as a branch of policy-oriented social science within the parameters of an unquestioned capitalist world order, but as a field of inquiry about the contemporary dynamics of that order itself, with imperative policy implications for the survival of civilized and decent life and not just in the ex-colonial countries.' Moreover, he continues, 'if, as I fear, it seems that not much scope for change exists – especially for small, severely underdeveloped countries – without a radical subordination of capital to democratic control, development theory will … have to be about this, and agents capable of undertaking it.'[37]

II. RESOLUTIONS

(1) The limited variants of 'reform'

'A radical subordination to democratic control': this might be taken to represent a call to socialist revolution, a theme to which we will return in our concluding section. First, however, we must note that it has become apparent even to many of those who look favourably upon capitalism as an acceptable and defensible global system that, in its neo-liberal articulation, it doesn't work quite as well as might have been hoped, especially for the poorest of the poor. The terrain of proposed global 'reform' of this system has been trenchantly mapped by Patrick Bond in many of his numerous publications.[38] I will merely note here, by way of summarizing the topic, three rather differing 'reformist' responses from groups that have particular global resonance. The first group focuses on the social distemper (Arrighi's 'systematic chaos') that this failed system has produced on the 'periphery' – the fundamentalisms and xenophobias, the internal chaos and occasionally unpredictable dictators, that haunt such countries – and casts the resultant problem principally in terms of 'security concerns' (and especially the security concerns of the American state). Of course, the proponents of such a perspective do not view see this as representing the failure of global capitalism. For the practitioners of this neo-conservative security doctrine (as exemplified by the current Bush team) are in fact devotees of the virtues of capitalism, their own ties to the oil, military and construction sectors of capital being well-known.

Moreover, when their house-intellectuals conceptualize empire in the language of security they also invariably make a heartfelt, in largely unexamined, bow to the virtues of 'globalization' – with the global capitalist economy, as a kind of residual category, assumed to be churning away benevolently under everything else, its bounty to be fully realized once the various irrationalities of Third World politics are cleared away. For them, it is the peoples of the South who have failed capitalism, not the other way around. Sometimes this understanding is cast in quasi-racist terms, the celebrated work of Robert Kaplan being a case in point.[39] But whatever the rationale, the need to take action to impose order is the bottom-line, and the projection of this task can sometimes attain breath-taking proportions. Thus, for American security advisor Thomas Barnett, 'disconnectedness [from globalization] defines danger': 'Saddam Hussein's outlaw regime', he continues, 'is dangerously disconnected from the globalizing world, from its rule sets, its norms, and all the ties that bind countries together in mutually assured dependence.' It lies, in short, in 'the Non-Integrating Gap', in those vast stretches of the world outside 'the Core' which are simply 'not functioning'[40] – and that is why war against it 'is not only necessary and inevitable, but good.' More generally, Barnett continues,

> a simple security rule set emerges: a country's potential to warrant a U.S. military response is inversely related to its globalization connectivity ... [I]t is always possible to fall off this bandwagon called globalization. And when you do, bloodshed will follow. If you are lucky so will American troops.

Note, however, that it would be unwise to see the assertive actions taken by such proconsuls and ideologues of 'empire' as being merely some direct emanation of the logic of capital. *Raison d'état* and moral/religious self-righteousness are important ingredients here in and of themselves and help determine that the kind of globalization they advocate – the brute neo-liberalism (paradox intended) of Bush and his cronies – comes most readily out of the barrel of a gun.

A second group of 'reformers', perhaps best described as being, at least in the first instance, denizens of the world of 'Empire' rather than of 'empire' (although, needless to say, they are also strongly inflected in their policies by pressures from the American state and the interests behind it), are more polite and less inclined to favour the overt use of force. True, in practice they have been equally concerned to bat down, when necessary, the tendency of even the least corrupt of Third World states to intrude their unacceptable, 'rent-seeking' ways into the market-place. But for them – and for the sectors of capital, in the financial, technology and industrial spheres, that are least comfortable with the hard-ball politics of empire – discipline in the interests of capital can be expected to flow primarily from the 'invisible hand' of the market-place (a pretty effective system of power in its own right, of course). Much has been made of the shift of the IFIs, albeit more the World Bank than the IMF or the WTO, away from the baldest forms of free-market messianism. And one can indeed track the increased saliency of such non-economistic additions to the Bank's preferred discourse as 'poverty alleviation', 'local empowerment', 'social capital',[41] and 'good governance' (the latter, for example, seeking to recite the virtues of an more effectively 'enabling state' as necessary to the facilitating of capitalist activity[42]). This battery of footnotes to neo-liberalism, the palest of reforms of the current system, is seductive to some, notably within the world of the NGOs, both Southern and Northern. But, in the end, such footnotes do little to qualify the extent to which the IFIs' still-in-place 'Washington consensus' continues to see development for Third World countries as calling above all for debt repayment, the embrace of their 'comparative advantage' as suppliers of primary products and a limited range of industrial output, and the rendering of themselves as open and attractive as possible to foreign investment.

Just how much should we make of this distinction between Bush and the Bank, in any case? For neither possesses a vision designed to produce a capitalism any less parasitic, any more positively transformative, of the material lot of the vast majority of people of the South. From within the camp of 'Empire' there is, however, a third group, one which advances a more sweeping vision of possible reform – albeit a vision that, like the much more saccharine offerings of the World Bank, is primarily cast in economistic rather than security terms. Not that members of this group are indifferent to the various political 'irrationalities' that now stalk the world of failed capitalism or even perhaps to the deepening plight of the global poor. But they are more preoccupied with contradictions felt to be internal to the capitalist accumulation process that the ascendant Washington consensus (whether dressed out in military mufti or in business suits) now threatens, they fear, merely to exacerbate. For they wonder aloud whether policies flowing from this consensus can really hope to maximize the system's drive to realize itself as a transformative (and, in the long term, ever more profitable) engine of expanded reproduction. As Robert Biel has argued from the left, the problem centres on the tension between short-term profit and 'the long-term conditions (economic – the reproduction of labour – and socio-economic) for future exploitation.' Thus, from the late 1970s on, protagonists of neo-liberalism developed as a Southern strategy the use of 'the "debt" as a lever to break resistance there to the demands of the new accumulation system. But this leaves a big question: [Structural Adjustment Programmes] may have been good at destroying the old, but this does not mean they could provide a basis for a stable self-reproducing set-up even within the confines of the current accumulation regime.'[43] For it is the virtual impossibility of the present system – now driven as much or more by the speculative activity of holders of financial capital than by the pursuit of 'productive investment' – to act 'rationally' at the aggregate level term that is crucial here.

Our third group expresses, but from within the world of capital, similar concerns regarding the current state of affairs. Master global currency manipulator George Soros provides an example here,[44] and Paul Krugman has also warned against the current salience of a 'depression economics' wherein, precisely, the possible means to plan, world-wide, the kinds of judicious interventions in financial markets and other spheres that might facilitate expanded reproduction have been dismissed on narrowly ideological (read: neo-liberal) grounds.[45] Moreover, such warning voices can also be heard from time to time within the IFIs themselves with respect to the dim prospects for the poorest of economies under the pressure of purely market-driven calculations: the views of Joseph Stiglitz,[46] Ravi Kanbur and Dani Rodrik have been significant in this respect (although we should also note just how quickly such figures are sidelined once the scarlet letter of Dissenter has been hung on them). However, even assuming for the moment the abstract potential of the model of disciplined capitalism that seems to drive such thinker/practitioners, what is the likelihood of their calls for latter-day quasi-Keynesianism being heeded, either nationally in the Third World or more globally? Not much, one suspects. For, on a global scale, the prospects are not strong for development of the political mechanism that could impose the (theoretically) expansive logic of capital on the largely destructive (from the point of view of the global poor) activities of multiple capitalists in real-life competition. Indeed, for the foreseeable future, the realization of any very meaningful form of 'global Keynesianism' must seem an even more utopian prospect than the realization of the least ambitious of socialist aspirations: actually existing global capitalism remains, as Przeworski once famously put it, profoundly 'irrational'.[47]

There are, of course, Third World elites who also play on the edges of these intra-establishment divisions, arguing 'the Southern case' for a degree of debt forgiveness, calling on the North to live up to its own pronounced principles of 'free trade' (the latter's tariff walls often structured, ironically, to make the entry of Third World goods more, rather than less, difficult) and making the unlikely case for economic transformation based on more foreign direct investment. The response has been meagre to even the mildest of Third World-sponsored reform efforts by the powers-that-be in the global economy: the Doha Summit of the WTO in 2001 and the 2003 summit of the G-8 in Evian, France, are cases in point. So, too, are such items as the token Northern support for the Heavily Indebted Poor Countries Initiative (HIPC), the unbending pressure on Southern countries (in the sphere of 'intellectual property rights', for example) to yield to intrusive WTO dictate, and the intense and continuing IMF directives against any form of control of exchange rates or capital movements. And yet, despite this record, initiatives like the capitalist-friendly New African Partnership for African Development (NEPAD), enthusiastically pushed by African leaders such as Thabo Mbeki (over the objections of many of their counterparts within 'civil society', be it noted), continue to be offered up.[48]

It is true that, as in the case of NEPAD, such assertions seem most often a ruse, their mild progressivism masking the deep incorporation of these elites (and their own class interests) within the 'inner circle' of Hoogvelt's social hierarchy rather than representing any real attempt on their part to meet the needs of the masses of the population of the disadvantaged countries for whom they profess to speak. Nonetheless, many development theorists and many development agencies have aligned themselves hopefully with such initiatives and such elites (the recent move to the right of OXFAM-International providing a case in point). They do so, they sometimes say, in a spirit of *realism*: in order to facilitate cutting a better deal for the global South within what has become the only game in town. A grim and unpromising choice to feel compelled to make, if so.

(2) The challenges of 'revolution'

In sum, there is little evidence that the global capitalist system can or will be reformed in such a way as to deflect the spread of global inequality or permit any meaningful development for the vast mass of the world's population: instead, it seems destined to produce profits for the few alongside grinding poverty for the many for some time to come. Nor is there anything inevitable about the over-throw of such a system. Indeed, as the morbid symptoms of its unchecked power multiply (manifested in the South, for example, in fundamentalisms and xeno-phobias of almost every variety) it is tempting analytically to see capitalism and barbarism as more likely outcomes, across the globe and in the foreseeable future, than socialism and development. Nonetheless. it is the task of the left to make such an understanding of the sorry pass to which the world has come on capi-talism's watch as much a staple of the common-sense of people's thinking as possible. And we must also ask ourselves, finally, just what are the countervailing tendencies that might yet be expected to keep the struggle to transform the existing system of virulent capitalism on the agenda in the current period.

Perhaps some general direction can be drawn from the writings of Robert Biel, whose point of entry on these matters is close to my own[49] and is premised on understanding the present global system as one that has sought to establish in the 'Third World' the ever more unmediated rule of global capital and the solitary imperative of capital accumulation. This is a system, he argues, in which policy has been downgraded merely to 'a question of "adapting" a country in the South to fit into the system by creating local conditions (for example, reducing interference from local bureaucrats) so that capital could find its way without hindrance to the most promising sectors.'[50] At the same time, however, Biel suggests that this new system is also one that has created a fundamental problem for 'the North' and, since it has placed the legitimacy of the Third World state under such pressure, this is true not merely in economic terms: 'The "national economy" is one of capitalism's best inventions because it provides a good basis for social control', he writes, and 'the new form of direct rule which I am calling "post-neo-colonial" [is therefore] very risky.' As he then elaborates the point,

> The new vision may appear plausible to elites, since it presents the North and South as united within a single free-market economic model (in contrast to the division between Keynesianism for the North and development economics for the South which was characteristic of the post-war regime). But in reality the free market is an expression of profoundly unequal power relations, and the practical consequences of this are all too obvious to the masses: to give only one example, it leads to a virtual monopoly by the North of mass consumption.[51]

'All too obvious to the masses': would that things were so simple. But they are not completely hidden from them either, as the level of emergent world-wide contestation of the claims of global capitalism begins to suggest.

There are clues regarding the possible nature of such contestation in previous sections of this essay, and other pertinent literature has also been cited.[52] As noted earlier, I will therefore limit myself here merely to suggesting some of the most pressing considerations regarding site, agency and imaginary that could help further define and advance effective radical resistance to global capitalist rule. As regards the most appropriate *site* (global, national, local) of struggle, for example, we have discussed some of the seemingly unavoidable tensions that arise between global and national scales in this respect, especially as regards Third World countries. In the current epoch, the emphasis is often put somewhat differently, however. Thus the liberal-left slogan 'Think globally, act locally' has proven to have considerable appeal for those who seek to challenge the global system more fundamentally. For it is struggles cast in local terms against the most proximate depredations – against the grossest of exploitation and raping of the environment, from the demands of the Zapatistas to the resistance to Shell Oil by the Ogoni people of the Niger delta – of global firms, imperial states and their local intermediaries that have captured much of the radical imagination in recent years.[53]

Such activities – 'militant particularisms', in David Harvey's evocative phrase – are then argued to be the building blocks of the most effective of global assertions. Yet even if this is the case, it is also true that some brands of emphasis on the virtues of the local can be advanced quite negatively by the World Bank and its ilk as part of their highly suspect anti-state agenda. And a localist preoccupation can sometimes serve the most extreme versions of left anti-developmentalism as well, casting excessive suspicion on more large-scale, potentially hegemonic forms of anti-capitalist endeavour. Once again, the allure of false binaries must be avoided, just as they must be in thinking through the best ways of linking local assertions and national projects. On this latter issue, for example, South Africa's leading social movement activist, Trevor Ngwane, could almost be quoting the arguments of Bienefeld, Graf and Panitch as cited above when he asserts, on the basis of his own experience, that

> ... the issue of political power remains crucial. Some people attack the idea of targeting state power – the argument that globalization undermines the role of the nation state gets translated into an excuse for avoiding the fight with your own national bourgeoisie. But we in South Africa can't not confront the ANC and Mbeki. American activists can't not confront Bush. The COSATU leadership, the SACP, are happy to fight imperialism everywhere except here at home. Its been good to demonstrate against world summit meetings in Seattle, Genoa, even Doha, but there are problems with following the global elite around – it's not something poor people can afford to do .... The point is, we have to build where we are.[54]

And, beyond the nation-state itself, there are also sub-global arenas of potentially progressive action, focusing resistances that manifest themselves at regional level (the African Social Forum, for example, and a range of parallel organizations in Asia) and even on a pan-Southern basis.

As regards the question of *agency*, those who most dramatize the purely globalizing nature of the current capitalist moment are also inclined to focus most exclusively on the sheer diversity of resistances, Castells in a wildly eclectic and unfocused way and Hardt and Negri in terms of an almost poetic invocation of the awakening strength of 'the multitude'. Others approach such issues more soberly, while similarly emphasizing the broad front across which diverse identities (in terms of race, gender, ethno-nationalism and religion) and localities are both negatively affected by, while also capable of acting to confront, the realities of global inequality as they impinge upon them in the forms of exploitation, exclusion and the rampant commodification of basic necessities. This humbling diversity of situation is said to find most effective expression in a rich diversity of 'social movements', with the latter in turn capable of comprising what Naomi Klein has termed 'a movement of movements', the (loosely) collective actor that surfaces in Porto Alegre and Seattle and also feeds more focused and cumulative global claims around issues of water, health, indebtedness and the like.[55] Certainly there is something to this, and, as I have pointed out elsewhere, Marxists and socialists would do well to heed the voices of diversity and of local definition of needs, possible modes of action and cultural integrity more effectively than they often have.[56]

At the same time, the celebration of diversity and spontaneity (the revolt against oppression but also against the undemocratic modes of political practice that is too much the legacy of the left, not least in the case of various 'Third World socialisms'[57]) must not blind us to the need for an increasing measure of effective organization and clarity of ideological thrust in confronting so powerful a system – especially since, at every site, locally, nationally and globally, that system can rely, when necessary, on powerful states to reinforce the irrationalities of the market-place. Thus, as Leys has argued in emphasizing the necessary emergence, *qua* agent, of 'unified' and hegemonic projects:

> Looked at in one way it will necessarily be a multiplicity of projects, in different sectors, nations and regions, [representing] the aspirations of different groups, movements and peoples. Yet unless these unite to confront the political and economic power of the transnationals and the states that back them, they will ultimately fail .... As a minimum it will require nation-wide movements and/or parties capable of exercising state power, and making it felt in supra-national institutions.[58]

Nor should diversity obscure the crucial importance of a class-based comprehension of agency, actual and potential,[59] including the key role that Southern workers and their trade unions have continued to play in keeping anti-capitalist and anti-imperialist themes firmly in the mix of global resistance.[60] At the same time, we should also avoid the temptation to abuse Marxist categories by glibly incorporating the vast numbers of the unemployed and marginalized that populate the South into the category of 'reserve army of labour' in order to save the hypotheses of 'proletarian revolution' and of the emergent movement's necessarily socialist vocation. As noted, such populations resist in terms of a wide variety of identities and grievances (even if they are also subject, in their desperation and in the absence of more progressive alternatives, to mobilization by the most self-defeating of fundamentalist and xenophobic ideologies). Nonetheless, some bridge to militant class awareness for the majority of Southerners might be found in the kind of expansive definition of class advocated some years ago by Post and Wright:

> The working out of capitalism in parts of the periphery prepares not only the minority working class but peasants and other working people, women, youth and minorities for a socialist solution, even though the political manifestation of this may not initially take the form of a socialist movement. In the case of those who are *not* wage labourers (the classical class associated with that new order) capitalism has still so permeated the social relations which determine their existences, even though it may not have followed the western European pattern of 'freeing' their labour power, that to be liberated from it is their only salvation .... The objective need for socialism of these elements can be no less than that of the worker imprisoned in the factory and disciplined by the whip of unemployment. These prices are paid in even the most 'successful' of the

underdeveloped countries, and others additionally experience mass desti-
tution. Finding another path has... become a desperate necessity if the
alternative of continuing, if not increasing barbarism is to be escaped.[61]

Note, however, that even the kind of 'class consciousness' implied in this paragraph is something that must be won politically, not merely assumed.

And what, finally, of 'imaginary' and the terms in which on-going struggle can
best be conceived and advocated? An emphasis on the range of 'disparate forces'
and 'multiple particularisms' from which more cumulative struggles of radical
provenance must be built has placed the issue of 'democracy' firmly on the
agenda of the contemporary left. Often the contrast with the past practices of
ostensibly working-class-based parties and national revolutionary movements is
self-consciously underscored in doing so. Moreover, the democratic imaginary
will be especially attractive to those who must confront, as is so often the case
in the Third World, the immediate reality of authoritarian state oppression (not
to mention the lack of transparency of most of the global institutions whose decisions have such a pronounced impact on people's fates). This, then, is certainly
a language of potential empowerment well worth clawing back from those, especially in the North, who manipulate it so unscrupulously. At the same time, any
temptation on the left to develop its project of resistance to oppression exclusively in terms of it – à la Laclau's notion of 'radical democracy' – should be
resisted, I think.[62] For, as important as such an emphasis is, and as responsive to
diversity as any emergent movement for radical change must be, a project cast
in terms solely of democratic claims (however 'radical') is risky: it courts
unfocused eclecticism and a blurring of the target of capitalism, of global
exploitation and commodification and of imperialist military and cultural assault
that we know to be so central to global inequality and underdevelopment.
Beyond democracy, 'naming the enemy', at minimum, in firmly anti-capitalist
terms provides an imaginary that is accurate and is, in any case, both implicit and
explicit in much Southern practice. It also has the potential of driving an ever
greater growth and consolidation of movements fighting commodification,
fighting exploitation, fighting exclusion and operating at various sites and scales:
'For all but a handful, capitalism has failed. For the rest of us, anti-capitalism
remains our only hope.'[63]

But what, one might ask, can this mean more positively, in terms of both
vision and promise? Some have argued effectively the need to complement 'anti-
capitalism' with a militant demand for 'social justice', for example.[64] And there
is also, I would suggest in conclusion, a continuing claim to be made on behalf
of the socialist imaginary – both as a plausible point of reference for struggles
against capitalist globalization and imperialism and as a feasible liberatory practice for advancing Southern claims against inequality and for genuine
development To be sure, the saliency of this once potent project has been downgraded in the eyes of many because of the internal weaknesses it has revealed and
the defeats and/or failures it has suffered in recent decades. Yet it will prove
neither possible nor wise for radicals in the South (or indeed anywhere else) to

refuse, as diagnosis of current problems and guide to future practice, the promise of what Greg Albo has termed 'realistic socialism' – a project which, in his discussion of the current parameters and likely prospects of global political economy, he has effectively contrasted to the claims of what he calls 'utopian capitalism'.[65] True, any such programme of 'realistic socialism' will not be realized quickly, in the form, say, of some kind of revolutionary 'big bang', as too often advocated rhetorically and abstractly on the left.[66] It will also have to be specified – globally, nationally, locally – not in terms of some pre-existing blueprint but by such social forces as mobilize themselves to place more progressive demands on the agenda. And, of course, it will not happen until even more people than at present, both in the South and in the North, embrace the fact that the existing market-dominated global order – driven by 'a minority class that draws its wealth and power from a historically specific form of production' – is (in Albo's words) 'contingent, imbalanced, exploitative and replaceable.' Nonetheless, Albo's broader premise – that positive outcomes 'can only be realized through re-embedding financial capital and production relations in democratically organized national and local economic spaces sustained through international solidarity and fora of democratic co-operation'[67] – seems a necessary starting-point.

NOTES

1   Although never quite given the prominence it deserves in most standard history books, this process has, nonetheless, been dissected effectively by a number of prominent western historians who provide their books with various suitably ironic titles: see Eric Wolf, *Europe and the People without History*, Berkeley and Los Angeles: University of California Press, 1982; V.G. Kiernan, *The Lords of Human Kind: Yellow Man, Black Man and White Man in the Age of Empire*, Boston: Little Brown, 1969; Sven Lindqvist, *'Exterminate all the Brutes'*, New York: The New Press, 1998; Richard Drinnon, *Facing West: The Metaphysics of Indian-Hating and Empire-Building*, New York: New American Library, 1980. Of course, this has also been done by 'Third World' scholars themselves (who tend to have a similar gift for to-the-point titling): Chinweizu, *The West and the Rest of Us*, New York: Vintage Books, 1975; Walter Rodney, *How Europe Underdeveloped Africa*, London: Bogle-L'Ouverture, 1972; Eduardo Galeano, *The Open Veins of Latin America: Five Centuries of the Pillage of a Continent*, New York: Monthly Review Press, 1973; and Edward Said, *Orientalism*, New York: Pantheon Books, 1978; there is also, more recently, Sophie Bessis, *Western Supremacy: Triumph of an Idea?*, London: Zed Books, 2003. Unfortunately, such history now stands in increased danger of being whitewashed and recycled for purposes of rationalizing the United States' own current bid for imperial legitimacy, one particularly worrying example of this trend being Niall Ferguson's *Empire: The Rise and Demise of the British World Order and the*

Lessons for Global Power, London: Allen Lane, 2002, itself linked to a successful television series.

2   Joseph E. Stiglitz, *Globalization and its Discontents*, New York: W.W. Norton, 2002, p. 5.

3   From the WTO's 1999 report, *Trade, Income Policy and Poverty*, as quoted in David McNally, *Another World Is Possible: Globalization and Anti-capitalism*, Winnipeg: Arbeiter Ring, 2002, p. 92.

4   'Three men own more than 48 countries', *Mail and Guardian* (Johannesburg), September 23, 1998, reporting on the annual Human Development Report of the United Nations; as that UN document continues: 'It is estimated that the additional cost of achieving and main-taining universal access to basic education for all, basic health care for all, reproductive health care for all women, adequate food for and safe water and sanitation for all is roughly $40-billion a year. This is less than 4% of the combined wealth of the 225 richest people'.

5   See, for overviews, the 'Afterword' (entitled 'Sustaining global apartheid' to Patrick Bond, *Against Global Apartheid: South Africa Meets the World Bank, IMF and International Finance,* Second Edition, London: Zed Press, 2003, Peter Waterman, 'The Global Justice and Solidarity Movement' (draft manuscript: forthcoming) and, for a range of diverse examples of concrete struggles, both McNally, *Another World* and Philip McMichael, *Development and Social Change: A Global Perspective*, Second Edition, Thousand Oaks: Pine Forge Press, 2000, esp. ch. 7, 'The Globalization Project and its Counter-Movements'. See also Stephen Gill, *Power and Resistance in the New World Order*, New York: Palgrave Macmillan, 2003.

6   Ankie Hoogvelt, *Globalization and the Post-Colonial World: The New Political Economy of Development*, Second Edition, London: Palgrave, 2001, p. xiv.

7   Beverley J. Silver and Giovanni Arrighi, 'Workers North and South', in *Socialist Register 2001*, London: Merlin Press, 2000, pp. 56-7.

8   Giovanni Arrighi, 'World Income Inequalities and the Future of Socialism', *New Left Review*, 189, 1991.

9   Giovanni Arrighi, Beverley J. Silver and Benjamin D. Brewer, 'Industrial Convergence, Globalization and the Persistence of the North-South Divide', *Studies in Comparative International Development*, 38(1), 2003; the same issue of this journal includes an exchange between Alice Amsden and the authors which serves, I think, to reinforce the latter's case.

10 Arrighi, 'World Income Inequalities', p. 65.

11 Arrighi, Silver and Brewer, 'Industrial Convergence', p. 26; a similar chasm, albeit one defined over a much longer period of time, separates Arrighi's prognosis for Africa in the 1960s, when, with the present author, he asserted that 'socialist construction is a *necessary* means to the end of development in Africa' (in Giovanni Arrighi and John S. Saul, *Essays on the Political Economy of Africa*, New York: Monthly Review Press, 1973) to the much more limited possibilities for change he now envisages for the continent in his

'The African Crisis', *New Left Review*, 15 , 2002.

12 See, importantly, Brian S. Smith, *Understanding Third World Politics*, Bloomington: Indiana University Press, 1996, ch. 1, 'The Idea of the "Third World"'; John Toye, *Dilemmas of Development: Reflections on the Counter-Revolution in Development Economics*, Second Edition, Oxford: Blackwell, 1993, ch. 1, 'Is the Third World Still There?'; and Fred Cooper and Randall Packer, eds., *International Development and the Social Scientists*, Berkeley and Los Angeles: University of California Press, 1997, 'Introduction'.

13 Manuel Castells, *The Information Age: Economy, Society and Culture*, in three volumes, Malden and Oxford: Blackwell, 1996, 1997, 1998.

14 Michael Hardt and Antonio Negri, *Empire*, Cambridge: Harvard University Press, 2000.

15 Leslie Sklair, *The Transnational Capitalist Class*, Oxford: Blackwell, 2001.

16 Gary Teeple, *Globalization and the Decline of Social Reform*, Aurora: Garamond Press, 2000.

17 James Petras and Henry Veltmeyer, *Globalization Unmasked: Imperialism in the 21st Century*, Halifax: Fernwood Books, 2001.

18 Leo Panitch, 'Globalisation and the State', *Socialist Register 1994*, London: Merlin Press, 1994, p. 63, and many of his subsequent writings.

19 Paul Hirst and Grahame Thompson, *Globalization in Question*, London: Polity Press, 1996, p. 189.

20 Colin Leys, *The Rise and Fall of Development Theory*, London: James Currey, 1996, p. 23.

21 Colin Leys, 'Africa's Tragedy', *New Left Review*, 204, 1994, p. 46.

22 The most symptomatic works in this vein have been written by Peter Evans, as, for example, his *Embedded Autonomy: States and Industrial Transformation*, Princeton: Princeton University Press, 1995, and numerous articles.

23 William Graf, 'The State in the Third World', *Socialist Register 1995*, London: Merlin Press, 1995, p. 159.

24 David Plank, 'Aid, Debt and the End of Sovereignty: Mozambique and Its Donors', *Journal of Modern African Studies*, 31(3), 1993.

25 Manfred Bienefeld, 'Nation State in the Dog Days of the Twentieth Century', *Socialist Register 1994*, London: Merlin Press, 1994, pp. 122-3.

26 Graf, 'The State in the Third World', p. 159.

27 Panitch, 'Globalisation and the State', p. 63.

28 There were also other Marxist theorists of 'underdevelopment', of course, some of whom chose to see – along classical lines – an unfolding process of global capitalist development that was necessary to produce genuine prole-tarian-based struggles in the longer run (Bill Warren's 'Chicago Marxism', as Fred Bienefeld once termed it, being a central point of reference here).

29 This 'counter-revolution' (to both 'Keynesianism' and orthodox 'struc-turalist developmentalism') has been well described in John Toye, *Dilemmas of Development*, where he skilfully evokes the roles played by the likes of Harry Johnson, Peter Bauer, Deepak Lal, Ian Little and Bela Belassa.

30 Amartya Sen, *Development as Freedom*, New York: Anchor Books, 1999.

31 See, *inter alia*, Jonathan Crush, ed., *Power of Development*, London and New York: Routledge, 1995, esp. ch. 11 by Arturo Escobar, entitled 'Imagining a Post-Development Era'.

32 For a strong statement of the weakness of much development theory in terms of gender see Catherine V. Scott, *Gender and Development: Rethinking Modernization and Dependency Theory*, Boulder: Lynne Rienner, 1995; see also Chandra Mohanty, 'Under Western Eyes: Feminist Scholarship and Colonial Discourses' in C. T. Mohanty, A. Russo and L. Torres, eds., *Third World Women and the Politics of Feminism,* Bloomington: Indiana University Press, 1991 and much subsequent literature.

33 Bob Sutcliffe, 'Development after Ecology', in V. Bhaskar and A. Glyn, eds., *The North, the South and the Environment: Ecological Constraints and the Global Economy*, London: St. Martin's Press, 1995.

34 Bob Sutcliffe, 'The Place of Development in Theories of Imperialism and Globalization', in Ronaldo Munck and Denis O'Hearn, eds., *Critical Development Theory: Contributions to a New Paradigm*, London and New York: Zed, 1999, pp. 150-2.

35 Cooper and Packard, *International Development*, p. 4.

36 Frans J. Schuurman, 'Paradigms Lost, Paradigms Regained? Development Studies in the Twenty-First Century', *Third World Quarterly*, 21(1), 2000, p. 14. See also Gillian Hart, 'Development Critiques in the 1990s: *Culs de Sac* and Promising Paths', *Progress in Human Geography* 25(4), 2001.

37 Leys, *The Rise and Fall of Development Theory*, p. 43.

38 See, *inter alia*, Patrick Bond, *Against Global Apartheid* and Walden Bello, *Deglobalization*, London: Zed Books, 2002.

39 Originating in his article, 'The Coming Anarchy', *The Atlantic Monthly*, February, 1994 and spun out as several subsequent books.

40 Thomas P.M. Barnett, 'The Pentagon's New Map: It Explains Why We're Going to War, and Why We'll Keep Going to War', *Esquire*, March, 2003. But this popular article is merely the most public face of this industrious Naval War College-based Doctor Strangelove whose career as consultant to policy-makers can be traced at his web-site: http://www.nwc.navy.mil/newrules/ThePentagonsNewMap.htm.

41 Ben Fine, 'The Development State Is Dead: Long Live Social Capital?' *Development and Change*, 30, 1999.

42 See Gerald Schmitz, 'Democratization and Demystification: Deconstructing "Governance" as Development Discourse', in D.B. Moore and G. Schmitz, eds., *Debating Development Discourse: Institutional and Popular Perspectives*, New York: St. Martin's Press, 1995 and David Moore, '"Sail on, O Ship of State": Neo-Liberalism, Globalisation and the Governance of Africa', *The Journal Of Peasant Studies*, 27(1), 1999. The often authoritarian and corrupt Third World state is, of course, a problem; it is just not the kind of problem that the IFIs prefer to see it is as being.

43 Robert Biel, *The New Imperialism: Crisis and Contradiction in North/South Relations*, London: Zed, 2000, esp. ch. 11, 'Permanent Subordination? Structural Adjustment as Control', pp. 231-2.

44 George Soros, *The Crisis of Global Capitalism*, New York: Public Affairs, 1998 and 'The Capitalist Threat', *The Atlantic Monthly*, 279, 1997, p. 48, where he argues the existence of a 'capitalist threat' that is causing 'intolerable inequalities and instability'. Indeed, he writes that 'unless [the doctrine of laissez-faire capitalism] is tempered by the recognition of a common interest that ought to take precedence over particular interests, our present system... is liable to breakdown'.

45 Paul Krugman, *The Return of Depression Economics*, New York: Norton, 1999.

46 See Stiglitz, *Globalization and its Discontents*, and for an even more advanced statement as to the need to 'start from scratch' in rebuilding more democratic and effective global financial institutions, see the report of Stiglitz's views in *Financial Times*, August 21, 2002.

47 Of course Przeworski (in his *Capitalism and the Market*, Cambridge: Cambridge University Press, 1991, p. 122) goes further, adding to his claim that 'capitalism is irrational' the disempowering reflection that 'socialism is unfeasible, in the real world people starve... the conclusions we have reached are not encouraging ones'!

48 For a searching critique of NEPAD, and of the role of the new South African political elite in promoting it, see Patrick Bond, ed., *Fanon's Warning: A Civil Society Reader on the New Partnership for Africa's Development*, Trenton and Cape Town: Africa World Press and AIDC, 2002.

49 Biel, *The New Imperialism*; I have also drawn on these arguments by Biel in developing a more detailed analysis of the possible revolutionary prospect for Africa in my article 'Africa: The Next Liberation Struggle', *Review of African Political Economy*, 96, 2003.

50 Ibid., pp. 232-3.

51 Ibid., pp. 242-3.

52 See, *inter alia*, the titles listed under footnote 5, above.

53 For an example of where an extreme emphasis on the appropriateness of a local focus can lead the development theorist, see the 'Conclusion' to Hoogvelt, *Globalization and the Post-Colonial World*; but contrast Giles Mohan and Kristian Stokke on the weakness (and possible cooptability) of such a tendency in their 'Participatory Development and Empowerment: The Dangers of Localism', *Third World Quarterly*, 21(2), 2000.

54 Trevor Ngwane, 'Sparks in the Township', *New Left Review*, 22, 2003.

55 See Naomi Klein, *Fences and Windows: Dispatches from the Front Lines of the Globalization Debate*, Toronto: Vintage Canada, 2002.

56 John S. Saul, 'Identifying Class, Classifying Difference', *Socialist Register 2003*, London: Merlin Press, 2002.

57 Cf. John S. Saul, 'What is to be Learned? The Failure of African Socialisms and their Future', in Robert Albritton, John Bell, Shannon Bell and Richard

Westra, eds., *Beyond Market and Plan: Toward New Socialisms* (forthcoming).

58 Colin Leys, 'Colin Leys Replies' [a reply to Jonathan Barker, 'Debating Globalization: Critique of Colin Leys'], *Southern African Report*, 12(4), 1997. I have explored at greater length some of the issues raised in this section of the present essay in my 'Africa: The Next Liberation Struggle'.

59 Cf. Neil Smith, 'What Happened to Class?', *Environment and Planning A*, 32, 2000.

60 See Ronald Munck, *Globalization and Labour: The New 'Great Transformation'*, London: Zed Books, 2002; Beverley Silver, *Forces of Labour: Workers' Movements and Globalization,* Cambridge and New York: Cambridge University Press, 2003; and the various essays in *Socialist Register 2001: Working Classes, Global Realities*, London: Merlin Press, 2000.

61 Ken Post and P. Wright, *Socialism and Underdevelopment*, London and New York: Routledge, 1989, pp. 151-2.

62 I have elaborated this point in my 'Identifying Class, Classifying Difference'.

63 J.C. Myers, 'What is Anti-Capitalism?' in Joel Schalit, ed., *The Anti-Capitalism Reader*, New York: Akashic Books, 2002, p. 34. On 'anti-capitalism' see also McNally, *Another World*; working along related lines, Amory Starr, in her *Naming the Enemy: Anti-Corporate Movements Confront Globalization*, London: Zed Books, 2000 emphasizes an 'anti-corporate' problematic as particularly appropriate for deepening the terms of popular struggle and coordinating radical activities.

64 Cf. Sam Gindin, 'Social Justice and Globalization: Are they Compatible?', *Monthly Review*, 54(2), 2002.

65 Greg Albo, 'A World Market of Opportunities? Capitalist Obstacles and Left Economic Policies', *Socialist Register 1997*, London: Merlin Press, 1997, pp. 28-30 and 41.

66 Drawing on the work of André Gorz and Boris Kagarlitzky on 'structural reform' I have sought to chart a possible course between 'mere reformism' and jejune 'revolutionism' in my *Recolonization and Resistance: Southern Africa in the 1990s*, Trenton: Africa World Press, 1993, chs. 4 and 5.

67 Albo, 'A World Market of Opportunities', p. 30; Albo himself suggests, for starters, the need for 'more inward-oriented economic strategies' and the devaluation of 'scale of production as the central economic objective' (p. 28).

THE LIMITS AND CONTRADICTIONS OF 'AMERICANIZATION'

EMAD EL-DIN AYSHA

The United States received a rude awakening on September 11, 2001, finally realizing that it was not as loved as it had once thought it was in the post-Cold War era, especially in the Middle East. The absence of a geopolitical and ideological counterweight did not automatically mean acceptance of the remaining superpower. Out of the cauldron of 9/11 emerged a new debate in Washington, DC about American 'soft power' versus 'hard power', reflecting a new understanding of just how unpopular the US was, and how ineffective America's supposed domination of the airwaves was in protecting it from popular opposition in the Arab-Muslim world.

The concept of soft power refers to a country's cultural and ideological 'appeal', its 'ability to get desired outcomes through attraction instead of force', working by ensuring that 'others want what you want'.[1] Hard power, by contrast, refers to more tangible power resources found essentially in the economic, demographic, military, and technological spheres.[2] Americans on the more liberal side of the ideological spectrum see soft power as the preferred way of managing America's position in the world. As Andrew Bacevich puts it, Americans 'count on the allure of the "American way of life" to win over doubters and subvert adversaries', a by-product of American exceptionalism, something that 'befits a nation founded on the conviction of its own uniqueness, [since] the American empire is like no other in history'.[3] Even radical critics of the invasion of Iraq have seen it as intended to clear the ground for the success of soft power in the Middle East. Perry Anderson, for instance, noting that Saudi Arabia is 'more barricaded against US cultural penetration than any country in the world after North Korea', has argued that while it is 'thoroughly subject to the grip of American "hard" power (funds and arms), most of the Arab world thus forms a kind of exclusion zone for the normal operations of American "soft power"'. Taking over Iraq would, he argued in 2002, give 'Washington a large oil-rich platform in the centre of the Arab world' leading to a role-model effect where Arab elites would finally be convinced of the 'need to modernize their ways, and Arab masses of the invincibility of America'.[4]

This essay will challenge the assumption that underlies the arguments of both American liberal imperialists and their critics – the assumption that once a part of the world is opened to 'globalization' it can be structured, thanks to globalization, in such a way as to openly embrace American soft power. Whereas many assume that a certain synergy exists between globalization and Americanization, such that the transnational economic forces of globalization remodel the world according to American ideological and cultural specifications, my argument is that the opposite is the case. Globalization, even if it certainly means commodification of culture, does not necessarily mean Americanization. On the contrary, as disproportionately important as the American contribution is to globalization, globalization can actually weaken America's cultural hold on the world. The world is much more immune to US influence than has been supposed.

SOFT POWER AND SEPTEMBER 11

In December 2002, Richard Haass, the State Department's Director of Policy Planning, admitted that past administrations had allowed the Middle East to become a 'democratic exception' and, consequently, 'breeding grounds for extremists and terrorists who target America for supporting the regimes under which they live'. After September 11th it was decided that it was 'not in the US interest … or that of Muslims, for the United States to continue this exception', as Secretary of State Colin Powell put it in his famous speech to the Heritage Foundation, talking about America's interest in promoting democracy and development in the region, and using his address to launch the 'US-Middle East Partnership Initiative' (MEPI) – commonly known as the Powell Initiative – with its emphasis on education, economic reform, private sector development, women's empowerment, and civil society promotion.[5]

For Powell, soft power means the use of public diplomacy to market America, quite literally, with the emphasis on 're-branding' the United States to the world.[6] The 'queen of branding', Charlotte Beers (the legendary ad executive who headed Tatham-Laird & Kudner, Ogilvy & Mather, and J. Walter Thompson), was hired to do the job, filling the post of Under Secretary of Public Diplomacy and Public Affairs soon after 9/11. Her main task involved changing the perceptions of 'disaffected populations' in the Middle East and South Asia about America, countering the global image of the US, the 'world's only "hyperpower"', as a 'boorish bully, intimidating its allies and unable to comprehend the hatred it inflames across the Arab world', as Ms Beers herself put it.[7] She followed the dictates of consumer research with focus groups and audience segmentation, engaging in weekly meetings with American Muslims and meeting Arab opinion-formers in Britain, Egypt and Morocco. Her ideas ranged from the State

Department booklet, 'Muslim Life in America', to Muslim American adverts during Ramadan, to a proposed partnership with the Smithsonian Institute to build a 'virtual reality American room where overseas looky-loos can experience a walk down an imaginary American street … [and] the local library, shopping mall or touring bus'.[8]

Beers resigned her post in March 2003 after only a little over a year in office. The state of her health was the official reason given, but soon after leaving office she complained that the rest of the government was uncooperative, making it impossible for her to do what she had been hired to do. An unnamed American official informed CNN that the White House 'has been distancing itself from Charlotte since day one'.[9] This certainly had something to do with the power of the superhawks in the administration. Beers was derided by the right-wing press and think tanks closely associated with the administration, who thought that treating America like a brand 'would debase us to be "sold" like soap'.[10] Although many of these critics have no qualms about Beers herself, or her techniques, which they find laughable but not too harmful in themselves, they believe that America's negative image among Muslims is because of a 'deficiency not merely in information but in the skills of reality-testing … The problem is not our "brand"; it is their buying habits'.[11] The superhawks would rather operate through generalized 'information warfare', a concept (developed and popularized by Donald Rumsfeld and his advisors at the Pentagon soon after 9/11) that combines purely military techniques of disabling enemy information systems, and demoralizing its troops through traditional psychological warfare (propaganda broadcasts, leaflet dropping), with 'public information management' (controlling the dissemination of 'true' information about wars the US is conducting).[12]

But the petty controversies around Beers' appointment and departure are really symptomatic of a much larger problem, namely that the US has gradually been stripped of its soft power resources by larger structural developments around the globe that are best summarized, ironically, under the label of 'globalization'. What September 11th really raised is the question of the type of world American power operates in; the question of how resistant this world is to the causes and consequences of American unipolar dominance. As the Cold War historian Michael Cox eloquently puts it, 'crises have the capacity to separate the conceptual wheat from the rhetorical chaff', drawing a 'clear line between the world as it is and the world as some imagine it to be'.[13]

'GLOCALIZATION' AND THE DILUTION OF AMERICAN CULTURE

Widely-held assumptions regarding Americanization take it that, for instance, eating at McDonald's is a 'political act', an act involving cultural or identity politics whereby 'one positions oneself socially and personally with global modernity'. When Americans eat at McDonald's, surveys show that they place the emphasis on the speed, efficiency and rationality of the fast-food industry, things they associate with twentieth century American life. This positions them as modern but not global. For people in the Third World one would expect the situation to be completely different. In eating at McDonald's they would position themselves in modern *and* global terms, wishing to 'consume a modernity they see as lacking in their own societies' but found in America and its products.[14] But while McDonald's does offer a 'standardized' menu, it is adapted to 'local' environments. McDonald's serves a berry-based drink in Brazil, a fruit-based shake in Malaysia, Singapore, and Thailand, coconut, mango, and tropic mint shakes in Hong Kong, vegetarian Maharaja Macs in anti-beef India, mutton potpies in Australia, and uses Asterix instead of Ronald McDonald to promote burgers in France. According to marketing guru and international consultant Paul Herbig much the same is true, to varying degrees, of the marketing strategies of Wrigley, KFC, Burger King, Wendy's, Coca-Cola, Pepsi-Cola, Marlboro, Revlon, Levi's, and Pizza Hut.[15] It is true that such corporations have changed the habits, tastes and mentality of customers around the world, but these homogenizing effects have not done away with local cultures. This allows non-Americans to eat fast food in a way that makes them different than before – 'modern' – but without thinking of themselves as Americans.

One can see evidence of similar non-Americanizing marketing processes at work in the entertainment industry. The very growth of the global market for American cultural products has exerted a 'homogenizing feedback effect on the creative process' in which many American movies are 'now produced with an eye on the foreign audience and often with the help of foreign investors'. As one critic complained, such films 'might as well come from the moon or the Cayman Islands' as from Hollywood.[16] Such feedback effects of globalization have already decisively made their way into the music industry. MTV is no longer split three ways between MTV America, Europe, and Asia, but now – thanks to digital technology – consists of: MTV Brazil, MTV Europe, MTV2 Europe, MTV Canada, MTV China, MTV France, MTV Germany, MTV2 Germany, MTV Holland, MTV India, MTV Italy, MTV Japan, MTV Korea, MTV Latin America, MTV Nordic, MTV Poland, MTV Russia, MTV South East Asia, MTV Spain, MTV Taiwan/Hong Kong, and MTV UK. Each segment of MTV almost exists in a world of its own, catering to the tastes of each market in its own language, using its music, arts and advertisements.

Thus American pop culture is not as all-pervasive as many think, given that the most popular television programs in most countries are nearly always local productions, while local pop groups are more than capable of competing with American bands in their home countries and even in the American market. In the Arab world, for instance, regional satellite channels dedicated to airing Arabic music videos – such as MTV Lebanon, Melody Hits TV, the Mazzika channel and Egypt's Dream TV, among others – have flooded the airways with their produce and directed Arabic-speaking audiences away from Western channels. Moreover, not all American pop culture that reaches the Third World comes from satellite broadcasts originating in the West. As a consequence the programs, shows, and movies broadcast through terrestrial outlets are heavily 'filtered' to local standards of morality. When episodes of the hit sitcom *Friends* were broadcast on Egyptian television a significant amount of material was removed, especially anything pertaining to homosexuality. Knowing how central homosexuality was to the storyline, one can imagine the amount of damage done. The censors were able to squeeze two half-hour episodes into a half-hour timeslot, with commercial breaks!

Similarly CNN, which broadcasts the 'American world view', is not a 'signpost on the road to a universal civilization' but an 'ephemeral artifact of America's present lead in communications technologies', as John Gray argues: only media companies that 'vary their product to suit different cultures, such as MTV, may expect to remain global'.[17] The CNN homepage does boast CNN.com Asia, CNN.com Europe, CNNenEspanol.com, CNNArabic.com, and some language services, but all of its broadcasting is in English, represents the American world view, and consists mostly of domestic news that does not interest foreign audiences. In fact, thanks to the domestic focus of CNN and the isolationist mentality of its predominantly American audience, CNN only reaches 3 per cent of the world's population and is 'struggling to make live global coverage its trademark'.[18] The paradox here is that for America to get its message across it must either dilute it (as in the case of movies) or stop broadcasting that message completely (as in the case of MTV). American pop culture is being *de-Americanized* by the very forces of globalization that supposedly thrive on the universal appeal of American culture.

The label that encompasses this contradictory state of affairs is 'glocalization', a business term invented by the Japanese in order to 'emphasize that the globalization of a product is more likely to succeed when the product or service is adapted specifically to each locality or culture it is marketed in'.[19] Glocalization attacks the process of Americanization at its very heart because it resists all homogenizing cultural tendencies, American or otherwise. As Roland Robertson says, '*indigenization* is the other side of the coin of the *homogenizing* aspects of globalization'.[20] Increasingly in this new globalized age the popularity of commodities is tied less and less to the culture of the country they originate in, and more and more to brand names. As Francis Rocca, former editor of the *American Spectator*, reminds us, how many of us know – or care – that Benetton is an Italian company, or that the Swatch logo is the flag of Switzerland, or that Nokia is Finnish? 'Korean youngsters', notes Rocca, are 'joyfully surprised to find, when visiting the States, that Americans have McDonald's, too'.[21]

This is not a particularly new process. Pasta – the symbol of Italian cuisine – is Chinese in origin. Baseball, the all-American game, is really a version of the British game of rounders. Cultures have always absorbed the products of other cultures, stripped them of their 'foreign' quality, and then conveniently forgotten their origins in order to make them something distinctly and uniquely local. The only difference now is that this process is driven by global capital; the foreign itself 'wishes' to become local. The structure of distribution and consumption in the global economy is 'distinctively American', but the 'content of global mass culture is multinational in origin and universal in character', robbing American goods of what is distinctively American about them. The end result is that there are 'fewer and fewer normative American tastes, making it harder to define American identity, and harder to adopt it'.[22] The global reach and appeal of American goods actually depends on the fact that what it exports globally is *not* seen to be American, or representative of any other culture for that matter. In Peterson's terminology, goods produced by American multinationals are culturally 'modern' but not 'global' because they are localized by these multinational corporations and by the populations that buy these goods.

One of the positive by-products of globalization is that by forcing local firms to conform to global standards of management and product quality it actually helps improve the competitiveness, and so the resilience, of local cultural industries in the face of foreign competition. One of the most successful cases of Third World cultural industries taking up Western standards and out-competing Western corporations is Al-Jazeera Satellite Channel. Al-Jazeera is modelled on CNN, aiming to be the premier 24-hour news channel of the Arab world, while most of its programs and broadcasting style are modelled on the BBC World Service, whence most of its employees originate.[23] Al-Jazeera was able to broadcast pictures from inside Afghanistan that no other network had access to, forcing the Western world to look at things from the perspective of the Taliban and al-Qaeda, and effectively bringing to an end the 'CNN age' that began with the first Gulf War. And in the 2003 US invasion of Iraq, as Jonathan Alter and Martha Brant say, 'Al-Jazeera [was] to the Iraq war what CNN was to the 1991 gulf war - the primary source of information', almost single-handedly ruining months and months of US planning for a huge propaganda war alongside the actual war.[24]

It is true, of course, that the multiple cultural roots of American society give the country's culture an advantage over all other countries in the soft power game; its European component appeals to Europeans, its Latino element appeals to Latin Americans, its African-American to Africans, its Asian to Asians.[25] But because the cultural identity of globalization is surprisingly fluid and malleable, it helps to shield consumers from the deleterious effects of American consumer and pop culture. The global marketplace is also the world of the Swatch Swiss watch, Mexican soap operas, Hong Kong Kung Fu movies and Japanese anime and computer games. The most popular game in the world is still football, a non-American sport that is finally beginning to become incorporated in the consciousness of the American population; and most people around the world still call it 'football', instead of the American word 'soccer'. The largest movie industry in the world is not Hollywood but Bollywood. The Indian movie industry has not faced any problems competing on its home ground with American movies, and has been very successful abroad and among Indian migrant communities in both the Third and the First Worlds, as have Indian music videos. In Egypt local movies are more profitable to cinemas than foreign films, and the Chinese have been so successful in exporting their brand of cinema that an increasing number of Chinese actors and directors work in Hollywood, with many American movies adopting their style of filmmaking (e.g. the *Matrix* movies, *Mission Impossible 2*).

Even at the level of language America's cultural ascendancy is not guaranteed, as pointed out by linguist Joshua Fishman. Despite the unprecedented reach of English as the new *lingua franca* of the globalizing world, this does not confer much (or at least not lasting) power on the US, because English 'actually reaches and is then utilized by only a small and atypically fortunate minority' while the 'kinds of interactions identified with globalization, from trade to communications, have also encouraged regionalization and with it the spread of regional languages'. The global predominance of English undoubtedly confers advantages on American firms from a marketing perspective, but its political utility as an instrument of imperialism is exaggerated. The fact that they spoke English did not prevent American colonists or the Irish from fighting and defeating their English (cultural) masters, any more than their continued usage of English has threatened their continued independence. People around the world are increasingly taught English by non-native speakers, with young people in particular developing their own slang dialectics which mix English and local languages. As Fishman reminds us, just because a great many 'young people around the world may be able to sing along to a new Madonna song does not mean they can hold a rudimentary conversation in English or even understand what Madonna is saying'.[26]

A relative once complained to me about how her son, who was enrolled in a foreign language school in Egypt, pronounces the world 'circle' as 'kurkle'. Even though the boy knew the proper pronunciation, he had to pronounce it with a 'k' because that was how the teacher pronounced it – and the teacher would not change her mind when he told her the proper pronunciation. People in the Third World – I speak from my own personal experience in the Arab world – often 'lump together' what is American, Western, European, Northern, white, and modern. Elite groups in Egypt still insist on speaking French as a sign of being 'developed' and 'modern' (a product of Egypt's unique affinity with all things French since the days of the Napoleon's invasion of Egypt and Mohammad Ali's attempt to modernize Egypt along French lines), even though English has long ousted French as the language of 'civilization'. Young people in the Arab world do wear T-shirts carrying the logos of 'Ralph Lauren' and 'Armani', but when questioned they do not attach any fashion significance to these particular brands – all 'Western' T-shirts are the same to them. They are just as likely to wear T-shirts with a picture of Che Guevara on it or the words 'JIHAD is the only solution'.

The crude kind of English that people speak in the Third World often forms a linguistic barrier to the cultural-ideological effect of Americanizing pop culture goods. People watch American movies or eat American food, but still do not get the point, cannot grasp the totality of the American experience. They often inter-pret things in a selective way that reinforces their biases and prejudices, believing that it confirms what they have known all along. Pursuing the concept of glocalization to its logical conclusion does not produce a homogenizing, Americanizing world but one that is being increasingly 'unified' and 'fragmented' at the same time.[27]

THE COUNTER-FORCE OF RELIGION

Already in 1970 Zbigniew Brzezinski suggested that people were searching for a 'more intimate linguistic and religious community' to overcome the impact of living in an increasingly 'congested, overlapping, confusing, and impersonal' global environment, drawing inward to escape a sense of 'global congestion'.[28] One consequence of this has been the addition of 'localization' to the list of the forces eating away at the global dominance of English. The world is teeming with voluntary language preservation movements and governments that find linguistic diversity acceptable and even desirable. The end result is that there have never been as many standardized languages as there are today: roughly 1,200, with the development of multilingual societies around the world grounded in a 'linguistic division of labor' where different languages serve different social func-tions and so do not displace each other.[29]

The end result is a world that, as Brzezinski argued, is more like a 'global city' than McLuhan's famous 'global village', because rather than 'the personal stability, interpersonal intimacy, implicitly shared values, and traditions that were important ingredients of the primitive village' what exists is a 'nervous, agitated, tense, and fragmented web of interdependent relations'. As Brzezinski points out perceptively, these are the dominant features of city life (where 'interdepen-dence... is better characterized by interaction than by intimacy') and not village life.[30] And this interaction can be and often is violent, given that globalization generates anti-global sentiment, and often allows anti-global forces to take advan-tage of what globalization has to offer, reinforcing their power and their ability to send shockwaves through the world. This is because one of globalization's boasts is that it 'increases choice', including the choice to 'live life according to your own lights'. An example used by Micklethwaite and Wooldridge to prove this is a religious group – the Bruderhof – who do not approve of radio, televi-sion, feminism, and homosexuality. But, despite this they 'established a highly successful global toy business using a mixture of Japanese management techniques and American technology'.[31] This gave them all the money they needed to keep their community intact and make it successful, so that they did not have to abandon their way of life. The Zapatista movement in Mexico is not alone in having made very successful use of the Internet: even the Taliban, who banned the Internet and television in Afghanistan, had a website of their own and were surprisingly successful at using satellite television to broadcast their version of the American war to the world.

Indeed religious fundamentalism of all colours is to a considerable extent a by-product of globalization, and at several levels. It is partly a 'search for stable values amid alienation from the harsh economic realities and materialism of the late twentieth century' – the revival of Christian fundamentalism in America in the wake of Reaganomics being a case in point.[32] Even more than materialism, however, fundamentalism is a reaction against Americanism seen as an attack on beliefs and institutions – gender, sexuality, identity, the definitions of marriage and family – that were once thought to be fundamental and unalterable. Fundamentalism mobilizes religious sentiment in an effort to preserve what people see as normal, and often drives them to push the clock back to a time before these challenges developed.

So religious belief thrives in the 'de-localizing' world created by globalization. At the level of identity globalization is fundamentally a 'process of exile', uprooting people from locally grounded sources of personal identification, making them into 'global citizens' with spatially-temporally dislocated 'portable identities'. Such dislocation is much less relevant in the religious context since religion, with its 'appeals to the hereafter ... does not recognize this post-modern dislocation, since it never, in the first place, was involved in a[n] empirical timetable', nor is it tied down to any geographic-social totality.[33] Religions are, at least in the case of the great missionary religions like Christianity and Islam, 'world religions' aimed at converting the whole human race to their message, creating a uniform world religious community with few distinguishing geographic identities, other than a few holy lands and places of worship that satisfy the need for some geographic bearings.[34] When the homogenizing forces of globalization are combined with the equally global but anti-materialist forces of religion, the result is a glocalizing world.

THE DARKER SIDE OF US CULTURAL EXPORTS

What is also often missed in discussions over Americanization is the fact that how America presents itself to the rest of the world is not always good. The American penchant for 'national self-absorption and self-congratulation goes hand-in-hand with a remarkable taste for self-exposure and self-criticism'. Therefore, the 'same satellites that beam each breathlessly awaited episode of *Dallas* or *Beverly Hills 90210* into untold millions of households also carry live, uncensored coverage of urban riots and self-immolating religious cults'. It could very well be these negative images that 'linger longest in the minds of external observers'.[35] Also, not every breathlessly awaited American TV show is politically pro-American (see for example *The X-Files*), while many American movies are often explicitly radically critical of US culture or politics (see for example the work of Spike Lee and Oliver Stone). Everyone watched Clinton's humiliating, confusing and inexplicable Monicagate 'trial' on CNN. Arabic and Muslim audiences in particular interpreted Clinton's attacks on Afghanistan and Sudan as an attempt to keep the scandal under raps by distracting Congress with foreign adventures. The pervasiveness of the race issue in America was brought to the world courtesy of the riots in Los Angeles after the brutal police beating

254 SOCIALIST REGISTER 2004

of Rodney King, and the live coverage of the O. J. Simpson trial. The slogan of American anti-Vietnam War protestors that 'The Whole World is Watching' seems to have become truer today than ever before.

This is why Joseph Nye, the author of the concept of 'soft power', worried that America's status in the world is 'endangered by the growing international perception of America as a society riven by crime, violence, drug abuse, racial tension, family breakdown, fiscal irresponsibility, political gridlock, and increasingly acrimonious political discourse'.[36] According to the Pew Global Attitudes survey for 2002, 'What the World Thinks in 2002 – How Global Publics View: Their Lives, Their Countries, The World, America', America is 'nearly universally admired for its technological achievements and people in most countries say they enjoy US movies, music and television programs', yet at the same time the 'spread of US ideas and customs is disliked by majorities in almost every country included in this survey'. It seems that opinions about the US are 'complicated and contradictory' because people 'around the world embrace things American and, at the same time, decry US influence on their societies'.[37] But this hardly captures the underlying problem revealed in a recent research report of a study of 1,259 middle-class teenagers from twelve countries: Saudi Arabia, Bahrain, South Korea, Mexico, China, Spain, Taiwan, Dominican Republic, Pakistan, Nigeria, Italy, and Argentina. With the exception of the Argentinians, young people in these countries saw Americans as violent, materialistic, domineering, disrespectful of people unlike them, sexually amoral (particularly women), not concerned about the poor, lacking family values, and generally prone to committing crime.[38]

The most important aspect of these findings, however, is that almost all of this was a result of their access to movies, television and pop music *made in* America. Such results suggest that 'pop-culture *rather than* foreign policy is the true culprit of anti-Americanism'.[39] Moreover, globalization is implicated in this, given that teenagers have been able to form these opinions from American pop culture, even in countries where most American movies and pop arts are banned, because entrepreneurs download this material and rent or sell it on videotapes or DVDs. The study discovered that even in 'very poor villages in Pakistan, where there is only one TV receiver', young people gather together, drink tea and watch this contraband material and 'discuss the evil nature of Americans'.[40] This is the impression they got from discussions with most of the students studied, not just those in Arabic and Muslim countries. This contradicts the view of those (whether they are American liberal imperialists or their critics, such as Anderson) that the Middle East 'excludes' American culture. The most negative attitudes the study came across were in Saudi Arabia. Saudi Arabian people are not anti-American because they are culturally barricaded in by their state, but because they aren't barricaded in enough.

AMERICANIZATION CONTRA AMERICAN
HEGEMONY

Brzezinski's concerns ran even deeper than Nye's, seeing the end of the Cold War era as representing a metaphysical transition from the age of 'coercive utopia' to an age of 'permissive cornucopia'. Too much control has been replaced by too little 'control over personal and collective desires, sexual appetites, and social conduct'.[41] What concerned him more than the negative image of America projected to the world by the USA's own media outlets were the 'corrupting effects' of American pop culture on foreign audiences, precisely to the extent that they embraced it. James Kurth has similarly noted that the 'ideal human type' promoted by American popular culture is the 'popular entertainer or sports star', based on the qualities of 'inherent talent, self-centeredness, energy, and aggressiveness' which are 'not the distinguishing qualities of a mature person', but of an 'adolescent'.[42] Are such people willing to make sacrifices for a national ideal? The every-man-for-himself philosophy preached by much American pop culture is hardly capable of encouraging loyalty to anything, let alone to some far-off country that may make demands on them to oppose their own governments. These are not the idle theorizations of conservative intellectuals but very shrewd and perceptive points that bear a strong relationship to reality.

Shortly after September 11th I personally witnessed a number of highly Westernized, 'Americanized' Egyptian youths making jokes – of the kind found on the Internet – about the New York and Washington attacks. They were not taking a political stance against America; politics was the farthest thing from their minds. They just saw the event as funny, something akin to the (steady diet of) videogames and actions movies they grew up on. These youngsters were just as capable of enjoying American movies that demonized Islam as they were of finding pictures of the planes hitting the Twin Towers exhilarating. This ambivalent attitude to the September 11th attacks is not verifiable by extensive empirical studies but to judge from my teaching experience with the more Westernized youth in the Arab world at the American University in Cairo, this attitude does seem quite common.

Admittedly, such local responses clearly also need to be related to the effects of a pre-existing local culture of alienation. The Egyptian youth only became Americanized after the Arab nationalist-African-Third World focus of Egyptian identity, built up during the Nasserist era, fell apart under the onslaught of Camp David and Open Door economics under Sadat. But the point is that this Americanization grounded in local alienation did not produce the required pro-American results, demonstrating that Americanization and globalization, even in the absence of a rival indigenous ideology, can still be highly counterproductive to American hegemony. American pop culture is exporting its culture of indifference, cynicism and apathy, a sort of post-modern detachment of the individual from any other concerns than his/her own, with the surrounding reality turning into an unreal, entertaining freak-show. Increasingly, many young people around the world are beginning to live in the world portrayed by Oliver Stone in *Natural*

Born Killers, where the 'good guys' and 'bad guys' exchange roles; a world where real violence and human tragedy become entertaining and an opportunity to make money. And, to be sure, such malaise is highly profitable.

The positive side of American pop culture, ironically, does not bode anything better for America's global position either. This is because mass communication and education create greater expectations – 'for which the material wealth of America provides a vague standard' – that simply cannot be met by these societies. 'Americanization' thus creates, as Brzezinski saw, 'common aspirations and highly differentiated reactions' whereby the US 'unifies, changes, stimulates, and challenges others – often *against* [America's] own immediate interests'.[43] Assuming that American pop culture promotes support for American foreign policy is like supposing that gangster rap promotes respect for the Los Angeles police force.

The export of America's education system to the world, particularly higher education, can also be positively destructive of US foreign policy initiatives. As Robert Switzer suggests, we should not expect American educational institutions to lead to a 'cloning of the American mind' abroad. Insofar as they teach people *how* to think instead of *what* to think they can also liberate students abroad 'from foreign occupation by the thoughts and values of others'.[44] The Islamic Revolution in Iran included among its militants many university students who were educated in America, some of whom later broke into the American Embassy in Tehran and took its employees hostage. The protest marches in the Arab world in support of the second Intifada, many of which were led by youths who did not witness the Arab-Israeli wars and grew up in the CNN/MTV age of the (Americanized) global village, are proof of the ineffectiveness of Americanization. And some of the most active protesters in Egypt have been students of the American University in Cairo.

CONCLUSION

Thanks to the dialectical interplay between the forces of globalization and localization, America's presence in this world, as an economic-informational-cultural totality, makes the global system chaotic and unstable and directs the general animosity found in the world towards itself. This is an unintended product of 'Americanization', of America's soft power resources. The assumption that after the fall of the Soviet Union the US dominated and managed a global village – a world that would perpetuate its message and posture with no contradictions – was false. In reality what existed was a global city, an entity that does spread American culture, values, tastes, ideals, but in a way that engenders resistance.

In such a volatile context, American double standards – over democracy, human rights, proliferation, peace – and the country's unilateral pursuit of its interests, often in disregard of international law, let alone the interests of others, were bound to lead to a violent backlash. September 11th needs to be seen in this perspective. From a more strictly political perspective, America's mismanagement of the global city is rooted in its inability – so far – to construct a viable world order in the aftermath of the Cold War order. And a war on terrorism pursued unilaterally in defence of American interests and rationalised by these double standards will further destabilize the world.

It is perfectly natural for the dominant powers of the world to want to impose their values and interests on others, and it's just as natural for everyone else to resist. But it is not enough, as Obododimma Oha puts it, that the victims of globalization merely 'construct and narrate their own victimhood.' Resistance must first take the form of challenging the Third World's 'own perceptions of ... inferiority'. Those who complain about the homogenizing effect of globalization have not been able to come up with an alternative, such as trying to reconcile such foreign goods as 'democracy' with indigenous political practices and ideologies. The onus is now on the populations of the Third World. They have the responsibility – the system will not correct itself – to impose their values and interests onto globalization on their own home ground. The only other alternative, if globalization and Americanization are as all pervasive as some claim, is to 'live like Unoka, the character in Chinua Achebe's "Things Fall Apart"', who went back to the 'evil forest with only a useless flute in the hand and a sorry history behind'.[45]

There is no such thing as 'cultural purity' and there is nothing to fear from interacting with foreign cultures given that 'intercultural transfer' is not 'primarily a politically based, one-way phenomenon – a cultural monologue rather than a dialogue'.[46] As for Americanization, it is its own worst enemy; there is nothing to fear simply because it can never come to pass.

NOTES

Special thanks to Melvin DeFleur for his kind comments and useful clarifications, and thanks also to Helen Rizzo and Hugh Nicol for proofreading this paper.

1   Joseph S. Nye Jr., 'The Challenge of Soft Power', *Time Canada*, 153(7), 22 February 1999, p. 30.
2   Joseph S. Nye Jr., 'The Changing Nature of World Power', *Political Science Quarterly*, 105(2), 1990, pp. 177-192; Nye Jr., 'What New World Order?', *Foreign Affairs*, 71(2), 1992, pp. 83-96.
3   Andrew J. Bacevich, 'New Rome, New Jerusalem', *Wilson Quarterly*, 26(3), 2002, p. 50.
4   Perry Anderson, 'Force and Consent', *New Left Review*, 17, 2002, pp. 5-30.
5   Richard Haass, quoted in Andrew J. Bacevich, 'Don't Get Greedy! For Sensible, Limited War Aims in Iraq', *National Review*, 55(2), 10 February 2003, p. 31.
6   Victoria De Grazia, 'Bush Team Enlists Madison Avenue in War on Terror', *International Herald Tribune*, 26 August 2002.

7   *Economist*, 'From Uncle Ben's to Uncle Sam', 362(8261), 23 February 2002, p. 70.

8   Nancy Snow, 'Reweaving Charlotte's Web', *CommonDreams.Org*, 27 December 2002, http://www.commondreams.org/views02/1227-05.htm/, p. 1.

9   Elise Labott, 'Bush's Muslim Propaganda Chief Quits – U.S. Official: "She didn't do Anything that Worked"', *CNN.com*, 4 March 2003, http://www.cnn.com/2003/US/03/03/state.resignation/, p. 1.

10   Allen Rosenshine, 'Now a Word from America', *Advertising Age*, 73(7), p. 15; another excellent source on these disagreements is Franklin Foer, 'Flacks Americana: John Rendon's Shallow P.R. War on Terrorism', *The New Republic*, 226(19), 20 May 2002, pp. 24-29.

11   Joshua Muravchik, 'Hearts, Minds, and the War Against Terror', *Commentary*, 113(5), 2002, p. 29.

12   William M. Arkin, 'The Military's New War of Words', *Los Angeles Times*, 24 November 2002.

13   Michael Cox, 'September 11th and U.S. Hegemony – Or Will the 21st Century Be American Too?', *International Studies Perspectives*, 3(1), 2002, p. 54.

14   Mark Allen Peterson, 'Languages of Globalization: Modernity and Authenticity', *Globalization: Blessing or Curse?,* Proceedings of the Fifth Annual AUC Research Conference, 29-30 March 1998, Cairo: AUC Press, p. 119. To be fair, Peterson's analysis of glocalization accounts for a significant degree of variability in the goods and corporations in question. Peterson shows that the recipient determines the degree of glocalization, and which culture gains more emphasis and imposes its values on the product. The customer is not a passive receiver, whereas the multinational corporation is more interested in profits than any 'cultural project'.

15   Paul Herbig, 'International Promotion: Standardization or Adaptation?', *Paul Herbig's Working Papers*, 1997, http://www.geocities.com/Athens/Delphi/9158/paper49.html/, pp. 1-21.

16   Aaron L. Friedberg, 'The Future of American Power', *Political Science Quarterly*, 109(1), 1994, p. 12; Todd Gitlin, 'World Leaders: Mickey, et al.', *New York Times*, 3 May 1992, quoted in Friedberg, 'The Future of American Power', p. 12.

17   John Gray, *False Dawn: The Delusions of Global Capitalism,* London: Granta Books, 1998, p. 60.

18   Claude Moisy, 'Myths of the Global Information Village', *Foreign Policy*, 107(Summer), 1997, p. 81.

19   *SearchEBusiness definition* (2002) 'Glocalization', http://searchcio.techtarget.com/sDefinition/0,,sid19_gci826478,00.html/, p. 1.

20   Roland Robertson, 'Comments on the "Global Triad" and "Glocalization": Globalization and Indigenous Culture', *Globalization and Indigenous Culture Conference*, Institute for Japanese Culture and Classics, Kokugakuin University, Higashi, Shibuya-ku, Tokyo, Japan, 1997, http://www.koku-

gakuin.ac.jp/ijcc/wp/global/15robertson.html/, p. 2; italics in original.

21 Francis X. Rocca, 'America's Multicultural Imperialism', *American Spectator*, 33(7), 2000, p. 37.

22 Rocca, 'America's Multicultural Imperialism', p. 37.

23 Rick Zednik, 'Inside Al-Jazeera', *Columbia Journalism Review*, 40(6), 2002, pp. 44-7.

24 Jonathan Alter and Martha Brant, 'The Other Air Battle', *Newsweek*, 141(14), 7 April 2003, p. 38; see also James Poniewozik, Matthew Cooper, Douglas C. Waller, Lina Lofrano, Azadeh Moaveni, and Amany Radwan, 'The Battle for Hearts and Minds', *Time*, 158(18), 22 October 2001, pp. 68-70, and James Poniewozik, Aparisim Ghosh, Amany Radwan and Pelin Turgut, 'What You See Vs. What They See', *Time*, 161(14), 7 April 2003, pp. 68-9.

25 Bruce Cumings, 'Still the American Century', *Review of International Studies*, 25(5), 1999, pp. 271-299.

26 Joshua A. Fishman, 'The New Linguistic Order', *Foreign Policy*, 113(Winter), 1998-99, pp. 26, 28.

27 Armand Mattelart, *Mapping World Communication: War, Progress, Culture*, Minneapolis: U of Minnesota Press, trans. by Susan Emanuel and James A. Cohen, 1994.

28 Zbigniew Brzezinski, *Between Two Ages: America's Role in the Technetronic Era*, New York: Viking Press, 1970, p. 55.

29 Fishman, 'The New Linguistic Order', p. 32.

30 Brzezinski, *Between Two Ages*, p. 19.

31 John Micklethwaite and Adrian Wooldridge, 'The Globalization Backlash', *Foreign Policy*, 126(September-October), 2001, p. 21.

32 Jonathan Clarke, 'The Conceptual Poverty of U.S. Foreign Policy', *The Atlantic Monthly*, 272(3), 1993, p. 61.

33 Ernest Wolf-Gazo, 'Globalization and Identity', *Globalization: Blessing or Curse?* Proceedings of the Fifth Annual AUC Research Conference, 29-30 March 1998, Cairo: AUC Press, pp. 89-90.

34 Liliane Voyé, 'Religion in Modern Europe: Pertinence of the Globalization Theories?', *Globalization and Indigenous Culture Conference*, Institute for Japanese Culture and Classics, Kokugakuin University, Higashi, Shibuya-ku, Tokyo, Japan, 1997, http://www.kokugakuin.ac.jp/ijcc/wp/global/12voye.html/, pp. 1-13.

35 Friedberg, 'The Future of American Power', p. 16. A good example of how ineffective pop culture is as an instrument of cultural imperialism is afforded by the views of one of the new generation of pop stars, Shakira. In an interview on MTV Shakira commented, when a caller from Israel contacted the show, that she would rather talk to a 'pig' than to someone from Israel. It is true that her views are partly dictated by her Lebanese origins, but one would think that being immersed in an Americanizing pop culture world – being at the centre of it in her case – would have blinded her to the double

standards of US foreign policy, dulling her sense of ethnic identity and historical rootedness.

36 Joseph S. Nye Jr. and William A. Owens, 'America's Information Edge', *Foreign Affairs*, 75(2), 1996, p. 36.

37 'Introduction and Summary – What the World Thinks in 2002 – How Global Publics View: Their Lives, Their Countries, The World, America', *The Pew Research Center for the People and the Press*, 2002, http://people-press.org/reports/display.php3?ReportID=165, 4 December, pp. 1, 3.

38 Margaret H. DeFleur and Melvin DeFleur, 'The Next Generation's Image of Americans: Attitudes and Beliefs Held By Teen-Agers In Twelve Countries – A Preliminary Research Report', 2002, http://www.bu.edu/news/releases/2002/defleur/report.pdf.

39 Melvin DeFleur, quoted in *Foreign Policy*, 'Pop Anti-Americanism', 134(January-February), 2003, p. 17.

40 Melvin DeFleur, email to the author, 9 February 2003.

41 Zbigniew Brzezinski, *Out of Control: Global Turmoil on the Eve of the Twenty-First Century,* New York: A Robert Stewart Book, 1993, p. 203.

42 James Kurth, 'The Adolescent Empire: America and the Imperial Idea', *The National Interest*, 48, 1997, pp. 14, 15.

43 Brzezinski, *Between Two Ages,* p. 53, my italics.

44 Robert Switzer, 'Globalization and Liberal Education: Cloning of the American Mind?', *Globalization: Blessing or Curse?* Proceedings of the Fifth Annual AUC Research Conference, 29-30 March 1998, Cairo: AUC Press, p. 74.

45 Obododimma Oha, '[globalization] African narratives', http://www.green-star.org/butterflies/Glocalization.htm, 13 May 2000: Email on the Internet, hosted on *Sweatshops and Butterflies: Cultural Ecology on The Edge,* by Michael North and Paul Swider, Greenstar Corporation, p. 1.

46 Craig Latrell, quoted in Richard Schechner, 'Performance as a "Formation of Power and Knowledge"', *TDR: The Drama Review*, 44(4), 2000, p. 5.

CROSSING BORDERS IN THE NEW IMPERIALISM

BOB SUTCLIFFE

In words which seem uncannily relevant today, two mid-nineteenth century fugitives (in today's language, asylum seekers) wrote that 'the bourgeoisie has through its exploitation of the world-market given a cosmopolitan character to production and consumption in every country'.[1] This cosmopolitanization (or in today's vocabulary globalization) turned out to be neither as continuous nor as complete as they expected. By the beginning of the following century other emigrant followers of these two men began to argue that the full economic integration of world capitalism would be prevented by strife between the industrialized countries. Imperialism in this sense seemed to mean that globalization would be a task for post-capitalist society.

This appeared to be confirmed by the following half century of war, protectionism and deep economic crisis until, in the middle of the twentieth century, cosmopolitan capitalism made its big comeback. Globalization is, more than anything else, the feature of today's capitalism which leads many to argue that there is a new imperialism, or even that imperialism has been replaced by something else (for instance, by 'post-imperialism' or by 'Empire').

The real newness of the present is, however, debatable. In trying to discern the character of an age, it is tempting to argue that everything has been totally transformed and a qualitatively new epoch has dawned. It is usually more accurate to say that there are new combinations of already known things. Most of the global or international characteristics of capitalist exploitation have existed throughout its life; it is the specific forms which these aspects assume which change and fluctuate. In other words imperialism in a broad sense both preceded and survived Imperialism in a narrower sense. At least four elements stressed in old socialist ideas about imperialism retain their relevance: the economic competition and occasional political conflict between developed capitalist states as well as the conditions under which they cooperate; the global polarization of power and income between those few developed states and the rest along with the division of labour between them; the predatory expansion of capitalist relations of production to absorb non-capitalist places and activities; and global cultural conflict. Through a combination of secular and cyclical change in these four dimensions the international aspects of capitalism evolve from one period to another creating new combinations rather than qualitatively different epochs. The salient characteristics of the present period may be new from a short term perspective but quite old from a long term one.

THE NEW GLOBALIZATION

To be more specific, capitalist economies are now certainly more economically integrated, in trade, investment and finance, than they were in 1950; but it is much less clear that they are strikingly more integrated than they were in 1900.[2] Hegemony is another feature which seems to shift back and forth. After 1950 we got used to thinking of the USA as the overwhelmingly hegemonic power. In the 1980s all the talk was of its waning hegemony. But then the collapse of the USSR seemed to produce a second coming for US hegemony. If that is true it cannot be put down to economics. The simplest statistical measure of a country's relative power is its share of the world's production. In the case of the USA this fell from about 27 per cent in 1950 to 22 per cent in 1973, since when it has hardly varied at all.[3] The 'new economy' boom of the late 1990s seemed to promise a new dominance based on US supremacy in high-tech industries. Subsequently, however, the fragility of that boom and the exaggerated expectations about the US economy which emerged from it have become clearer.[4] If trends of the last twenty years were maintained the USA would be replaced as the largest economy in the world in about 2009 – by China. If that country seems set to be the USA's most probable future challenger, further doubts about US hegemony were raised during the preparations for the 2003 invasion of Iraq when, for the first time in decades, a group of large developed countries (with some support from China and more from Russia) dared to launch a sharp if so far limited political challenge to US foreign policy. At the same time the European Union is adopting an increasingly confrontational approach to trade and other disputes with the USA. Perhaps the present swaggering unilateralism of the Bush administration is partly an indication that it does not possess the degree of hegemony which others perceive it to have.

The impulse behind the new world economy is often seen as coming from multinational corporations. Once again both their newness and their size tends to be exaggerated. In 1990 the 100 largest multinational companies (according to the value of their foreign assets) produced something like 7 per cent of the total value of world production and this had risen by 2000 to about 7.5 per cent.[5] Some things did change, however, during that decade. In 1990 all of the 100 corporations were from developed countries; by 2000 the number of US and

European companies in the top one hundred had declined, that of smaller developed countries had grown and five came from developing countries. This reflects something much more general: a new dynamic capitalist development of parts of the Third World, especially in Asia but also in isolated pockets in Latin America. There has been a noticeable if limited shift in the division of labour towards a selection of industrializing countries (of which the most important is China and the most advanced are Korea, Taiwan, Hong Kong and Singapore). Once again all this implies important but hardly as yet epochal change.

Something else which is new arises from factors already mentioned — the fact that now, even by the restrictive definitions of capital flows used by international financial institutions, 'developing countries export capital to high income countries'.[6] This is independent of the flows such as debt service, the repatriation of profits by multinational corporations or unequal exchange which have meant, as many socialists have argued, that poor countries have always financed richer ones in various ways. For several years Third World governments and capitalists have been net acquirers of assets (shares, bonds, foreign exchange and bank accounts) while the United States in particular has been incurring equivalent liabilities. Since the mid-1980s the USA has fallen ever deeper into debt. Its growing excess of national spending (on imported consumer goods, investment, military expenditure and so on) has to be financed by foreign savings, especially of Japan, China and other East Asian countries. A hegemonic power which is seriously and increasingly indebted to the rest of the world is certainly a novelty whose consequences are still not foreseeable.

MIGRATION AND THE WORLD ECONOMY

Many people also see international migration as a new element in the present conjuncture of imperialism. Modern capital accumulation and industrialization has produced an immense and universal increase in one form of migration – namely from country to town, although even now only about half the world's human population is classified as urban dwellers and being some kind of a peasant is still the world's most numerous occupation (followed by being an employee in a service industry).[7] But mass migration of people across frontiers is, like other aspects of globalization, nothing new in the history of capitalism (let alone, of course, in longer term history during which humans have shown themselves to be habitual long distance migrants). The forced migration of slaves and then indentured workers from Africa and Asia and the vast migrations from Europe to North America all played important roles in the history of capital accumulation and imperialism. The migration of recent decades is certainly more varied in its forms and more inclusive regarding the countries involved than previous major migrations. A judgement about its size depends on the perspective from which it is seen.

About 2 per cent of the world's population, according to rough estimates, now live in countries of which they are not citizens. The percentage might rise to a maximum of 3 per cent if it were possible to calculate the number of people who live in countries where they were not born. Is this percentage large or small? It certainly seems small compared with other indicators of globalization. For instance, on average about 20 per cent of what residents of each country consume is imported from another country. And international migrants as a percentage of the population have been rising much more slowly than international trade as a proportion of production. While nearly all governments now declare themselves to be in favour of the maximum freedom of movement for goods, capital and finance, no government has opened its borders to people, indeed most countries of immigration are trying hard to close them to many kinds of immigrant. In addition, while vast legions of intellectuals, politicians and bureaucrats argue for free trade and free capital movements, and international organizations like the IMF and the WTO exist to bring about these goals, the number who argue for the free movement of human beings is extremely limited and no international organization promotes it, unless one counts the International Tourism Organisation. Some of the theoretical high priests of free trade and capital movements (including Milton Friedman and Gary Becker) have explicitly declined to apply their arguments to the international movement of labour.[8] Among the pillars of neoliberal ideology, the *Wall Street Journal*, in advocating the elimination of national borders, stands as a rule-proving exception.

Even without encouragement, however, the increasing integration of world production and finance and a large number of political upheavals has inevitably produced a rise in both forced and voluntary migration across international frontiers. This rise is driven by a combination of three factors. First are those which push people to consider leaving the place where they are: poverty, hunger, war, unemployment, lack of economic opportunity, physical danger and persecution by states, priests, parents, husbands and others. Whether or not such conditions are growing or diminishing, there is certainly no shortage of them in the world. Second are the pull factors: economic growth and demand for labour in other countries and in many cases direct international labour recruitment by companies or governments, in addition to a host of non-economic dreams and aspirations. And third there are the facilitating factors such as the wider spread of information along with the availability of cheap travel, designed originally for businesses and tourists but increasingly available to migrants. Migration tends to be self-reinforcing in that the establishment of communities of migrants or their descendants in the countries of destination makes it easier for new migrants from the same places to establish themselves and find help and acceptance. These frequently become authentically multinational communities, containing millions of multinational families whose members move in two-way flows between country of origin and country of destination. Finally, there has been an expansion in the number of people who organize international migration, varying from modern slave traffickers to people simply providing services such as hiring out their boat or truck, guiding people over a dangerous frontier or forging a document.

The 2-3 per cent of the world's population who live outside their country of origin are not, of course, randomly distributed. They come disproportionately from certain countries and groups and go disproportionately to others. A few countries, because of their political or economic situation, as well as that of their neighbours, are places of significant immigration and emigration at the same time (in recent years these have included Jordan, Somalia, Paraguay, the Dominican Republic, Poland, Burkina Faso, Bolivia, Sudan, Botswana, South Korea, Egypt, Tunisia, Iraq and Iran).[9] But in general most are countries either of emigration or of immigration. And within the latter immigrants are often concentrated in particular areas, especially in a growing number of 'world cities'.[10]

Theories of imperialism focus on the hierarchy of nations, but some of them see it in the context of the other factors – class, gender, colour, culture and so on – which go to make up the system of interlocking hierarchies which compose capitalist society. Mass migration across national frontiers, in particular from less to more developed countries, adds a new complexity to this way of looking at things. To some extent such migration breaks down the previous geographical clarity of the hierarchy of nations. Workers from Latin America living and working in the USA are geographically no longer in the Third World but are directly exploited in the First World and are part of its population, perhaps even full citizens. Their inferior position in the social hierarchy is now explained less by nation or geographical position, more by class, and perhaps also by other factors like language, colour or religion. Yet part of the old situation remains: workers may retain close contacts with their families who may even be economically dependent on them. Their position in society will also be affected by cultural factors which relate to national origins, language or colour. Immigrants are not a new class or layer of society. But they become incorporated within the multiple and superimposed nature of hierarchies in their new country of residence while often retaining a position in other hierarchies in their old country.

THE CHARACTER OF THE MAJOR MIGRATION FLOWS

A major proportion of the world's migrant population consists of forced migrants fleeing genocide, political persecution or economic catastrophe. Of the twelve million people counted as international refugees and asylum seekers by the UNHCR at the end of 2001 the largest absolute numbers were (in descending order) in Pakistan, Iran, Germany and the USA. Eight countries, none of them developed, housed refugees amounting to more than 2 per cent of their own population (Armenia, Congo Republic, Yugoslavia, Djibouti, Iran, Zambia, Guinea and Tanzania). The number in Britain, where complaints about their presence are so strident, was only 0.31 per cent, much less than Germany (1.2 per cent), slightly less than Ireland and slightly more than France. The great majority of refugees are not in developed countries at all but in developing ones neighbouring the country from which they have fled.[11]

There is no simple dichotomy between forced and voluntary migration since most migration choices are probably constrained in some ways; though it also seems too reductive to say, as some do, that all migration is forced. The flows of migration which have developed in recent years have to an important degree been determined by the migrants themselves as subjects. Among these flows are several between developing countries (for instance between Indonesia and Malaysia, or between countries of West Africa) and three major flows from less towards more developed countries: first, to Western European countries, largely from their ex-colonies (the Caribbean, South Asia, North Africa, Tropical Africa) and from Turkey; the second from Central America and subsequently East Asia to the USA; the third from West and South Asian countries to the oil-producing countries of the Arabian/Persian Gulf.

After the early 1970s the newly super-rich oil states embarked on ambitious plans to transform their infrastructure, and workers from all over Asia (especially South Asia) were recruited, to the point where they came to outnumber the local population in some small countries. Virtually the whole working population consisted of immigrants and the local populations were converted into a rentier class. This was very different from migration to Europe or the USA. From the beginning it was regarded by the Gulf states as temporary; workers lived tightly controlled lives and family migration was not allowed. Governments tried to maintain a strict apartheid between nationals and foreign workers and the latter had even fewer political and civil rights that the former, if that can be imagined. They wanted workers, not people. For some regions of India, however, Kerala in particular, the employment and resulting flow of funds became important and played a role in Kerala's ability to maintain relatively high levels of state provision for health and education, even though the local economy was not very developed. This is an example among many where the new migration led to economic benefits but also to a new dependence on migration.[12]

While in modern history large-scale immigration is new to Europe and the Middle East this is not true of the USA (or Canada). Between 1820 and 1996 63 million immigrants entered the USA; during the first fifteen years of the twentieth century migration was adding about 1 per cent a year to the country's population, considerably more than today. Restrictions after the First World War, and the increasingly racist structure of immigration laws, then produced fifty years of very low immigration. After the repeal of racist immigration quotas in 1965, immigration, primarily from Central America, but later from Asia and virtually all other parts of the globe, accelerated. That already mentioned canny pair of nineteenth century asylum seekers saw very clearly how mass immigration was the US ruling class's weapon of mass destruction against European hegemony:

> Precisely European immigration fitted North America for a gigantic agricultural production, whose competition is shaking the very foundations of European landed property – large and small. At the same time, it enabled the United States to exploit its tremendous industrial resources with an energy and on a scale that must shortly break the industrial monopoly of Western Europe, and especially of England, existing up to now.[13]

Despite the official US ideology of openness, attempts to curb immigration abound, but they have usually failed to achieve the desired result. High immigration continues and, given the relatively rapid economic assimilation of immigrants, helps to maintain the growth in the size of the US economy compared with its rivals, as some of its advocates have realized.[14] As in Europe, US immigration practice has led to a polarized kind of immigration in which highly qualified and very unqualified labour predominate. Since the mid-1990s spending on illegal migration control has sharply increased. This is reflected in the stepping up of border controls between the USA and Mexico, and after the attack on the World Trade Center also on a vast increase in port and airport security and the large scale arrest and detention of Arab and Islamic men. The budget of the US immigration service tripled during the years 1980-2000; yet during the same time the number of foreigners illegally in the USA is estimated also to have tripled from 3 million to 9 million.[15] This is in spite of the fact that intensified frontier policing, as intended, makes migration physically more dangerous and has led to a marked increase in the numbers of migrants dying from starvation, drowning and shooting along the US-Mexican border. The number estimated to have been killed rose steadily from 87 in 1996 to 499 in 2000.[16] If recent US history repeats itself the 9 million illegal immigrants will at some point receive an amnesty and immigration control will begin again from scratch, although it is a possibility that such actions will now be seen as inconsistent with the fight against terrorism.

The origins of post-1950 migration into Western Europe can be found in the combination of the collapse of colonialism and the economic boom during the 1950s and 1960s. Efforts, especially by Britain and France, to turn their previous colonial empires into a Commonwealth or Communauté for a time fostered relatively liberal immigration and citizenship regimes. And rapid economic growth created growing demand for labour. Germany had to improvise an ex-empire, choosing Turkey as its honorary ex-colony.

The overall numbers of immigrants in Europe are hard to compare with those in the USA since most European countries count foreign citizens while the USA counts residents born outside the country (a figure which tends to be higher due to past naturalizations). France, however, gives figures for both concepts: about 5 per cent of the population have foreign nationality while 10 per cent were born abroad. This difference is larger than in most countries since the rate of naturalization of foreigners is relatively high. In Britain, where naturalization is more difficult, the number of foreign nationals is about 4 per cent; in Germany, where naturalization for people who are not ethnically German is even harder, foreign nationals are 8.9 per cent of the population. In the USA 10.4 per cent are foreign born, implying perhaps 6 per cent with foreign nationality. So to this extent the US and Western European figures are not too dissimilar.

The USA, of course, is a more ethnically diverse country due to earlier migrations. In several European countries, however, as in the USA, one nationality dominates recent immigration. Thirteen per cent of the US population are considered 'hispanic', most of these being immigrants from Mexico or their descendants. People born in Mexico and resident in the USA are equal to 7 per cent of the Mexican population. No European country shows such high concentrations: the Turks in Germany are nearly 4 per cent of the Turkish population and nearly 3 per cent of the German. About 3 per cent of the population of the three Magreb countries are resident in Europe where they represent 2.6 per cent of the population of France and smaller proportions of the populations of Spain, Belgium and the Netherlands.[17] All of these have become multi-national communities in which many members move back and forth between their country of origin and country of residence, as have South Asians and Caribbeans in the UK. These figures give little indication as to the ethnic composition of populations since many immigrants are white and many people of colour have become citizens and so are not included in figures for foreign nationals. And other people of colour are both citizens and were born in the country. The 2001 census in Britain found that 9 per cent of the population were not white.

Since the late 1960s migration policy and the presence of immigrants has inexorably moved up the political agenda in many Western European countries. Neo-fascist, racist and right-wing populist politicians and groups have used the presence of immigrants as the centrepiece of their argument and at various moments have gained some political ground. They have had considerable success in raising the presence of immigrants as a threat to existing populations and blaming them for an extraordinarily long list of evils: violent crime, disease, drugs, environmental degradation, unemployment, the deficiencies of the welfare state and more. The fact that the evidence for most of these claims is either non-existent or even suggests the opposite has little effect. In Britain it was Enoch Powell who, in 1968, in what seems in retrospect a turning-point in British politics, established the idea that there should be a limit to the proportion of 'citizens of the new commonwealth and their descendants' (i.e. people who were not white) in the population. He predicted that without a major change in policy, by the year 2000 the proportion would rise to 10 per cent and that the result would be 'the Tiber foaming with much blood'. Margaret Thatcher when prime minister later reduced the supposedly critical percentage. More recently the percentage has been raised by some anti-immigration commentators but the argument has not changed. In Britain at least the extremist racist parties have not thrived because mainstream politicians, media, think tanks and intellectuals have adopted more reasonable-sounding expressions of their ideas. As early as 1961 the Labour Party had abandoned its commitment to free immigration for all commonwealth citizens. Powell was sacked from the British shadow cabinet by Edward Heath, but it was Heath's government that introduced the Commonwealth Immigrants Act in 1971. Labour promised to repeal it but failed to do so when in office from 1974 to 1979.

This change in the conventional approach to the immigration issue was hastened from the mid-1970s onward by increasing unemployment levels throughout Europe after a long period of high employment, although there is no evidence that the rise in unemployment had anything to do with immigration. But governments were becoming impressed with another economic argument: the idea that the supply of particular kinds of skilled workers (especially in high-technology sectors), increasingly known as human capital, was the key to stimulating growth and exports and attracting foreign capital, in short to international competitiveness. This was to lead to more liberal immigration policies towards skilled workers, as well as foreign students, who were increasingly encouraged to stay and work in the country of study: Britain was the most notable practitioner of this policy and presently holds the world record for the highest number of foreign students per head of the population (about 1 in 250). These areas of migration policy, however, are becoming more conflictive: Indian IT firms recently claimed that their technical workers were suffering increasing discrimination by immigration authorities when working on short term contracts in developed countries; and post September 11th controls have led to a large backlog of graduate student applicants for entry to the USA.[18] And finally the collapse of the communist regimes and increasing hardship, political disorder and freedom to move away from it led at the start of the 1990s to a brief increase in immigrants from the east seeking asylum in Western Europe, most of them being ethnic Germans entering Germany.[19] The more recent substitution of asylum applicants from Eastern Europe by applicants from other places (such as Iraq, Somalia and Zimbabwe) has in the first years of the present century provoked a new crisis in European migration as a whole which centres on the questions of asylum and illegal migration.

GOVERNMENT POLICY AND ASYLUM APPLICANTS

In recent years in Europe changes in migration policy have tended to be frequent and sudden. This results from several factors: governments want to increase some kinds of migration while at the same time reducing others; they are trying to please contradictory parts of the electorate (some wanting more and some less immigration); they have found that expensive efforts to increase the policing of frontiers do not seem to work and may even have perverse effects (discouraging people from leaving once they have successfully arrived); alternatives to immigration such as aid to source countries also seems to have perverse effects; and finally they vacillate about enforcing the high level of repression both at and within borders which rigid migration control would require.

Nearly all countries now wish to encourage the immigration of skilled workers, both for their key skills and because increasing skilled workers is part of encouraging foreign investment. Legal unskilled immigrants in developed countries are not very numerous but some sectors of low productivity agriculture are dependent on them and so reducing their number might have severe regional economic consequences in parts of countries such as the USA, Spain and even the UK, which has recently authorized an increase in temporary unskilled migrant agricultural workers. The right to immigration of family members of legal residents is also difficult to curtail. In some countries this composes the major part of current legal immigration. It has been roughly calculated that the immigration multiplier (the total number of subsequent legal immigrants for each legal primary migrant) is about 1.2, that is every 100 primary immigrants implies 120 additional legal immigrants within ten years.[20] In the long run this element of immigration can only be reduced by reducing other forms of legal immigration; in the short run it can only be reduced by forbidding immigrants to live with their close families, which violates an ideological tenet of most western governments and might be expected to engender serious protest and would discourage the migration of skilled workers.

With these three legal categories of immigration difficult or impolitic to reduce, the attack on immigration must focus on two remaining categories – asylum applicants and illegal immigrants. The right to asylum from persecution, however, has been (as long as it is resorted to in moderation) one of the defining rights of the 'free world'. It was used in this way particularly during the Cold War when the West was secure in the knowledge that while those in the unfree world had the right to asylum they would be prevented from taking it up by the strict control of exit by the communist regimes. Asylum applications increased with the fall of the Berlin wall and panic increased even faster.[21] When that crisis ultimately subsided asylum applications remained relatively high, partly because others now followed the East European example. Western countries have, therefore, tried to cut the number of asylum applications without abolishing the right to asylum as such, something which would threaten their credibility as 'free nations'.

Various ways have been sought to go back to the good old days of the Cold War when asylum was a principle but not so much a practice. In the first place, a rapidly expanding list of countries has been designated as places from which no asylum applications will be accepted since they are already 'free' and therefore persecution is by definition ruled out. It will be interesting to see what happens when Anglo-American occupied Iraq (the leading country of origin of asylum applications in developed countries between 2000 and 2002) is declared 'free'. Secondly, applying for asylum has been made more difficult. The British government's attempt to restrict valid applications to those made at the moment of entry to the country, however, has, at the time of writing, failed. Third, the living conditions of asylum applicants have been made more arduous in order to dissuade applications. Applicants are forbidden to work; financial support has been cut and some applicants are obliged to live under conditions of detention while their applications are processed. Fourth, the processing of applications has been speeded up so that in principle failed applicants spend less time in the country. Fifth, the rate of forcible deportations of failed applicants has increased, although most are not deported. An unknown number leave of their own accord. By the end of 2002, however, measures such as these had not had the desired effect of reducing the number of applications. In Britain, in particular, they reached record levels.

In view of this failure it is not surprising that many governments, especially in Europe, have become attracted by a more radical approach, advocated especially by the British Labour government. This would involve not allowing any applicants to enter the country where asylum is sought but obliging them all to register their application from transit camps (officially known as International Transit Centres) outside the country. For this the British Conservative Party, like its Australian counterpart, favours small islands, which are easy to isolate; instead the British Labour Government has proposed countries like Albania which are outside the EU but which might like to make some money by housing asylum applicants, becoming a kind of international Group 4 (a British private security company with contracts to manage some prisons and asylum applicants detention centres).

Applications would then be processed at a distance. Failed applicants (who presumably, as today, would be the great majority, presently in Britain around 90 per cent) would be deported from the transit area to their country of origin or some other country which would accept them. Successful applicants would be admitted to the country of asylum but burdened with a debt, equivalent to the cost of their upkeep in the Transit Centre, a burden which it is hoped might dissuade them from seeking asylum in the first place.[22]

If and when asylum seekers are thereby eliminated as part of the resident population the anti-immigration campaign will have to concentrate on illegal immigrants. This will require police campaigns to find and if necessary forcibly eject thousands of failed asylum applicants who are still present (a policy recently recommended by the home affairs select committee of the British House of Commons), and to detect others who have overstayed the limiting date of their visas or who have entered clandestinely without papers of any kind. It is impossible to imagine that such a policy could be carried out effectively throughout Europe without enormous police intrusions on the 'innocent' as well as the 'guilty'. If no more asylum applicants are allowed to enter the country then there will probably be a rise in attempted illegal entries. This can only be prevented by a much stronger policing of the borders. This is already happening in the sea crossings between Spain (including the Canary Islands) and Morocco. Greater enforcement has brought similar results to those already mentioned for Mexico. Expenses have risen, the number of detained migrants has not risen substantially, the estimated number of successful illegal entries has risen and so has the number of deaths due to drowning and exposure during the crossing. Estimates by the Association of Moroccan Workers in Spain (ATIME) put the death toll in the seas between Morocco and Spain at about 4000 during the five years 1997-2001, a figure that is broadly in line with the one appearing in the Spanish press.

Already coast guards and port police forces have been strengthened and in some places the military also takes part in border control. NATO forces have directly assisted the policing of frontiers in Italy and probably elsewhere. In a speech shortly after taking office the NATO Supreme Allied Commander Atlantic, General William Kernan, argued in 2000 that 'In the future, the task will not only be to defend the borders (of its member states) but to fight against ethnic violence, international crime and illegal immigration.'[23] A recent report, written for the International Organization for Migration, estimates that the world's twenty-five richest countries 'are probably spending US$ 25-30 billion a year on immigration enforcement and asylum processing mechanisms',[24] a figure which is about two-thirds of their total spending on development aid and one which is rising fast while development aid stagnates.

The plea to curb immigration in the interest of preventing too much ethnic and cultural diversity for the nation to maintain internal order is offered up as a conservative argument for a peaceful status quo. But in fact it can only be achieved by a radical change in the nature of the state, involving a major reduction of human rights and a large step towards a more repressive state, from which not only would-be immigrants will suffer. It turns out to be a great error to think that transport and communications can be revolutionized and that borders can be opened to goods, capital and money but not to people, if only because, unknown to many governments, people are much smarter than goods or money. The designers of the European Union were aware of this and have to some extent accepted its consequences by allowing relative freedom of movement of citizens within its borders. But the designers of a globalized world have not.

At present, the major capitalist countries compete for one kind of migrant but they seem to be united on the need to exclude others (asylum applicants and most unskilled workers and in particular illegal immigrants). It is not at all clear, however, that they will be able to establish a common strategy against unwanted immigration, using their increasingly divided alliance, NATO. The bitter, although finally settled, conflict between the British and French government over the Sangatte refugee camp[25] was an example of the problems which they will encounter. In any event, tighter migration control seems inconceivable without a major increase of state repression and an equivalent loss of civil rights.

MIGRATION AND REDISTRIBUTION

The distribution of income between the countries of the world was more unequal at the end of the twentieth century than it was at the end of the nineteenth.[26] There has been little enough redistribution within the developed countries themselves; on a world scale it has been negligible. Official development assistance has fallen to the negligible level of about 0.2 per cent of the national income of developed countries. President Bush's appropriation bill to pay for the first six months of the 2003 invasion of Iraq was worth about eight times as much as annual US official development aid to the rest of the world. Protectionism and dumping continues to damage poor primary producing countries, and many countries are burdened with an immense debt service obligation, often to pay off loans which have accumulated in the foreign bank accounts of the privileged or which have paid for state repression. With the very partial exception of the Nordic countries, there is no evidence that the richer capitalist countries take the question of extreme world inequality seriously. It is natural that many citizens of poor countries look to temporary or permanent migration to rich countries as a way of redistributing income through individual action.

If loans, aid and trade in present conditions are at best extremely limited as motors of development in poor countries, the possible positive effects on world equality of the migration of poorer people to richer countries are also limited by a number of factors. First, there is not a close correlation between poverty and successful migration. It is not yet the very poorest countries which provide the largest numbers of migrants; nor do migrants usually come from the most deprived classes. The many needy people who might benefit from the ability to migrate for work are hindered by the cost of migration which is itself greatly increased by anti-migration policies and laws in the richer countries. This situation is made worse by the trends in migration policy described above.

Despite this, many millions of people from poor countries have been able to improve their and their families' economic position by migration. There is much evidence also that it has helped the economic situation of their country, by increasing foreign exchange availability, by raising the skills of the labour force when migrants return, by raising the wages in the countries from which the migrants come and by the transfer of part of the emigrants' earnings. Some of these effects are seen in the figures for the constantly rising flow of migrants' remittances from richer countries back to their countries of origin. In the year 2000 the total of remittances registered by the World Bank was US$ 80 billion (almost certainly an underestimate), of which about one quarter went to India and Mexico and about one third originated in the USA. This means that the individual decisions of individual migrant workers lead to considerably more money being transferred to poorer countries that all the development aid provided by the world's richest countries (including the multilateral agencies) which has been stuck at about US$ 50 billion (an overestimate) for several years. In the case of the USA remittances are estimated at 2.5 times the level of development assistance. While the distribution of remittances reflects the relative economic position of those who are able to migrate successfully, it is still almost certainly better distributed than development aid, much of which is lost in corruption and bureaucratic inefficiency. The ending of migrants' remittances would now be a much more catastrophic event than the ending of official development aid.

European governments and the European Union have for some time been toying with the idea of using development aid as an antidote to immigration: aid would be concentrated on areas which produced a disproportionate number of migrants and on projects expected to curb migration, either because they provided alternative economic opportunities or because they were used explicitly to boost emigration control in the country of origin. The idea has not really got off the ground, partly because Third World governments are often happy for migration to take place, either to ease various pressures or because they lead to future remittances, and because several studies have suggested that the effect of aid on migration will, from this point of view, be perverse. Aid between two countries, along with trade and investment, serves to increase knowledge of opportunities in the richer country, to build the contacts which make migration networks possible and to produce the resources to finance migration. The USA dropped the idea of aid against migration some years ago which is one reason why its aid budget remains so low.[27] The European pursuit of stronger border control suggests that EU governments have drawn the same conclusions.

In theory it might be expected that any positive effects on inter-country distribution would be offset by the negative effects of more immigration on workers in the developed countries. The effects of immigration on employment and wages have been quite widely studied by economists but they have failed to reach a consensus. One careful comparative evaluation of economic studies of this question concludes that 'the growing body of empirical research on the economic impacts of immigration has produced many and various findings, but there does not seem to be any consistent evidence of broad net negative effects on wage or employment levels among native born workers'.[28] The absence of the expected effect is often explained by arguing that the labour market is not a simple, single entity but a whole series of relatively segmented markets. The effects of immigration may be only on one of these, rather than on the level of wages and unemployment as a whole. In particular, many immigrant communities, once they reach a critical minimum size, form partially self contained economic enclaves with their own partly separate economies. Immigrants themselves, however, often suffer discrimination when they try to integrate themselves in the economic life of the destination countries. Many of them receive lower wages and suffer higher levels of unemployment than the population as a whole, though it should not be forgotten that immigrants are an increasingly bipolar category, divided between the more than averagely skilled and the less than averagely skilled with relatively few in the middle skill categories. In Britain a higher proportion of immigrants have low educational qualifications than the population as a whole; but also a higher proportion of immigrants have especially high educational qualifications.[29]

There is something which economic studies have missed. Virtually all of them have looked at the effect on wages and employment of the *number* of immigrants. Few, if any, have looked at the effects of the *legal status* of immigrants. Whatever is the economic consequence of the amount of immigration it is predictable that the criminalization of part of the migrant population will have a serious effect on inequality. It obliges immigrants to pay enormous sums in order to enter destination countries, it renders them victims of criminal traffickers or bosses who super-exploit them, it leaves them particularly vulnerable to threats if they do manage to migrate and find employment, it renders them more liable to be robbed, injured or killed during the journey, and it makes them accept non-enumerated, sweated, or even illegal and low-paid work.

Criminalization not only reduces the gains to immigrants themselves, it is also likely to threaten the wages and conditions of already resident workers. Nothing is more damaging to the bargaining power of the working class as a whole than the existence of a significant fraction of it which suffers worse conditions, whose ability to organize is completely negated by their illegal status, and who live with the constant threat that their presence will be denounced to the authorities by employers or rivals. So it is by no means obvious that lifting immigration barriers would have a negative effect on wages and conditions in the labour market. And more positively it would enhance the possibility of drawing immigrant workers into the organizations of the labour movement.

MIGRATION AGAINST IMPERIALISM

The history of migration is an important part of the history of imperialism. Imperialist expansion in many parts of the world went hand in hand with the forced migration of slaves and indentured workers. The havoc wreaked by imperialist occupation has made many areas of the world unable to support human life and so produced the conditions of more migration. The greatly increased inequalities produced by colonialism left a huge incentive for emigration when colonialism ended. The long series of alliances of convenience between imperialist countries and oppressive dictatorships in Third World countries has also increased the political pressures to migrate. A large share of today's asylum applicants are fleeing the actions of some government put or kept in power by the great powers of the international community. It is not possible to deny, let alone to roll back, the long history of imperialism which has help to produce the pressures which today result in migration.

International migration at the start of the twenty-first century is still intimately tied up with the main mechanisms of imperialism. The liberalization of immigration for highly skilled workers and international corporations reflects the needs of the protagonists in the increasing competitive struggles between capitalist powers in a very imperfectly globalized economy. The worsening of conditions of migration for poorer migrants and asylum applicants is one aspect of the polarizing tendencies of the world economy, partially but very inadequately compensated by the rising flow of migrants' remittances. The continued rise in migration, despite the fortresses and obstacles which confront them, is certainly part of the continuous incorporation of the whole world into the commodity economy. And immigration often leads to cultural assimilation and sometimes impoverishment. The realities of immigration, however, are not only part of imperialism but also an aspect of the struggle against it. Immigration in part represents an assertion of rights to share in prosperity by those whom the fortresses seek to keep out. Immigration sometimes leads as much to cultural preservation, creativity and interchange as to cultural destruction. Migration often permits progressive citizens to survive the persecution of dictators. And, despite all the problems associated with it, it makes some contribution to breaking down the destructive traditions of ethnically based nationalism which have created or fuelled most of the conflicts of the last century and more.

The restriction of migration runs counter to the interests of poorer countries and poorer people and in some ways to the economic interests of the workers of developed countries. That does not mean that unlimited immigration is preferable to more balanced development of the world or to a more basic solution to the problem of inequality and exploitation. But in the context of a capitalist world economy with virtually no commitment to the elimination of world poverty the freedom for all workers to move freely across borders increases equality. For that reason alone it is a freedom which socialists should defend.

Nevertheless, it is not enough to assert the abolition of borders as a socialist principle; a way needs to be found, especially in today's developed countries, to translate it into a set of policies which can command popular support. Such practical utopianism will need to focus on migration and citizenship laws, economic and welfare policy, anti-racism and foreign policy.

Dismantling the physical and bureaucratic barbed wire with which rich countries are increasingly surrounding themselves would contribute to meeting some needs of many poor and persecuted people. But their welfare also depends on the rights which they possess once borders are crossed. If it takes them a long time to acquire the same rights which existing inhabitants enjoy, then migrants will continue to suffer political persecution and economic super-exploitation which will also weaken sections of the existing resident working class. Immigrants should be able to gain full rights of access to work, protection by wages and hours legislation, to social services and benefits and full rights to organize. It is important for existing workers' and socialist organizations to support these rights for immigrants and to fight alongside them. Migration requires the development of a kind of portable citizenship, where citizenship is seen less as membership of a national community and more as endowment with a number of rights. It would help if formal citizenship were made easier to acquire. The rate of naturalization as a percentage of the estimated foreign population in recent years is nowhere very high: it is less than 3 per cent in Germany, Spain and the UK, more than 7 per cent in the Netherlands and Sweden with France and the USA somewhere in between. Many migrants need to have dual nationality, which is becoming more possible (even in the USA), but again the pace of change is slow.

To contemplate the opening of borders is to confront the real state of the world — its conflicts, injustices and inequalities. Fears inevitably arise that more immigrants will simply mean more conflicts for a limited number of jobs and resources. The possibility of such conflicts cannot be wished away. But jobs and resources are not an unchangeable quantity. They are influenced by the economic policy, of firms, of states and of supra-national entities. The economic problems faced by large numbers of workers in developed countries during the last twenty-five years have resulted not from immigration but primarily from the neoliberal policies of privatization, deflation, labour market 'flexibilization' and cutbacks in the social services. Attention has been focused on reducing the financial cost of social policy not on the changes and expansion in social spending which are necessary complements of rising immigration.

The insecurities of the sections of the non-immigrant working class most affected by neoliberalism have naturally been exploited by the racist right. It has been too easy to spread the idea that it is immigration which has been responsible for economic hardship. The governments responsible for the economic hardships have either tacitly allowed the connection to be made, or have sometimes argued it explicitly. What should be a conflict about economic policies with class at its centre has been converted into one about immigration policies with race and nationalism at its centre.[30] Governments could still, globalization notwithstanding, do a great deal through their economic policy to ensure that any growth in immigration does not threaten jobs, public services, housing standards and the environment.

There is no necessity that large scale immigration of people of other ethnic or national groups or colours will result in more racism and xenophobia. Pervasive as racism is in the world the worst inter-ethnic conflicts are not especially associated with recent immigration. They often occur after communities have lived together for centuries. But today immigration is exploited by racists to sow conflict. Although racism is not simply economically determined, it is likely that if employment and other economic policies work then many typical racist arguments will be more difficult to use. But it is impossible to imagine the racist and xenophobic threat being defeated without directly confronting it politically and ethically. Fears of conflict, opportunistically generated and not based on any real differences of interest, cannot be allowed to govern a society's policies on immigration.

Many of the situations which now produce forced migration and the need for asylum result directly and indirectly from the foreign policies of the countries which are now energetically trying to exclude immigrants. The ending of support for tyrannies and international economic policies which create greater inequality and obstruct the development of poor countries would reduce the pressures to emigrate from many countries. But socialists should be very clear that the purpose of foreign policies is not to reduce migration. Some proponents of more international aid have used that argument, but it tacitly accepts the anti-immigration prejudice. A less imperialist foreign policy would create fewer forced migrants. But, by encouraging more democratic societies, perhaps with more successful economic involvement with the rest of the world, with opportunities for education and more knowledge of the world, a less imperialist foreign policy might also create more voluntary migration. There is every reason for socialists to argue for a massive transfer of economic resources to poorer countries (though not in the form of what now passes for development aid), but it should be on its own merits regardless of the effect which it has on the scale of migration.

Although some migrations reflect politically and economically pathological conditions and events in the world, migration in itself is not, as the anti-immigration coalition claims it to be, pathological. It can be part of a healthy, living cosmopolitan society. In particular it is a phenomenon which can help the world's working class to escape from the nationalist strait-jacket in which the intermittently cosmopolitan bourgeoisie has always tried to confine it.

There is another immediate reason why socialists should give priority to resisting immigration controls: immigration is threatening to become the central issue of politics in Europe, and a very important one elsewhere. Opposition to immigration is the leitmotif of the far right in all European countries; despite many oscillations in its fortunes, it has recently been gaining ground. In the last five years the extreme anti-immigration right has gained a foothold on power in several European countries: Austria, Denmark, Italy and the Netherlands. And in France the advance of the National Front has not ended with Le Pen's defeat in the presidential election. The vast majority of mainstream political thinking, of the so called centre right and centre left, rejects part of the rhetoric of the extreme right's project but increasingly adopts its content. Its response to ultra-right mobilization around immigration has been to implement a panic-driven programme of measures which criminalizes much immigration and vilifies many immigrants. Fortress Europe will lead to consequences which should be unacceptable to socialists. It can only be enforced by the militarization of borders, the worsening of conditions for many migrants and a growing number of deportations. Such a trend threatens not only immigrants but all citizens. It is impossible to repress one section of the population without repressing others. And it will worsen relations between existing communities in Europe. Fortresses are not by nature peaceful or democratic.

Immigration controls are a macrocosm of the pass laws of apartheid and the justifications for them which are given are the same in substance as those historically given by the ideologues of the white minority in South Africa. Yet South Africa has abolished its pass laws, while Europe is looking to strengthen them and seems even to be heading towards the establishment of a new kind of Bantustan for asylum applicants. Some European governments are already also envisaging making the offering of humanitarian assistance or refuge to illegal immigrants into a criminal offence.

Cosmopolitanism (the word so often used now by Le Pen and formerly by his infamous predecessors to characterise their enemies) seems to me integral to socialism, as it did to the two nineteenth century asylum seekers already quoted. They foresaw a socialist future in which those who did not own capital would build a cosmopolitanism to challenge and supersede that being constructed by those who did. Proletarian cosmopolitanism, the fight against imperialism and national separatisms, today means fighting for, among many other things, the end to the criminalization of poor people crossing borders. In a broader sense it remains a central weapon against the new imperialism (and the old).

NOTES

Many thanks to Andrew Glyn for comments on this article.

1   Karl Marx and Friedrich Engels, *The Communist Manifesto*, 1848, available at http://www.anu.edu.au/polsci/marx/classics/manifesto.html.
2   For a detailed argument see Bob Sutcliffe and Andrew Glyn, 'Measures of Globalization and their Misinterpretation', in Jonathan Michie, ed., *The Handbook of Globalization*, London: Edward Elgar, 2003 (an extension and updating of 'Global but Leaderless? The New Capitalist Order', *Socialist Register 1992*, London: Merlin, 1992).
3   Angus Maddison, *The World Economy: A Millennial Perspective*, Paris: OECD, 2001; World Bank, *World Development Indicators*, CD-ROM edition, Washington DC, 2002. These figures are measured at purchasing power parity.
4   Robert Brenner, *The Boom and the Bubble*, London: Verso, 2002.
5   Sutcliffe and Glyn, 'Measures of Globalization'; UNCTAD, *World Investment Report 1993*, Geneva: UNCTAD, 1993; UNCTAD, *World Investment Report 2002*, Geneva: UNCTAD, 2002.
6   World Bank, *Global Development Finance 2003*, Washington, DC: World Bank, 2003, p. 49.
7   Deon Filmer, *Estimating the World at Work*, Background Report for World Bank World Development Report 1995, Washington DC: World Bank, Office of the Vice President Development Economics, 1995.
8   Vernon M. Briggs Jr., 'International Migration and Labour Mobility: The Receiving Countries', in Julien van den Broeck, ed., *The Economics of Labour Migration*, Cheltenham, Glos and Brookfield, Vt: Edward Elgar, 1996.
9   Bob Sutcliffe, *Nacido en otra parte*, Bilbao: Hegoa, 1998.
10   Saskia Sassen, *The Global City: New York, London, Tokyo*, Princeton: Princeton University Press, 2001.
11   For more details and a searching analysis see Stephen Castles, 'The International Politics of Forced Migration', *Socialist Register 2003*, London: Merlin, 2003.
12   John Willoughby, 'Ambivalent Anxieties: Towards and Understanding of the South Asian - Gulf Arab Labor Exchange', draft, 2000.
13   Karl Marx and Friedrich Engels, Preface to the Russian edition of *The Communist Manifesto*, 1882 available at http://www.anu.edu.au/polsci/marx/classics/manifesto.html.
14   Julian Simon, *The Economic Consequences of Immigration*, Oxford and Cambridge, Mass.: Blackwell, 1989.
15   Philip Martin, *Bordering On Control: Combating Irregular Migration in North America and Europe*, Geneva: International Organization for Migration, available for browsing at www.iom.org.
16   Wayne Cornelius, 'Death at the Border: Efficacy and Unintended

Consequences of US Immigration Control Policy', *Population and Development Review*, 27(4), December, 2001, pp. 661-685.

17   All figures in this paragraph come from SOPEMI, *Trends in International Migration 2002 edition*, Paris: OECD.

18   Edward Luce and Khozen Merchant, 'Visas and the West's "Hidden Agenda"', *Financial Times*, 9 April 2003; Alan Leshner, 'America Closes the Door to Scientific Progress', *Financial Times*, 30 May 2003.

19   Castles, 'International Politics'.

20   Douglas Massey et al., 'Theories of International Migrations: A Review and Appraisal', *Population and Development Review*, 19(3), September 1993.

21   Castles, 'International Politics'.

22   Financial Times, 'UK Asylum Proposals Draw Mixed Reponse', *Financial Times*, 29/30 March 2003; Alan Travis, 'Blunkett Backed on Asylum Centres', *The Guardian*, 22 April 2003; Theo Veenkamp, Tom Bentley and Alessandra Buonfino, *People Flow: Managing Migration in a New European Commonwealth*, London: Demos, 2003, available at http://www. demos.co.uk/uploadstore/docs/MIGR_ft.pdf.

23   Statewatch, Statewatch News on Line, September 2000, available at www.statewatch.org/news/sept00/06nato.htm.

24   Martin, *Bordering On Control*.

25   Sangatte, near Calais, was a temporary reception centre for asylum applicants to which the British government objected on the grounds that its proximity to the entrance to the Channel Tunnel facilitated illegal entries into the UK. After a long dispute between the British and French government it was finally closed in December 2002. A limited number were offered residence in the UK while the rest were redistributed to other parts of France.

26   Bob Sutcliffe, 'A More or Less Equal World? The World Distribution of Income During the 20th Century', *Indicators*, forthcoming.

27   Commission for the Study of International Migration and Cooperative Economic Development, *Unauthorized Migration: An Economic Development Response*, Washington, DC: US Government Printing Office, 1990; Georges Tapinos, 'La coopération internationale peut-elle constituer une alternative à l'émigration des travailleurs?', *mimeo*, Paris: OCDE, 1991.

28   Gregory DeFreitas, 'Immigration, Inequality, and Policy Alternatives', in Dean Baker, Gerald Epstein and Robert Pollin, eds., *Globalization and Progressive Economic Policy*, Cambridge: Cambridge University Press, 1998.

29   SOPEMI, *Trends 2002 edition*.

30   See Hans-George Betz, 'Xenophobia, Identity Politics and Exclusionary Populism in Western Europe' and Jorg Flecker, 'The European Right and Working Life: From Ordinary Miseries to Political Disasters', in *Socialist Register 2003*, London: Merlin, 2003.

Socialist Register – Published Annually Since 1964

Leo Panitch and Colin Leys – Editors
2003: FIGHTING IDENTITIES – Race, Religion And Ethno-Nationalism

"these contributions... show a left able to avoid both economic reductionism and post-modern identity-fetishism in confronting and understanding a world of mounting anxiety, instability and violence." Stephen Marks, *Tribune*.

Contents: Peter Gowan: The American Campaign for Global Sovereignty; Aziz Al-Azmeh: Postmodern Obscurantism and 'the Muslim Question'; Avishai Ehrlich: Palestine, Global Politics and Israeli Judaism; Susan Woodward: The Political Economy of Ethno-Nationalism in Yugoslavia; Georgi Derluguian: How Soviet Bureaucracy Produced Nationalism and what came of it in Azerbaijan; Pratyush Chandra: Linguistic-Communal Politics and Class Conflict in India; Mahmood Mamdani: Making Sense of Political Violence in Postcolonial Africa; Hugh Roberts: The Algerian Catastrophe: Lessons for the Left; Stephen Castles: The International Politics of Forced Migration; Hans-Georg Betz: Xenophobia, Identity Politics and Exclusionary Populism in Western Europe; Jörg Flecker: The European Right and Working Life- From ordinary miseries to political disasters; Huw Beynon & Lou Kushnick: Cool Britannia or Cruel Britannia? Racism and New Labour; Bill Fletcher Jr. & Fernando Gapasin: The Politics of Labour and Race in the USA; Amory Starr: Is the North American Anti-Globalization Movement Racist? Critical reflections; Stephanie Ross: Is This What Democracy Looks Like? -The politics of the anti-globalization movement in North America; Sergio Baierle: The Porto Alegre Thermidor: Brazil's 'Participatory Budget' at the crossroads; Nancy Leys Stepan: Science and Race: Before and after the Genome Project; John S. Saul: Identifying Class, Classifying Difference

396pp, 234x156mm

0 85036 507 4 hbk £29.95   0 85036 508 2 pbk £16.95

Canada: Fernwood Publishing; USA: Monthly Review Press; UK and Rest of World: Merlin Press

Leo Panitch and Colin Leys – Editors
2002: A WORLD OF CONTRADICTIONS

Timely and critical analysis of what big businesses and their governments want, and of the problems they create.

Contents: Naomi Klein: Farewell To 'The End Of History': Organization

And Vision In Anti-Corporate Movements; André Drainville: Québec
City 2001 and The Making Of Transnational Subjects; Gérard Duménil
& Dominique Lévy: The Nature and Contradictions of Neoliberalism;
Elmar Altvater: The Growth Obsession; David Harvey The Art Of Rent:
Globalization, Monopoly and The Commodification of Culture; Graham
Murdock & Peter Golding: Digital Possibilities, Market Realities: The
Contradictions of Communications Convergence; Reg Whitaker: The Dark
Side of Life: Globalization and International Crime; Guglielmo Carchedi:
Imperialism, Dollarization and The Euro; Susanne Soederberg: The New
International Financial Architecture: Imposed Leadership and 'Emerging
Markets'; Paul Cammack: Making Poverty Work; Marta Russell & Ravi
Malhotra: Capitalism and Disability; Michael Kidron: The Injured Self;
David Miller: Media Power and Class Power: Overplaying Ideology; Pablo
Gonzalez Casanova: Negotiated Contradictions; Ellen Wood: Contradictions:
Only in Capitalism?

293pp, 234 x156mm

0 85036 502 3 hbk £30.00   **0 85036 501 5 pbk £16.95**

Canada: Fernwood Publishing; USA: Monthly Review Press; UK and Rest of World: Merlin Press

---

Previous volumes:

Leo Panitch and Colin Leys – Editors
2001: WORKING CLASSES, GLOBAL REALITIES

Socialist Register 2001 examines the concept and the reality of class as it effects
workers at the beginning of the 21st Century.

"an excellent collection". Bill Fletcher, *Against The Current*

Contents: Leo Panitch & Colin Leys with Greg Albo & David Coates: Preface;
Ursula Huws: The Making of a Cybertariat? Virtual Work in a Real World ; Henry
Bernstein: 'The Peasantry' in Global Capitalism: Who, Where and Why?; Beverly J.
Silver and Giovanni Arrighi: Workers North and South; Andrew Ross: No-Collar
Labour in America's 'New Economy'; Barbara Harriss-White & Nandini Gooptu:
Mapping India's World of Unorganized Labour; Patrick Bond, Darlene Miller &
Greg Ruiters: The Southern African Working Class: Production, Reproduction and
Politics; Steve Jefferys: Western European Trade Unionism at 2000; David Mandel:
'Why is there no revolt?' The Russian Working Class and Labour Movement;
Haideh Moghissi & Saeed Rahnema: The Working Class and the Islamic State in
Iran ; Huw Beynon & Jorge Ramalho: Democracy and the Organization of Class
Struggle in Brazil; Gerard Greenfield: Organizing, Protest and Working Class Self-
Activity: Reflections on East Asia; Rohini Hensman: Organizing Against the Odds:

Women in India's Informal Sector; Eric Mann: 'A race struggle, a class struggle, a women's struggle all at once': Organizing on the Buses of L.A.; Justin Paulson: Peasant Struggles and International Solidarity: the Case of Chiapas; Judith Adler Hellman: Virtual Chiapas: A Reply to Paulson ; Peter Kwong: The Politics of Labour Migration: Chinese Workers in New York; Brigitte Young: The 'Mistress' and the Maid' in the Globalized Economy; Rosemary Warskett: Feminism's Challenge to Unions in the North: Possibilities and Contradictions; Sam Gindin: Turning Points and Starting Points: Brenner, Left Turbulence and Class Politics; Leo Panitch: Reflections on Strategy for Labour.

403pp, 232 x155mm

0 85036 491 4 hbk £30.00   **0 85036 490 6 pbk £16.95**

Canada: Fernwood Publishing; USA: Monthly Review Press; UK and Rest of World: Merlin Press

Leo Panitch and Colin Leys – Editors
2000: NECESSARY AND UNNECESSARY UTOPIAS

What is Utopia? An economy that provides everyone's needs? A society which empowers all people? A healthy, peaceful and supportive environment ? Better worlds are both necessary and possible. "This excursion to utopia is full of surprise, inspiration and challenge". Peter Waterman

Contents: Preface; Transcending Pessimism: Rekindling Socialist Imagination: Leo Panitch & Sam Gindin; Minimum Utopia: Ten Theses: Norman Geras; Utopia and its Opposites: Terry Eagleton; On the Necessity of Conceiving the Utopian in a Feminist Fashion: Frigga Haug; Socialized Markets; not Market Socialism: Diane Elson; The Chimera of the Third Way: Alan Zuege; Other Pleasures: The Attractions of Post-consumerism: Kate Soper; Utopian Families: Johanna Brenner; Outbreaks of Democracy: Ricardo Blaug; Real and Virtual Chiapas: Magic Realism and the Left: Judith Adler Hellman; The Centrality of Agriculture: History; Ecology And Feasible Socialism: Colin Duncan; Democratise or Perish: The Health Sciences as a Path for Social Change: Julian Tudor Hart; The Dystopia of our Times: Genetic Technology and Other Afflictions: Varda Burstyn; Warrior Nightmares: Reactionary Populism at the Millennium: Carl Boggs; The Real Meaning of the War Over Kosovo: Peter Gowan.

301pp, 232 x155mm

0 85036 488 4 hbk £30.00   **0 85036 487 6 pbk £14.95**

Canada: Fernwood Publishing; USA: Monthly Review Press; UK and Rest of World: Merlin Press

Leo Panitch and Colin Leys – Editors
1999: GLOBAL CAPITALISM VS. DEMOCRACY

The essays here not only examine the contradictions of both neo-liberalism and 'progressive competitiveness', but demonstrate that no democracy worth the name can any longer be conceived except in terms of a fundamental break with it.

Contents: Preface; Taking Globalisation Seriously: Hugo Radice; Material World: The Myth of the Weightless Economy: Ursula Huws; Globalisation and the Executive Committee: Reflections on the Contemporary Capitalist State: Konstantinos Tsoukalas; Contradictions of Shareholder Capitalism: Downsizing Jobs; Enlisting Savings; Destabilizing Families: Wally Seccombe; Labour Power and International Competitiveness: A Critique of Ruling Orthodoxies: David Coates; Between the Devil and the Deep Blue Sea: The German Model Under the Pressure of Globalisation: Birgit Mahnkopf; East Asia's Tumbling Dominoes: Financial Crises and the Myth of the Regional Model: Mitchell Bernard; State Decay and Democratic Decadence in Latin America: Atilio Boron; Comrades and Investors: The Uncertain Transition in Cuba: Haroldo Dilla; Unstable Futures: Controlling and Creating Risks in International Money: Adam Tickell; Globalisation; Class and the Question of Democracy: Joachim Hirsch; The Challenge for the Left: Reclaiming the State: Boris Kagarlitsky; The Public Sphere and the Media: Market Supremacy versus Democracy: Colin Leys; The Tale that Never Ends: Sheila Rowbotham

364pp, 232 x155mm

0 85036 481 7 hbk £30.00   **0 85036 480 9 pbk £14.95**

Canada: Fernwood Publishing; USA: Monthly Review Press; UK and Rest of World: Merlin Press

Leo Panitch and Colin Leys – Editors
1998: THE COMMUNIST MANIFESTO NOW

Essays on the Manifesto's legacy and analysis of working class responses today. It also features brilliant essays on the making of the Manifesto, a reprint of the Manifesto itself and a reproachful letter to Marx from a socialistfeminist.

Contents: Preface , Dear Dr.Marx: A Letter from a Socialist Feminist: Sheila Rowbotham; The Political Legacy of the Manifesto: Colin Leys & Leo Panitch; The Geography of Class Power: David Harvey; Socialism with Sober Senses: Developing Worker's Capacities: Sam Gindin; Unions, Strikes and Class Consciousness Today: Sheila Cohen & Kim Moody; Passages of the Russian and Eastern Europe Left: Peter Gowan; Marx and the Permanent Revolution in France: Backgound to the Communist Manifesto: Bernard Moss; The Communist Manifesto and the Environment: John Bellamy Foster; Remember the Future? The Communist Manifesto as Historical and Cultural Form: Peter Osborne; Seeing is Believing:

Marx's Manifesto, Derrida's Apparition: Paul Thomas; The Making of the Manifesto: Rob Beamish; The Communist Manifesto: Marx & Engels.

278pp 232 x155mm

0 85036 472 8 hbk £25.00   **0 85036 473 6 pbk £14.95**

Canada: Fernwood Publishing; USA: Monthly Review Press; UK and Rest of World: Merlin Press

Leo Panitch – Editor
1997: RUTHLESS CRITICISM OF ALL THAT EXISTS

"it is all the more clear what we have to accomplish at present: I am referring to ruthless criticism of all that exists, ruthless both in the sense of not being afraid of the results it arrives at and in the sense of being just a little afraid of conflict with the powers that be."– Marx, 1843

Contents: Preface , A World Market of Opportunities? Capitalist Obstacles and Left Economic Policy: Gregory Albo; Financial Crises on the Threshold of the Twenty-first Century: Elmar Altvater; Green Imperialism: Pollution, Penitence, Profits: Larry Pratt & Wendy Montgomery; China's Communist Capitalism: The Real World of Market Socialism: Gerard Greenfield & Apo Leong; Taking Stock of a Century of Socialism: George Ross; The Marginality of the American Left: The Legacy of the 1960: Barbara Epstein; Clinton's Liberalism: No Model for the Left: Doug Henwood; The Ideology of 'Family and Community': New Labor Abandons the Welfare State: Joan Smith; The Decline of Spanish Social Democracy 1982-1996: Vicente Navarro; Cardoso's Political Project in Brazil: The Limits of Social Democracy: Paul Cammack; The State as Charade: Political Mobilisation in Today's India: Ananya Mukherjee-Reed; Marxism, Film and Theory: From the Barricades to Postmodernism: Scott Forsyth; Cyborg Fictions: The Cultural Logic of Posthumanism: Scott McCracken; Restoring the Real: Rethinking Social Constructivist Theories of Science: Meera Nanda; Post Colonial Theory and the 'Post-' Condition: Aijaz Ahmed.

381pp 215x 135mm

0 85036 465 5 hbk £25.00   **0 85036 466 3 pbk £12.95**

Canada: Fernwood Publishing; USA: Monthly Review Press; UK and Rest of World: Merlin Press

Leo Panitch – Editor
1996: ARE THERE ALTERNATIVES?

Contents: Preface; The British Labour Party's Transition from Socialist to Capitalism: Colin Leys; Developing Resistance and Resisting 'Development': Reflections from the South African Struggle: Patrick Bond & Mzwanele Mayekiso; The Use and Abuse of Japan as a Progressive Model: Paul Burkett & Martin Hart-Landsberg; A Kinder Road to Hell? Labor and the Politics of Progressive Competitiveness in Australia: John Wiseman; In Defence of Capital Controls: Jim Crotty & Gerald Epstein; The Challenge for Trade Unionism: Sectoral Change, 'Poor Work' and Organising the Unorganised: Anna Pollert; The Tower of Infobabel: Cyberspace as Alternative Universe: Reg Whitaker; 'Sack the Spooks': Do We Need an Internal Security Apparatus?: Peter Gill; Sport, Gender and Politics: Moving Beyond the O.J. Saga: Varda Burstyn; Socialist Hope in an Age of Catastrophe: Norman Geras; Are There Left Alternatives? A Debate from Latin America: Carlos Vilas; Socialists, Social Movements and the Labour Party: A Reply to Hilary Wainwright: Barry Winter; Building New Parties for a Different Kind of Socialism: A Response: Hilary Wainwright

307pp 215x 135mm

0 85036 455 8 hbk £25.00   **0 85036 456 6 pbk £12.95**
Canada: Fernwood Publishing; USA: Monthly Review Press; UK and Rest of World: Merlin Press

Leo Panitch – Editor
1995: WHY NOT CAPITALISM?

Contents: Preface; Ralph Miliband, Socialist Intellectual, 1924-1994: Leo Panitch; A Chronology of the New Left and Its Successors, Or: Who's Old-Fashioned Now?: Ellen Meiksins Wood; Saying No to Capitalism at the Millenium: George Ross; Once More Moving On: Social Movements, Political Representation and the Left: Hilary Wainwright; Globalizing Capitalism and the Rise of Identity Politics: Frances Fox Piven; Europe In Search of a Future Daniel Singer; The Yeltsin Regime: K. S. Karol; The State in the Third World: William Graf; The 'Underclass' and the US Welfare State: Linda Gordon; 'Class War Conservatism': Housing Policy, Homelessness and the 'Underclass': Joan Smith; Capitalist Democracy Revisited: John Schwartzmantel; Parliamentary Socialism Revisited: John Saville ; Harold Laski's Socialism: Ralph Miliband; How it All Began: A Footnote to History: Marion Kozak; Ralph Miliband, A Select Bibliography in English

299pp 215x 135mm

0 85036 449 3 hbk £25.00   **0 85036 448 5 pbk £12.95**
Canada: Fernwood Publishing; USA: Monthly Review Press; UK and Rest of World: Merlin Press

Ralph Miliband and Leo Panitch – Editors
1994: BETWEEN GLOBALISM AND NATIONALISM

Contents: Preface; Thirty Years of The Socialist Register: Ralph Miliband; Edward Thompson, The Communist Party and 1956: John Saville; Richard Rorty and the Righteous Among the Nations: Norman Geras; Globalisation and the State: Leo Panitch; Capitalism and the Nation State in the Dog Days of the Twentieth Century: Manfred Bienefeld; Globalisation and Stagnation: Arthur MacEwan; 'Competitive Austerity' and the Impasse of Capitalist Employment Policy: Gregory Albo; Globalism, Socialism and Democracy in the South African Transition: John S. Saul; The Development of Capitalism in Vietnam: Gerard Greenfield; The Decline of the Left in South East Asia: Kevin Hewison and Gerry Rodan; The Left in Russia: Poul Funder Larsen and David Mandel; Workers and Intellectuals in the German Democratic Republic: Patty Lee Parmalee; Germany's Party of Democratic Socialism: Eric Canepa.

349pp, 215x 135mm

0 85036 441 8 hbk £25.00   **0 85036 440 X pbk £12.95**

Canada: Fernwood Publishing; USA: Monthly Review Press; UK and Rest of World: Merlin Press

Ralph Miliband and Leo Panitch – Editors
1993: REAL PROBLEMS, FALSE SOLUTIONS

Contents: Preface; The Nature of Environment: Dialectics of Social and Environmental Change: David Harvey; Old Themes for New Times: Basildon Revisited: Christopher Norris; Illusions of Freedom: The Regressive Implications of Post-Modernism: Marsha A. Hewitt; False Promises: Anti-Pornography Feminism: Lynne Segal; The Rights Stuff: John Griffith; Why Nationalism?: Michael Löwy; Rethinking the Frelimo State: John S. Saul; After Perestroika: K. S. Karol; The Left and the Decomposition of the Party System in Italy: Stephen Hellman; Why Did the Swedish Model Fail?: Rudolf Meidner; Borders: The New Berlin Walls: Saul Landau; In Defence of Utopia: Daniel Singer.

256pp, 215x 135mm   **0 85036 430 2 pbk £12.95**

Canada: Fernwood Publishing; USA: Monthly Review Press; UK and Rest of World: Merlin Press

Ralph Miliband and Leo Panitch – Editors
1992: NEW WORLD ORDER?

Contents: Preface; The New World Order and the Socialist Agenda: Leo Panitch and Ralph Miliband; Global Perestroika: Robert W. Cox; Globalization: To What End?: Harry Magdoff; Global but Leaderless? The New Capitalist Order: Andrew Glyn and Bob Sutcliffe; The Collapse of Liberalism: Immanuel Wallerstein; Security and Intelligence in the Post-Cold War World: Reg Whitaker; US Military Policy in the Post-Cold War Era: Michael T. Klare; Europe in a Multi-Polar World: John Palmer; The Emerging World Order and European Change: Stephen Gill; Japan in a New World Order: Makoto Itoh; Africa: The Politics of Failure: Basil Davidson; The Gulf War and the New World Order: Avishai Ehrlich; Ruptured Frontiers: The Transformation of the US-Latin American System: Roger Burbach; Post-Communist Anti-Communism: America's New Ideological Frontiers: Joel Kovel; Hollywood's War on the World: The New World Order as Movie: Scott Forsyth.

285pp 215x 135mm

0 85036 427 2 hbk £25.00   **0 85036 426 4 pbk £12.95**
Canada: Fernwood Publishing; USA: Monthly Review Press; UK and Rest of World: Merlin Press

Ralph Miliband and Leo Panitch – Editors
1991: COMMUNIST REGIMES: The Aftermath

Contents: Preface, The Communist Experience: A Personal Appraisal: John Saville, Perestroika and the Proletariat: Leo Panitch and Sam Gindin; A Future for Socialism in the USSR?: Justin Schwartz; The Struggle for Power in the Soviet Economy: David Mandel; Perestroika and the Neo-Liberal Project: Patrick Flaherty; "Real Socialism" in Historical Perspective: Robert Cox; The Roots of the Present Crisis in the Soviet Economy: Ernest Mandel; Privilegentsia, Property and Power: Daniel Singer; For a Socialist Rebirth: A Soviet View Alexander: Buzgalin and Andrei Kalganov; Marketization and Privatization: the Polish Case: Tadeusz Kowalik; From Where to Where? Reflections on Hungary's Social Revolution: Peter Bihari; Nicaragua: a Revolution that Fell from Grace of the People: Carlos Vilas; Soviet Rehearsal in Yugoslavia? Contradictions of the Socialist Liberal Strategy: Susan Woodward; The Socialist Fetter: A Cautionary Tale: Michael Lebowitz; What Comes After Communist Regimes?: Ralph Miliband

389pp 215x 135mm   **0 85036 420 5 pbk only £12.95**
Canada: Fernwood Publishing; USA: Monthly Review Press; UK and Rest of World: Merlin Press

Ralph Miliband and Leo Panitch – Editors
1990: THE RETREAT OF THE INTELLECTUALS

Contents: Preface; Seven Types of Obloquy. Travesties of Marxism: Norman Geras; Marxism Today: An Anatomy: John Saville; The Uses and Abuses of 'Civil Society': Ellen Meiksins Wood; Defending the Free World: Terry Eagleton; Postmodernism and the Market: Fredric Jameson; The Eclipse of Materialism: Marxism and the Writing of Social History in the 1980s: Bryan D. Palmer; Statism, New Institutionalism, and Marxism: Paul Cammack; The Welfare State: Towards a Socialist-Feminist Perspective: Linda Gordon ; Intellectuals against the Left: The Case of France: George Ross; Derrida and the Politics of Interpretation: Eleanor MacDonald; Should a Marxist Believe in Marx on Rights?: Amy Bartholomew; Liberal Practicality and the US Left: John Bellamy Foster; Intellectuals and Transnational Capital: Stephen Gill; Why we are Still Socialists and Marxists After All This: Arthur MacEwan; Eulogy beside an Empty Grave: Reflections on the Future of Socialism: Richard Levins; Counter-Hegemonic Struggles: Ralph Miliband.

365pp 215x 135mm   0 85036 395 0 hbk only £20.00

Canada: Fernwood Publishing; USA: Monthly Review Press; UK and Rest of World: Merlin Press

---

New Books of interest to readers of Socialist Register from The Merlin Press

David Coates – Editor
PAVING THE THIRD WAY: The Critique of Parliamentary Socialism
A Socialist Register Anthology

The parliamentary road to socialism has held the attention and loyalty of much of the Left in the UK for more than a century. But has the strategy worked, and could it yet work? Writings on Parliamentary Socialism inspired by Ralph Miliband provide an important answer to these questions, and in the process throw new light on the history of the British Labour Party.
In this book David Coates brings together key original texts, adding critical commentary, annotation and some of his own writings, to contributions by Ralph Miliband, John Saville, Leo Panitch, Colin Leys, and Hilary Wainwright. Given the centrality of the Third Way to social democratic politics globally, this collection will be of interest to students and practitioners of left-wing politics in all advanced capitalist economies.

Contents: Acknowledgements; Introduction; Part 1: LABOURISM AND ITS LIMITS; Ralph Miliband: Introduction; Ralph Miliband: The Climax of Labourism; Ralph Miliband: The Sickness of Labourism; John Saville: Labourism and the

Labour Government; Ralph Miliband: Postscript; Leo Panitch: Conclusion; David Coates: The failure of the socialist promise; PART 2: FROM OLD LABOUR TO NEW LABOUR; Leo Panitch Socialists and the Labour Party: A reappraisal; 9.Ralph Miliband Socialist Advance in Britain; Leo Panitch: Socialist Renewal and the Labour Party; Colin Leys: The British Labour Party's transition from socialism to capitalism; David Coates: Labour Governments: Old Constraints and New; Parameters; PART 3: MOVING ON; Hilary Wainwright: Once More Moving On; Hilary Wainwright: Building New Parties for a Different Kind of Socialism: a Response; 15. David Coates and Leo Panitch: The Continuing Relevance of the Milibandian Perspective.

2003 234x156mm   270pp   0 85036 512 0 pbk £16.95
Canada: Fernwood Publishing; UK and Rest of World: Merlin Press

John Saville
MEMOIRS FROM THE LEFT

Autobiography: Early life, joining the Communist Party at the LSE, travels in France and Nazi Germany, war service as an Anti-Aircraft Gunnery Sergeant-Major, WW2 army life in India, colonialism and the Communist Party, teaching at the University of Hull. Notes on the crisis of the British Communist Party in 1956, following the Soviet invasion of Hungary and on people and co-thinkers: the MI5 agent planted at his home in Hull, John Griffith, Stuart Hall, Philip Larkin, Doris Lessing, Ralph Miliband, Sir John Pratt, Raphael Samuel, EP Thompson. Life in Hull, perspectives on a the rightward drift of Labour and last word on war in Iraq, etc. Includes a bibliography of writings by J. Saville.

"a stirringly humane and for the most part honest account of a life on the left in the 20th century from an independent socialist who remains true to his early Marxist beliefs" Mike Davis, Chartist
"a fascinating look at British political developments over the last 70 years" Mike Ambrose, Morning Star
"a joy to read… …by contrast with Eric Hobsbawm's recently published memoirs, Saville's account shows someone who has not only remained on and contributed to the left, but has done so actively. He concludes the book by noting his opposition to war with Iraq and to US and British imperialism in general. It will repay reading by historians and activists alike." Keith Flett, Socialist Review

"Much of the contemporary British left can trace its origins to that moment. [1957] We live in an intellectual space that others freed for us. Memoirs from the Left is a brilliant introduction to that history." Red Pepper

2003220x157mm   208pp   0 85036 520 1 pbk £14.95
Canada: Fernwood Publishing; UK and Rest of World: Merlin Press

Ralph Miliband
MARXISM AND POLITICS

What is class conflict? How do ruling classes and the state reproduce capitalism? What is the role of the Party? and what are the differences between reform and revolution? This is a readable and engaging survey: mainly of key Marxist texts – Marx, Engels and Lenin- and of Marxist political experience. Miliband believes in a socialism which defend freedoms already won: and to make possible their extension and enlargement by the removal of class boundaries.

Reviews of the previous edition: "This is probably the best introduction to Marx's Politics currently available and is as non-sectarian as the subject allows." Teaching Politics
" A job excellently done…" New Society. "the best primer on Marxism and politics ever written and Miliband's best book."
Leo Panitch: Professor of Politics, York University, Toronto

Contents: Introduction: Class and Class Conflict: The Defence of the old Order 1: The Defence of the old Order 2: Class and Party: Reform and Revolution: Bibliography: Index.

220x157mm   viii+ 200pp
Late 2003   0 85036 531 7 pbk £10.95

Canada: Fernwood Publishing; USA: Monthly Review Press; UK and Rest of World: Merlin Press

Michael Newman
RALPH MILIBAND AND THE POLITICS OF THE NEW LEFT

Based on exclusive access to Miliband's extensive personal papers and supplemented by interviews, this book analyses the ideas and contribution of a key figure in the British and international Left from the Second World War until the collapse of communism. Miliband's life and work form the central focus, but the book also provides an interpretative history of the evolution, debates and dilemmas of socialists throughout the period, and of the problems they faced both at work defending academic freedom and in society at large.

"comprehensive: scholarly: sensitive and readable: ..one of the kindest men and the best minds in our generation" from the Foreword by Tony Benn:
"admirably clear in its construction and scrupulously researched..."
"Miliband's own interventions in his time live on: in his books and essays: but his personal writings, amply extracted here, give a vivid sense of the man behind them-making this a good book to have." New Left Review:
"not just a biography of one of the great socialist minds of the 20th century, it is the history of an entire period of Leftist activity, buffeted as it was by WWII: Vietnam

and the decline of the Communist bloc........ a full and incisive a biography as he could have wished" Red Pepper

Contents: Introduction; Socialism and Identity (1924-1946); Apprenticeship (1946-56); The New Left and Parliamentary Socialism (1956-1962); The Sixties (1962-69); Free Speech and Academic Freedom; The State in Capitalist Society and the Debate with Poulantzas; Marxism and Politics (1970-77); An Uphill Struggle (1977-91); In Pursuit of Socialism; Conclusion: Ralph Miliband Today; Notes on Sources & Bibliography; Index.

2002 234x156mm   384pp. 8 pages of photos   **0 85036 513 9 pbk £15.95**
Canada: Fernwood Publishing; USA: Monthly Review Press; UK and Rest of World: Merlin Press

Ursula Huws
THE MAKING OF A CYBERTARIAT: Virtual Work in a Real World
with a foreword by Colin Leys

A new global labour force is being created working in call centres, homes and electronic sweatshops. New technologies are also transforming daily life. This book presents a coherent conceptual framework within which these developments can be understood. This book explains the impact of technology on the workplace, and relating its arguments and analyses to the work-situations of real people, showing how larger trends influence daily activities and shape the possibilities for collective action. It portrays working conditions experienced by both men and women, but focuses especially on the double impact on women, as workers and as consumers.

Contents: Foreword by Colin Leys, Introduction, Chapter One — New Technology and Domestic Labor Chapter Two — Domestic Technology: Liberation or Enslavement? Chapter Three — Chips on the Cheap: How South East Asian Women Pay the Price, Chapter Four — Terminal Isolation: The Atomization of Work and Leisure in the Wired Society, Chapter Five — The Global Office: Information technology and the Relocation of White Collar Work, Chapter Six — Challenging Commodification: Producing What's Useful Outside the Factory, Chapter Seven — Women, Health, and Work, Chapter Eight — Telework: Projections, Chapter Nine — Material World: The Myth of the Weightless Economy, Chapter Ten — The Making of a Cybertariat: Virtual Work in a Real World, Notes, Index.

Winter 2003-2004 213x135 mm: 208pp.   **0 85036 537 6 pbk £13.95**
UK: Merlin Press; Canada: Fernwood Publishing; USA: Monthly Review Press

Patrick Bond and Masimba Manyanya
ZIMBABWE'S PLUNGE: Exhausted Nationalism, Neoliberalism and the Struggle For Social Justice

Zimbabwe must explicitly confront the myriad political-economic contradictions that bedevil both nationalists and neo-liberals. An alternative political project is sketched out, drawing upon the Zimbabwean people's own struggles for social justice. " a comprehensive summary of the recent political developments…"
Johannesburg Star

Contents: Preface - A History Of Uneven Development - A Brief Pre-Independence Political Economy - Who Really Owed What To Whom? - Economic & Political Constraints- Globalisation's Constraints- Conquering The Constraints: Movements For Justice -Zimbabwe's Options - Conclusion: Scenarios for Social Change. Appendix 1: ZANU's ESAP/MERP Debate; Appendix 2: The MDC's ESARP; Appendix 3: Declaration of the National Working People's Convention; Appendix 4: Jubilee South's Pan-African Declaration on Poverty Reduction Strategy Programmes. References, Index.

2002 228x151 276pp.   0 85036 517 1 pbk £14.95
UK: Merlin Press; Rest of the World: University of Natal Press

Patrick Bond
UNSUSTAINABLE SOUTH AFRICA: Environment, Development & Social Protest

Why can multinationals build Africa's largest dam, and price water at levels that many Johannesburg residents can't afford? Why are illegal electricity connections so common in Soweto? Why is South Africa amongst the world's worst emitters of greenhouse gases? Critical perspectives on post-Apartheid South Africa's 'sustainable development' experience, and on the neo-liberal, market-oriented strategies adopted by central government and most municipalities since democracy dawned in 1994. Maps, tables and photos.

Contents: Preface; Introduction: 'A World in One Country'; PART ONE : AN UNSUSTAINABLE LEGACY; The Environment of Apartheid-Capitalism: Discourses and Issues; PART TWO : UNSUSTAINABLE PROJECTS; The Development of Underdevelopment in Nelson Mandela Metropole: Coega's Economic, Social and Environmental Subsidies; Lesotho's Water, Johannesburg's Thirst: Communities, Consumers and Mega-Dams; PART THREE : UNSUSTAINABLE POLICIES; Eco-Social Injustice for Working-Class Communities: The Making and Unmaking of Neoliberal Infrastructure Policy; Droughts and Floods: Water Prices and Values in the Time of Cholera; Power to the Powerful: Energy, Electricity, Equity and Environment; PART FOUR :

ENVIRONMENT, DEVELOPMENT AND SOCIAL PROTEST; Conclusion: Environmentalism, the WSSD and Uneven Political Development; Refs; Index.

2002 227 x 152 449pp.   **0 85036 522 8 pbk £18.95**
UK: Merlin Press; Rest of the World: University of Natal Press

---

In case of difficulty obtaining Merlin Press titles outside the UK, please contact the following:

Australia: Merlin Press Agent and stockholder:
Eleanor Brash: PO Box 586, Artamon: NSW 2064 Email: ebe@enternet.com.au

Canada: Co-Publisher and stockholder:
Fernwood Books, 8422 St. Margaret's Bay Rd, Site 2a, Box 5, Black Point, Nova Scotia, B0J 1B0
Tel: +1 902 857 1388: Fax: +1 902 422 3179 Email: errol@fernwoodbooks.ca

India: Merlin Press Agent:
Parrot Reads Publishers Merlin Press Agents, 14-Dakshinapuram, J N U, New Delhi 11006
Tel. and Fax: +91 11 2617 4382 Email: jharajiv@now-india.net.in

South Africa: Merlin Press Agent:
Blue Weaver Marketing
PO Box 30370, Tokai, Cape Town 7966, South Africa
Tel. and Fax: +27 21 701 7302 Email: blueweav@mweb.co.za

Publisher:
University of Natal Press, Private Bag X01, Scottsville 3209
Tel: +27 33 260 5226 Email: cowleyg@press.unp.ac.za

USA:
Merlin Press Agent and stockholder: Independent Publishers Group, 814 North Franklin Street, Chicago, IL 60610.
Tel: +1 312 337 0747   Fax: +1 312 337 5985 frontdesk@ipgbook.com

Publisher: Monthly Review Press:
Monthly Review Press, 122 West 27th Street, New York, NY 10001
Tel: +1 212 691 2555 promo@monthlyreview.org